(continued from front flap)

But what are these key elem
the executive breakthrough pa
Mr. Uris follows each case history with
the lesson behind the success — such
things as seeking out the action, learning the business of business, "mentor
cultivation" (getting to know the right
people), discovering how to raise
money for capitalization, and working
hard for the pay-off.

In addition, there are chapters on
such topics as "The Entrepreneur vs.
The Organization Man" and "Big Company vs. Small Company — are opportunities equal?"

Auren Uris is an experienced and
prolific author of books for people in
business and management. His titles
include *Developing Your Executive
Skills, The Efficient Executive, Discover Your Inner Self* and, most recently, *The Executive Job Market*.
Presently an editor with The Research Institute of America, Inc., he
lives in Grandview-on-Hudson, New
York.

THE
EXECUTIVE
BREAKTHROUGH

Other books by Auren Uris

THE
EXECUTIVE
BREAKTHROUGH

21 Roads to the Top

AUREN URIS

Doubleday & Company, Inc., Garden City, New York
1967

Library of Congress Catalog Card Number 66–17417
Copyright © 1967 by Auren Uris
All Rights Reserved
Printed in the United States of America
First Edition

CONTENTS

Contents

BOOK III

INTRODUCTION

In 1932 nineteen-year-old Tom O'Ryan, fresh from Ireland, applied for work with a New York section gang. He got a job—digging a subway tunnel. Thirty years later, Thomas O'Ryan had the pleasure of seeing his company's advertising posters decorating the subway trains for which his earlier work had provided a track. His position: chairman of the nation's largest transit advertising firm, O'Ryan & Batchelder. Rex Wood started his business career by putting up five hundred dollars—his entire savings—for a rundown service station. It didn't pan out. After moving aimlessly from one undistinguished job to another, a chance street encounter got him started selling jewelry door to door. Fifteen years later, Wood was president of the company, Sarah Coventry, Inc., director of a twenty-two-thousand-woman sales force, and responsible for achieving a multimillion-dollar sales volume. O'Ryan and Wood are unlike in temperament, skills, careers. Yet they are alike in one essential: each scored a breakthrough, made it to the top.

HOW DID THEY DO IT?

Meeting an exceptionally successful person, one automatically thinks: What sets him apart from others? What factors led him to fame and fortune, when men and women of seemingly equal talents continue to struggle along in the ruts of mediocrity? Outward appearances seldom yield the answer. A successful businessman *may* be aggressive, articulate, self-confident, personable—but he may also be quiet, diffident, badly dressed and unprepossessing.

Nor does the secret become known by going to the source. Reporters and writers often ask of wealthy and powerful businessmen: "Mr. X, to what do you attribute your success?" But the answer is usually disappointing. For the same reason that it's futile to ask a centipede how it walks, it's usually hopeless to ask a successful businessman how he got that way. He probably doesn't know.

Recently, eleven winners of Horatio Alger awards for outstanding accomplishments in business were asked to name the factors behind their success. Their responses, reported by the *New York World-Telegram and Sun,* might have come straight from Horatio himself: "Faith, hard work, belief in people, and service to others." Scrutiny of any one of the eleven careers would certainly reveal far more fascinating explanations.

How did they *really* do it?

One ready answer: motivation. There's no question that almost every self-made success has been propelled by inner drive. Yet, strong motivation is much more widespread than success. Says King Whitney, president of the Personnel Laboratory, a psychological services firm: "We Americans pursue success with the same sense of mission that sent knight errants of old from their castles to seek the Holy Grail." And Whitney adds, "Success is not so much a goal as it is a universal *direction.* In our culture, in our time, it is as natural for us to seek success as it is for us to breathe."

The question persists: How did they do it? Is it mainly luck? Unusual opportunity? Drive and ambition? Special techniques? There must be an answer, because some people *do* score spectacular breakthroughs. Because success comes about through their own efforts, the explanation then must lie in their behavior, in *what* they do and *how* they do it.

TWENTY-ONE PATTERNS OF SUCCESS

In the following pages the lives of a group of successful men and women will be analyzed, the ups, downs and turning points in their fortunes explored. The objective: to identify the factors that propelled these individuals into achievement.

The people selected come from widely diverse backgrounds. They have achieved their breakthroughs in a broad cross section of industries and service fields—from heavy industrial equipment to doughnuts, from the clothing business to marketing research. Both individual entrepreneurs and corporation executives are represented. At one extreme is John M. Fox, president of the vast United Fruit Company enterprise, which racked up $400,000,000 in sales last year. At the small-business end of the spectrum stands Amelia Lobsenz, president of her own twenty-five-man public relations agency.

Directly after each person's story is what might be called the story behind the story—the unique pattern of factors that led him to the top in his field. The final chapter takes up in detail the factors that recur—to pinpoint the elements that seem to be common to the behavior patterns of successful people.

In selecting the people for case histories, three criteria were set up:

1. The individual must have reached a level of accomplishment or acquisition that *would be judged by most people* as unquestioned success. No dollar limit was set. No type of company, size, number of employees or other measure was used. Rather, the objective was to gather as varied a group as possible, in terms of company size, type of industry and so on.

2. The second criterion was that the individual must have made it to the top *through his own efforts*. This does not mean that he or she had to do it alone. On the contrary, one of the common threads running through the biographies is the ability to utilize the help of others. Strictly ruled out, however, were individuals who started their business careers with one foot well up the ladder. For example, "sons of" and close relatives of company founders were eliminated. So were those with family fortunes who could buy their own ladder. Many capable and successful businesswomen also were disqualified because their husbands—sometimes through death—had been the cause of their entry into the world of business at a high level.

3. The third consideration was that *no "creative genius" need*

apply. The success of an Edison or a Steinmetz generally holds few surprises within the context of this book. Where a business enterprise was formed as a result of a creative idea—such as Stanley Arnold's, for example—the focus of the biography has been not on how the idea was originated but rather on how the idea was put to work.

One point deserves special explanation. In analyzing the histories of these successful businessmen and -women, a number of phrases have been developed to distinguish various traits: "achievement escalation," "dead-end avoidance," "opportunity awareness," and so on. These terms may sound like jargon on first reading, but they will be helpful for two reasons: First, specific terms are useful for labeling particular actions or phenomena so that they can be clearly identified and discussed. Second, key elements in the pattern of the successful individual can be seen most clearly and simply when the parts are separated and tagged.

How did they do it? The pages ahead hold some of the answers.

BOOK I

1 { Joseph Katz –
HE WRAPS UP CHRISTMAS

The Pittsburgh flood of 1936 swept Joseph Katz into the path by which he eventually got to be president of the Papercraft Corporation, a twenty-million-dollar company that is the world's largest manufacturer of gift wrappings. "Papercraft is an ideal business for a man of my temperament," says Katz. "It has yielded personal wealth. It is small enough for me to control personally, but big enough to make a mark in the financial community." (When Papercraft went public in 1958, it became one of the hottest growth stocks on the over-the-counter market.) "It operates at a constant pitch of excitement—literally all of our fortunes depend on one day alone, Christmas. Then, of course, all of our products go up in smoke."

*　　*　　*

"I was the oldest of six children of immigrant parents who settled in Pittsburgh, Pennsylvania, in 1913," Katz relates. "Like many other immigrant families of that era, mine arrived with very little money, but with the ambition to become a vital part of this new country. Our family was closely knit and very happy, but the strain of making ends meet was always there. It was the desire to ease this strain that pushed me from the beginning."

At age ten, Joe Katz took his first job, selling the *Saturday Evening Post*. But he soon discovered that the financial reward was not enough—a characteristic that was to play a vital part in his later success. "The company awarded a plaque to the boy who was able to sell the greatest number of subscriptions," Katz recalls. "There was a tremendous spirit of competition. I felt I *had* to be the one to win the plaque, and I had to do it, not only by selling the most subscriptions, but by breaking the all-time record. It was only when I had broken that record that I was satisfied to look for a better job."

The panic that began on Wall Street in October of 1929 took only seconds to reach Pittsburgh, and it affected Katz deeply. "There wasn't anyone old enough to read and to reason who wasn't affected by that day. While our family wasn't hit directly by the crash, we all knew that life would never be the same again. Suddenly I realized that as long as I sold someone else's product I was not free. I had been making good money while a high-school student, averaging as much as many families live on—but I was dependent on an employer. I saved one hundred dollars, bought equipment and went into business for myself—making corn fritters." Profits from the corn-fritter enterprise were good. Katz soon averaged one hundred dollars a week. But the business wasn't interesting enough, particularly for a boy who gobbled up biographies of early American industrialists and longed to emulate their enterprise.

CYRUS CURTIS WINS A DISCIPLE

It was a biography of Cyrus Curtis, founder of the Curtis publishing empire, that started Katz on his first serious business activity and gave him a yen to enter a field that nearly became his lifetime occupation, journalism. When Curtis was a boy, Katz read, he had published his own magazine for other boys, *Young America*. If Curtis could do it, why couldn't Katz (now fifteen years old) do it too? He had a ready-made audience: youngsters all over the world whose interests and activities he shared at first hand, so Katz began to publish his own magazine. He divided his time between the writing (which he did under various pseudonyms so that his readers would envision a large staff), soliciting advertising and doing odd printing jobs such as menus, invitations, bills, and memo pads. The small printing jobs were done on his own press to help pay the bills incurred through the publication of *Boys' Ideal*. His own press was too small to handle the magazine, so that business was given to a mail-order printer who had the facilities.

"My situation was not unlike that of many publishers today. I had to subsidize my main publication with the income from a less interesting but more profitable business. My biggest financial problem arose from the fact that I had advertised subscriptions at only twenty-five cents a year, and I was constantly running out of money to pay for postage. Boys from as far away as Egypt, Iraq and China were reading the magazine. I tried to solve the problem by printing some impressive-looking business stationery and soliciting advertising on a national basis. I actually did get a few advertising accounts this way, but *Boys' Ideal* was still in the red."

Katz considered giving up the magazine, but being a publisher and editor offered such a challenge that he decided to keep publishing as long as his own press kept turning out the dull but profitable printing jobs for local businessmen. During his last year of high school, Katz says, he finally had to face reality. "I wanted to go on to college, and this meant I would need time both for study and for work to pay my tuition. Rather than let *Boys' Ideal* die, I merged with another publication and assured the readers that they would have the advantages of both magazines in one."

After entering college, he expanded his printing business until he had a full-scale plant in the family garage. He employed students from various schools in Pittsburgh, paying them a commission, and he soon had his presses working a full eight-hour day (at night)!

During his last year in college, Katz had an opportunity to get practical experience by working as a part-time reporter without pay for the *Pittsburgh Press,* the city's major newspaper. Along with the usual assignments given to novices on newspapers, he was offered the opportunity to write an occasional small feature for the Sunday edition. A simple business fact of life influenced Katz greatly at this point. He was shocked to discover that the head of his department, a man of long experience and great editorial ability, was forced to take a cut in pay. It was the height of the depression, and newsmen, along with millions of others, had to accept such pay decreases—or face the possibility of having no job at all. His editor was making only thirty-five dollars a week, while truck drivers were making at least 20 per cent more. Joe Katz's own printing business was providing him a better income. "That," according to Joe Katz, "was the end of my journalism career. I knew that newspapers could take their pick of men and begin them at only twelve dollars a week.

"Once I realized that journalism was not to be my career, I became impatient with my life as it was and decided to leave the University of Pittsburgh. Although I had only one year to complete for my diploma, that term would cost three hundred dollars in tuition. After talking it over with one of my professors, I decided that I had neither the time nor the money to invest. I had gone to school for an education, not the diploma."

In 1934, two days after leaving college, Joseph Katz rented a small loft in downtown Pittsburgh, formed a partnership with Harry Kanarek, an old friend, and set up in business as the "Beacon Press." Both men were twenty-one. Assets were a press, a paper cutter, some stands of type and less than one hundred dollars. They printed small advertising booklets, circulars, menus and dozens of other jobs needed by small businessmen in a community. Joe satisfied his creative bent by designing and writing brochures.

The business proved to be a shaky one at best. Finances were strictly a day-to-day affair, a matter of forever trying to collect from customers in time to pay production costs. There was never any working capital and no opportunity to expand beyond the confines of the small printing shop. If the printing business meant opportunity, Katz could not see any in *his* limited operation.

THE GOLDEN TRIANGLE GOES UNDER WATER

Opportunity came at last, but it turned out to be only peripherally related to Katz's printing business. The date was March 17, 1936, famous in Pittsburgh's history as the day when the Great

Allegheny Flood put Pittsburgh's renowned business area, the "Golden Triangle," under twelve feet of water.

"I was making my way downtown, walking in the rain," recalls Katz, "when I suddenly realized that the Golden Triangle was slowly disappearing, giving way to a vast river. The further I walked the greater the ravages became. People were out in canoes, rafts and rowboats, trying to make their way in and out of buildings. Many people were in a state of shock, as if they could not believe their own eyes. Yet all kinds of people were taking photographs, and I realized immediately how important these pictures would be, not only to residents, but to the newspapers. I didn't have a camera myself. I offered to buy the exposed film from every passerby I saw. Soon my pockets were filled. I was sure I had a gold mine."

In his enthusiasm, however, Katz had failed to take account of the fact that there was no place to develop the film because all of Pittsburgh's power lines had failed. Heading back to high ground, Katz contacted his partner, they hopped into a car and headed for the first town where power was available. "We ended up in a twenty-four-hour drugstore in nearby Monongahela where we spent the rest of the night developing pictures. As the prints emerged, one by one, I realized that we had the makings of a one-shot news magazine. From radio reports, we knew that it would be days before anyone could print our material. So Harry and I took a train to Cleveland. We arrived there that afternoon with only twenty dollars between us, not knowing a single person who could vouch for us. We went through the Yellow Pages calling printer after printer. They all turned us down. Finally, as we were nearing the end of the alphabet—and our hopes as well—we found one who understood the value of our pictures. He agreed to do the job on credit. Within twenty-four hours we had one hundred thousand copies of our magazine printed and loaded onto a baggage car, on its way back to Pittsburgh."

The magazine, selling at ten cents a copy and similar to *Look* in format, was out on the streets the next day, scooping the Pittsburgh newspapers by four days. It was sold out within the week. Katz's flood souvenir, *The Pittsburgh Flood,* earned him four thousand dollars, more money than he had ever seen—enough to pay his bills and leave him with his long sought-after stake, one thousand dollars of working capital.

INTO BUSINESS VIA THE BACK DOOR

At this point, the partners decided to go their separate ways and Katz started looking around for a "somewhat more lofty" business to enter. Reasoning that he would be in a position of greater control if he produced the product instead of the service, he decided to enter the paper business. Katz visited mills in the Holyoke and Springfield areas and soon discovered that a paper business was not to be started on a shoestring. Paper wholesalers were people who had capital and substance. Distribution was franchised, and all major brands were contracted on an exclusive basis. There was no room for a newcomer, particularly one whose financial resources were limited.

But Katz was stubborn. "I could see," he says, "that the paper field, despite the drawbacks, offered more opportunity than printing. It was bigger and there were fewer people in it. I decided I would try to enter it through the back door—buying up over-runs, seconds and close-outs, which I would then sell to printers.

"The challenge of handling something more difficult to sell than standard brands appealed to me. For example, I recall one time buying a railroad car full of purple cover paper. Ordinarily you couldn't give it away. But I found other uses than just cover paper. That was the year when the students in Pittsburgh covered their books with purple, businessmen ordered their blue-plate special from a purple menu, and department stores made purple the vogue for bill enclosures. On another occasion I took a load of white coated paper that was so badly curled it couldn't go through a printing press. But it was good paper and I knew that I'd figure out a way to sell it. I did, too. I devised a way to clamp it so that the edges could be fed to the presses."

Getting into the paper business even by the back door wasn't easy. Katz simply did not have enough capital to buy up the needed inventory. The banks refused a loan and the paper mills turned thumbs down on extending credit. A company that was new to the industry and which could not offer a guaranteed distribution was not exactly a good risk.

One man came to the rescue. He was Alfred Srere, the president of the Miami Valley Coated Paper Company in Franklin, Ohio. When Katz walked into his office one spring day and offered to give him four cents a pound for four carloads of close-outs, Srere accepted the deal. Then came a rough moment. "Mr. Srere," said Katz, "I have no money right now. But I am an old hand in the printing business and I know I can sell these four carloads. Can you give me a ninety-day credit?" Srere, impressed with Katz's general air of competence and honesty, agreed to extend the credit. What Katz didn't know at the time was that the Miami Valley Coated Paper Company was in the hands of a receivership, making the risk that Srere took more than an ordinary one. The bank which was responsible for the receivership took sharp exception to the deal. Srere, however, refused to go back on his commitment and in the end his judgment proved right. Katz paid back the entire amount before the ninety-day period was up. Not only did he continue as a substantial customer of Srere's, but some years later was able to repay Srere's faith by lending him capital with which to expand what is now a flourishing paper mill.

During the years from 1936 to 1942, Katz's company, operating under the name "Printer's Paper Supply Company," did relatively well. While annual gross rose moderately, the payroll grew to ten employees. One of these, pert, blonde, Agnes Roman, was Katz's secretary. In 1937 he married her, and in 1939 their first child, a son, Marshall Paul, was born. A daughter, Andrea Tina, was born in 1945.

As Katz recalls, the germ of the idea that was ultimately to be the Papercraft Corporation sprouted just before his wedding. He remembers walking into Agnes' home one night and seeing a group of unopened wedding presents on a table. The gift wrappings were of poor quality paper, and the design and colors were downright bad. Yet, they were the best gift wraps available. Gift wrapping as such was a new product in those days. White tissue and thin ribbon were standard, whether the gift was for Christmas, weddings or birthdays. Only the color of the ribbon was sometimes changed. The use of paper with printed designs grew out of the depression, when people's budgets left little or nothing for extras. A pair of socks, a kitchen utensil were gifts, and the use of a gift wrap was one way to add a bright touch to a utilitarian gift.

A reasonably successful man by now, Katz was still restless and discontented. It was not only that the business was small and the income relatively modest, but that the operation itself was too limited. "I was still on the outside. I was only a middleman, selling raw material from which others made a product. This wasn't control. I wanted a business I could run from start to finish."

THE "PITTSBURGH FLOOD" REPEATS

With the beginning of World War II came the opportunity, the big one, which turned Katz's business into a million-dollar operation and gave him the financial freedom he had always sought. In May of 1942, while waiting for a lunch date with a friend on the staff of Kaufmann's Department Store, Katz noticed a crowd of customers gathering around the stationery counter. Always curious, he worked his way through the crowd to see what the big attraction was. It turned out to be stationery with a military emblem. People were lining up to buy it, along with leatherette writing pads, to send to relatives and friends in the service.

"It suddenly occurred to me that the two items could be combined to make a stationery kit for soldiers. The stationery box could be made of extra-durable cardboard, with a blotter on top, so that the fighting man, wherever he was—on board a ship, an airplane, in camp, or in the desert—would have a ready-made, instantly usable portable desk, complete with stationery, pen and blotter."

Within a matter of minutes, Katz sketched a rough drawing of his idea, named it "Rite Kit," and took it up to Morris Sanger, Kaufmann's merchandise manager. Sanger was interested, asked Katz to bring him back a final design. The next day Katz turned up with the completed drawings, and Sanger ordered a gross, sight unseen.

During the next ten days, Katz whirled around in a storm of activity. He applied for a design patent on his Rite Kit. He lined up a boxmaker to make the cardboard "desk" and found an envelope manufacturer to produce the envelopes. He engaged a printer to print the paper with the military emblem (he himself would supply the paper); located a source of pens; reorganized his shop to assemble the whole operation; got permission to photograph and use pictures of soldiers in uniform for advertising purposes. At the same time, in a flush of what Katz now refers to as "blind optimism," he made preparations for expanding his business. He drew up a 17-inch by 22-inch advertising circular with an order blank inside, and sent it to every department store in the country.

Meanwhile the gross had been delivered to Kaufmann's, and the Rite Kits went on sale. They turned out to be that unbeatable combination—a good product offered at the right time. Not only was Kaufmann's gross sold out in short order, but the response from sixteen hundred department stores was phenomenal. One hundred thousand dollars' worth of orders came rolling in. Three months later, in August, when Katz took stock of the operation and projected his shipments for September, he realized that the impossible had happened. His net profits for the month would read ten thousand dollars. He had really hit the jackpot.

For the next three years until the end of the war, Rite Kit proved a bonanza. Katz's annual gross (including other types of military writing kits and stationery items) totaled $1,500,000. Profits were, as Katz cautiously phrases it, "quite substantial"—30 per cent net. His income rose to $400,000. "The funny thing," he says, "is that anybody could have done it. Truthfully, a boy could have sold those products just as well. I just happened to have a good idea and the temerity to carry it out."

Significantly, almost as soon as he had launched Rite Kit, Katz began making plans to enter another business. "I realized that Rite Kit was strictly a war baby," he says. "By the end of the war, it had already served its main purpose—providing the capital to start a new enterprise."

SEARCH FOR PROFIT ITEMS

Sticking close to home, Katz decided to enter the paper industry again—this time through the *front* door. "During the war years," he says, "I conducted a thorough investigation of paper products, searching for a likely one to manufacture. I looked at more things made of paper than you can imagine—all the way from wallpaper to candy wrappers. I finally narrowed the field down to two: gift wraps and greeting cards. The established companies in both industries were relatively small and the business techniques rather unsophisticated, so there was ample room for a newcomer. There were other attractions too. I had fallen in love with selling to the consumer on a nationwide basis; these were both consumer industries. Both were also dependent on design and art for their success, and this satisfied a long-felt urge of mine to put my knowledge of art to practical purposes." He finally settled on gift wraps, and in 1945, the Papercraft Corporation was formed with a capitalization of ten thousand dollars.

This time success was far from instant. In its first month of operation, Papercraft made exactly seventy-five dollars. At the end of a year, the gross was a few thousand dollars. After two years, things weren't much better. Papercraft was doing a business of only a few hundred thousand dollars annually and it looked as if it had no place to go.

"Everything we did was wrong," says Katz. "We were unknown. We were the smallest company in the field. Our line was poor; we had nothing but feeble geometric designs which clearly didn't appeal to the consumer. We were inexperienced in rotary printing, and we ran into all kinds of troubles with production. The business we obtained was grudgingly given to us by condescending buyers. Trouble was, I had been operating as if the wartime seller's market still existed, when, in fact, it had already been replaced by a hard, competitive buyer's market. We had come in too late, to the wrong place, with the wrong product."

What was needed, Katz realized, was a radical change that would turn Papercraft from a second-rate "me-tooer" into an industry leader. This change, he reasoned, would have to be one that exploited the dynamics of the new postwar market. The single most important element in this new market was retailing self-service, the marketing concept that lay behind the success of the supermarket and later the self-service department stores. What was the chief ingredient of the self-service selling operation? Katz asked himself. Wasn't it . . . packaging, that magical marketing component that enabled a product to display, advertise and sell itself at the same time? In 1949, Katz decided to put Papercraft gift paper into supermarkets in a radically new type of package—a continuous roll in place of the old flat wrap of folded paper. The Papercraft rolls would also be distributed through a new type of middleman, the rack jobber, whose operations had impressed Katz.

The idea was a good one, Katz was convinced. But in the first year of operation he had once again to reckon with a heartbreaking failure. "We did miserably," he says, "and this time, we really couldn't figure out why. I was still confident that rack jobbing was the best method of supermarket distribution for us—these men were masters at setting up displays which capitalized on impulse sales. I was sure that the supermarket was the right place to be. And I still believed that the continuous roll was a tremendous improvement over the old package. It allowed the consumer to make a gift wrap of any size she wanted. In a market where convenience was becoming a magic word, it just had to succeed."

TWO ELEPHANTS ARE A BIG BARGAIN

One day as he prowled the supermarket, he passed by a candy display, and was struck by a flash of intuition. "Our mistake was in not carrying the new packaging concept to its logical conclusion. We had been selling in single packages when we should have been following the principle used so successfully by the candymakers— selling in multiple packs. It was the old story of the door-to-door salesman who offered elephants for sale. When he tried to entice customers with the amazingly low price of $150 per elephant, nobody wanted elephants. It was only when he offered *two* elephants at the bargain price of $175, that the customer bought. This was the operating principle of the supermarket—mass buying, not single-item purchases."

Repackaged in boxes containing multiple rolls, selling at ninety-eight cents for three rolls, Papercraft wraps went back into the supermarket in 1951. Katz's idea clicked. Papercraft rolled up a tremendous Christmas sale that year.

From then on, it was pretty much clear sailing. Papercraft grew to its present twenty-million-dollar size, selling to some 200,000 retail outlets throughout the country, including supermarkets, discount stores, drug- and variety stores. The multiple packaging concept has been further expanded; Papercraft now offers the buyer a complete kit of everything she needs for Christmas wrapping—paper foils, bows, ties, tapes and tags—all displayed on a single Papercraft stand, carefully calculated to catch the shopper's eye. Americans spend from four to six dollars per family on Christmas wrapping paper and Papercraft thinks it accounts for the largest portion of these sales.

From a neophyte who lacked even elementary know-how in the field, Katz has turned into a grand master of the industry. His printing machinery is among the finest in the U.S. His designs— carefully calculated to appeal to the ephemeral quality known as mass taste—rarely miss. "We try to hit somewhere between Park

Avenue and Main Street, because this is the point on the taste spectrum where the average (meaning 85 per cent of the population) customer is inspired to buy."

Last year Katz realized a long-delayed ambition when Papercraft began manufacturing greeting cards. Applying the hard-earned and hard-learned techniques of merchandising from the gift-wrap field, he marketed his greeting cards in the newer and more heavily trafficked retail outlets. Like gift wrap in the fifties, greeting cards in the sixties are still largely sold in stationery and department stores. The initial line, introduced during Christmas, 1964, proved so successful that the greeting-card division was sharply expanded in 1965. Manufacturing and storage space has been increased from 50,000 to 100,000 square feet, and the line itself has been doubled. "It is not inconceivable," says Katz, "that one of these days our greeting-card division may be the tail wagging the dog."

In 1965, Katz turned his eyes abroad, where Papercraft's first European plant was recently completed near Brussels. It's a thirty-thousand-square-foot factory which will manufacture the Papercraft product mix for the European market. The European market, he points out, is ripe for American-type merchandising. The newer retail outlets are already there—they are just waiting for gift wraps and greeting cards. What's more, he adds, the European operation, with its lower labor and overhead costs, can't help but be profitable. The fact that Papercraft will be able to use last year's American designs, thus reusing its engraved rollers, which cost twenty-five hundred dollars per design, will help too.

And what of the many-faceted Katz personality? During these years of success, he has used his multiple skills for both pleasure and profit. From a practicing artist, he has become an art collector. In the course of some forty-five trips to Europe, he has acquired a fine collection of paintings which hang in his Pittsburgh house and his apartment in the Hotel Pierre in New York. It includes works by Renoir, Picasso, Chagall, Utrillo, Vlaminck, Dali and Dufy. He collects art for fun, not for money. "Art is not always the best investment," he points out with typical practicality. "I collect art because paintings give me, as nothing else can, a sense of total tranquillity."

With Papercraft earning millions of dollars and expanding every year, Katz certainly has no need to work for personal income. Yet he gets as steamed up about the company's new projects as when he was just getting the business on its feet. Asked why he still works as hard as ever, Katz gives an answer that is perhaps not untypical of the successful entrepreneur: "The motivation is certainly not money; it's the challenge to do a better job and the challenge of my ego, perhaps, to enrich the thousands of shareholders who had enough faith in me and my company to invest their own hard-earned dollars in Papercraft Corporation stock."

BEHIND THE JOSEPH KATZ STORY

The Competitive Spirit. Americans, being largely a nation of sports enthusiasts, are used to playing games to win. For Joseph Katz, a competitive situation automatically led him to tremendous goal-directed exertions. Even as a youngster, when the reward to be won was a plaque for selling the greatest number of subscriptions to the *Saturday Evening Post,* Katz felt he *had* to win. And even winning wasn't enough. He set out to break the all-time sales record. It was only success in this lofty goal that satisfied his need to compete.

Some individuals because of their backgrounds or interests commit themselves to competition in a single line of business activity. For example, only machines and things mechanical appeal to Thomas Coe of Wakefield Engineering. However, for some individuals *any* opportunity represents a challenge. In his early years Joseph Katz demonstrated that for him variety was the spice of enterprise. Whether it was drawing cartoons or selling corn fritters, if he had a chance of "winning" in the sense of achieving some financial and psychic reward, he would undertake it. Essentially the difference between a Thomas Coe and a Joseph Katz is the difference between the specialist and the generalist. Coe's specialty was engineering. Katz, too, had technical training—in the printing business. Yet for him it almost didn't matter which version of the "business game" he played. As long as it was some recognizable version, he became a dedicated player.

Katz's personal testament provides an interesting insight into the psychology of the entrepreneur. Some people have said that the entrepreneur becomes one because of his urge for independence. Katz says, in so many words, "I realized that as long as I sold someone else's product, I was not free." To him, the lure of being his own boss had the great appeal of personal freedom. He tended to champ at the bit when the reins were held by somebody else.

Reality Recognition. "The ability to accept a harsh fact when it hits one in the face," says one executive, "is exceedingly rare." Katz had the ability to recognize reality without waiting for it to hit him in the face.

"The analysis of the ordinary," said Alfred North Whitehead, "requires an extraordinary mind." In a deceptively simple situation, Katz was able to put two and two together and draw a sound conclusion: He decided to end his journalism career when he realized that his editor-boss was making thirty-five dollars a week while truck drivers were making at least 20 per cent more. He saw nothing wrong with the higher pay earned by truck drivers. However, he just didn't see himself following a profession that got the short end of things.

Opportunity Spotting. Perhaps the single most revealing incident in Katz's biography is that involving the Pittsburgh flood. His quickness to realize what was happening and its implications represent an alertness to opportunity of the highest order. His actions, although seemingly simple and logical, are also a model of creative action. Note the sequence of actions, each creative in itself, that made his big scoop possible: buying the exposed film from the Pittsburgh shutterbugs; seeking for the means by which to develop the film; next, making up the one-shot news magazine; and finally, finding a printer who could be persuaded to do the printing job on credit. As inspired as each one of these separate acts was, of course they are all derived from the basic inspiration that struck him at the very outset: the sales appeal of a flood souvenir to the people who had experienced it. To have foreseen this potentiality even while the floodwaters were still gathering represents the recognition and development of opportunity in its most creative form.

The famed Harvard industrial psychologist F. J. Roethlisberger used to say, when presented with a slippery problem, "It's a spherical s.o.b.," pointing up the difficulty of coming to grips with the situation. Joseph Katz was faced by a spherical s.o.b. in trying to break into the paper business. His lack of capital and the reluctance of the paper mills to extend credit seemed to offer insuperable obstacles. Yet Katz persisted, finally found a point of entry, a "handle" by which to grasp the problem—in this case, Alfred Srere's willingness to do business with him on a credit basis.

From time to time a businessman, whether he's the head of his own enterprise or an executive in someone else's company, must be willing to take risks. The difference between the successful risktaker and the failure is that the former knows *when* to set down his chips. Katz, too, was willing to put his bets on the line when he developed his Rite Kit. He took the gamble and he won. Yet the "gamble" was not a jump off the deep end. Katz had good reason to believe that his idea would be successful because he had correctly assessed the consumer appeal of a similar item. His Rite Kit provided the key elements to the consumer that were so much in demand at that time.

Snowballing. Katz leapfrogged his initial successes. Having operated successfully in the gift-wrapping field, Katz looked for new worlds to conquer. The "new world" was related to the old. Still working in the paper and printing business, he decided to expand into the greeting-card field. This element is repeated in the patterns of many individuals on our roster. There comes a point in one's success when, in effect, the individual asks himself, "Shall I continue with more of the same or expand?" For the most part, the decision will be to venture into a broader field of endeavor. But this undertaking of a new challenge is not the same as a similar decision by a novice. The successful individual has already proved himself. Bringing his past experience with him is often sufficient guarantee that if the game's at all the same, he stands a better-than-even chance to win out.

Owen K. Murphy—

2 THERE'S MONEY IN CIRCULATION

Owen K. Murphy is president and founder of Niagara Therapy Corporation of Adamsville, Pennsylvania. The firm manufactures health equipment and furniture which incorporate "cyclo-massage" motors. It's a $25,000,000-a-year business that has enabled Murphy to acquire the Manatee Yacht Club and Marina in Port Salerno, Florida, and a $1,000,000 art and art object collection, consisting of ivory, jade, and crystal.

Niagara's product is an interesting example of the offbeat, and is a reminder that the old, traditional items that come to mind when one thinks of "going into business" don't make up the whole list of possibilities by a long shot. The output of Murphy's Niagara Therapy Corporation ranges from a flat pad containing a cyclo-massage motor and heat element, to matching living-room furniture, lounge chair and sofa, also equipped with cyclo-massage and heating units. Exactly how Murphy got the business going, and made it prosper, is an example of enterprise coupled with imagination— and a few other special ingredients.

*   *   *

There was little doubt in the minds of those who knew seven-year-old Owen K. Murphy that this was a boy destined to find his way to the top. What convinced his fellow residents of Carmel, Pennsylvania, was that while there was nothing unusual about a schoolboy running a paper route, it was rare to find a youngster of such tender years working not one but *two* routes.

There were only eight or nine thousand people residing in Carmel, and Owen calculated that he could increase his sales if some of these folks would subscribe to out-of-town papers. His judgment about this market proved correct. Philadelphia newspapers were brought into town by train at 4:40 A.M. each morning. He picked them up, and he distributed them to his customers by bicycle while on his school lunch hour. The Carmel paper he delivered to his customers after school hours. Neither route interfered with the other. The seven-year-old had already figured out the principles of time scheduling.

Why was a boy of such tender years willing to devote his leisure time to working and earning money? Was there a desperate need for the income at home? Was he driven to work by the demands of parents at home? Not at all, explains Murphy. The reason for his enthusiasm and drive for earning money was inspired by his father. Supporting a family of six in the early twenties was a task. Owen's father's situation was not much different from that of other heads of families. The senior Murphy was more than ordinarily ambitious, however. Employed as a fireman on the Pennsylvania Rail Road, Mr. Murphy managed to learn electrical engineering through night school and correspondence courses. In addition, Owen's father operated a small general store in Carmel. Mrs. Murphy and the other children pitched in as sales help. The combined income from his jobs and from his store provided a comfortable living for the family.

"One fact my father was fond of repeating to me," says Owen Murphy. "No one could get anywhere in this life without work. If you managed eight hours of honest labor you could probably take on sixteen just as easily. I figured that if Pop could do it, so could I. I was always proud of my father. I guess I patterned myself after him."

Murphy senior was a devoted parent, but he wanted his children to grow up standing on their own feet. If the family could have used part of the income that Owen was bringing home, it was not made known. This money was put into a savings account for the boy's future.

While Owen was in the second grade, Mr. Murphy was offered a lucrative job by the Underwriters Laboratories in Clearfield, Pennsylvania, a small town not too distant from Carmel, as an inspector of coal mines and industrial plants. He accepted the offer. With the family move, entrepreneur Owen had to forfeit his going newspaper business. But not without a profit. He sold his routes to two other enterprising youths.

He was not long idle in his new home town. It took only three days to track down a job as a gas station attendant. A few years later, when he was in junior high school, he arranged his schedule so that he could start the job at 4 P.M. and work till midnight. Doing this, he was able to earn as much as thirty-five dollars a week, a sum that an average family could live on in those days, back in the twenties.

LOYAL—BUT ALERT

In any work he has ever undertaken, Murphy says, he has always tried to do his best. Yet, at the same time, he felt it was important to remain alert to a better opportunity, should it appear. And indeed, when he heard about a job at Church Brothers, a stationery factory in town, he left the gas station job for the new opportunity. On school days he worked during the noon hour and at night; on Saturdays he worked all day in the shipping room, packing boxes and cleaning machinery. During the summer he made plans to work full time. As a sturdy young man, with excellent health, stamina and vigor, long hours never were a bother or inconvenience to him.

One afternoon, in 1925, Owen was in a diner passing the time of day with the owner, Gene Bishop, who mentioned that he was thinking of selling the restaurant. Then he asked, "Why don't *you* buy it?" Murphy was seventeen.

"I guess that was the moment that I got the real bug to become a financial success," says Murphy. "My dad had bought me a book,

Think and Grow Rich, by Napoleon Hill. Maybe it sounds cold-blooded, but I looked in the bathroom mirror after I read that book and told myself I was going to get rich!

"I had always dreamed of owning a boat, a car, maybe even an airplane. My father never laughed at my exalted dreams. He just made it clear that I stood a chance of having these acquisitions and more if I worked for them, but that that would be the only way I could get them."

When Gene Bishop offered to sell him the restaurant, Murphy decided this was his opportunity. There was only one, classic hitch: insufficient funds. With a small inheritance plus savings, he had amassed an astonishing ten thousand dollars since his newspaper route days. But the asking price for the luncheonette was exactly double. Without consulting anyone, young Murphy confidently approached the only person he knew in Clearfield who might help him—Charlie Kurtz, his former employer at the stationery factory.

FOUND—A BACKER

The experience of asking for his first and only loan left a vivid impression on Owen Murphy. "When I approached Charlie Kurtz he was in his private office. With him was his male secretary, a Mr. Ward. Kurtz, who was always very gruff in his dealings, barked at me, 'What do you want?'

"First, I said, I wanted the secretary to leave the room, for I would not speak in his presence. This didn't sit too well with Charlie Kurtz since he considered Ward somewhat of a confidante. Anyhow, I stood my ground and finally the secretary left us alone. I said my piece. I told Mr. Kurtz there was a business in town that I felt I could make a success out of.

"All Kurtz said was, 'Stop beating around the bush. What do you want?' I blurted out that I wanted five thousand dollars. He almost jumped out of his chair but finally quieted down long enough to ask me what I had in mind. He told me to leave and come back later in the afternoon.

"When I returned my heart sank when Mr. Kurtz said, 'Well, I've decided not to lend you that money.' But before I had a chance to react further, he added: 'You have to have twice that much.' He had gone down to look at the Bishop place and decided that as long as I was going to get it, the luncheonette would need a new soda fountain, new flooring, a paint job, and other repairs. He wanted me to start off right. I never forgot his faith in me. More than ever, I wanted to show him I could succeed."

Once again Murphy was in his own business. He convinced the principal of his school that he would serve his fellow students well-balanced meals and at a more attractive price than any competition in the neighborhood. He also promised that he would not neglect his own studies. On this pledge, his school schedule was arranged so that he could leave early to tend to his luncheonette. Before long, he had drummed up a steady trade.

Murphy soon felt, however, that he should be getting more out of the business. The logical move was to expand operations, but how? An idea flashed: the ice cream company that supplied his store made the best product in the area. Why not canvass private homes and take orders to deliver ice cream between 11 A.M. and 2 P.M.? He invested in a Model T Ford, arranged for his brother and his mother to handle walk-in trade, and took over the job of creating direct sales in the home. Business clicked immediately. Then Murphy found that there was a demand for candies, peanuts, and other refreshment products for bridge parties. He moved in on this extra business and found himself with a catering service.

The enterprising young man enjoyed two years of managing and running his multi-interest luncheonette. In this short time, he was able to pay back Mr. Kurtz in full and still retain a small profit. "I was thrilled that I could wipe off my debt," reminisces Murphy, "and know, at the same time, that I could run a business at its maximum possibilities. But I was restless now. I wanted something else although I wasn't sure what."

RESTLESSNESS OR AMBITION?

A change of scenery might invite new ideas or opportunities, he thought. He traded his Model T for a new Model A Ford and, with ample funds in his pockets, left for Texas, a spot to which he was attracted because of the climate and the promise of opportunity. The time was 1929 and jobs were scarce. After a week or two of scanning the local Houston papers, Murphy found an ad calling for laborers. Pay was four dollars a day. With nothing else in view at the moment, young Murphy answered the call and was hired to work on a project building portable exhibits for state and county fairs. But salaried jobs of any kind had never appealed to Murphy; they were too confining and he was anxious to "go places" as fast as he could. He figured there was no harm in asking the top brass if he might run one of the exhibits. As luck would have it, they agreed. Murphy ran his concession successfully for eight months. Then one night, he decided this was not a career for him. Although wooed by the fair's management to stay, Murphy once again took to the road.

His travels brought him to Minneapolis and it was here that twenty-year-old Murphy had his first exposure to the direct sales field. He called upon a company headed by Chester Krum, a former New Yorker, to apply for a job selling men's apparel from house to house.

Murphy had heard that "to be a good salesman, you have to have the desire to be one." "Truthfully," he confides, "I was drawn to the field because I like to make money. A salesman can do just that. The harder he works, the longer hours he puts in, the more dollars he can pile up. His working life is not timed by punching a clock. His future depends entirely on his own initiative. I liked that."

Murphy recalls that he had picked up a Dale Carnegie book while driving to Minnesota. He read it carefully and gave considerable thought to the contents. "My feeling was," he says, "that I could learn everything covering ten years of a man's life by investing only a couple of hours of reading. Surely I could afford that! I learned from Carnegie, and I believe it, that in order to sell yourself, or a product, people have to like you. I felt that if I had a good product to sell and I was permitted to enter a person's home and talk to them, to make them like me, to find we had a couple of common interests, if I could give them something more for their money than they were paying, I would make a good salesman."

Fortified by the words of Dale Carnegie, Owen Murphy launched himself into a career with Chester Krum, selling men's wearing apparel. It wasn't long before Murphy was sent to Washington, D.C., Boston, Pittsburgh, St. Louis, San Francisco and fifteen other cities to open up offices for the clothing firm.

$25,000 AT TWENTY-TWO—IS IT ENOUGH?

Although his salary had reached the $25,000-a-year level by now, and he was barely twenty-two years old, overnight he made up his mind to quit. His decision was based on the fact that he could not see enough growth in the business. Before deciding what career to pursue, Murphy wanted a vacation. He headed for Miami Beach, Florida, to loaf for a couple of months in the sun and meditate on his future. "I guess an active mind never rests," he reflects, "especially when you haven't found yourself, and I hadn't. Subconsciously, I was always on the lookout for something out of which I could form a business."

That something happened quite unexpectedly. The national craze for jigsaw puzzles was just starting. Murphy noticed men and women alike, young and old, lounging around on the beaches, putting together large pieces of puzzles. He noticed, also, a photographer who strolled around the beaches every day taking pictures of the vacationers. That's all his fertile brain needed to put an idea into action. Why not make puzzles of the photos of actual people?

Murphy drove back to Pittsburgh. He contacted Freddy Burger, a photographer, who agreed to make photographic enlargements at a nominal price. Murphy also ran ads in the local papers looking for all jigsaw operators who had machines that would cut puzzles out of plywood. He was lined up for action now. There was one thing left to do—test his brainstorm. The logical and fastest way was to advertise. Murphy bought space in metropolitan dailies across the United States, selecting key cities where the response would be greatest. The ad proclaimed that for one dollar and a photograph enclosed in an envelope, the sender would receive a hundred-piece personalized jigsaw puzzle.

In anticipation of the response to the ads, Murphy rented desk space in an office on the north side of Pittsburgh. All he could do was to sit and wait for the first Sunday ads to break. Would there be a response? By the following Tuesday morning six hundred envelopes were delivered to him. By the close of the week more than ten thousand pieces of mail, holding one dollar each, were piled high on his desk.

It looked like a bonanza. But, in his anxiety to capitalize on the jigsaw rage, Murphy had neglected to make certain that he could deliver when the orders came in. In the rush to produce the quantity of puzzles demanded, Murphy faced a major problem. The photo paper being used would not adhere to the plywood. He had to make good or return the mountains of dollars he'd received. He searched frantically for an experienced man to help him out of the dilemma and, fortunately, located a man who knew adhesives. Working day and night for most of a week, Murphy and the expert finally solved the problem.

Riding the crest, Murphy rented a store at the corner of Fifth and Market streets in Pittsburgh, calling it the Premier Puzzle Shop. He engaged three operators to sit in the front windows cutting out photographs, then sat back again and waited for the rush. But, just as the jigsaw-puzzle craze had risen from nowhere, so did it fade. The fad had simply gone.

Nevertheless, Murphy emerged from the experience with a profit and his spirits high. He was ready to latch on to something new again, something on which to build a solid future.

Shortly after the collapse of the jigsaw business, while he was attending a party in Pittsburgh, Murphy met a representative of A & B Smith Company, agents for a Hoboken, New Jersey, firm manufacturing engineering supplies. Murphy made an impression on the company man and he was asked to join A & B as sales manager. "It was real depression time by now," says Murphy. "Jobs were hard to get so I accepted the offer. It was a wise choice. I knew nothing about engineering equipment or supplies, but I knew that my prospective customer, an engineer, certainly would. I felt that if I had a good product, he'd buy without too much selling."

An unorthodox sales approach—but it worked.

Murphy concentrated on developing a sales force and expanding the sales territory for the company. Within a few years the volume of business for A & B Smith had more than tripled, jumping from $300,000 to $1,000,000. A major portion of the credit was attributed to Murphy's initiative. He had set up an efficient sales organization, opened up new territories for sales and then climaxed his efforts by bringing in the all-important new accounts.

By 1942 World War II had broken out and Murphy found himself in the Navy as a pharmacist's mate. He was assigned to Bethesda, Maryland, for training in the medical corps, where he worked eventually with plastic surgeons. Here he developed an avid interest in physical medicine, and became fascinated by the reconstruction skills of the physicians with whom he worked. His stint of three years in the armed services and an observation he made while on duty was to be worth millions to him later.

GENESIS OF AN IDEA

"One thing impressed me more than anything else," Murphy says. "I learned that if we couldn't get circulation in certain parts of an injured GI's body, that man stood a good chance of losing an arm or leg. This bothered me terribly. I wished there were some way to help increase blood movement."

His three years of service completed, he returned to work for his former engineering supply firm. The company had kept him on the payroll while he was in service so he felt it was no more than fair to go back to his old work. One weekend early in 1946, Murphy met a Mr. Wettlaufer while attending an antiques auction on a farm in upstate New York. Wettlaufer mentioned that he held patent on a unique product which, he claimed, increased blood circulation. Murphy forgot the auction and the antiques and asked to see the item. Wettlaufer gave a demonstration and soon Murphy was on his way home, minus $395 but with a crude-looking unit that reminded him of an electric chair. This chair had straight wooden arms with a motor built underneath that vibrated the seat and sitter.

Murphy began sampling the action of the motor by sitting in the chair for a few minutes a day. He discovered that it made him "feel good." By adjusting a dial at one arm of the chair, he would receive a massage that seemed to make his body lose its tenseness. The intensity of the massage could be increased by turning up the control dial. This stepped-up action seemed to exhilarate him. For several weeks he kept testing his reaction to the chair. He kept a record of how long the effects of the massage lasted. He tried it out on a friend who had complained of sore muscles in his shoulder. The latter's reaction was enthusiastic. He told Murphy he'd buy a unit that day, if they were for sale.

Murphy thought to himself that if a man could respond this quickly to the product it must have merit. More than that, he believed that he had finally come upon that "something" that he had dreamed about ever since he left the Navy, the useful device that would help stimulate and increase blood circulation. This was the moment in which his future "became crystallized." Murphy was going into his own business and this time he would devote his lifetime to something he felt would help other people.

All Murphy had to start with was the crude-looking chair he'd bought on a hunch. This alone gave him no license to begin a manufacturing business. First, he had to get hold of the patents and the name, Niagara—and who knew if the owner was willing to sell?

Murphy was living in Adamsville, Pennsylvania, which was a short way from Buffalo, where William Wettlaufer, the developer of the massage motor, lived. Wettlaufer was rather a well-known name, since he's also invented an industrial shaker for coal, gravel and sand. Murphy called on the man and, with what appears to have been a combination of good fortune and masterful business tactics, purchased the patent for $150,000.

"Wettlaufer drove a hard bargain," says Murphy. "He knew he was in the driver's seat. Like other shrewd sellers he capitalized on the advantage of his position. He knew I was anxious to get hold of the patents, so he was determined to stand pat on his asking price. I was just as determined to own Niagara. We closed the deal at his figure. I gave him thirty thousand dollars down and agreed to pay off the balance within five years, which I did. The $150,000 bought only the patent. It included no tools, no stock, no inventory—nothing. All I'd really bought was a motor and a name—Niagara. I knew I had a tough job ahead of me."

A BABY FALLS BEFORE IT WALKS

The Niagara patent was purchased in the spring of 1948. Murphy immediately converted an old barn behind his house into a manufacturing plant and office. He hired three local men to build the Niagara motors and the furniture. When the first few units were completed, he decided to make the rounds of the beauty shops in nearby Meadville, seemingly a natural market for the chair. This notion proved wrong. Beauty-shop owners didn't believe that the action of the motor could meet the claims. They just weren't interested in the product.

The budding manufacturer then decided to approach a few hospitals. He reasoned that if the machine was to perform a therapeutic service, what could be a more appropriate market than a hospital, where many patients suffered from poor circulation. Accompanied by two registered nurses who were to demonstrate Niagara, Murphy visited local hospitals in and around Reading, Pennsylvania. Here he met another obstacle. He was told that without any research to back up the claims of mechanical massage, it could not be accepted. Hospital officials pointed out there was no factual evidence to substantiate what the Niagara motor could do. This was a blow to Murphy. However, his faith in Niagara was undiminished. If proof was needed, he'd get it.

This meant medical research and Murphy knew this would take a lot of precious time. Meanwhile, other developments were shaping up for Niagara. One afternoon as he was coming into New York on a train, he chanced to read an article in *Fortune* magazine about two men who'd been mustered out of the armed services and who had built a flourishing silverware business by canvassing house to house. They romanced their product by presenting it to the potential customer by candlelight, displayed on the family dining-room table.

Direct selling? Murphy hadn't considered it until this moment, although he had experience in the field when he worked with Chester Krum, back in the thirties, selling men's apparel. Why not take a chance and try to sell Niagara via direct sales? The first man to answer the ad that Murphy ran in the *New York Times* calling for distributors, turned out to be a man known in selling circles as a "live wire." He was Al Leo, a twenty-five-year-old who had a direct selling organization of his own in Harrisburg, Pennsylvania. Murphy was attracted by the spirit of the young man and his knowledge of selling. Murphy gave Leo a demonstration, let him use the chair, spent an hour or more explaining the great potential of the health equipment. "I thought I'd sold him on my product," says Murphy, "but I was left a little awe-struck when this young man said to me, 'If I'm interested, I'll get in touch.'"

Leo returned in five hours with a surprising story. When he had left the hotel, he was unable to get a taxicab so he had to walk about fifteen blocks. He said his feet hardly touched the pavement, he felt he was bouncing along. He could only attribute this condition to the workout with the Niagara equipment—encouraging words for Owen Murphy.

That incident marked the beginning of the first direct-selling campaign for Niagara. Leo placed an order for twenty-four units with Murphy; in a week he ordered twelve more. Within ten years Al Leo made one million dollars selling Niagara. "He's no longer with me," says Murphy, "because he couldn't go any higher. He couldn't own my company. He couldn't run it. I was doing that. He left me, but he's still in the direct selling field."

SUCCESS—WITH LIMITATIONS

Although Al Leo was the first of more than three hundred Niagara distributors, and although sales of Niagara hand units, foam-rubber pads and furniture were increasing monthly, Murphy was still disturbed by the fact that he had not yet cracked the hospital market or achieved recognition in the medical field. It was becoming increasingly important that he gain this recognition because Niagara was being advertised nationally in magazines such as *Good Housekeeping, House and Garden, Life, Look.* Copy and claims were coming under the eagle eye of the Food and Drug Administration.

Murphy had two choices in trying to convince the medical profession of the worth of Niagara products. He could let sales continue as they were going, "make a fast killing," then get out of the manufacturing business. Or, he could pull in the reins on sales and soft-pedal claims until he had enough clinical evidence to substantiate them.

RESEARCH BUILDS THE FUTURE

Murphy chose the latter—and has reason to cheer his decision. Murphy heard that a Dr. John R. Mote, former associate professor of medicine at Harvard University, had earned a reputation as a brilliant researcher, and that he was one of the men responsible for introducing the wonder drug cortisone to the commercial market. This was the kind of man Murphy felt he needed on his medical team. He induced Dr. Mote to head up a medical research program. From a modest start, the research projects have continued and expanded. More than one million dollars has been invested in this phase of the business in just the last few years alone.

There was only one moment after he engaged Dr. Mote in which he says he could have "thrown in the sponge." Actually it was Dr. Mote, whose background covered a list of impressive accomplishments in academic medicine, government work, pharmaceutical development, and industrial medical work, who tried to discourage him. The consultant told him that research was expensive and might prove that the product was not of great medical significance, after all. But Murphy's belief in his unique massage motor never wavered. He gave the order to go ahead no matter what the results.

In short order, the Niagara Research Institute was established, with executive offices in New York. The first research program was set up in the physics department in a college in Greenville, Pennsylvania, to determine the actual physical characteristics of Niagara. What made it different from any ordinary vibration? What motion or activity did it generate to produce such beneficial relief from symptoms?

Research found that Niagara products did, indeed, develop a unique action. Instead of the harsh, thumping stroke of a common vibrator, Niagara units operated with a pleasant, rolling, cycloid motion. The action was referred to as "cyclo-massage," combining a vertical, horizontal and circular motion that reached into bone and muscle; helped relieve minor aches and pains and to relax tense muscles. Further experiments confirmed and extended the findings of the first study. After this, Owen Murphy's Research Institute made grants to hospitals, teaching medical centers and clinics throughout North America to evaluate the medical and physiological potentials of the health equipment he manufactured. Results of the studies were published in such medical publications as the

American Journal of Physical Medicine and the *Archives of Physical Medicine,* among others. One team reported that "the application of Niagara resulted in an increase in blood circulation."

This was what Murphy had banked his hopes on, risked his money for, given his time and effort to. Niagara was in the clear now. The few claims made by the product could be upheld. He hired expert engineers to keep perfecting and improving the Niagara motors. He expanded his advertising program. And the salesmen bringing Niagara to the consumer were ringing up dollar after dollar for themselves and Murphy in sales. More than that, mail was pouring in from all parts of the country, lauding Murphy's products.

When Murphy bought the first unit from Mr. Wettlaufer for $395 he didn't realize that he was founding a new industry. Until then there were no chairs and no other furniture constructed in the United States with built-in massage motors. Niagara was the first.

But not the last, it seemed. By the time his first national ads were breaking in consumer publications, competition had already begun to spring up. Soon, more than fifty manufacturers of some kind of chairs and hand-massage units were ready to share the market with Murphy. So they thought. It took only one year for thirty-eight of these companies to go bankrupt. "They probably thought they'd come in for a fast kill," says Murphy, "but they hadn't learned, as I had, that the FDA would be on top of them because they hadn't backed up their claims—many of them fantastic—with medical research. With this kind of a beginning there is seldom chance for a second time around. Once the buying public loses confidence in you it's the death knell of the business."

FAILURE IS WHAT YOU MAKE IT

In looking back over his career, Murphy is quick to admit that he's made more than his share of mistakes. He doesn't describe them as failure, but mistakes. Some of them were made because of overzealousness, particularly in his rush to expand operations. Some are attributed to impulsiveness, a trait that the industrialist some-times has difficulty in controlling.

One of his most recent blunders resulted from his overanxious-ness to sell Niagara products in England. A dealer in Bermuda who had been buying the cyclo-massage merchandise for some time told Murphy he would like to open a dealership in London. Murphy was overjoyed at the prospect, particularly when the gentleman placed an order for fifty thousand dollars worth of Ni-agara units.

A thousand units had been paid for and shipped when the fire-works began. A transatlantic phone call informed manufacturer Murphy that in testing, the first unit produced electrical interference on British television and radio frequencies. All of the merchandise had to be taken back. And, to top it all, a thirty-pound fine (about ninety dollars) was levied upon the dealer. Niagara, of course, doesn't like to lose a customer. Murphy placated the dealer and reimbursed him for the fine. He instructed the plant to produce new motors, compatible with the BBC radio and television signals, then shipped the units back at company expense.

Another mistake which Murphy admits readily, proved even more costly. For years he argued with dealers that the health benefits his furniture offered were more important than fashion or design. He believed implicitly that styling was of secondary interest to Niagara's customers compared to the therapeutic value. When sales began to drop, Murphy was finally convinced that his factories must produce furniture that was fashionable as well as beneficial. He scanned the market for designers to upgrade the lines and fabrics of the leisure lounge chairs, chaise longues, and sofas. It may have been an expensive mistake, but by correcting it Murphy expects to more than double the volume of business within the next few years. In fact, he hopes to realize his one recurring dream, to see cyclo-massage furniture in every American home as standard household equipment, as essential as the telephone, the refrigerator, and the television set.

Niagara's president doesn't mind too much the mistakes that he or his employees make. He still believes to err is human. Sure, he says, it can and does cost the company money. But, over-all, mistakes don't add up to more than a temporary hindrance. At least, that's how this businessman looks at it.

BEHIND THE OWEN K. MURPHY STORY

The career of the President of the Niagara Therapy Corporation demonstrates what might be called "rungs-upmanship." His progress is marked by a constant series of moves, each one taking him higher up the ladder than the last. This particular element in Murphy's pattern existed even when he was a youngster. When his family moved into a new town, young Murphy looked about for a new type of work instead of seeking to duplicate a job he had already mastered. For example, after his gas attendant's job had provided the experience he wanted, he was ready to move on to a factory job with better pay and more challenge.

The strong motivation that characterizes most of our successful people is especially clear in Murphy's case. The average youngster who delivers papers after school is usually considered to be highly motivated. Murphy one-upped this stereotype by having not one but *two* newspaper routes. Not only was he willing to work, he also had a strong awareness of opportunity. He almost seemed to be able to smell it out. Even as a youngster, Murphy had the ability to appraise a situation and uncover an exploitable angle. His development of a group of subscribers to out-of-town papers illustrates this talent.

Youngsters vary considerably in the direction in which they expend their energies. The sports-oriented lad will devote hours to pitching a baseball, kicking a football, or practicing a racing stroke in the school pool. The studious-minded youngster will spend his leisure time in reading. Young Murphy exhibited an intense interest in a single area of activity: commerce.

There is an interesting parallel between Murphy's pattern as a young man and the findings of a recent study of six thousand newsboys conducted by Dr. Mortimer R. Feinberg, President of BFS Psychological Associates. The study cast a revealing light on the parental treatment that helps youngsters toward responsibility and maturity. Dr. Feinberg found that the most dependable youngsters had the following characteristics:

They are allowed to spend (or save) their earnings, according to their own desire. Their parents don't try to tell them what to do with their money. Nor are these boys urged to "chip in" to the family kitty when the family is in financial need. Many mature boys insist on helping their families out of financial jams, but they do it on their own in individually satisfying ways. Apparently when a young man contributes his earnings to a family general fund, his ambition and drive are stunted; his earnings lose personal significance. By doing something *he* wants to do with his money, his initiative is rewarded. Young Murphy fitted this pattern. Money he earned was his—to save, as happened to be the case—but his alone.

They are not necessarily from poor families. Dr. Feinberg's research shows that a history of economic deprivation may *decrease* reliability on the job. Unlike the children of poverty-stricken immigrants two generations ago, the youth of today is not challenged by economic deprivation. Dr. Feinberg found that the higher the economic and educational level of his parents, the greater the likelihood a newsboy would stay on a job and succeed at it. In one sense, this negates the theory that children of wealthy parents are often spoiled and irresponsible.

They are accustomed to doing things with their parents. Boys who are successful, mature and responsible say they attend ball games, go to shows and circuses, visit museums and such, with their parents. Those boys who are unsuccessful indicate that their parents generally have little interest in "doing things" with the children.

Another new finding, concludes Dr. Feinberg, is just beginning to emerge and will bear further examination before the study is complete: *The boy who thinks he will succeed at selling newspapers usually does.* Further, he seems to have a plan about how he will tackle his selling challenge. For example, he may plan to sell first to his family, then to his friends. Then, having gained confidence, he plans to sell to strangers.

Psychologists repeatedly point out the importance of parental influence. As his biography indicates, Murphy's father helped his enthusiasm and his sense of self-sufficiency. Murphy himself says, "I was always proud of my father. I guess I patterned myself after him." Psychologists tell us that this type of identification with the male parent is often the emotional foundation of the secure and self-confident individual. It undoubtedly represents a major factor in Murphy's emotional development.

In addition to these major elements in Murphy's success pattern, the following are also important keys:

Idea Mating. There is at present a great deal of interest in creativity. Articles with titles like "How to Be an Idea Man," "How to Increase Your Creativity" abound. Murphy's story provides two excellent examples of just how an idea is born. There are apparently two types of idea men: The "genius," who is an original groundbreaker, a man who innovates in fresh areas; and the rearranger, whose brainstorms, often as worthy as that of the genius, recombine previous ideas and represent something new. Murphy developed two ideas by this latter method. The first instance occurred in Miami Beach, when he got the idea for making jigsaw puzzles of the enlarged photographs of actual people. His combination of two things—the jigsaw puzzle craze and interest in one's own photo—made it possible for him to develop a unique and attractive product.

The second idea led to the birth of his company. During his Bethesda hospital experience, he first became aware of the importance of increasing blood circulation for therapeutic reasons. Seeing Wettlaufer's motorized chair and hearing the inventor's claims for its circulation-increasing capabilities, immediately gave Murphy the idea that here was the answer to the need. In his own words, "his future was crystallized." The two ideas, coming together almost like male and female gametes, gave birth to an important and viable third idea that resulted in the founding of his million-dollar enterprise.

The "Whittington Augury." It's an amazing fact that the successful person often has an augury of his future triumphs. This was certainly the case in young Murphy's life. As he describes it, he confronted himself in the bathroom mirror and assured himself that *he was going to be rich*. This incident ties in with the findings mentioned by Dr. Feinberg, that the boy who *thinks* he will succeed usually *does*.

This "foreknowledge of success" has been dramatized in the story of a poor orphan named Dick Whittington who went to London in the late years of the fourteenth century to seek his fortune. Reduced to starvation, defeated and forlorn, he was about to leave the city when the famous Bow Bells rang out and seemed to say to him, "Turn again, turn again Dick Whittington, thrice lord mayor of London." And he stayed and lived to see the augury of the bells fulfilled. He won great wealth, married his master's daughter, was knighted and three times was elected Lord Mayor of London—in 1397, 1406, and 1419.

Many successful people recall an incident in their own lives, a moment of foresight, clairvoyance—call it what you will. An inner voice tells them that they will succeed just as Owen Murphy looked into the mirror and "told himself" that he was going to be rich. Here again, parental influence offered a strong assist: "My father never laughed at my exalted wishes," says Murphy. As a matter of fact, the elder Murphy did more than not laugh. He encouraged his son to make the efforts to make the augury come true.

The Direct Approach. In one of his first big business ventures, Murphy had the opportunity for what he thought would be a remunerative deal—the buying of Gene Bishop's restaurant. He himself lacked sufficient funds to swing the deal. In this situation, Murphy's thinking was precise and to the point. He asked himself, "Who among the people I know could help me buy the restaurant?" Charlie Kurtz, owner of the stationery factory in which Murphy had worked, was the answer. And having arrived at that answer, notice the directness of Owen Murphy's approach.

The quality of directness is extremely important here. A lesser person might have had qualms. Hesitations might have forced him to make a fumbling and unpersuasive request. Murphy was not hampered by such attitudes. He could approach Kurtz directly— that is to say matter-of-factly—for two reasons: first, confidence in the proposal; and second, a mature understanding of the fact that the proposition he was making was a matter of *business* in the best sense of the word. Kurtz was obviously going to be free to accept or reject the proposal.

This ability to be direct, to be matter-of-fact with people in business situations—leaving out such negative emotions as shame, worry, indecisiveness—was an important element in Murphy's makeup and his approach to people.

Asset Exploitation. Many of us have assets both tangible and intangible which we are content to possess passively. Owen Murphy's exploitation of his newly acquired asset, a luncheonette, illustrates a productive, even imaginative extension of the benefits of this asset. He wasn't content to run the restaurant in the same way his predecessors had. Instead of sitting back and letting customers come to him, Murphy developed the idea of building up the business. Casting about, he decided that the students in the neighboring school were a logical group to attract. Next, he used the restaurant as the center of operations for a catering service, creating direct sales in adjoining areas.

The Restlessness of Insufficient Challenge. Murphy's feelings of restlessness usually coincided with a situation in which he did not see a sufficiently bright future. Although earning twenty-five thousand dollars a year at the age of twenty-two—certainly impressive by any ordinary standard—he decided to give up selling men's clothing because he could not see enough growth in the business. One might describe these fits of discontent of Murphy's as the "restlessness of the uncommitted entrepreneur." Not finding sufficient opportunity in what he was doing, he undertook a search for a more promising and rewarding occupation.

Perhaps the most decisive factor in Murphy's rise, however, was a quality that must go hand in hand with this restless, searching attitude: the ability to know when to settle down. Murphy never let his rambling take his mind off what he was really looking for— and he had the courage to stick with his fledgling company once he had recognized that it was his big opportunity.

3 { Donald M. Kendall –
HARD CASH IN A SOFT DRINK

Many successful people spend considerable time in their early years "finding themselves." They grope, stumble, go through a variety of jobs, often undistinguished ones, until they eventually grasp their main chance. The story of Donald M. Kendall's breakthrough is an interesting example of the successful man who placed his foot firmly on the right road at the outset. The story describing the particular elements of Kendall's breakthrough also offers an inside view of the growth of one of America's peppier corporations.

*   *   *

Lt. (j.g.) Donald M. Kendall, on terminal leave from the United States Navy in the fall of 1947, had two subjects uppermost in his thoughts. One was a long-anticipated fishing trip to Nova Scotia. The other was finding a job. Kendall and the girl he had married while he was in the Navy were visiting the Long Island, New York, home of his wife's family. He had spent five years in the Navy. A patrol bomber pilot in New Guinea and the Philippines, he had been award the Distinguished Flying Cross and two Air Medals. Now, somewhat later than most World War II servicemen, he was preparing to re-enter civilian life.

An eager and vigorous young man of twenty-five, Kendall was determined to make good in the American tradition. He felt strongly that he had something of value to offer the business world. The idea of the give-and-take competition of the market place excited him. He liked people and liked doing business with them. He had learned the rudiments of office procedure while serving in the administration headquarters of the flying unit to which he had been attached. He was ready to meet opportunity. He no doubt would have spelled the word with a capital *O*.

AN OUTFIT CALLED PEPSI-COLA

A friend told him of a sales job that might be just what he was looking for. This job was in the Queens plant of an outfit called the Pepsi-Cola Company. The friend advised Kendall that the soft-drink bottling concern had done well in the past but had been on the downgrade since the war. While its product was good, the company had been plagued with management problems. It was so far behind its competition, that there wasn't even a race. But the potential was there. This was the kind of company, his friend thought, in which he might go up fast. A bigger, more solid company would offer opportunities, too, of course, but they would be slower in coming. And Kendall was in a hurry.

He was interviewed by Edward Loughlin, vice-president in charge of fountain syrup sales. Loughlin, impressed by the enthusiasm and ambition of the tall, good-looking young man, hired him. "Come to work Monday," he said. That was a Friday. Kendall's fishing trip was scheduled to begin the next day. Not one to beat about the bush, he expressed his chagrin with rueful humor. Loughlin was sympathetic. "I'm a fishing nut myself," he said. "Go ahead, then, and come in a week from Monday."

The fishing excursion was all that Kendall had hoped for, and on the appointed day he reported with high anticipation to the job with the only company he was ever to work for.

Although without business experience, he knew the meaning of the word "work." Born on a dairy farm near Sequim, Washington, he had worked on the farm as a boy. During his last year of high school in Calhoun, Kentucky, and as a student at Western Kentucky State College, he had held summer jobs. One was as a workman on a gang clearing right of way for an electric power company. Another summer he ran a creamery route in the daytime, picking up cans of cream at dairies and hauling them to a central point. At night he switched hats and went to work for the transport company that took the dairy products to the processing plant. This kind of labor developed the boy's physical strength and gave him the stamina that was to serve him well in hectic demanding later years.

WHEN EMPLOYEE AND COMPANY JELL

In Queens, during the closing months of 1947, Kendall threw himself zestfully into the learning stage of his new job. From the first, he knew this was the business for him. "I was lucky beyond belief to walk into that Queens job," he said later. "I could have wasted four or five years with the wrong company. I would have been farther behind than ever. I wanted a company that I could stay with, and it was my good fortune that I found it on the first try. Pepsi-Cola and I jelled right from the beginning." This "jelling" was not difficult to explain. Pepsi was a company that was trying not merely to get back where it had once been but to surpass past performance. Kendall was a man with the will and the spirit to ride upward with the company. They belonged together.

Kendall had told Loughlin in their initial conversation that he was much more interested in a chance for advancement than in what his starting salary would be. The salary agreed on was four hundred dollars a month—three hundred less than the young lieutenant (j.g.) was getting as terminal pay. He soon found that his pay was being increased regularly at six-month intervals. The money meant less to him than the knowledge that he was moving up.

The young salesman brought a potent combination of energy and excitement to his work. He was soon out on the road, calling on franchised Pepsi-Cola bottlers throughout New England and the Middle West. He was charged with getting the bottlers into the company's fountain program, a high-profit segment of the soft drink business. Part of the job was to help local bottlers in getting Pepsi-Cola fountains installed in new locations.

On entering a territory, Kendall would spend a day calling on

proprietors of drugstores and snack bars and convincing them that
he offered a product that would make money for them. Then he
would go back to the bottler and say, "Look—I've sold this many in
just one day. Think what you can do from that beginning."

Placed in charge of a crew going into a bottler's territory to sell
soft drink dispensers, Kendall made it a point to sell more than any
other crew member. He never stopped making calls until he had
accomplished this aim.

"Why?" he was asked.

The significant reply was shot back unhesitatingly: "Because I
wanted to be number one!" He went on to explain his conviction
that the boss, at whatever level, has to prove himself better
than any man working under him. "You can't send a man out to do
a job you can't do yourself," he said.

On his sales trips Kendall worked inordinately long hours. The
work included talking shop by the hour to anyone in the business
who was willing to talk with him. His objective was to learn everything there was to know about the soft drink business in general
and the Pepsi-Cola Company in particular. "I spent a lot of time
with our bottlers," he recalls, "and it was time well invested. One
thing I learned of great value to me ever afterward was that these
realistic-minded, independent businessmen used their own individual approaches in running their affairs. These approaches might
be different, even when the problems involved were similar. I found
out that there is no such thing as a standardized way of attaining
success. There is no sure-fire formula. Each man has to do it in his
own fashion and by his own methods."

Kendall remembers with gratitude the assistance and advice extended him by such men as Walter Dossin, the veteran bottler who
held the Pepsi-Cola franchise for the state of Michigan, and Joe
Lapides, the Baltimore franchise holder. They and others were
never too busy to talk shop with the pleasant, hard-driving young
salesman.

He drew on customers as well as bottlers for his continuing
business education. He learned promotion techniques from theater

owners who stocked his product. He studied the marketing methods of the chain stores where Pepsi-Cola was offered. He learned early that a good salesman had to be a good listener. He listened hard, eventually concluding that another prerequisite was the ability of a good listener to separate the useful from the merely showy.

"YOU CAN BE PRESIDENT . . ."

Along with the salary increases that came with gratifying regularity, Kendall received encouraging words from Ed Loughlin, who quickly realized that he had hired a man of unusual capabilities. "You can go to the top," he said near the end of Kendall's first year with him. "You can become president of this company." This was a heady thought, but to Kendall at the time it seemed an unrealizable dream. But if the presidency should be beyond his reach, advancement on a lower level could certainly be attained. He applied himself to achieve what he regarded as the possible.

The apprenticeship and journeyman phases of his career were soon behind him. He became manager of syrup sales for all company-owned plants. Shortly afterward, in 1951, he went to the national sales department as assistant national sales manager. He was still learning. He taught himself how to read a balance sheet and took a correspondence school course in accounting. Most of his business education continued to come from his associates. He kept up his practice of talking shop, and he studied the art of salesmanship as practiced by other men in the company.

In 1952, five years after he had "lucked into" the job in Queens, Kendall was named vice-president in charge of national sales. Four years later he became vice-president in charge of marketing. His new duties included jurisdiction over all sales, advertising and promotion. Now the knowledge he had gained out in the field from bottlers and customers proved its value. He had become a moving force in the company.

His great opportunity opened in 1957, when he was chosen to be president of Pepsi-Cola International, Ltd. This was the company division that handled overseas sales of Pepsi-Cola. At the time of Kendall's assumption of the presidency, the division was operating in sixty countries. This was foreign ground to him in every sense of the term. He had visited Europe twice and Mexico once as a tourist, but he knew nothing about overseas business operations. As president of Pepsi-Cola International, he found himself spending up to half his time abroad. A new learning process started.

THREE STEPS TO NEW MARKETS

Pepsi-Cola International was not living up to its potentialities. His search for reasons why soon convinced Kendall that a basic flaw existed in the overseas division's method of operation. A man who felt that flexibility was the key to success in modern business, he decided that the New York headquarters of the parent company was keeping far too tight a rein on the overseas division.

To open a new market abroad, three steps had to be taken. First, it was necessary to make a survey to determine the market potential, the required investment and the probable return on the investment. Then a prospective bottler had to be found and convinced of the profit potentialities. Finally, everything else having gone well, the planned expansion had to be implemented by the construction and equipping of a plant. These steps were essential, Kendall realized, but the trouble was that each one had to be outlined and the outline submitted to New York for approval before the next step could be taken. This time-consuming process left little to the judgment of the man on the site, although it was he who presumably had the best-grounded knowledge of the various factors involved.

Kendall completely reorganized the overseas division. He decentralized the operation so that once the budget was set the local manager could go ahead pretty much on his own.

In addition to his administrative duties, the president of Pepsi-Cola International devoted much time to personal selling. To him selling was the perpetual adventure. At times his sales trips led to other adventures. There was the time in 1958, for instance, when he left Iraq only two days before the king was overthrown and rioters attacked and killed several Americans and Europeans who were guests in the hotel where Kendall had been staying. On another occasion when there was trouble in Lebanon he arrived before the Marines had landed and had to get a military escort to accompany him from the airport to the hotel. Once there, he and a companion decided to have a swim. They left the water in haste shortly after they had entered it, being chased out by shots from low-flying planes.

KHRUSHCHEV ORDERS A SECOND CUP

Kendall also had the experience of introducing Nikita Khrushchev, then head man in Soviet Russia, to Pepsi-Cola. This was at the fair held by the United States in Russia in 1959. At the request of the Department of State, Kendall arranged for his company to set up a booth to hand out samples of soft drinks. When Khrushchev visited the booth, steered there by Vice President Richard M. Nixon, he first drank a bottle of Pepsi-Cola produced in New York and brought over especially for the fair. He was then given a cup of the drink produced in Russia from syrup brought over from the United States. To the surprise of no one, Nikita avowed that the Russian product was better and ordered a second cup.

Pictures of Khrushchev drinking Pepsi-Cola were published all over the world. It was the kind of public relations coup that Kendall delighted in scoring—particularly since he had encountered some difficulty in convincing a top Pepsi executive of the value of the company's participating in the fair.

Beneath his controlled exterior, Kendall was never a sedate man. His mind swarmed with ideas, plans, and programs—all designed to advance the company's interests. The soft-spoken man who had started his business career as a district fountain syrup salesman in Queens now had all the world (excepting only the

United States and Canada) as his sales territory. He joyously made the most of it.

The results of his reorganization and revitalization of the overseas company, plus his personal sales efforts and, as he says, the dedicated work of many people, were sensational. During Kendall's presidency of Pepsi-Cola International, which continued until September, 1963, the number of foreign countries in which the company's products were sold zoomed upward from 60 to 103. Sales tripled. Profits from the foreign operation soared five times above what they had been.

HIGH VISIBILITY OF A COMER

Kendall's rapid rise in the Pepsi-Cola organization had naturally attracted the attention of company insiders. He had help from many, including in particular two company presidents. He credits Alfred N. Steele, president from 1949 to 1959, with teaching him how to sell on a massive scale. Herbert L. Barnet, Steele's successor, was his greatest tutor in corporate finance. These men knew they had a comer on their hands. Now the entire soft-drink industry was aware of the transformation brought about in Pepsi-Cola International under his leadership. Soon, it became clear that his genius was needed at home. On September 6, 1963, on Barnet's recommendation, Kendall was elected by the board of directors as president and chief executive officer of the Pepsi-Cola Company. The date was almost exactly sixteen years from the time he had applied for the job in Queens.

The success of which he had dreamed was his. He stood on the top rung of the golden ladder. But he had no intention of resting there. In his new post, Kendall continued to think in terms of company expansion. Pepsi bought a small company that was producing a locally distributed soft drink called Mountain Dew, which quickly gained widespread consumer acceptance. It developed Diet Pepsi, which soon captured approximately a third of the burgeoning low-calorie soft-drink market. On June 8, 1965, Frito-Lay, Inc., Dallas-based producer of nationally distributed snack foods, merged with Pepsi-Cola Company. It was a foreordained marriage—between a soft-drink concern and a producer of foods that made people thirsty. To accommodate all these companies, a new parent organization, PepsiCo, Inc., was created, with Kendall as president and chief executive officer.

No one can question that this is a company chief who infused a new spirit—his own spirit—into a once-ailing organization. No one can question that the new spirit paid off. During Kendall's first full year as president, the company reported all-time record sales and earnings, exceeding the previous year's level by the greatest actual increase in more than a decade. Sales for that year of 1964, with the new management team in charge, totaled $252,544,000—up 16 per cent over the 1963 figure. Net earnings after taxes and adjustment for foreign activities were $18,577,000, an increase of 15 per cent over the 1963 earnings. Pepsi-Cola Company was a giant—and still growing.

BEHIND THE DONALD M. KENDALL STORY

The approach of the larger company to problems and opportunities continues to reflect the business philosophy of the man at the top. And the philosophy of the mature, although still young, Donald Kendall grew out of the precepts to which he attached himself—or did they attach themselves to him?—at the beginning of his career.

Basic in Kendall's nature is an intense desire to be *involved*. He would never be content to sit on the sidelines. He was always that way. He wanted to be in military service during the war because he could not endure the thought of missing something that so deeply affected his generation. When he went into business he immediately had to get out among the people who were engaged in that business; these were the people with whom he felt most at home. As he advanced in the company, he was pushed from below and pulled from above by men who believed in him because he had proved himself among them.

Kendall holds a strong faith in the basic honesty and integrity of man. Recent fiction tends to foster a belief that corporate executive life is one of continual backbiting and intrigue. Kendall has never found it so. Nobody, he observes, has ever been out to "get" him.

If possible, he believes, the man in every key job should be "smarter than the head man." He is especially insistent on surrounding himself with men who possess different talents. Sitting with them around the conference table, he does not seek agreement but instead incites differences of opinion. The ideas he wants are generated in sessions where the participants go at one another hammer and tongs.

Young people entering the business world today face much

stronger competition, according to Kendall, than they did when he started in 1947. They must be better prepared if they hope to be successful. This means, first of all, that a college education is essential. After graduation from college, the business aspirant should attend one of the good business schools. "The young businessman probably will have no great need for what he learns in business school during the first five or ten years of his work," Kendall concedes. "But later, as he advances, he will need it badly. This is especially important in marketing and finance. That is where the backlog of knowledge gained in business school pays enormous dividends."

He feels people should be enthusiastic about their work. In fact, he values enthusiasm as fully as adequate training and native competence. If a man finds himself in a job about which he cannot be enthusiastic, he should start all over. "Cut your losses and get out," Kendall advises. "Don't waste more of your time by sticking with the job."

He remembers an admonition from a former president of his company. "Al Steele used to tell me, 'Don't forget to say hello to the man running the elevator,'" Kendall recalls reflectively. "It was the best advice I ever got in a single sentence. If you don't stay human, if you don't say hello to the man on the elevator, you lose touch with people—and that is the biggest failure of all."

The rise of the president of PepsiCo is a classic example of the executive who makes his mark in a particular business function. In Kendall's case, it was sales. In the case of James Connaughton of Wheelabrator, it was production. In the case of others, it's been finance, or engineering. To reach the president's chair, however, more than expertness in one area of executive performance is needed: the man must also have the capability to expand his horizons, to become a generalist, versed in the broad-gauge thinking required of a corporate "first man."

In Kendall's breakthrough, the elements of his success almost form a series of steps, leading one after another to the top spot:

Tip From a Friend. Kendall's entry into the Pepsi-Cola Company came about through the recommendation of a friend with the intelligence and understanding to see that Kendall's capabilities might have a particular value to a company with a great potential, suffering a temporary slump. Utilization of one's friends is a frequent element in an individual's success. However, a hazard exists in the well-meaning but inept friend who makes an inappropriate suggestion, based on an unrealistic appraisal of a situation. Kendall apparently was able to make the distinction.

Job Affinity. Kendall knew almost immediately that the job was for him. As he put it, "Pepsi-Cola and I jelled right from the beginning." The man who has a feeling of "rightness" about what he's doing, who likes his work and his job, has a decided edge on his competition. It's not only a matter of being able to work more effectively as a result, but of being willing to make the effort needed to perform at a superior level. The individual who simply "does a job" has no incentive to deliver at other than a get-by standard.

Success Compulsion. Kendall, too, had a hunger for success that had to be satisfied. He started at the bottom, selling store to store. He wanted to "sell more than any other crew member" when he called on drugstores and snack bars to take on Pepsi-Cola. And he didn't stop making calls until he succeeded. This element became a continuing aspect of his performance.

Vision of Success. "You can go to the top," his boss, Ed Loughlin, told Kendall. If Loughlin's encouragement didn't put the provocative thought in the young salesman's head, it certainly strengthened his conviction that the top spot was within range. This phenomenon, that an individual almost sees the president's chair through the cross hairs of his personal "sighting" device, is common among people who eventually hit the bull's-eye.

Trouble Analysis. Every company or organization has problems. The man who can satisfactorily analyze and solve the difficulties has the best chance of making his mark in the organization. There is little doubt that Kendall's ability to find out why Pepsi-Cola Interna-

tional wasn't living up to its potential, and the resulting solution
he devised for a more effective marketing approach, was an important key to the promotion that followed.

Allies at the Top. "Nobody was ever out to get me," says the
PepsiCo president. In the days when the "business jungle" is an accepted phrase, and a "knife in the back" is not an uncommon
fate for the aspiring executive, Kendall's remark is noteworthy.
Perhaps one cannot avoid making enemies, or at least suspicious
competitors, as one seeks to forge upward within an organization.
Nevertheless, it's important to make friends, and to develop well-
wishers. Alfred N. Steele and Herbert L. Barnet were two allies
who looked with favor on the outstandingly capable young executive, and were more than willing to give him a leg up.

Team Building. In modern business, few people ever make it to
the top entirely on their own. Help can come from many quarters
—an understanding and encouraging wife, interested superiors.
Another source, for the businessman, is the group of people he
creates around himself, to help him operate. Kendall's team, he
points out, was made up of a variety of differing talents. He took
advantage of their knowledge, not by seeking agreement, but by
getting them to develop their points of view in discussion and argument. In the sparks that ensued, much light was shed on company
problems.

The "Touch." Executives like to talk about the "touch," by which
they mean the human touch that distinguishes the successful leader's
ability to make contact with their subordinates. Kendall reveals
that one of his mentors, Al Steele, told him, in a single sentence,
the essence of developing the "touch": Steele told him, "Don't
forget to say hello to the man running the elevator."

Into this simple statement must be read some implied ideas. Not
meant, for example, is the suggestion that one can substitute the
formality of a casual, unfelt greeting for a genuine interest in "the
elevator man" as a fellow human being. Steele's words underline
the need for the would-be leader to establish contact with his sub-

ordinates, from the elevator operator to the receptionist, secretary, and on through the dozens of job categories that make up the modern corporation. When this contact is real, the leader draws as much strength from it, as the subordinate may draw pleasure and satisfaction from getting a friendly word from "the big boss."

4 { Thomas O'Ryan –
ADVERTISING ON WHEELS

A nineteen-year-old Irish immigrant applied for work with a New York section gang in 1932. "O'Ryan, eh?" the hiring boss said. His critical eye assessed the youth's six-foot-four, 240-pound frame. "All right. Draw your tools. You're on day wages." The job: digging a subway tunnel through Manhattan's bedrock. Thirty years later, a new advertising poster went up in New York subways: "An O'Ryan & Batchelder Operation." It was the same O'Ryan.

In the years between, Thomas Michael O'Ryan had become chairman of the nation's largest transit advertising firm. When he was awarded the New York subway advertising franchise in 1962, the one-time subway laborer had run full cycle. Three decades from subway laborer to subway advertising czar traces Tom O'Ryan from poverty to business success. His story begins in Ireland.

* * *

Thomas Michael O'Ryan, second of six sons born to Edward O'Ryan and Mary Cusack O'Ryan in Limerick City, Ireland, didn't exactly begin life with a silver spoon in his mouth. But he does remember fine Irish lace curtains on the windows, and his father, Edward O'Ryan, who had a highly respectable position as manager of a retail furniture department. Young Tom, ambitious to become a barrister, attended boarding school. Since his allowance covered everything, afterschool work was no necessity. During one vacation, he managed a trip to the Continent. On other vacations, he tinkered as a hobby on a farm operated by his second cousin,

Christopher McCurtain. Tom liked the rolling country estate. He also entertained the idea of managing it someday. Money worries didn't touch him. "In 1928, I remember buying six new pairs of pants rather than send my clothes to be cleaned," O'Ryan says. "It seemed easier. I didn't think about the expense."

Then came the family financial crisis. The elder O'Ryan's business plunged downward. Mary O'Ryan, an active and assertive woman, decided to attack the problem frontally. Her plan: to open a small hotel. Edward O'Ryan's wrath was classic, old-fashioned—and quite Irish. "No matter what happens, a woman's place is in the home," he raged. The rift between the parents grew —and spread. Relatives began taking sides, some with one faction, some the other. Living at home became difficult and soon impossible. Tom's older brother left for America. Tom felt he must leave, too. His only question: where to go?

STREETS PAVED WITH GOLD

At seventeen, Tom O'Ryan made up his mind: he'd go to Australia—and stop off in the U.S. en route. With his savings, augmented by family contributions, he booked passage. He arrived in New York in 1929 with four hundred dollars in his pocket. America appealed to him from the start. "I wanted to be independent," O'Ryan recalls. "I didn't like the idea of not being able to take care of my family. I felt I could manage things if I could only rely on myself. America, I found, was that kind of place."

Within two weeks, he was hired as a file clerk for Union Indemnity Company. O'Ryan joined nineteen other youths in the insurance company's main records room. His salary: $27.50 every two weeks. America! Indeed, the streets were paved with gold. "That first year, I had more money than I was to see for many years to come," O'Ryan says.

Easy money was everywhere. In fact, Tom's co-workers asked, did he know a game played with dice—called craps? He didn't.

Time to learn, surely. Easy money. In one hour, Tom lost his first week's salary. He went back the next Friday. This time, it took four hours to lose his week's pay—and to gain a lifelong lesson. "I resolved never to shoot craps again," O'Ryan says. "And I never have."

Throughout the U.S., prosperity reigned. Elevator operators and shoeshine boys played the stock market. The slogan "every day in every way I'm getting better and better" typified national optimism. One month later, the stock market crashed. *Variety* carried its now-classic headline: "Wall Street Lays an Egg." Union Indemnity, a house of cards, collapsed. Tom O'Ryan was out of a job. The Era of Wonderful Nonsense skidded to a fast stop. Job-hunting became the national pastime. O'Ryan found himself facing a new and urgent battle: survival. He wasn't helped by his futile experience in job interview lines. In crisis, bitterness seeks a scapegoat and his fellow job-seekers picked O'Ryan. "Look at that Irish immigrant taking jobs away from good American citizens!"

His response was characteristic. He filed citizenship papers immediately. But there was to be a long difficult period before he even approached the first rung on his career ladder. For example, he had a persistent sore throat that never seemed to get any better. "Bad tonsils," the doctor said. "Better have them out. Ten dollars." At that point, Tom didn't have ten cents. But he did have a family heirloom from Ireland, a gold watch chain. He charged off to a pawn shop. After examining the chain, the pawnbroker quietly produced a ten-dollar bill.

Later, with odd-job money in hand, Tom went to redeem the chain. "Sorry. We had to sell it," the pawnbroker said. "You failed to live up to your contract." As Tom left the shop, head down, looking at the cobblestone streets, they didn't look like gold any longer.

He continued to look for work without success. Even the police department—a traditional Irish haven—was closed to him because he was still a noncitizen. The job didn't appeal that much to O'Ryan. There were eighteen thousand college graduates with police applications ahead of him. He was looking for opportunity. Finding little hope for permanent work, O'Ryan was happy to get spot jobs to pay daily expenses. It was one of these that led indirectly to his present career. While making a delivery by Radio City Music Hall, O'Ryan observed the doorman—a massive fellow, easily six feet six. Figuring his size as an asset, O'Ryan applied for a job as doorman. "Sorry," the Music Hall's chief of service said. "You're big—but you're not quite big *enough.*" Would there be an usher's job available? "Unfortunately, you're *too big* to qualify as an usher," the employer told him.

Size *did* prove helpful in landing the subway tunneling job, the one that O'Ryan regards with some amusement today. The work was soon completed, however, and he found himself once more scratching for any work that was available. "Odd jobs and working for companies that collapsed convinced me I would have to work for myself, sooner or later," O'Ryan said. "I needed to control my own future."

DO-IT-YOURSELF SALES AND ADVERTISING

It was during a Wall Street messenger job that O'Ryan racked up his first sales and advertising experience—though no one called it that at the time. O'Ryan delivered a package to an insurance adjustment firm on Maiden Lane. The company has just acquired a consignment of damaged men's suits. To recover costs, the company was trying to sell them. The young messenger volunteered to take on the job and the office manager gave him the contract. (After all, who wants to buy a damaged suit?) O'Ryan thought differently —he knew all too well that in lean times men were looking for bargains.

Imbued with enthusiasm for his first sales venture, he invested his last few dollars in printed brochures describing the merchandise.

Each time he made a delivery to a company, O'Ryan would seek out the office manager. His sales pitch was simple: he'd make special rates on suits available to executives in exchange for permission to demonstrate his wares to the office staff. Soon he was holding sales meetings at lunchtime, handing out brochures, taking orders. "Within twenty days, I had sold several hundred suits," O'Ryan said. "The insurance man was shocked. But one fellow was even more surprised—me."

BITTEN BY THE BUG OF FREE ENTERPRISE

With twenty dollars borrowed from a druggist-friend, O'Ryan turned his hand to what might be called vegetable retailing. Actually, it was peddling produce from a rickety cart. He rented a horse and wagon for four dollars per day, with the agreement that he would feed the horse as well. So equipped, O'Ryan would arrive at Washington Market—New York's wholesale vegetable center—at 4 A.M., buy a load of produce, then clop-clop over the Brooklyn Bridge to supply the housewives of Brooklyn. However, the profit picture was a little unstable for the budding entrepreneur. "On a good day, I made enough to buy food for the horse," O'Ryan said. "On a bad day, we were both on short rations."

Something had to be done, and a friend suggested, "Why not specialize?" This sounded logical, so O'Ryan picked his specialty —rhubarb. O'Ryan bought stocks of rhubarb, storing it in his landlady's basement. He watched his inventory grow. Soon he'd dominate the rhubarb market. But he hadn't reckoned with the hot water pipes in the basement. They generated fermentation within the rhubarb and the house took on a most distinctive smell. When pedestrians began crossing the street as they went by, O'Ryan's landlady traced the problem to its source. She was irate. Only O'Ryan's native charm—and his offer to whitewash her cellar free of charge—saved the day.

Then, to the envy of his friends, O'Ryan got a full-time job:

elevator operator at Saks–34th Street department store. He continued to make friends. Older women on O'Ryan's elevator were impressed with his genial good humor. A typical joshing comment: "Sure, he's a fine Irish lad and he's going to take us right to the top with him." O'Ryan soon caught the eye of management and in time he was promoted to floorwalker.

Since arriving in the U.S., O'Ryan had been fascinated by Wall Street, the financial nerve-center of the American economy. To succeed, he decided, a man needed financial district experience. When he heard that a brokerage house was hiring runners—messengers who run from office to office—he took the job. In addition to the valuable experience, O'Ryan figured investment opportunity might be a side benefit for him. After all, stock prices in the early 1930s stood at all-time lows. Some issues must be due for a rise.

On the job, he was soon investing money. Whenever he made a few dollars, he plowed it back. Soon he accumulated close to five thousand dollars merely by "buying low and selling dear." O'Ryan was elated. He began to think of what the money would buy. He'd once shipped out to the Caribbean and he had dreamed ever since of living on a tropical island. Only why not go to a *real* island paradise—Hawaii! Why not, indeed. In mid-depression, five thousand dollars was a fortune. He quit his job and booked passage to Hawaii. "It was indeed an idyllic paradise," he said. However, he soon became restless. He started teaching school part time in the Islands. Money steadily dwindled. When he got down to passage money, he sailed for San Francisco. He then crossed the continent in his entire fortune: an automobile with Hawaiian plates. In 1936, he returned to Saks–34th Street store—flat broke, sun-tanned, wiser.

"I never regretted my trip to the Islands," O'Ryan said. "I've continued to travel as a business investment ever since. Travel adds to stature and broadens outlook. It's valuable to anyone. But looking back to my Hawaiian trip, I soon realized I could have gone there and invested my money at the same time. I made the mistake of living off capital. I never did that again."

Saks was happy to get its personable floorwalker back. By 1937, he had been promoted to assistant to the dress buyer at seventy-five dollars per week. But he wasn't happy.

ENTER: TRANSIT ADVERTISING

Long before Tom O'Ryan left Ireland, Barron G. Collier had established an empire in the U.S. in the field of transit advertising. Collier had started selling streetcar ads in Memphis in 1890. By the 1930s, Collier was selling and servicing advertising in transit vehicles throughout the U.S. O'Ryan heard through a friend that Collier was hiring salesmen. Since retailing didn't offer fast-enough advancement, he decided, he made an interview to see Collier the next day. The sales manager raised his eyebrows at the thick Irish brogue.

"Ever sell transit advertising?"

"No."

"Know anything about advertising?"

"Well, I haven't worked in the field, but—"

"Look, fellow, we're turning down *experienced* salesmen," the manager said. "What makes you think you can do it?"

"I'm willing to work," said O'Ryan, turning red. "If I don't sell anything, don't pay me. I'll finance myself. Try me and see. I can do it."

The Collier executive nodded his head. If a man offered to pay his own expenses, he must at least have confidence. "All right, you're on," he told O'Ryan. "Twenty-five dollars per week draw."

O'Ryan joined several new men in a two-week training course. On-the-job training included some experience in merchandising. O'Ryan helped arrange displays in retail stores—posters that duplicated the transit advertising campaign. Retail customers, seeing a Sunkist display, were reminded of earlier impressions received from Sunkist transit ads. The emphasis on point-of-sale merchandising impressed O'Ryan. "It taught me our role is moving products out of stores into homes. I've stressed strong merchandising programs to accompany transit campaigns ever since."

After training, the Collier organization announced new men would be given out-of-town territories. Although he hadn't planned to leave New York, O'Ryan immediately applied for New England. "Irishmen were getting on well up there," O'Ryan reasoned. "I'd have a built-in welcome."

"Your territory is Georgia and the Carolinas," O'Ryan was told. "You leave tonight." O'Ryan had never been there. But he suspected the people would not react favorably to a greenhorn Irishman. However, admitting defeat before trying was not O'Ryan's style. He caught the train south. His mission: selling advertising space in streetcars. (Transit ad firms hold contracts with transit operating companies. Admen sell and service the eye-level spaces, plus other special positions provided in each car.)

O'Ryan will never forget his first prospect—a local bakery famous for Craig's Honey Bread. On Monday, O'Ryan called on the president. "Young man, we've never used your advertising, and we don't intend to start now," he said. Tuesday O'Ryan was back with a smile—and a new advertising idea. No sale. He came back Wednesday, Thursday, and Friday. On Saturday, he arrived at noon. The proprietor was getting ready to close for half holiday. O'Ryan took a new tack.

"I've been taught to answer all sorts of objections to transit advertising," he said, spreading his sales literature on the table. "It's all in here somewhere. Anything you ask I'm sure we can find— even if I don't know the answer."

The baker looked at the literature, back at the determined O'Ryan, then sighed: "Well, this looks like something I'm going to *have* to have. Reckon you'd better sign me up." O'Ryan wrote up his first customer.

"Looking back on it, I think he bought so he could close up and go home," O'Ryan said. "But it gave me a big lift. After that, I started *selling* advertising." He soon turned his Irish brogue into a plus. People remembered him. He became a distinctive personality. Sell he did. In 1938, O'Ryan ranked number one in the nation among Collier salesmen in bringing in five-year contracts—the longest term sold. The industry had a new ace salesman. He didn't know novices aren't likely to lead the pack. He did it anyhow.

By the end of 1938, O'Ryan would not consider any business other than transit advertising. "Nobody explained the averages to me," O'Ryan recalls. "I tried to sell one contract a day. I thought that was expected." In 1939, O'Ryan's outstanding sales record won him promotion to Collier district manager for Tennessee, Mississippi and Arkansas. His future seemed assured.

OUT OF TRAGEDY, NEW OPPORTUNITY

In 1940, shortly after the death of founder Barron G. Collier, the Collier organization went bankrupt. "We were stunned to find how shaky financial management had been," O'Ryan recalls. "The company had done a fine job selling its service. But financial management had been decaying from within." Investigation showed funds from the advertising business had been used to finance disastrous real-estate ventures. "The moral was clear," O'Ryan said. "A company can do well in its specialty but go broke if finances are mismanaged."

With the Collier collapse, Tom O'Ryan faced a pivotal fork in the road: should he join forces with a new national firm—or form his own? His decision grew out of three factors. He felt the industry would be healthier with a larger firm rather than many small companies. He felt more executive experience—particularly in administering a staff—would benefit him. And he lacked capital to finance a new firm at the time. So O'Ryan decided to join the newly organized National Transitads.

He became Southern division manager of National Transitads in 1942; vice-president of the company two years later. He moved the Southern headquarters to Memphis, site of his home and business ever since. He also launched a series of projects that made permanent contributions to the transit advertising field:

- In Oklahoma City when all interior transit space was sold, O'Ryan developed the first exterior bus poster. (Exterior transit ads had been carried by streetcars. This was the first exterior bus poster.) It was a far-reaching development. Today, 65.9 per cent of transit's volume comes from exterior-vehicle posters.
- O'Ryan expanded the exterior poster into the prototype of today's king-size poster, the mass-display panel on the left side of buses throughout the U.S.
- O'Ryan organized and served as first dean of National Transitads first sales school.
- He assumed responsibility for promoting the medium throughout the nation.

Over the years, however, differences of opinion between Tom O'Ryan and other National Transitads principals became a problem. The controversy: was national or local concentration the route to future growth? Strong local companies, O'Ryan felt, must grow and serve local advertisers. On this basis, national advertising can be sold. His colleagues felt national should come first, in the traditional Collier manner.

THE TOM O'RYAN ADVERTISING COMPANY

By 1947, O'Ryan decided to go a different way and he resigned from National Transitads. In 1948, he formed the Tom O'Ryan Advertising Company. He began by signing an exclusive agreement to manage advertising throughout the Memphis bus system. In 1949, he acquired the Atlanta franchise. In 1951, Tom O'Ryan developed another new concept for transit advertising—the Merchandising Bus. He was looking for a dramatic way to help Libby Foods get distribution for a new product. His reasoning: buses provide the physical medium for transit ads. Why not load up a bus with samples of advertising *and* the product—then drive around and present wholesalers and retailers? The result: the first Merchandising Bus. Since that time, O'Ryan has directed dozens of Merchandising Bus promotions. Other transit ad firms have put the concept to work, too.

O'RYAN AND BATCHELDER

In November, 1953, a transit system serving nine cities in the Carolinas called for advertising bids. O'Ryan's firm was invited to quote. So was the Transit Advertising Company of Peoria, Illinois, operated by Joseph H. Batchelder, Jr. O'Ryan, who knew Batchelder from industry meetings, phoned to see if he planned to attend the presentation in Charlotte, North Carolina. Batchelder did. O'Ryan welcomed the opportunity to confer with Batchelder because he hoped to avoid competition that might hurt both firms.

"Why not come by Memphis and we'll go together?" O'Ryan suggested. Batchelder agreed. On the plane from Memphis to Charlotte, O'Ryan and Batchelder found considerable common ground in their respective philosophies of transit advertising. By the time the plane landed in Charlotte, the two men had made an important decision: they would put in a single bid as O'Ryan and Batchelder. The new combination got the contract. O & B was under way.

By 1955, O & B was offering transit advertising in Charleston, West Virginia, Indianapolis, Louisville, Milwaukee—plus nineteen other cities. By 1960, Cleveland, Philadelphia, Boston and Baltimore had been added. Chicago was signed in 1964. Today, O & B holds franchises in seventy U.S. urban areas. Advertising coverage throughout nearly twenty-five thousand vehicles makes it the nation's largest transit advertising company. O & B sales volume during 1966 was sixteen and a half million dollars.

For Tom O'Ryan, achievement continues. He has been chairman of the Transit Advertising Association, his industry's trade group. He has been a prime mover in formulating the World Transad Association with members in the United States, France, Italy, Canada. He represents his industry as board member of Brand Names Foundation. But for O'Ryan—a most active chairman of the O & B network—the best recognition came that day in 1962 when his firm acquired the New York subway franchise. The immigrant Irish laborer had returned to the subways—in style.

BEHIND THE THOMAS O'RYAN STORY

One cannot read Thomas O'Ryan's biographical sketch without noting its almost rollicking and good-humored keynote. O'Ryan's ability to accept the bad as well as the good with equanimity, even humor, shows up repeatedly. At the very outset, his flamboyance becomes clear. For a seventeen-year-old youth to leave home, even for that bright and mythical land of America, required a spirit both of independence and self-reliance. But then O'Ryan soon showed himself capable of making decisions reflecting a considerable degree of self-control. Consider his brief encounter with crap shooting. Another individual might very well have resolved to "stick it out." O'Ryan, despite his youthful brashness, was able to say "No" to gambling. Clearly he had decided this was one type of enterprise for which he was not well suited. And he was able to beat a retreat without either ill will or a feeling of failure.

The birth of the entrepreneurial spirit is not always easy to pinpoint. However, for Tom O'Ryan, the sequence of events seems clear. A series of failures and turndowns of getting a job one day and losing it the next, as an employer went out of business, eventually brought him to a firm resolve—that he should work for himself, because as he himself said, "I wanted to control my own future."

We have been told that one of the distinguishing marks of the successful individual is that he can identify opportunity's knuckles rapping at the door. However, it is quite likely that many people fail to hear opportunity because the lady uses a variety of knocks, raps, and rhythms. O'Ryan's history suggests that if the successful individual responds quickly to the knock at the door, it is because he himself has composed the cadence. Note, for example, O'Ryan's capabilities in this matter:

Opportunity Proliferation. Once O'Ryan got the idea that he wanted to go into business for himself, the "businesses" he started proved to be startlingly diverse. Within a comparatively brief period, he undertook to sell several hundred men's suits that had been damaged in a fire. Shortly thereafter, he was selling vegetables from a horse and wagon. Next, he attempted to be a "rhubarb king"— until he found he couldn't fight biology.

Personal Appeal. The element of personal attractiveness is always difficult to assess in the success pattern. In many instances, it obviously plays no part at all, either because the individual is without any notable personal appeal or these qualities never emerge as a factor in his progress.

However, at several points in O'Ryan's story, his general good humor clearly created a favorable response in the people with whom he came in contact. At least, in one specific instance, it got him a promotion from elevator operator to floorwalker.

The Planning Eye. One capability that appears frequently in the behavior pattern of the successful man: he looks about him in the business scene and makes an evaluation or a judgment that results in the setting of a goal. In the case of Owen Murphy, this gambit developed when he saw the model of the mechanized armchair. O'Ryan's appraisal was of an entirely different kind although the pattern was the same. In the latter case, he decided that Wall Street would be for him an important training ground. Accordingly, he kept his eye out for a Wall Street job and eventually found one. The wisdom of his choice became clear when he was able to accumulate five thousand dollars by what he learned about stocks and the vagaries of the stock market.

Action Hunger. The Hawaii period in O'Ryan's story is both unexpected and instructive. One would not have thought that a man as intent on achieving success as he was would break the pattern, merely for the purpose of indulging a whim. But the interesting thing is that even though he found Hawaii the idyllic paradise he expected, what soon developed was that an idyllic paradise was just not his cup of tea. Because O'Ryan could thrive only in an environment that offered him the challenge of money-making opportunities, he soon returned to where the action was.

Capital Conservation. There's an interesting difference between the successful businessman and the gambler. Although they both take risks, the typical gambler often will stake all his available funds on the turn of a card, but the businessman, while he may take risks, usually will do so with "risk money"—that leaves him a sizable and untouched reserve. This was the lesson that O'Ryan learned in Hawaii.

The Right Gamble. "What makes you think you can sell?" the manager asked.

"I'm willing to work," said O'Ryan. "If I don't sell, don't pay me." In a way O'Ryan was making as big a gamble in taking on the job with the Collier Advertising Company as a wealthy man risking thousands. However, the unique aspect of O'Ryan's gamble was that he knew he could influence the outcome. At last the truth was out. He *was* willing to gamble, not on the roll of a pair of dice, but on himself.

5 ⎰ Charles A. Berns –
⎱ HOW "21" BECAME A FAMOUS NUMBER

An appropriate coat of arms for Charles A. Berns, chairman of the board of "21" Brands, Inc., would be a genial gourmet rampant on a field of business skill holding the heraldic symbols of good food and drink.

Berns achieved fame and fortune in the most colorful tradition of the great restaurateurs and liquor merchants. His renown, as co-founder of the "21" Club, the posh Manhattan restaurant and gathering place for celebrities, was firmly established by the time he was thirty. Yet, barely two years later, in 1933, he put his success on the line to form "21" Brands, wine and liquor merchants and distillers. The initial success of "21" Brands rested on the strength of a handshake between Charlie Berns and an emissary of Scotland's ancient House of Ballantine's Scotch.

Characteristically, Charlie Berns didn't sit around waiting for this plum to fall into his lap. Prohibition had just ended and, because Berns knew that many liquor importers with well-established names would be competing for the Ballantine franchise, he put a nervy plan into action. He sent his new company's salesmen out to scour the country and drum up orders for a Ballantine product they didn't even have. Those orders turned out to be his trump card when he met with the emissary Ballantine's had sent here to choose an importer. The bargain was sealed by a handshake, and a "21" Brands representative was dispatched to Scotland to work out the details.

Since the Ballantine's coup, "21" Brands has progressively added other fine liquors to its roster, including Tribuno Vermouth, Hine Cognac, Bobadilla sherries, and Constantino ports from Spain and

Portugal. The finest of California premium wines are also "21" Brands—Louis M. Martini and Wente Bros. From the company's old-fashioned distillery in Kentucky come Ezra Brooks Bourbons, Benson's Creek Bourbon, and "21" Club Special. More recently, the Benedictine Monks of Assumption Abbey selected Mr. Berns's company as exclusive national distributor for their brandy.

*   *   *

Charlie Berns didn't start out with much. Born and raised on Manhattan's immigrant-crowded West Side early in the century, young Charlie sold newspapers while attending P.S. 69 and DeWitt Clinton High School. His newsstand at 55th Street and Eighth Avenue is still there. It was at that newsstand that he first exhibited his flair for business. Soon he had other kids in the neighborhood working for him, delivering laundry and groceries as well as papers. During summer vacations he took steady jobs. As he recalls, "I was a strong and powerful boy—robust you might say—and my summer jobs reflected it. The summer of 1915 was a hot one for me. I worked as a blacksmith's helper, hauling tools and keeping the forges going."

With his parents' encouragement he determined to enter New York University. To help pay his way he got a job as a shoe clerk. Another shoe salesman in the same store, a very successful one, was his cousin Jack Kriendler. "That shoe store," Charles Berns says, "will always remain a vivid memory for me. The best thing about it was Jack Kriendler; I already knew him well and I liked and admired him. He was extremely popular and a real charmer, especially with the girls. He was the best salesman in the store.

"Our families came from the same place in Austria. As a matter of fact, when his family immigrated to this country, they stayed with us until they got settled on their own. The feeling of helping one another was instilled in us early, and we never forgot it. My parents always told us, as little as you think you have, there are other people with far less, and it's your responsibility to help them.

"Then there was the boss of the store, a man named Duncey.

He used to say that he just couldn't understand how a 'college boy' could be such a poor shoe salesman. I'd never amount to much, he kept saying. Years later Duncey operated a liquor store and we became friends. He was a good man and a good customer. He used to tell me that I had destroyed his confidence in his ability to judge human nature.

"I was determined to show Duncey, back in that shoe store, that I wasn't the complete dunce he judged me to be. It wasn't easy. But I needed that job and I managed to hold it. I have always been determined to finish whatever I start to do, and I think that that has played a major role in my career. I was determined to get my university degree, and then my law degree; and I was determined to become a success. But I never succeeded in being anything other than a *poor* shoe salesman."

START OF A FAMOUS PARTNERSHIP

When Charlie graduated from New York University's School of Commerce in 1922, he faced a problem: how to finance his further education at New York Law School. The opportunity to finance those studies soon presented itself. It grew out of Charlie's willingness to help Jack Kriendler out of a business difficulty. Jack Kriendler had left the shoe store and had teamed up with a fellow student at N.Y.U. to go into the restaurant business near the campus in Greenwich Village. The place was called the "Redhead." Kriendler was great when it came to attracting and pleasing patrons, but neither he nor his partner were strong in business management. They asked Charlie Berns, School of Commerce graduate and now a part-time accountant, for help.

"Before I knew it, I was not only keeping their books, but advancing them the money they needed to pay their bills. They couldn't pay me back, let alone pay me for my work, so they made me a partner. Soon the books began to balance without red ink and the business was paying its way. We were on our way." Thus two college students in Greenwich Village formed the celebrated partnership of Jack and Charlie. The Redhead was only the first in a succession of restaurants. No matter what their names, patrons always referred to each of them as "Jack and Charlie's." The nickname finally became official many years later when the restaurant settled into its permanent home at 21 West 52nd Street, becoming the world-famous Jack and Charlie's "21."

WHAT JACK DIDN'T KNOW, CHARLIE DID

From the start, it was evident that there was a natural division of talents between the two partners—Jack as the front man, Charlie as the busy beaver behind the scene. "Jack supplied looks, charms and brains while I supplied only brains," Berns says with a chuckle. It soon became apparent that the two young men were doing well. Nevertheless, Charlie continued his law school studies for the three years it took to get his law degree.

"My father was not too pleased that I went into the nightclub business while still in school even though it helped ease his financial burden. He was afraid my education would get sidetracked. In his and my mother's eyes, education came first, then money. I gave him my word that I would earn a law degree, and I was determined to keep it. Actually Jack Kriendler and I regarded commercial ventures as a way of financing our education as well as contributing to the financial support of our respective families. Our ventures were initially intended as a means to that end."

Charlie's determination to get his law degree created a problem. He was carrying a full schedule at law school and also devoting full time to the restaurant. "The solution was, by necessity, quite simple," he cheerfully explains. "I slept less. I learned to budget my time, concentrate my energies where they counted most, and pace myself. I still sleep less than six hours a night and still have the habit of grabbing quick catnaps.

"Another, more sinister problem, suddenly erupted. This was the strange era of prohibition. The Redhead, like many restaurants of that period, was part speak-easy. The hoodlums spawned by prohibition were one of the early problems that Jack and I faced. I learned early that the direct approach is often the best . . . not to avoid a showdown . . . that you have to fight for what you believe in. For example, take the day some goons walked into the Redhead and demanded a piece of it. We didn't try to compromise. We fought. I was in the hospital for ten days and still carry a razor scar on my neck. The point is that we threw them out, and the word spread. It was many years before we were bothered again."

THEY FAILED IN HARRISBURG—BUT CAME BACK STRONG

"A friend," Berns recalls, "named Bill Hardey had been a professional dancer around New York, and he'd worked for a fellow who owned a dance hall in Harrisburg. This fellow wanted to retire, and we agreed to take over with Hardey. We sort of regarded ourselves as young business geniuses out to conquer the world. But everything went wrong. To be perfectly blunt, Harrisburg was a complete fiasco, a thorough flop. It almost wiped us out financially. Harrisburg taught us a lesson that we never forgot: we weren't geniuses after all."

Before they leaped into their next business adventure, the two took a careful look. In the mountains where Rip Van Winkle once slept, an enterprising family had created a colorful mecca for New Yorkers—the famed Grossinger's Catskill Mountain resort. The Grossingers invited Jack and Charlie to run certain concessions and they accepted. In short order they were renting rowboats, selling newspapers, sundries, candy, soft drinks and sandwiches. One of their first acts, as their concessions began to flourish, was to extricate their friend and associate Bill Hardey from the ruins of the Harrisburg fiasco and bring him to Grossinger's to run their horse-renting concession. The Grossinger episode proved profitable for everyone and cemented a close, affectionate relationship between the Grossinger and "21" clans that has endured ever since.

After two or three years with the Redhead, the two young men had moved their operation to 88 Washington Place, still in the Village, calling it the "Fronton." When the Sixth Avenue subway construction forced them out of the Fronton, they decided to go farther uptown and bought a handsome brownstone, with an elegant iron gate, on West 49th Street. They also acquired a new employee, Jack's younger brother Mac. His credentials included a college degree and a splendid voice. Mac's impromptu singing performances and Chuck Wagon Glee Club, an elite group of patrons who helped him serenade guests, became a tradition. Mac was the first of the brothers to be admitted into the business under the strict rule that required members of the family to be university graduates in order to be even considered. Like all the others he had to start at the bottom—in his case, the "butcher shop," or meat section of the restaurant.

The new brownstone restaurant was officially christened the Iron Gate, but it still was universally known as Jack and Charlie's. A policy of carefully screening customers gave the new place a reputation in the New York of the 1920s as a place where the "best people" went. Dorothy Parker and especially Robert Benchley, who adopted the place as his hangout, quickly attracted to the Iron Gate many of the literary figures, Broadway stars, and other creative personalities. One day Benchley showed up with a friend named Benedict Quinn who took one startled look and exclaimed, "My God, this was the house I was born in!" Thereafter, Quinn, a Yale man, returned regularly, introducing all of his colleagues to what became known among Yale grads as "Ben Quinn's home."

Suddenly, one night in 1927, the place was raided—a common disaster among the best, as well as the worst, restaurants and speakeasies of that era. The raid, by federal agents, instead of ruining the restaurant, contributed materially to furthering the careers of its management. The raiding special squad confiscated all of the liquor and subjected samples to tests. They were found to be as represented—genuine. New York newspapers found out about it and publicized the findings. Jack and Charlie reopened to a landslide business and a firmly established reputation for integrity.

In 1929 Jack and Charlie had to move again to make way for

the construction of Rockefeller Center. On their last night at the old Iron Gate, they invited a special guest list of "trustee members" including Bea Lillie, Robert Benchley, Gilbert Kahn, Broadway producer Alex Aarons, the Irish poet Ernest Boyd, and others. When the guests arrived they were handed crowbars and shovels, and spent a hilarious evening demolishing the place. Then they paraded through the streets, accompanied by carts loaded with pots and pans, jockey statues and even the famed iron gate, to what was destined to be "Jack and Charlie's" permanent home.

"21" IS BORN

The following night Jack and Charlie's were open for business in their new establishment at 21 West 52nd Street, an elegant dining institution so celebrated that it needs only the number of its address —"21"—to be instantly identified. Prohibition was still in force and the new place was elaborately equipped with dumping devices whereby push buttons and chutes could instantly send all the liquor in the bar crashing into a rocky culvert leading to a sewer main. Reserve stocks were kept locked behind a two-and-a-half-ton electrically operated stone door that could be swung open by inserting a long iron wire into a certain hole, the hole rendered inconspicuous by some hundred others exactly like it. Other doors were similarly locked by a short-circuit button. None of the several raids on "21" ever produced a drop of evidence, though on one occasion federal agents spent twenty-four hours searching the premises.

Gangland began once again pressuring for admittance to partnership. Legs Diamond, kingpin of the New York underworld, sent three toughs around to talk to the management. Another fight ensued, and Charlie, Jack, and their doorman, Jimmy Cosgrove, beat up the three hoodlums and threw them out. That took not only strength but nerve. "We were lucky," Charlie says, looking back, "Legs Diamond was shot to death by the underworld before he had a chance to retaliate."

At last came repeal, which put an end to some of the problems, though not to all. It's not generally known, but the "21" Club almost went bankrupt following prohibition. During the first six or seven months after repeal, clients wanted to try the new places that were opening up. Restaurants and hotels pirated the highly trained "21" help. The "21" pulled through only because a small nucleus of employees and customers remained loyal and the partners poured every cent of cash and credit they could muster into keeping up the quality standards of food and service which had made the establishment famous.

"The lesson we learned," says Berns, "was that in a crisis you must make your decisions and have the courage to stick to them. It also illustrates that you have to work for a long haul, not the short profit. The "21" Club survived its crisis principally because of a record and reputation that were built up long before. You stand or fall on your foundations. Wit and luck help, but it's what you have accumulated in terms of what you really are and represent that makes the difference in the long run. Selectivity and quality were always the keys to our business, in the restaurant and in '21' Brands."

The spring of 1933 saw a wave of bank closings climaxed by the famous national bank holiday. That day, Jack and Charlie printed their own scrip which patrons could use at "21" in lieu of money. They had always made a point of keeping a large sum of cash on hand for emergencies, including momentarily embarrassed but solidly solvent patrons.

A DISTRIBUTING COMPANY NAMED "21"

The year 1933 marked the founding of "21" Brands to distribute the favorite liquor brands of the elegant restaurant's exclusive clientele. The new company moved into the town house next door. Fittingly, Mr. Berns's office is what used to be the dining room. The Old World atmosphere of the mansion has been retained practically intact, a pleasant exception to the soaring skyscrapers which surround it. Laws set up to govern the nation's liquor industry after repeal required the restaurant and the liquor company to be separated. By 1936 these statutes came into full force and the famous partnership of Jack and Charlie was dissolved. Their personal connection remained as strong as ever, and to this day Charlie Berns quits his office next door and lunches at "21." His early lunch hour is a carry-over from the days when he used to taste the food himself before serving it to the clients.

"I do not believe in the popular notion that business and pleasure don't mix," says Berns. "I have always enjoyed doing business with people that I like and admire and whom I want to be with socially. One of my basic principles of personal philosophy has been, in relations with people, to try to do more at a personal or social level than the person expected in the normal course of a business relationship."

BEHIND THE CHARLES A. BERNS STORY

Charles Berns started life in the New York tenement district surrounded by the squalor and harsh realities of poverty and hunger. Out of these social and economic pressures grew young Charles's first buddings of business enterprise. He sold newspapers, an early activity of many successful men. The "selling newspapers" element of a youthful background is important because it reflects a vital decision. The individual decides that he will cope with the demands of a harsh environment by means of work.

Another major element in Berns's success pattern: he scored his achievements as a member of a team, known as "Jack and Charlie." It is not unusual for successful men to mount the ladder as part of a team. In Berns's case, however, this was more than a passing phase. It lasted for years, and many upward steps. An important aspect of the Jack and Charlie duo: it exemplifies the traditional "inside man–outside man." Jack Kriendler was the outside man, the "salesman." Charlie was the inside man, the "businessman," who kept one eye on the books and the other on running the establishment. The logic of this pattern is a key aspect of its effectiveness. In this type of two-man team, there is a powerful reinforcement factor. One man's capabilities in one area is complemented by his teammate's proficiency in another. As a team, they are much more effective together than they would likely be individually. And certainly, their combined capabilities are more formidable than those of the ordinary individual, operating on his own.

Success Hunger. As you read this story, you are aware of Berns's need to keep working, fighting, and striving. He loves challenge and he seemingly has to seek it out if it fails to come to him. Some people spend many years waiting for opportunity to knock. Berns appears to have been short on waiting time. He created his own opportunity. He knocked on the outside of his door, then ran inside to answer the knock.

Failure Response. Young Charlie Berns didn't do well as a shoe salesman. As a matter of fact, he failed miserably. The meaning of this early experience should not be misinterpreted. Failure can be a very strong selection factor. A man who does well in every job he undertakes may well end up a success but at a low level of satisfaction. In other words, had Charlie been a good shoe salesman, he might have ended up owning his own shoe store—but not much more.

Failure as a shoe salesman was a learning experience. He became aware that there were some things he could do well, some things he could do better and some things he couldn't do at all. Once this awareness sank home, he responded to this realization by moving into the areas in which he functioned best.

Goal-Setting. Berns grew up in a family that believed that if life was not the way you wanted it, you took active steps to do something about it. You set yourself an objective which, when accomplished, would revise the *status quo* upward.

Berns was part of an immigrant family that uprooted itself and moved a vast distance across the planet to rectify what was unsatisfactory in its life. The Bernses clearly did not believe in accepting lesser standards when they might find something better. Here we see both the incentive for setting high goals and a personal philosophy that encouraged the efforts to achieve them.

Team Play. That Berns was part of a two-man team has already been pointed out. He was also a member of a larger team, that of family and friends. It was not so much a member of the family that set out to find his fortune, it was the entire family unit. Whether one member succeeds or fails, he does so as part of the family, with others to support him, pick up the pieces, offer encouragement, and so on. This team approach is significant because it probably accounts for Berns's willingness to accept assistance when he needed it, and to offer assistance to others when the need arose. A man like this isn't likely to suffer the traditional "loneliness at the top." Talk to Berns today, and his warm jovial manner, his easy sociability, back this assumption.

Monument-Building. The monument to Berns's accomplishment is fairly tangible—a world-renowned restaurant and a distribution organization that deals with a substantial product. For Berns, the symbol of success is the effectiveness of a man's work efforts. He was willing to stake everything he had in order to build and maintain his "monument." This attitude explains his pitched battles with the hoodlums who threatened his lifework—where others might have yielded.

What isn't sufficiently clear in Berns's story is why he was able to survive the changes brought about in the restaurant business by repeal. Remember, there were literally dozens of other "clubs" or speak-easies, some as big or bigger than Jack and Charlie's spot. Berns asserts positively that it was his "education" that gave him the edge. He means this literally. And, to the extent that his college and law school training made him more aware of currents of change, it seems likely that his explanation comes close to the mark. Just add, to "education," the concept of quality foods and service, and the capability of "21's" owners to forge close friendly relationships with their patrons, and the reason for Berns success becomes clear.

6 $\left\{\begin{array}{l} \text{J. Leonard Reinsch} - \\ \text{SERVICE IN THE AIR} \end{array}\right.$

On the morning of September 27, 1960, the John F. Kennedy forces were a shade short of delirium. It was the morning after the historic first Kennedy-Nixon television debate that many people now consider the turning point in the 1960 Presidential campaign that elected John F. Kennedy the thirty-fifth President of the United States. Among those celebrating Kennedy's television victory was J. Leonard Reinsch (pronounced "wrench"). Veteran broadcaster and executive director of the Democratic National Convention, Reinsch had labored through fifteen tension-filled meetings to negotiate the historic first and subsequent debates.

Reinsch's political activities are but an extension of his business interests. His career encompasses three industries within broadcasting: the birth and maturation of the radio industry; the birth and development of the television industry; and today, a third industry, community antenna television (CATV), which Reinsch (and Cox Broadcasting), along with other pioneers, are developing.

His election as president of Cox Broadcasting Corporation in 1964 at an annual salary of $100,000, his ownership of 110,000 shares of Cox Broadcasting stock (valued at $2,750,000 in mid-1965), his board membership in Broadcast Music Incorporated and in the National Community Television Association, highlight Reinsch's success as a broadcasting executive.

* * *

He was twelve years old and in the eighth grade, Reinsch recalls, when he first mapped out his career. His profession would be that of an advertising copywriter. And he would someday be in advertising's hall of fame. How this ambition to become a successful copywriter germinated, Reinsch does not know. No one in his family wrote for a living, or was interested in advertising.

His father, Henry Emil Reinsch, of Joliet, Illinois, was an engineer on the Atchison, Topeka and Santa Fe Railroad. His mother, nee Grace Lillian Funk, housewife, had been a country schoolteacher. There was always a love of learning in his home, a respect for intellectuality.

Reinsch's desire to become a successful copywriter is more understandable when viewed in the context of the times. From World War I through the 1920s, copywriting held the same prestige that astrophysics does today. These were the golden years of copywriting. Professionals like Claude C. Hopkins, Bruce Barton, Raymond Rubicam, John E. Kennedy, John Orr Young, Ernest Elmo Calkins moved mountains of merchandise with slogans like:

"99 44/100% pure—it floats"

"They laughed when I sat down at the piano, but when I started to play . . ."

"The Prudential has the strength of Gibraltar"

These men turned trade names into household words, helped to raise unknown companies into national prominence.

Wearing knickers and still in grade school, Reinsch set out to master the copywriting art. He studied ads in national magazines such as *Boys' Life, Collier's, Saturday Evening Post;* drew his own crude layouts, wrote copy, mailed his roughed-out advertisements to General Foods, Ralston, Procter & Gamble, and other prominent corporations only to be met with silence at the other end. But this did not deter Reinsch from flooding the mails with his layouts and copy.

Along with writing, Reinsch was a voracious reader. During summer vacations, when the Chicago library system permitted students to check out ten books at a time, he took his full quota. Reinsch still retains his love of reading. In one month he may read six books, ranging from current novels to social, historical or scientific works, along with trade journals and newspapers.

Attending Chicago's Harrison High School, Reinsch discovered that the library subscribed to *Printer's Ink,* then advertising's foremost trade journal. He was Balboa discovering the Pacific. *"Printer's Ink* opened a whole new world I didn't know existed," says Reinsch. "The seed to be a copywriter was already there. *Printer's Ink* nurtured it."

When Reinsch broke into the communications field in April, 1924, it was as a radio performer, appearing as interlocutor in a minstrel show on Chicago's station WLS. He was sixteen and a high-school senior. He was also an amateur pianist, and he produced a variety show on WENR. In those days of rampant experimentalism, performers oftentimes forgot their scores. Music had to be hastily rearranged and introductions ad-libbed. Performers sometimes failed to show up. Each new program contributed to Reinsch's education in radio. Meanwhile, Reinsch attended high school and worked as a church janitor to earn money for college.

In the early 1920s, radio, operating in what Reinsch describes as a "state of disorderly confusion," was more gadgetry than an industry. Radio stations were set up by corporations to sell their own products, by religious groups to proselytize; by personalities and groups eager to promote themselves.

In the fall of 1924, Reinsch entered Crane College in Chicago, still fired with ambition to achieve success as a copywriter. In 1927, he dropped out of college to earn tuition to continue his education, meanwhile poring over catalogs to find a university where he could major in advertising. Northwestern University had an outstanding advertising department, founded by Dr. Walter Dill Scott who, in 1904, had started what was probably the first academic course in advertising. Entering Northwestern as a junior in 1928, Reinsch majored in writing and copywriting. Motivation and motivation studies were the vogue during this stage of advertising's development, and Reinsch took courses in psychology.

In 1928, Reinsch was hired on a part-time basis by Chicago's WLS, then owned by the *Prairie Farmer Magazine*. The management knew Reinsch from his guest appearances at the studio. They were impressed with the young man's ability to perform, to put programs together, to improvise and keep programs going when performers or announcers failed to show up, and by his coolness under pressure.

Like many others in this new field, Reinsch started as general handyman around the studio. He began on the switchboard, then moved into writing copy for commercials, next was assigned to announce a cooking school program sponsored twice weekly by Midland Milling Company. Reinsch not only did the commercials, he also wrote and prepared the recipes—although, as he admits, he knew absolutely nothing about cooking. He remembers this job with special pleasure. On Friday noon, WLS broadcast directly from the kitchen of the College Inn, with Chef Magliano cooking and narrating his favorite recipes in broken English. When the meal was cooked, Reinsch got the "run of the house," which meant he ate well indeed.

Reinsch *needed* nourishment to keep up his schedule. Carrying a full course of study at Northwestern, he worked at WLS in the evenings, Saturday, and Sundays. Classes started at 8 A.M. On weekdays, he finished at the radio station at 11 P.M. or midnight. On Saturdays, Reinsch arrived at the radio studios at 10 A.M. and finished his stint at midnight, announcing a barn dance broadcast. He always carried his textbooks to the studio, studying between announcements. When the engineer would tap on the window for Reinsch to rise for a station break or a commercial, he was usually deep in a marketing or business organization problem, or writing copy.

WLS shared its frequency with two other stations: WENR, owned by Samuel Insull, later to gain notoriety as a pyramider of utility companies, and WCBD. The latter station, transmitting from Zion, Illinois, had one distinction. Its founder, Wilbur G. Voliver, was dedicated to the belief that the earth was flat. In the formative days of radio, "frequency raiding" was quite prevalent. When WENR applied for full-time on WLS's frequency, therefore, a hearing was called before a government agency. Although Reinsch was only twenty-two, he was assigned by the station management to prepare WLS's defense. Preparing WLS's rejoinder required Reinsch to familiarize himself with the rules and regulations governing the operation of radio stations—an experience which later proved invaluable in furthering his career.

GOLF AS A SOCIAL TOOL

Between a full college schedule and working at the station evenings, Saturdays, and Sundays, Reinsch had little time to make the necessary business contacts and friends, to learn the techniques of leadership, and executive methods. Reinsch realized this; ability and energy would carry him just so far, but not far enough. One had to know important people, to mingle with them socially, if one wanted to be taken as an up-and-coming young man. And so Reinsch set out on a systematic campaign to make friends and contacts, to learn executive skills and graces.

In the twenties, golf was, as it is today, a great social equalizer, a sport which brought together gas station attendants, executives, and royalty. Golf also bore the stamp of success. Golf would be the medium through which the twenty-two-year-old student and aspiring executive would cultivate social and business contacts. He could, of course, scarcely afford membership in a golf club. In a flank attack on this obstacle, Reinsch concluded an agreement with the *Midwest Golfer,* a large, plush magazine carrying photographs and news of individual golfing clubs. In return for writing a four-page advertising insert, Reinsch received two memberships, one in the Elmhurst Country Club, another in the Edgewood Valley Country Club, both in Chicago. His contacts were primarily corporate advertising managers and advertising agency officials. One of these, Walter Wade, who headed his own agency, later gave Reinsch his first contract when Reinsch joined WHIO in 1934.

While Reinsch was in his junior year at Northwestern in 1929, he worked up to a full-time position in WLS's commercial department. This meant switching to night college during his senior year. It would be five years before Reinsch would complete his senior year and attain his degree.

He worked at WLS for three years before resigning in 1932 at age twenty-four, to take a six-month assignment which proved to be a major leap forward in his career. He sacrificed a full-time job in an expanding company for a short-term assignment promising nothing more than broader experience—and an opportunity to manage. The assignment was to reorganize and manage WMBD ("World's Most Beautiful Drive") in Peoria, Illinois, until older hands could take over. "I was amazed that they would entrust a station's management and a staff of twenty people to me," says Reinsch. "But I have never been one to duck responsibility, or avoid making a decision, and I welcomed the assignment. Responsibility is the final test of ability."

HOUSECLEANING AT WMBD, PEORIA

When Reinsch arrived at WMBD in Peoria, he found the staff operating the station in Mack Sennett fashion—and this at a time when the whole broadcasting business was sinking rapidly. Advertisers were pulling in their horns; profits were razor-thin or nonexistent.

WMBD, sharing its frequency with another station, was scheduled to operate until 2 P.M., when it signed off. If the WMBD announcer ran out of programing or felt like "knocking off," he would sign off at 1:00 or 1:15 P.M. This not only meant unproductive time, but loss of audience. This was the first abuse Reinsch corrected: the announcer stayed at the microphone until the station signed off for the day. Reinsch took on the job of re-educating the staff, and when a few turned out to be ineducable, he dismissed them. "In Peoria I received a practical lesson in handling people, a lesson in adjusting to a new community," says Reinsch. He further learned how to make difficult decisions, and to carry them out with a minimum of upset to those involved.

He learned that being quick to praise and being genuinely enthusiastic were ways to motivate people. He learned that assigning tasks with a specific date set for their completion and delegating responsibilities were indispensable to getting things done. The WMBD assignment gave him practical experience in getting the best performance out of people; in setting up a full schedule of programing; in developing promotion techniques to publicize the station; in salesmanship and selling advertising time; and in the accounting end of radio station management. More than this, Reinsch's first experience as an administrator would shortly lead him to switch his career objectives from copywriting to broadcasting.

Reinsch did not return to Chicago laden with the proverbial fortune, but the value of his tenure at WMBD could hardly be measured.

A PIONEERING THESIS: RADIO ADVERTISING

His next hurdle was completing his college education, begun eight years before. This meant writing a thesis, and the subject Reinsch chose was radio advertising.

In the 1920s there were intimations that radio might develop into a significant advertising force. But corporations and retailers were skeptical of putting their advertising dollars into such a nebulous medium as wireless. Advertisers were dubious that a huge audience was "out there in the nowhere," listening to their messages, with dollars ready to buy their products. Institutional advertising by radio stations was virtually unheard of. The art of writing radio commercials was primitive. On many stations, announcers read newspaper ads or ad-libbed commercials.

Reinsch's thesis, exploring this new field, won the D. F. Keller competition at Northwestern. When Reinsch won the Keller competition, Dean Harrington, of Northwestern's Medill School of Journalism, invited Reinsch to act as consultant in setting up the first curriculum in radio journalism at Northwestern. Setting up the curriculum gave him additional insights into the operations of radio stations.

AFFILIATION WITH JAMES M. COX

The following year, 1934, was a decisive one for Reinsch. Having decided on an executive career in radio, he mapped out for himself a step-by-step plan to ascend the corporate ladder. His first move was to look for a managerial position in a radio station serving a community of 200,000 to 300,000 population. A smaller town would not afford him broad enough scope to exercise and enlarge his skills. And in a large city station, he would be hamstrung, forced to specialize.

Reinsch embarked on a letter-writing campaign seeking employment. Then one day he spotted a blind advertisement in *Broadcasting* magazine: "Manager, to direct a new station to be built in Dayton, Ohio." Dayton fell precisely into the 200,000–300,000 category. The advertiser, as Reinsch soon learned, was James Middleton Cox, twice governor of Ohio, Democratic presidential candidate in 1920 (running mate: Franklin D. Roosevelt), and owner of a newspaper chain. Cox was now expanding his communications empire into radio.

At twenty-six, Reinsch, the youngest applicant, won the job. "In retrospect," he says, "the development seemed inevitable." He joined WHIO on November 11, 1934. One of the factors that persuaded Cox to hire him, the Governor later disclosed, was Reinsch's pioneering thesis on radio advertising. Other factors were Reinsch's enthusiasm for radio as a communications medium, his intensity of purpose, his interest in current events, and his comprehensive knowledge of radio station management. (Reinsch's book *Radio Station Management,* written in collaboration with E. I. Ellis and published by Harper & Row—1948; revised edition, 1960—is the standard text in the field.)

Governor Cox handed Reinsch a sheaf of architect's blueprints for the station to be built—or rather rebuilt from an existing structure. Studying these, Reinsch discovered that the architect was unfamiliar with radio station construction. That night, Reinsch and the chief engineer went into the building (a former dress store) with a broom, swept the floor, and with colored chalk laid out studios and offices. The next morning, Reinsch showed Governor Cox his layout and explained why the architect's plans should be altered. The plans were revamped.

On February 8, 1935, radio station WHIO started transmitting with Governor Cox scheduled to appear on the inaugural program. "The Governor asked me how long he should speak," Reinsch recalls. "I told him about sixty to ninety seconds." He looked me in the eye and said, 'Young man, I don't get started in ninety seconds.'" Reinsch pointed out that long-winded oratory would drive the audience away. The Governor settled for two minutes. It was a ticklish situation: a twenty-seven-year-old newly hired employee standing up to a former presidential candidate and governor, a disciple of old-time evangelistic oratory. (Reinsch's prescription: "Keep it short," is standard operating procedure today at political conventions.)

WHIO operated on the National Broadcasting System with 1000 watts of power. Its competitor, WLW, operating out of Cincinnati on the same network with 50,000 watts and staffed by a large organization, completely overshadowed WHIO in power, experience, availability of talent, and resources.

Taking inventory of the staff assigned him, the young manager discovered that some people were not pulling their weight, some practices and programs were not holding audiences. Demonstrating the talent which he had shown at WMBD three years previously, Reinsch acted decisively. He called a staff meeting and spoke for ten minutes. "I explained that I was the station manager, that I had the responsibility for direction until Governor Cox indicated to the contrary and that I expected their cooperation and loyalty," Reinsch says.

"We expected to have a top-flight radio station in which we could all take pride. Anyone who did not share that feeling would not stay long with the organization. I closed the meeting with no discussion. Fortunately I hit the right note, and the WHIO organization today has a solid base of people who were with me at that time."

As Cox acquired additional radio stations, Reinsch was assigned to manage them. In December, 1939, Reinsch was named executive director of WHIO and of recently acquired WSB in Atlanta and moved permanently to the latter city. Three years later when WIOD was merged into the Cox chain, Reinsch became executive director of three radio stations.

F.D.R. PUTS IN A CALL

The following year the Senate Interstate and Foreign Commerce Committee under the chairmanship of Senator Burt Wheeler of Montana launched an investigation of the Federal Communications Commission.

Reinsch was asked to testify as a representative of the broadcasting industry. At the conclusion of his testimony, Senator Albert Hawke, a New Jersey Republican, declared: "Mr. Reinsch, you have made the finest presentation I have ever heard of any witness before this committee." Word of Reinsch's competence sifted over to the White House. In 1944, President Roosevelt called Governor Cox asking for "your man Leonard Reinsch to direct convention radio programing."

Reinsch welcomed this opportunity to enter politics. By 1944, he was straining at the leash. He had organized or reorganized three broadcasting stations. They were operating smoothly. "I didn't have any challenge and was feeling restless," he says. During 1944, Reinsch barnstormed with Senator Truman, the Vice-Presidential candidate. After President Roosevelt's death, in 1945, Reinsch was delegated by President Truman to be his White House press secretary. Reinsch's tenure lasted a short two weeks—just time enough for

Governor Cox to realize that he was losing his right-hand man in radio. Cox almost literally yanked Reinsch back into his corporate job.

With the war's end, Reinsch was again feeling restless. He had achieved a degree of success, but found that radio was losing its dynamism and hence its challenge for him. Then television burst on the scene.

The new medium presented challenges—technical, managerial, and artistic—that were more overwhelming than the advent of sound in motion pictures. Scores of Hollywood stars never made the transition into talking pictures. History repeated itself. Hundreds of radio performers and technicians, unable to cope with the new medium, never made the transition into TV. Reinsch was one of those who started fast in television. Cox Station WSB-TV in Atlanta went on the air September 30, 1948, the first television station in the South. The following year WHIO-TV began programing in Dayton.

Reinsch says of this era: "We knew intuitively that television would be the greatest social, political, and educational force, the greatest communication medium in mankind's history. But we had no equipment, no organization, no tradition, no standards to go by. We improvised, borrowed from radio, the stage, motion pictures, the newspaper city room.

"We sent camera crews into the street to conduct sidewalk interviews. We took pictures of the local high-school football games. We set up spelling bees with civic clubs competing against each other. We held crossword puzzle matches. We inaugurated a promotional program called 'Meet the Boss,' in which executives and their families were interviewed." When a transit strike crippled Atlanta, Reinsch installed programing facilities in Richard's Department Store, displayed—over WSB-TV—items for sale, conducted fashion shows, ran the camera over the street floor display windows. So successful was the program in selling merchandise, that the settees and desks used as background for the set itself were sold.

TV IN POLITICS

Television, as historians are aware, has transformed the art of the political campaign, and Reinsch played an important role in this transformation. He began speeding up conventions, making them more dramatic in 1952 when he was radio-tv director of the Democratic National Convention. In 1960, Reinsch had a vision of what one could do with a vigorous political personality on television. "I knew we had an outstanding candidate in Kennedy who would swamp his opponent in a television debate. The feat was to bring him together with his Republican opponent." After repeated efforts, Reinsch was successful in arranging face-to-face confrontations on television between presidential candidates Kennedy and Nixon. The rest is history.

Reinsch's acquaintance with literally thousands of political figures, his knowledge of FCC regulations and the directions in which federal agencies were going in regulating radio and television were undoubtedly factors in elevating him to the presidency of Cox Broadcasting Corporation in 1964. This was the same year in which he guided the newly founded corporation through a public offering of its stock to a listing on the New York Stock Exchange.

Reinsch could well rest on his laurels today. Instead, he is constantly on the go, seeking acquisitions for Cox, setting up new ventures, making contacts, developing a new industry, community antenna television. This latter medium, incorporating radio, television, background music, and commercial services will, in Reinsch's view, supplant television as we know it today within the next decade or two.

BEHIND THE J. LEONARD REINSCH STORY

Leonard Reinsch's story is as much a capsule history of a time and an industry as it is of a person. As one follows Reinsch's career, there emerges vivid and insightful flashes of the birth and development first of radio, then of the TV industry.

Too often when the historian speaks of an event or development, it's described as though it took place in a vacuum without people. Certainly, there will be many histories written of the growth of radio and television as though radio stations proliferated and grew as a result of some kind of mushroom-like genesis. But in Reinsch's biographical sketch, we see through his eyes and his career some of the forces—and problems—involved in the development of the radio-TV industry, from puny beginnings to a lusty giant covering the planet.

Elements like these account for the important role Reinsch was able to play in the management end of radio-TV:

Core Learning. One sees in Reinsch's career an element common to many successful people. He benefited from his early exposure to a milieu that provided an important basic business education. At the age of twenty-two, he was given the opportunity of preparing radio station WLS's defense in litigation with another station. In preparing the case for WLS, Reinsch became intimately familiar with the regulations governing radio station operation. It was both a milestone and a keystone in his career.

Action Program. "Successful people are doers," goes the saw. But it's often difficult to figure out exactly what the successful person does. Leonard Reinsch provides a clear-cut example of the achiever as a doer. In thinking about his career, he decided that he must make contacts, get to know important people. Having made this decision, he set about planning moves that would get him a nodding acquaintance with important individuals. The fact that membership in a golf club was the means to the end shows that, in some instances, the answer to an abstract question—"How does one go about meeting important people?"—can have a perfectly simple and matter-of-fact answer.

Did Reinsch's "action program" pay off? Apparently it did. In addition to meeting "people who mattered," he met Walter Wade, who proved to be an important business contact for Reinsch when he was beginning at WHIO.

Loss for Gain. From time to time a businessman finds himself in a losing situation. Then he must decide when to take his losses to end the drain of the disadvantageous situation.

Reinsch's affiliation with WLS was not, strictly speaking, a "losing" situation. As a matter of fact, he had profited considerably in terms of experience gained. Yet, in his case, he pulled out of a winning situation, took on the job of managing radio station WMBD on a short-time assignment, essential to gain the opportunity of managing a station.

Taking over the management of radio station WMBD, Reinsch found himself with a dying organization on his hands. Advertisers were cutting down expenditures, inefficiency was a serious cost drain. Reinsch had to make a tough decision. It was the kind of resolve that a doctor must sometimes make to cut out the source of infection in order to save the patient. This kind of stop-loss decision is not uncommon in business. What was unusual is that it was made by a twenty-four-year-old young man who acted with the sure instinct and resolve of a veteran.

The Art of Management. It was at Peoria's radio station WMBD that Reinsch learned how to manage people. This knowledge covered a number of specific executive techniques. He learned how to motivate people. He learned how to delegate. He learned how to make assignments and set up deadlines for their conclusion. And, especially difficult for a young man, he learned how to fire people when necessary. These techniques, well-learned once, became his for all time and facilitated his later management achievements.

The Success Lesson. Some people view a final crowning success as merely the last of a series of earlier successful achievements. In Reinsch's career, we see the importance of learning to appreciate one's own success as a means of repeating it.

Actually, the achiever learns from experience not only how to repeat success, but how to avoid repeating a failure. In the story of Charles Berns, for example, one sees how the world-renowned restaurateur learned that he was not cut out to be a shoe clerk and gave up trying to be one. Reinsch, whose boyhood ambition it had been to become a copywriter, switched when the opportunities of radio came his way. As his story shows, he scored an early and outstanding success as troubleshooter and administrator of a radio station. He never forgot the lesson—and continued pressing in the direction of his success.

Seek and Find. The Bible asserts the same idea that is frequently found in management literature: Seek and find. In other words, set a goal and take the steps necessary to achieve it.

Leonard Reinsch analyzed what he needed to do as a next logical step in his career. After he had finished his Ph.D. studies at Northwestern University, he had figured out, down to the detail of the size of the community, the kind of radio job he wanted. He then set about job-hunting and did not stop until he found precisely the station he had in mind.

7 { Eugene K. Denton –
A FORTUNE IN TASTE

Eugene Denton is the "dean" of Fifth Avenue merchants, the oldest active full-time store head whose career has been continuous with one firm. His store at 57th Street and Fifth Avenue, the "fashion crossroads of New York," is recognized as one of the leading women's specialty stores in the city and in the nation. It employs more than 350 persons, many of whom have been with The Tailored Woman for more than thirty years, and it is a flourishing example of the determination of one man to establish and perpetuate a retail operation according to his own high standards of taste and quality.

Because Gene Denton runs The Tailored Woman in his own way, his business practices antagonize some people but are admired by others. Suppliers respect him for paying bills promptly and not taking anticipation on special purchases. His bankers and accountants deplore this practice, for he loses thousands of dollars annually by not utilizing suppliers' credit. He prefers the good will of suppliers. Many of the merchandising techniques he developed evoked the envy of his competitors, who now follow the patterns he established.

His blue and beige office, overlooking the busy intersection five floors below, is not just an executive office but another working part of the store. There are racks of muslin patterns; there are original Paris fashions which he purchased and which he will "edit" for the store; there are bundles of rare mink which he will inspect expertly before sending them to the store's vaults; there are neat stacks of magazines and trade papers; and there are ad layouts, sketches and photographs for his approval. There are two desks, although he rarely sits at the more formal, ornately carved one, but prefers to work at a small square table. The walls are hung with portraits of prize-winning Aberdeen-Angus cattle, which he raised on his New Jersey farm; portraits of friends; and framed, giant-sized birthday and greeting cards signed by store employees.

Gene Denton is not only chief executive of The Tailored Woman but chief buyer, salesman, fashion authority, stylist, copywriter and self-styled elevator operator. The last position came about a few years ago when he commandeered one of the store's elevators for his personal use so that he could speed from floor to floor, department to department. His intense interest in the day-to-day operation of every part of The Tailored Woman—not just the financial aspect—stems from his conviction that a merchant must stay close to customers in order to understand and serve their needs. "My mother taught me always to go to the bottom of the facts—to the source. It's a practice that's necessary in business—and in life."

* * *

Denton's family lived in the Southern tradition of ease and comfort, and as a youngster Denton had few, if any, thoughts about business or work. But with changing economic and social patterns, the family had to sell their plantations and move to Nashville. When Gene completed high school, he had three choices: go on to college, work on a plantation, or get into some kind of business. With a twinkle in his eye, he claims that women were responsible for his decision to start in business and that they have been his business ever since. "In my teens I was something of a ladies' man. But my allowance wasn't enough to cover all my dates. I didn't want to go to college, I wasn't interested in working on a plantation. I solved the two problems by getting a job."

The job was with a local dry goods store, run by a family friend and part of a retail chain. Gene's older brother, Elroy, was head of the chain's Augusta, Georgia, outlet. "Once I started working, I loved the job," Gene says. "And I guess my enthusiasm showed, for a short while later I was sent to New York to learn the technical aspects of the dry goods business. Of course, I jumped at the opportunity."

In New York, Gene was assigned to the chain's big outlet, James McCreery & Co., the well-known department store. "I was probably the first executive trainee in retailing," he says. He believes he "got the greatest education in the world" for his future at the store. He spent time in every department, hounding buyers and executives with an almost insatiable curiosity about the ins and outs of retail operation.

"I tried to do more than what was expected of me and I wasn't afraid to offer a suggestion or give an opinion. Sometimes my ideas were laughed at or resented and I would shut up. But I learned to swallow my pride and, little by little, the buyers recognized that I might have something to contribute. I volunteered to work nights, often with the store's display department, which gave me great experience in draping materials."

ALL ABOUT SILK

Gene finally ended up in McCreery's highly esteemed silk department. The department was run by a rough-and-tumble Irishman named Joe Morrissey, who knew more about silks than anyone in the business. The forty Irish salesman under him were all good at their jobs but they knew little beyond their immediate areas of operation. One day Gene was called into Morrissey's office. "He scared the hell out of me," Gene recalls. "'Come here, kid,' he said, 'I'm going to teach you everything there is to know about silks and I want you to teach that dumb bunch out there.' And he did; and I did. I found very quickly that you can learn something from everyone—whether it's good or bad; and I also found that my enthusiasm for learning was catching."

A year later Gene was offered the job of silk buyer for the chain's Cincinnati outlet, the George McAlpin Company. "I was twenty-two at the time and all the buyers I have ever met were bewhiskered gentlemen, sixty or seventy years old." The head of the Cincinnati store was something less than enthusiastic about the potential abilities of a young upstart from New York. But Gene worked hard and fast. To the amazement of the store personnel, he carried hundred-pound bolts of fabrics with ease. He cleaned out old merchandise and brought in new materials. He quickly latched on to a promotion being staged by a manufacturer. (Management took a dim view until they learned that he had taken the goods on memo.) "And," he recalls, "the fabric 'walked out' of the store."

"Sometimes it's necessary to take chances," he says. "You just can't sit back and expect things to happen by themselves."

Business in the fabric department improved markedly and Gene was given the added post of buyer of woolens. Traffic in the department had increased to such an extent that it became necessary to move from the main floor to a second-floor annex. "This meant I had to work even harder to attract customers." But within five years there were five salesmen in the woolen department and twelve in silks, and the store's chief competitors, the H. S. Pogue Company and Shillito's, had begun to take notice.

SKIRTS TO ORDER

One day a Polish tailor called on the young buyer with an unusual plan. Many fabrics were sold in lengths designed to be sewn into skirts. Why shouldn't the store offer customers the chance to have these lengths made up into a skirt by the tailor for an additional two dollars? The idea appealed to Gene. "It was my first crack at the garment business," he says. "We tried it and it worked. Then I knew we could do even better. I learned that certain fabric mills sold remnants by the pound rather than by the yard, which made the cost very low. I went to the New York sales agency for one of the largest mills and made a deal with them. I spent my entire 'open-to-buy'—eighteen thousand dollars—for mill ends. It was a tremendous amount of fabric and there was some doubt that the floor of the store could support the weight. There also was some doubt about my sanity.

"We worked days, nights, and Sundays unpacking, measuring and marking pieces of fabric. Not only was I worried about moving all that material but I found out I'd made a mistake too. Many pieces in that mountain of fabric turned out to be just too small for skirts and we were stuck with them. But it all turned out. Women flocked to the store, and ordered so many skirts that we had to move the tailor and his assistants into the store to speed up service. The next load of mill ends I bought, I arranged for a cap manufacturer to take the small pieces."

The success of the venture prompted store officials to make Gene buyer of suits and coats. He began making frequent buying trips to New York where he became acquainted with many manufacturers and suppliers. They looked forward to seeing the genial Southerner with the determined quality, the ready smile, and definite opinions about style.

ON HIS OWN

In 1912, his brother Elroy suggested that he and Gene strike out on their own. Typically, Gene made the decision quickly. They established the Denton Company in Cincinnati with Elroy handling the administrative end of the business and buying for the first floor and Gene in charge of suits, coats, dresses, blouses, and skirts. They worked well together, with Gene quick to learn management techniques from his more experienced brother.

Gene Denton's future retailing concepts now assumed definite shape. As a child in the South he had been brought up in a conservative manner. The bizarre, the outrageous, the sensational were foreign to his family's teachings and to his nature. Even as a youngster he disliked the garish styles and colors which were familiar street sights of the time. In business with his brother, he was finally able to combine his taste for the conservative with his retail know-how, and put into practice his fundamental credo: "Good style, good lines, good quality, quiet colors."

Each time he came east he was more and more attracted by the possibilities New York City offered for retailing. He says, "I realized that I wouldn't be a success in my own mind unless I came to Fifth Avenue. That thought was always with me, from the very beginning."

After a number of successful business years with his brother, Gene began to express more and more interest in the move to New York. The older man was in complete sympathy with his younger brother's desire to establish a New York store, and gave Gene his blessing. He served as Gene's mentor not only during the formulation of plans but also for many years to follow while he continued to operate and expand the Ohio store.

One of Gene's friends, Morris Black, an important manufacturer of suits and coats, was anxious to have a New York outlet for his merchandise and he was impressed with young Denton's energy, enthusiasm, and determination. He also liked Gene's definite ideas about the type of store he wanted. Finally, Black and his brother-in-law, Max Hellerman, agreed with Denton that each would put up one-third of the necessary capital and that Gene would run the store.

THE INVASION OF FIFTH AVENUE

In June, 1919, he picked a site on Fifth Avenue between 49th and 50th streets, where Rockefeller Center now stands. The old shopping hub of Manhattan was 34th Street but retail expansion was moving northward on Fifth Avenue. Even "upper" Fifth Avenue was still dotted with the homes of the city's affluent residents and Gene was anxious to be near the type of customer he hoped to attract to his special kind of retail operation.

The theory behind establishment of the store, which was to be called The Tailored Woman, had been conceived by Gene throughout the years. The store was to be devoted to clothes of simplicity and good taste. At that time, this idea was not easy to sell. For the most part, ready-to-wear clothes of the day were poorly made and overdecorated. Gene Denton was convinced that fashionable women who subsidized "little dressmakers" or went to Paris for clothes, would buy ready-mades that were properly designed and carefully made. The first advertisement, which he wrote for the opening of the store, sought a certain type of customer, stated a policy from which he has never deviated:

"The Tailored Woman intends to earn a high place among the better grade shops on Fifth Avenue. It intends to earn that place by the service it renders. Its aim is: First: to exclude rigidly the bizarre, the extreme, the unworthy in style, fabric, or tailoring. Second: To include the most worthy, having ever in mind that good taste and good style are synonymous, and that both are dependent upon and interwoven with good quality. Through it all shall prevail the policy of fair prices. There shall be also the refusal to sell to any individual the inappropriate or the unbecoming. Good Style— Good Taste—Good Quality are the watchwords of our endeavor."

The thirty year old store owner didn't get much rest before The Tailored Woman opened on September 29, 1919. The night before the opening he singlehandedly was carrying stock tables from the basement to the first floor. "But," he says, "if you're the leader, you must lead. Did you ever try to push a string?"

During the first six months of operation, the store lost thirty-two thousand dollars. "Of course, I was disappointed," he says, "but it only made me more determined than ever. I didn't stop buying. We took additional newspaper ads to stress our quality concept. We took more expensive ads too in the widely read rotogravure sections—to get our message across. We put on fashion shows in various hotels. Little by little, people began to understand our purpose.

"During the second six months, our volume increased to the point where we reversed our losses and came back to break even for the year. I was fortunate in having the help and advice of my brother and my good friend, Andy Traina, probably the best dress manufacturer in the business and known for his part in the famous fashion firm of Traina-Norell."

To continue his policy, Gene went to Paris where he selected fashions of extreme simplicity and had his own private resources duplicate the elusive quality of taste and workmanship that distinguished made-to-order clothes from run-of-the-mill ready-mades.

A few years later when Saks Fifth Avenue was moving across the street, someone remarked that it would probably help his business. Gene proudly quipped, "I don't need their help"—and he didn't. The store has made a profit every year since its start with the exception of 1932. Both of Gene's partners died during the early years of business and he bought the outstanding interest. At thirty-five, he was sole owner of an up-and-coming enterprise.

Some years later, the store moved one block north on Fifth Avenue. Then when Rockefeller Center was to be established, all tenants in the area were asked to vacate and The Tailored Woman moved again, to the southeast corner of 57th Street and Fifth Avenue, diagonally opposite where it stands today. In 1939 the store moved once more to its present site on the northwest corner of the intersection. With each move new departments were added.

THE MODEL WHO DIDN'T BLINK

The last move created a major problem. At the time the west side of Fifth Avenue was not considered desirable since traffic favored the opposite side of the street. "Everyone said I shouldn't cross the avenue," Gene says. "My bankers told me I would go broke in the new location since there was no traffic. I told them I'd make traffic and I did, but not without getting into a couple of scraps with neighboring stores. One battle I had concerned our use of a live mannequin visible from the store windows. One of our show models had an uncanny ability to hold perfectly still without blinking for almost endless periods of time. She and I hit upon the idea of placing her in an open area inside the front entrance of the store along with regular display mannequins. She would sit or stand for fifteen or twenty minutes without moving a muscle. Then she would get up, move behind a screen to change her costume and reappear.

"People flocked from all over to watch; bets were made on which was the live model, and the police had to be called in to handle the traffic. "Of course," he adds cheerfully, "other stores screamed when they saw what was happening and the Fifth Avenue Association was finally forced to get the city to pass a ruling outlawing the use of live models visible from the street. The rule is still in effect today."

In 1950, The Tailored Woman again outgrew its surroundings and acquired an additional twenty-two thousand square feet by taking space in adjoining buildings. Again new departments were added and existing ones expanded.

For the first fifteen years of operation, Gene Denton did everything at the store. He bought for every department, acted as salesman and took time to pick scraps of paper off the floor, a practice he continues to this day. Although the store has expanded and responsibilities have been delegated, he still keeps a finger in every pie. Four times each year he jets to Europe to buy designs and patterns. He has made more than 110 buying trips to Europe since he founded the store. His theory of editing the more extreme styles of international couture to make them more practical for the active American woman is now an accepted technique in the fashion industry.

A WINNING FORMULA

The Tailored Woman's fur salon is one of the most successful in the country and Denton's special pride and joy, accounting for a substantial portion of the store's annual volume. Its development illustrates Gene Denton's operating pattern. In 1936, The Tailored Woman was an established entity in the New York retailing community. But Gene Denton was not satisfied. He added several departments, including furs. Since his previous experience with furs had been limited to a leased department in the Denton Company, he again leased the fur department. But from the outset, the operation did not please him; it did not come up to the quality standards set for the store. In his characteristic manner he determined to set things right. "I never had tried to master the fur business but I now realized I had to do so."

He decided to limit the stock to five types of fur, "as much as I felt I could handle at first." He met with ranchers, talked with trappers. He examined pelts, worked with fur craftsmen, learned fur techniques. "It wasn't easy," he admits, "taking on a whole new addition to a career, but I had to know the fur business—inside and out."

With this intensive self-training, Gene recognized that he was not satisfied with the typical manufactured fur product. Workmanship generally was far below what he wanted or expected. He found that in many of the intricate fur processes, short cuts were taken to save on expensive materials and labor. The result was garments which he considered ill-fitting and unattractive. As part of his crusade for more care in the manufacture of precious pelts, he coined a new phrase within the industry, "nailing in." It described how he wanted pelts to be handled, in place of the familiar "nailing out" process in which costly furs more often than not were stretched beyond reasonable limits to conform to the desired pattern.

Finally he resolved that The Tailored Woman would establish its own manufacturing system for furs. Using designs obtained in Paris, he had his own contractors make up garments from pelts he purchased personally. He supervised the entire operation. By bypassing dealers and wholesalers, he was able to produce high-quality furs at attractive prices. This procedure continues to be followed today, to the delight of customers, the envy of other retail stores, and the chagrin of certain elements of the fur industry.

He has flown to the backwoods of Labrador to seek rare wild mink and is a familiar figure at fur auctions all over the world. The store's vaults, deep beneath Fifth Avenue, contain almost one million dollars' worth of rare pelts, one of the largest retail inventories in the world.

Producing fine furs is all well and good, Gene Denton believes, but customers have to be attracted to the store. To achieve this he has resorted to some attention-getting devices in a city where the spectacular is often commonplace. He has, for example, hired glamorously befurred models to shovel the first snow of the season from the sidewalks in front of his store. He created a traffic-stopping, near-riot on Fifth Avenue by giving away a mink coat. Thousands of mink-mad women poured into the store but Gene admits he wouldn't attempt it again. "Too much pilfering went on."

He personally writes most of the fur advertisements, some of which take on an educational flavor and some of which assume a fighting, peppery form. Not long ago he was outraged when some stores and fashion writers promoted cowhide as fur. He promptly ran an ad that showed him standing next to one of the spotted cows on his White Gates Farms. The headlines read simply: "I never thought any woman would like to look like a cow . . . fun is fun, but not at Tailored Woman."

The store used to have two branches—one in Pittsburgh and another in Palm Beach—but Denton closed one and sold the other when he found that because he couldn't supervise them personally, they did not work out.

MORE STEAM

Recently he was quoted in a major New York newspaper as saying that he "hadn't put any steam into this business in the last year-and-a-half" and that he had begun a program of management staff expansion to put his business "on a stronger, more substantial basis for the future . . . and to ensure the continued growth of The Tailored Woman." But even with additional personnel, Eugene K. Denton has not slowed down his daily activities. He still puts in an eleven-hour day, arriving at 7:45 A.M. and rarely leaving before 6:30 in the evening. He calls his store his hobby, and his enthusiasm for it has never waned, nor has his energy or determination to maintain his principles ever faltered.

"People must believe in you and what you stand for," he says. "My earliest hopes for The Tailored Woman were based on that idea and I've tried to instill it in all my personnel. That's why I sign every one of the store's advertisements.

"I discovered early in business that there are two kinds of people —the good workers and the others. You need a good crew to help you over the hurdles, but you are the one who must make the important decisions. And just as vital, you must be willing to learn all the time because nothing is permanent except change."

Not long ago, Eugene Denton was awarded the Gold Cup of Le Comité du Bon Goût Français of Paris for outstanding taste in the selection of fashions for over forty years. In accepting the award he said, "In my opinion good taste is a merchandisable commodity. It has been The Tailored Woman's credo since its founding and we have not suffered from it."

BEHIND THE EUGENE K. DENTON STORY

In Eugene Denton we see an example of that rare breed, the old-style entrepreneur. Unlike many modern-style business proprietors, who limit themselves to (or overemphasize) one or another function of the business—e.g. finance or production—Denton spends time personally checking on all activities of his company. He makes clear his personal involvement, his unwillingness to relinquish control of any aspect of his enterprise to someone who might perform at a level lower than his own. The one-man business has obvious limitations. It cannot grow beyond a given size. It will tend to reflect the thinking of one man.

But in Denton's The Tailored Woman we see the strengths of the enterprise dominated by one man. Since Denton is obviously multi-talented, able to grasp such diverse business functions as finance, merchandising, advertising, selling, display, style, manufacturing technique, real-estate locations, competitive marketing—the limitations of his strong personality are practically nonexistent.

The decisive commodity sold at Denton's The Tailored Woman is good taste. Without this invisible quality the store would have been no better than any other of the fine women's stores on Fifth Avenue. But, because of the pervasive strength of Denton's personality, he was able to give a distinctive style to his store. When ladies shop there, they are not only buying clothes but are paying gladly for Denton's good taste as well.

The determination, the setting of a goal and the energetic follow-up with the actions required to achieve it is another strong element in Denton's career. His method of decision-making is particularly noteworthy. When Eugene Denton decided to undertake something—whether swimming or furs—it was not a spur-of-the-moment decision. His moments of resolve were arrived at slowly and carefully. Once the decision was made, however, he would not accept even the possibility of failure.

This broad pattern is filled out by specific factors like these:

Singleness of Purpose. When Denton decided he wanted to learn to swim, he practiced intensively until he had mastered the skill. Similarly, when he wanted to learn retail merchandising, he studied it day and night. When he decided to go into the retailing of furs, he set out to learn everything necessary to operate successfully. Denton shows the outstanding ability to involve himself completely and thoroughly in the activity required. He was a "direct actionist," never hesitating to plunge in and dirty his hands—he carried stock, took inventory, and so on. This not only helped get the job done, but it also set an example for others to follow—an important technique of leadership.

Most successful people develop this strong sense of self-reliance and ability to get involved. In Denton's case, his self-confidence apparently was built on a strong contact with the reality of things. When he became interested in a matter, he asked questions, demanded answers, proposed his own ideas and believed in his eventual success. Psychologist Bernice M. Gurvich of the Personnel Laboratory, Stanford, Connecticut, says: "Frequently, people with a realistic outlook have had a secure early family life, one in which the individual's qualities and abilities as a person were recognized and encouraged. Along with this also goes an atmosphere where freedom to express one's own needs and tendencies are permitted. In short, the individual is free to be himself as long as he does not violate the general rules of acceptable conduct."

Teacher-Student Symbiosis. Many successful people have had a relationship with a mentor from whom valuable lessons were learned. Denton had this type of fruitful relationship with Joe Morrissey, the silk buyer. Morrissey taught him what he had to know to make one of his early upward steps—the job of buyer when he was still only twenty-two years old. While the opportunity to learn from a brilliant teacher is often fortuitous, there are also instances in which individuals have sought out a mentor, precisely in order to gain special knowledge and experience from an apprenticeship.

Creativity. In Denton's case, brilliant strokes of originality are especially interesting, since he has a strong tendency toward caution and conservatism. But when motivated by the strong need to accomplish a result—such as attracting attention to his store—his mind produced fresh and unorthodox ideas. His use of a live mannequin in the store window, and his awarding a mink coat as a prize are two examples.

Self-Actualization. Psychologists use the term "self-actualization" to express the idea that each individual has a potential for development, and may develop it to a greater or lesser degree. What self-actualization means in ordinary terms, in terms of behavior, is that an individual makes a point of using his gifts and takes advantages of his opportunities.

Eugene Denton's pattern is essentially a combination of *action* and *control.* By his actions, he was able to direct himself and his energies in as many directions as he had talents and opportunities. But his efforts were always modified by his careful appraisal of situations in which he found himself, and his behavior was further modified by his sense of good taste, a quality that germinated in his childhood, but which he cultivated throughout his career.

Mildred Custin –
BONWIT TELLER'S BEST BUY

In 1963, the Man of the Year Award sponsored by the Chestnut Street Businessmen's Association of Philadelphia was given to a woman. The "Man of the Year" was Miss Mildred Custin, president of Bonwit Teller, a twelve-unit chain of women's specialty stores that includes the world-famous Bonwit Teller, New York. Miss Custin's road to the top leads rather unexpectedly through Boston's Girls' Latin School and Simmons College. While some of Miss Custin's teachers might be astonished at her eventual achievement, it is likely they would approve of the fact that she beat out the competition in rough-and-tough industry without abandoning either her aplomb or the social amenities.

*　　*　　*

During her junior year in 1926, her family had financial difficulties, and in order to remain in college, she did typing jobs for fifty cents an hour. She also served as receptionist for the head of the Secretarial School of Simmons. At that time, the school was receiving prospective employers looking for girls who were about to graduate. One such employer was a woman who was writing a sales training course for an insurance company. Miss Custin's manner and maturity impressed her and after interviewing some of the seniors, she offered the job to Miss Custin for thirty-five dollars a week. Since most of the graduates were receiving twenty-five to thirty dollars per week, Miss Custin decided that she didn't need any more college training and took the job. After six months away from college and classes, she realized, perhaps intuitively, that in later years her college degree might be of importance to her. So back to Simmons she went and asked the dean if she might resume her studies. The Dean agreed that if she got all A's she would be permitted to graduate with her class, even though she had missed the first semester. As it turned out, she graduated with her class.

THE OBSTACLE: "MIDDLE-CLASS MEDIOCRITY"

Her first job after graduation was secretary to a Boston patent attorney. It was not a very busy office and after reading *Corpus Juris* from A to M, she decided that being a legal secretary was not her cup of tea. It was just about this time, too, that she made a major decision which was to give direction to her entire life. She was twenty-one years old, living in what she called "middle-class mediocrity." She wanted out. There were two possible exits. Either she had to marry her way out—or work her way out. She elected to work.

Miss Custin heard about Macy's training program and decided to go down to New York. It seemed to be an opportunity to strike out on her own and get away from family ties. At the end of her first interview, the head of Macy's training squad informed her that she was not suited for retailing. Right then and there she determined to stay in New York, get a job at Macy's, and as soon as she became vice-president, fire the head of the training squad. She did get a job at Macy's in the controller's office, but she didn't stay long enough to fulfill the rest of her ambition. On a visit to New York, her mother took one look at the room she was sharing in a student's residence with two would-be actresses, packed her bags and whisked her back to Boston where she resigned from Macy's by mail.

In retrospect, she believes her mother was probably right. She was too young and naïve to be in New York. But her ten month's stint at Macy's, if it had done nothing else, inspired her belief in retailing as a rewarding career. She believed that there was money in retailing—and opportunity, too—even for women, although women at that time held few of the posts of responsibility. But her "feeling" about retailing has become a fact. Today, retailing is truly a woman's business and, as Miss Custin frequently points out, there are more executives per square foot in retailing than any other business known to man.

Maybe it was her clairvoyance about the potential for women in retailing that fired her with ambition to get into it. When a friend offered to give her a letter of introduction to Mr. Chamansky, President of Shepards Department Store in Boston, she accepted the offer. Mr. Chamansky had just hired a new general merchandise manager, Herbert Uline, who would need a secretary, and he offered this job to Mildred Custin. She started to work at Shepards on October 1, 1929.

THE CAN-DO GIRL

Around Christmas time, Mr. Uline thought it would be a good idea to gather gift items from all areas of the store and set up a gift shop. He asked Miss Custin to look around the store for someone to handle this job. A few days later he inquired whether she had come up with anyone and she said, "Yes, I'll do it." "Who will be my secretary?" he asked. Her reply: "I'll do both jobs." By her own admission, she was an eager beaver. She would try anything—do everything—and everyone knew it. She was eager, energetic, and endlessly enthusiastic—traits which have been constant throughout her career.

So successful was the Christmas gift shop that Miss Custin was given the job of gift buyer. Thus she was launched on a retailing career. Mr. Uline had confidence in her ability and despite the fact that she had no previous training or experience in buying or merchandising, she was a buyer at the age of twenty-three. To this day, Miss Custin believes that on-the-job training is the best way to learn. "Retailing," says Miss Custin, "is not a science but a series of practices."

And what did she learn on that first job? The fundamentals of buying, of course. But more importantly, perhaps, she learned that the customer is queen, and you bow to her every wish, or at least most of them. She remembers that if a customer were looking for something that wasn't in her first Christmas gift shop, she would run to get it. "Fortunately," she says, "no one asked for a refrigerator"—or she would have undoubtedly tried to carry it down single-handed. She learned too, to conceal her great drive. She found that people may respect you for it, but they do not necessarily like you for it. And if you want people to work with you and for you, it is important that they like you. She recognized her own sensitivity and realized that she, like most women, tended to react more personally than men to criticism and suggestions. She knew she must develop objectivity and she did so—quickly.

People who work with Mildred Custin do like her. She is not one to apple-polish top brass—nor does she flatter her colleagues and staff. She earns not only respect for her ability and admiration for her accomplishments, but people respond to her sense of humor, her counsel, her fairness and her own dedication to her job. Perhaps people work for her so willingly because she works with them so untiringly. As a gift buyer, it was a morning ritual for her to put on rubber gloves and work with her assistant and stock girls, dusting stock and rearranging displays. Even today, it is not unusual to find her behind the drawn curtains of the Fifth Avenue windows late at night, helping the display department accessorize Bonwit's mannequins for a new set of fashion windows.

Her ability soon commanded the attention of R. H. White Company—a neighboring department store—and she was wooed away from Shepards to become their gift, art needlework and lamp buyer. At R. H. White, Miss Custin really sharpened her merchandising teeth in hard times. Her first full-page advertisement for a sale of lamps appeared in the paper that carried the shattering headline: BANKS CLOSE. The next few years were not easy sailing for any buyer—and certainly not for one whose merchandise could be categorized as nonessential. But through astute buying and promotion campaigns, she survived the economic storm.

THE LADY FROM WANAMAKER'S

In 1935 one of the best gift-buying jobs in the country opened up. She was persuaded to apply for it, and she wrote a letter to the president of John Wanamaker in Philadelphia. She wasn't really too surprised that she received no reply. It was common knowledge that every buyer coming to the New York market was making the trip via Philadelphia to apply for the Wanamaker job. One day, however, a stately lady arrived in her department, announced that she was from John Wanamaker. She said she had come to look over Miss Custin's operation. Mildred was so busy at the moment that she didn't have time to weigh the importance of this call. She told her visitor that a fashion show of hand-knitted dresses was about to begin, and invited her to watch the show, after which she would be delighted to talk with her.

By coincidence, the name of the designer for the yarn company was "Custi*s*," and all during the show, the commentator referred to Miss Custi*s* as the creator of "these exciting designs." Apparently the lady from Wanamaker's thought that Miss Custi*n* was not only an excellent buyer, but a designing genius as well, for she could hardly wait to set up a date for Miss Custin to be interviewed by Mr. Shipley, president of Wanamaker's.

Miss Custin had been told by buyers who worked for Mr. Shipley when he was at Lord & Taylor that he would certainly ask her for facts and figures about her department. She took the sleeper from Boston to Philadelphia and sat up all night memorizing operating statements. After a twenty-minute interview—and no query about operations—she was hired. She—and everyone else—wondered how a complete unknown had walked off with the biggest art needlework and gift-buying job in the country. Months later she found out. After interviewing every buyer available, Mr. Shipley decided to hire the youngest one. As luck would have it, Mildred

Custin was it. Needless to say, Miss Custin believes a great deal in "luck" and also in the good fortune of being in the right place at the right time—or, in this case, at the right age.

SIGNS OF GENIUS

At Wanamaker's, Miss Custin had the opportunity to use her talents and her knowledge, and she began chalking up "firsts" that were to culminate in her becoming the First Lady of retailing in America. An example of merchandising sense at work: Knitting argyles was an extremely popular pastime in those days. Women would spend hours of their time—and a salesperson's too—selecting various color combinations of yarn. Miss Custin got the bright idea of prepackaging yarn in a variety of different color combinations together with the proper knitting needles and instructions for knitting argyle socks. The kits made it easier for the customer to make her selection and relieved salespeople of time-consuming assistance. They also increased unit sales considerably and racked up a pretty profit for her department—as well as the yarn manufacturer.

Ever since, Mildred Custin has been noted throughout the fashion industry for her ability to create and introduce new merchandising ideas, to discern fashion trends and promote them. She was the first to bring French and Italian designer fashions to Philadelphia in Wanamaker's Tribout Shop, for which she was buyer and later merchandise manager.

She was the first woman to be named vice-president of John Wanamaker, in 1951. She was thrilled, of course. Her first reaction, however, was not "Look what *I* did," but "Look what *they* did, *they* made me a vice-president." During the next seven years Mildred Custin helped to raise Wanamaker's fashion reputation from a low point in its history to a new peak. She acquired more and more responsibilities in more areas. She took over the merchandising of intimate apparel and ready-to-wear, children's shoes and millinery and all main-floor accessories—in all fifty-three departments representing about one-third of the most profitable part of Wanamaker's volume.

NEXT STEP: PRESIDENT OF BONWIT'S

In 1958 Mildred Custin assumed the presidency of Bonwit Teller and its two branches. She became the first woman to be named president of a major woman's specialty shop in the Philadelphia area. (At that time the Philadelphia Bonwit Teller stores were owned by Albert M. Greenfield and operated completely independent of the New York stores.)

Mr. Greenfield had approached Miss Custin several years prior to 1958 and asked her to be vice-president and general manager of the store. He indicated that he would prefer to have a man as president because he had reservations about appointing a woman. Miss Custin declined the invitation; she would not direct the store as second in command. By 1958, when Bonwit's volume had declined drastically, Mr. Greenfield overcame his reservations and named Miss Custin president. Much to his delight, not only did Miss Custin's performance justify his confidence in her ability to run the store, but her presence in the top spot proved to have great publicity and public relations value.

Miss Custin arrived on the scene to nurse back to health an ailing business. She found its fashion pulse weak, its physical appearance pale, its prestige count exceedingly low—and it was running a high fever of off-price promotions. She was sure that she could effect a cure even though complete recovery might take a long time. She made drastic changes in merchandising policies, advertising, and display—yet with a minimum of changes in personnel because the staff responded to her leadership. Miss Custin dislikes firing people, and she never does it without fair warning, and always without taking away the person's dignity or self-confidence.

"YOU DON'T HAVE TO BE TOUGH . . ."

She is a patient and understanding, soft-spoken and mild-mannered woman. When a subordinate is antagonistic or uncooperative, rude or ruthless, she always tries to determine what makes him act that way and then attempts to help him face up to his problem. This kind of tolerance was equally applicable to her relationships with superiors up the line. Her own business philosophy (and advice to women) is to demonstrate clearly a determination to complement the activities of men—rather than compete with them—and to show a desire to supplement men, rather than supplant them. She believes that men prefer women to act as women, even though some men still toss a verbal orchid to a woman who, in their opinion, "thinks like a man."

She is completely feminine. She dislikes the hard-driving, hard-boiled businesswoman. She does not believe that a woman has to be tough to be successful—but rather she must be tough-minded with firmness and the courage of her convictions. She is a real lady from the top of her silver-gray hair to the tip of her Bonwit Teller shoes. Four years ago when she was the first woman to be named "Man of the Year" by the Chestnut Street Businessmen's Association of Philadelphia, and was very formally informed by a delegation from the organization, she responded with a familiar line: "Oh, heavens, what shall I wear?"

BEHIND THE MILDRED CUSTIN STORY

Mildred Custin's pattern of success, after a few false starts, confined itself entirely to retailing. Her rise is a particularly interesting one because it dramatizes some of the similarities and differences that characterize the woman's pattern as compared to the man's. One outstanding example of her feminine approach: although highly motivated, she felt she had to conceal her great drive. A man in her same position might not have felt this same need. But for Mildred Custin it was a key to her approach to people. As she herself points out, "If you want people to work for you, it's important that they like you." It proved to be an important aspect of her personal leadership.

As is true of many successful people, she made a major decision early in life—when she was only twenty-one years old. Refusing to live in "middle-class mediocrity," she sought an out. There were two possibilities: to marry well or work her way to the top. She chose to work. This kind of self-confrontation takes place frequently in the lives of successful people, and the significance of the decision —to work to win—cannot be underestimated. It is this resolve that propelled Mildred Custin and many others up the road to achievement.

No Is No Answer. Again and again, Mildred Custin seemed to be marked for failure, but, through a combination of luck and determination, she kept moving ahead. An early example was her rejection by the head of Macy's training program as a trainee in retailing. Instead of crushing her, it strengthened her resolve. She decided to stay in New York and succeeded in getting a job at Macy's. Later, two advantageous breaks came Miss Custin's way. The first occurred when a representative of John Wanamaker's confused her with a Miss Custis, consequently attributing to Miss

Custin the abilities of both an excellent buyer and a designer as
well. The second instance: she was hired over many other con-
tenders by John Wanamaker's simply because she happened to be
the youngest candidate.

Working with People. Business leaders vary greatly in their approach to their colleagues and subordinates. But certainly there is
no question of the effectiveness of Mildred Custin's leadership
methods. By respecting the dignity of individuals, by welcoming
suggestions, by patience and understanding, she apparently is able
to get people to go above and beyond the call of duty. Even in that
most critical of situations, the firing of a subordinate, she apparently is able to function without robbing the individual of dignity or
self-confidence.

The way an executive fires a subordinate is always a giveaway of
character and evaluation of one's fellow man. People have been
fired by ranting bosses who sought to reduce them to a pulp which
could then be kicked summarily out the door. At the other extreme,
people have been fired by superiors so inhibited by their own insecurity and guilt that it was done by a formal note left by the
boss before he goes on vacation. Mildred Custin's approach is a
healthy middle ground, healthy because it is fair and shows no need
to vent a neurotic spleen on an essentially helpless subordinate.

Implicit in every successful businesswoman's behavior is a
method for overcoming what Mildred Custin describes as the male
feet in the aisle that attempt to trip a career-minded woman on the
way up. Mildred Custin's approach was not to play a man's game,
to attempt to win out by direct competition. Her business philosophy in her own words is to *complement* the activities of men rather
than to compete with them, to *supplement* men rather than to supplant them. Here is the perfect example of a woman who "thinks
like a woman" rather than a man and still succeeds in making it
to the top in a man's world.

9 { ENTREPRENEUR VERSUS ORGANIZATION MAN

"Should I start my own business, or take a job with General Motors?" (Or any one of the more than four million corporations that dot the American business landscape.) Clutching his new sheepskin or a recent inheritance, many an ambitious, success-minded young man confronts this basic question. The two alternatives are decidedly different in terms of working climate, opportunities, and demands on the individual. They are *so* different, in fact, that the man who goes into business for himself when he really has the makings of an organization man is almost bound to fail; and the man who might perform brilliantly as an entrepreneur often suffers the throes of a fish out of water as a member of a corporate team.

Business ownership has always occupied a special place in the American dream. Aside from the lure of personal profit unlimited, as measured against company-wide wage levels or a figure that will pass the scrutiny of a board of directors, it strongly appeals to the American emphasis on "independence" and "being one's own boss." The individualistic frontier spirit likes to feel he is the master of his own fate, accounting to no man—save the tax collector. A business of one's own also gives a man a chance to prove himself in a special way. The thought is, "If I run my own show, and have ability, initiative, and a bit of luck, I can prove my worth by means of a favorable balance sheet." And, of course, reap commensurate rewards.

Fortune magazine polled employees of a number of corporations on the question, "Would you like to go into business for yourself?" Approximately 50 per cent answered "Yes." Yet the fact is, there are many more people who don't go into business for themselves than who actually do, despite *Fortune*'s fifty-fifty response. What considerations separate the entrepreneurs from the organization men? Seldom is the choice made by chance. Both situational and personality factors, it seems, nudge an individual into the one road rather than the other.

SITUATIONAL FACTORS THAT FAVOR THE "OWN BUSINESS" CHOICE

In the case of Owen K. Murphy, it was the novelty of an idea that suggested a new business. Here the situation has two facets: first, it's often difficult, even risky to try to interest an established business in a new product or service. The risk lies in the possibility of having the idea "adapted." If it's not protected by patent, the inventor may have no practical recourse from an idea-hungry and unethical management. Second, a new idea, if it's commercially viable, suggests the possibility of a fortune to be made. Then why not make it for one's self?

Another situational factor becomes obvious when viewing the employment field in general. Some individuals may discover at a certain point that they are practically unemployable. They are forced to go into business for themselves because no one will hire them. Typical is a marketing manager who functioned as a capable executive until he had a severe nervous breakdown. After a year's stay in a mental hospital, he was pronounced cured and set out to resume his profession. Then began a series of grim disappointments. Whenever his interlude at the mental institution became known by a potential employer, the prospect of landing a job vanished. Finally he decided to try to cover up the detrimental episode. He was told by an employer that he was hired—pending a check of references and a pre-employment investigation. Subsequently his secret was discovered by the employer's investigating agency and he was turned down. "I had no recourse," said the executive bitterly. "It was either go into business for myself or starve."

Similarly, men may be considered unhirable because of health reasons, criminal record, unsatisfactory past performance for other employers—they may find that the only solution is to go into a business of their own, or to buy part ownership of an existing company.

Occasionally an executive who has acquired experience in a large company in some specialized area—it may be engineering, production, finance, research and development—may leave to start his own consulting business.

From time to time, one hears of a successful enterprise that grew from a hobby. In one case, a woman started designing clothes for friends. She had a flair for design, and enjoyed the activity as an escape from housewifely duties. Demand for her clothes soon outgrew her circle of immediate friends, and she eventually started her own custom dress shop. Similar interests and development of capabilities have led to the founding of antique shops, bakeshops, food-specialty plants. And, of course, on the masculine side, superior mechanical or manual skills have been the basis of starting up service stations, machine shops, and contracting firms.

One final reason should not be overlooked; the need for more money, or the desire to augment an unsatisfactory income. Feeling this prod, the individual looks for a business that can be operated in his spare time, with little capital investment. The mail-order business is one that has lured many would-be entrepreneurs. Home landscaping, where the man with a power lawnmower and a few hand tools can satisfy his enterprising spirit and at the same time be paid for easing the strain on the homeowner's back, is another. Ingenuity and imagination from time to time add other low-investment enterprises to the list.

SITUATIONAL FACTORS THAT FAVOR THE ORGANIZATION MAN

It was suggested earlier that for some people, the choice between self-employment and taking a job is a career crossroad which is consciously confronted at one time or another. This is true. But many individuals make the choice without a second thought. They are so preconditioned—usually by family or social contacts—that only one alternative is even considered. For instance, family or community tradition often make the employee road a foregone conclusion. "My family has always had its sons go to work for local industry," explains a Newark resident who reached the vice-presidential level in a plastics plant.

Interest in a specific type of endeavor is another motivation that may steer a man into company employment. If he has an interest in automobiles, it's natural to try to land a job with Ford, American Motors, and so on. The man who is fascinated by computers and their future potential will head for IBM, Remington Rand, or any of the dozens of computer organizations that have sprung up in recent years.

Jim Connaughton, now the president of the Wheelabrator Corporation (not a company that he founded, but one that hired him as president) is a good example of a highly successful businessman whose technical and managerial abilities are most valuable within the framework of a complex, already existing company. Connaughton is a production man who can examine the inner workings of almost any heavy production industry and then reorganize the setup to make it more efficient and more profitable than it was before. Working for a series of different companies as a "trouble shooter," Connaughton made a name for himself as a man with a great knowledge of technical production methods, engineering, financial structure and management techniques. Eventually he was asked by Wheelabrator to become their chief executive. Upon accepting the position, Connaughton was given over a year to familiarize himself with every aspect of the company's activities before he was formally designated president. Because of his knowledge of the fundamentals and his great ability to adapt to new organizations, he was able to assume full control in only four months. Talents like Jim Connaughton's seem tailor-made for the corporate structure.

A negative factor has forced the choice, however, for some organization men. "My brother opened a small lumberyard and building supply shop in a Chicago suburb," says a top executive of a food products company. "I saw his struggles to make it pay, and believe me, it was painful. After three years, he had to fold. Working for somebody else looked like heaven, compared to that."

PERSONAL DIFFERENCES BETWEEN BUSINESS OWNER AND COMPANY EXECUTIVE

The most obvious trait of the man who starts his own business is usually his desire to "be the boss," or "be his *own* boss," as the feeling is often expressed. But there's more to it than that. Psychological studies tend to show marked differences between the man who rises to the top through a company hierarchy, and one who makes it on his own. One such study, by Orvis F. Collins and David G. Moore, entitled *The Enterprising Man,* focused on a sample of over a hundred small manufacturers in the Michigan area. The "typical" small-business owner emerged from the study as follows:

"He's less likely to be native born." In the matter of national background, the authors found that 20 per cent of the group was foreign-born, 35 per cent more were U.S.-born with foreign-born fathers. These figures are particularly interesting when compared to the average business leader—that is, big-company executive. Of the latter group, only 5 per cent were foreign-born and 20 per cent were U.S.-born of foreign-born fathers.

"He's no Joe College." Only about 20 per cent of the small-businessmen were college graduates. A separate study of big-business executives showed a 57 per cent figure. Thirty-six per cent of the small-businessmen had not graduated from high school, as compared to 13 per cent of big-business leaders.

"He tends to be a rebel." The study indicates that interpersonal ties, such as those with an older man who is a teacher or mentor, tend to be short-lived. Say the authors, "The entrepreneur learns that he can live neither within the restrictions of large organizations nor within the restrictions of protégé-sponsor relations. Instead, he rebels."

"He's self-made—and it hasn't been an easy job." The old

Horatio Alger idea that anyone can succeed in business simply by trying is badly damaged in the Michigan study: "For most entrepreneurs, success in business was preceded by a long period of training and trial, often marked by periods of broken dreams and bankruptcy. It is in this crucible of experience that the entrepreneur develops his skills and learns his trade."

"He's a driven man." It's in the area of motivation that the study is particularly revealing. Our small-business entrepreneur is the antithesis of the organization man. He doesn't stay in an established company because he can't stand the atmosphere. The authors conclude: "The small businessmen are often driven men who have deliberately placed themselves in 'open' positions because they would rather face the impersonal forces of the economy than cope with interpersonal relations that they find in the established organization."

"He's creative." The authors conclude that the enterprising men they studied have made a definite contribution to society: "They found an outlet for their creativity by making out of an undifferentiated mass of circumstance a creation uniquely their own: a business firm."

In drawing conclusions from the Collins-Moore study, two limitations must be remembered: the businessmen studied were all from the Michigan area. A study from a different geographical area might very well turn out differently. Also, in getting the group together, no distinction was made as to the capability or degree of success being achieved.

WHAT PRICE DIPLOMA?

The Enterprising Man makes interesting generalizations about the educational backgrounds of the entrepreneur as compared to the company executive. The entrepreneur is best off when his education or training enables him to operate as a kind of one-man army in an open field. The theoretical outlook and rigidities that sometimes result from education, or overeducation, would hamper the entrepreneur in his flexibility and ability to buck the established order of things that is often his trademark. That's why a man who's to go it alone is best educated by being thrust upon his own at an early age. He learns to survive by his wits. He learns about life by living it. He learns about people by dealing with them, often in pressure situations. His ability to deal with people on a realistic basis is strengthened, because he builds a structure of relationships outside established organizations. There are no rules, and perhaps no genteel traditions that guide or limit what can be done.

By contrast, the company executives in the higher corporate echelons generally have sophisticated technical training—in engineering, finance, or a combination of disciplines. A study by Dr. Mabel Newcomer and *Scientific American* found that 38 per cent of a group of one thousand top executives either had degrees in engineering and the natural sciences or the equivalent in on-the-job experience. The study shows, further, that the proportion of top executives with degrees in science or engineering jumped from 7 per cent in 1900 to 20 per cent in 1950. The 38 per cent figure, a 1964 finding, confirms the long-range trend.

SHAPE OF THE UNIVERSE

The "models" of the world in which the businessman and the executive operate are quite different. Although each is dominant in his particular sphere, the "hill" of which each is "king" has different aspects. The enterprising man, by and large, builds his own world. He sees it not as a hierarchy, a pyramid with himself at the top, but rather as a kind of open market place, an activity of exchange and transaction, one that he put together by trading and making deals. Surprisingly, he doesn't see himself as a leader of men, but rather as a key figure in a network composed of buyers, sellers, arrangers, promoters, people to call on for help, people whose skills and capabilities are to be used to further his objectives. In comparison, the executive who makes it to the top of a corporate pyramid sees the world of business as an entirely different kind of place. First, he has achieved his success by rising through an established social and authority structure. He has had subordinates and superiors. To some extent, the successful paid manager has learned how to exploit both—not necessarily in a selfish or destructive way, but for the "good of the team"—for the sake of efficiency and company profit.

The self-employed entrepreneur sitting on top of the self-made mountain enjoys a very different kind of status from the pyramid climber. Being an owner endows him with a sense of feudal nobility. Elevator men, waiters, secretaries, subordinates react to him with a certain deference unconsciously engendered by the man's own bearing and attitude. He can actually behave as he pleases, for he's untrammeled by any big-company public relations policy that requires its top executives to act with democratic and even humble mien. On the other hand, the top executive in a corporation well knows he is not a free spirit. Even the president has a boss. It may be a board of directors or a group of stockholders. And this means, he dare not exercise power willfully, nor behave like "the king." The corporate image always comes first.

THE RISKS AND REWARDS

The entrepreneur and the company executives also operate with different feelings toward the vehicle of their success. To the executive, "the company" is an organization of which he is an important member, and toward which he feels loyalty and dedication. The entrepreneur's identification with "*his* company" is much closer, and stronger. The degree of ego-involvement can be tremendous. Certainly, it's often enough to keep him working long hours, seven days a week, to keep the business alive and growing.

The hazards of the entrepreneur are usually more threatening. The number of failures of corporations, given as 13,514 in 1965 by Dun and Bradstreet, remind the entrepreneur all too vividly, of the fate that awaits a single major slip or error in judgment. A verbatim statement by an entrepreneur—in this case, the proprietor of a small retail shop—gives a view, perhaps exaggerated, but at any rate colorful, of the basic outlook of the entrepreneur versus the company executive:

> Big-shot executives hand me a laugh. They're like big-game hunters operating in a zoo. Where's the risk? Look what I'm up against. It rains, or the temperature drops too far, and wham, my cash register is paralyzed, and Mama cooks old shoes. I gotta buy and sell and be my own mule. A big-business guy, he's got everything going for him. He's got secretaries and think machines and experts to hold his hand when he gets scared or lonely. When my business goes bad, I gotta worry about bread on the table. He only has to worry about how to make it look good to the stockholders or to the bank.

In the final analysis, the business owner is playing for big stakes. If he loses, he may be set back to the starting line—no cash, no prospects, no business. The fate of the company executive, in case of failure, is far less devastating. He may simply get "kicked upstairs." True, he is taken out of a position of authority, but he's often given a well-paying sinecure. And if his fall from grace is sufficiently serious to warrant firing—well, there's always the chance of a job in another company, possibly a competitor's, where he may well be welcomed with open arms, because of his experience in the enemy camp.

BOOK II

The "little business" started in a basement or garage is proverbial. Thomas D. Coe's story follows that tradition, but with a couple of original twists. For one thing, Coe's Wakefield Engineering Company of Wakefield, Massachusetts, was at the beginning a business without a product. It was a company created by an individual who wanted to go into business for himself—even though he wasn't sure just what the business would do, once it was created. Thomas D. Coe took the gamble. It paid off handsomely.

*   *   *

Tom Coe's first view of this world was of a dairy farm run by his mother's father, Nels Jorgenson. Nels came to the U.S.A. from Denmark at the turn of the century and located in Jamestown, New York. He established a plumbing and heating shop, and shortly thereafter, purchased a farm in nearby Stillwater, which became the largest dairy farm in southwestern New York. Later, when he saw that the automobile was here to stay, he established a Willys-Knight agency. He had three active businesses going at one time.

When Isabelle Jorgenson, Nels's daughter, and David Coe were married in the mid-twenties, they set up housekeeping in a home built on a plot next to the main farmhouse. It was a compact bungalow that Nels had copied from houses he saw on a trip to southern California. Even though there were only five rooms, it had most of the conveniences found in most homes today. The surroundings remained rural all during their son Tom's youth.

ENTER THE BOY MECHANIC

During the long, severe winters in the "snow belt," Tom sought something to absorb his time. It was his father who provided this impetus, with an investment in some tools and a small bench lathe. When Tom got into the Jamestown school system, he was influenced even further toward things mechanical. Jamestown, in the forties, was a major center for the furniture and woodworking business. It also is the home of many well-known metalworking industries such as Crescent Tool Company, Art Metal Construction Company, and Marlin-Rockwell Corporation. Of course, there were many tool and die shops and other metalworking facilities serving these large companies. Courses in sheet metalworking and woodworking were required in junior high school for all boys. Later, they were encouraged to do further shopwork in high school. Spotted by a Mr. Janowsky, one of the shop teachers, Tom was counseled to take as much shopwork as he could carry. In the Jamestown school system, the better students were given the opportunity to take electives beyond the required courses. Accordingly, Tom continued his shop studies.

Being an auto dealer, his father always drove a new company car, but like everyone else during the depression years, he had to work hard for everything he got. There was no excess in those days. His father would come home for supper and then go back to the garage to work until he closed it at 9 P.M. Tom thought that hard work and long hours was the normal routine for grown-ups. But these were not begrudged hours; his father and grandfather obviously enjoyed being in business for themselves.

A CONSTRUCTIVE DELAY, THEN COLLEGE

As it happened, Tom went overboard on his shop courses and then found he was lacking some college entrance requisites. This turned out to be a blessing in disguise. Shortly before graduation time he decided he wanted to get the best mechanical engineering degree available, possibly at Massachusetts Institute of Technology. Since he didn't meet entrance requirements, his father recommended a year at Choate School, Wallingford, Connecticut. At this well-known prep school, Tom picked up those courses he needed and got a running start on the demanding years of study to come at M.I.T.

When Tom entered M.I.T. he was well prepared in many ways for the rigors of the school. He did not feel lonesome, like so many boys, when he had to spend long hours over his books without much entertainment. Tom was used to being alone—in the woods, on a lake, setting his trap lines, in the basement over his lathe and tools and working late at the high-school shop. The independence that he had seen in his mother, father and grandfather as well as his own intellectual capability and preparation, fostered an unusual degree of self-reliance in Tom. He never failed a subject in four years and he received his mechanical engineering degree with an A— average.

M.I.T.'s Lincoln Laboratory in Lexington, Massachusetts, was the focal point in the Boston area for the best that was new in electronics. The school promoted this aggressively both within and without, propagated to a large extent by the missile industry and later by the need for large-scale radar warning systems for the cold war. Like many others, Tom Coe read the signals. To the usual mechanical engineering courses he added electrical and electronic studies. Accordingly, he became one of the first of a new kind of engineer, the electromechanical engineer. Today, an engineer of this kind is considered the sophisticate on the new frontier of engineering. He has the capability of combining mechanical systems with electronic actuations and controls.

After World War II ended, there was a big question mark hanging over the head of every eligible young man—military service. This confronted Tom Coe as well, and he decided to enlist in the Air Force. Because of his qualifications, he was commissioned and sent to Air Force Cambridge Research Center, next door to Lincoln

Laboratory, to work on radar and the early warning systems. Here he found three major influences of his life: Jane Shriver, who later became his wife; Joseph Bianco, who became his partner in the business; and a modern laboratory, which gave him the best and most modern electronic education possible. He also made business contacts that helped keep bread on the table during the lean days to come.

During 1955 and 1956, Tom and Jane became good friends, then married in 1957. Jane was a physicist at Lincoln Lab and was able to comprehend Tom's love of engineering. During this same period, because of his energy and aptitude for the work, Joe Bianco befriended him. Joe was the civilian engineering group leader on the Air Force project to which Tom was assigned. They were both outstanding producers, a fact that made them unpopular with some co-workers. This external force pushed the two men closer together.

"LET'S START A BUSINESS . . ."

One night shortly before Tom's release from service, Joe approached Tom and Jane with the idea of starting their own business. The three reached rapid agreement as to the desirability of the idea, but then reality had to be faced. What kind of business would this be? Something electronic or mechanical? Where would a product be obtained? What would be used for manufacturing and where? Where would the money come from? Tom and Jane had saved up about four thousand dollars, which might pay for some used equipment. Could they buy an existing business? And on and on this went, over many weeks. Finally, some answers started to come.

Since they did not have enough money to buy a company or a product line, they would have to start from scratch. Joe determined to look for a better job. He soon found a fine position at a substantial income, far beyond what he could expect to earn out of their own firm for years to come. Then Jane came up with the solution. After they got married, she would continue to work and contribute her income so she and Tom could set up housekeeping. Although this meant sacrifice, they were interested, excited, and ambitious. The second part was that Joe's new position paid more than he needed to survive. So he would take the excess and put it into the business at a rate commensurate with the time that Tom put in. It looked as if they all could exist and progress.

Joe had a conviction that affected the business in many ways. He believed that when one man got a new idea, it was apt to come to competitors about the same time. Therefore, the individual or company first to act on the idea would be ahead and could succeed with the product. Both Tom and Joe concurred that the more enmeshed they were in some good activity, the greater would be the opportunity to be exposed to possible ideas. Additionally, by having a going small firm, they would be more flexible and could move faster than large outfits that got the idea the same time they did. The location of the new business would be determined partly by the availability of low-cost floor space that had heat. It also had to be close to Joe's home so he could consult and do some engineering at night. And they wanted to remain in the Boston area because they knew sometime they would need engineering assistance. However, being realists, they also knew it would be years before they could hire needed engineering talent. But this talent would be available to them on a part-time basis from their friends.

They finally found the space in a small frame structure on the property of a large manufacturer. It had an added advantage—a concrete floor that could support heavy machine tools. The upper floor was already occupied by a man with a small stamping facility. They had two machine tools, the bench lathe David Coe had bought for Tom in the forties and another lathe Joe Bianco had purchased on the surplus market some years earlier.

NOTHING TO SELL? SELL SERVICE

They were going to need an immediate income and any product line would take years to develop. They certainly couldn't afford to buy an existing product. What other avenue was available? How about a machine shop? Job work was available and Joe had one or two other contacts where work was being farmed out. So this became the avenue of first intent. They next went to used machinery dealers and selected the best they could afford. This meant a Bridgeport miller, another two heavy lathes, a hand turret lathe, a cutoff saw, and some drill presses. They both pitched in to clean out the building, make a small office, wire in the equipment and lighting, plus doing some painting. They then went out to get orders so they'd have work for two machinists they wanted to hire. They got the jobs and the machinists. Early in 1957 they finally got under way: Tom at the shop day and night, Jane at her job plus assisting with assembly or paper work at night, and Joe at his new position with his contribution of time nights and weekends, plus his cash comparable to Tom's input of time. Since they did not know what their product line would eventually be and since the shop was in Wakefield, Massachusetts, the company name became Wakefield Engineering, Inc.

They decided to only add good men as they could afford it, and then let these men do the jobs as they knew they had to be done. Minimum supervision and limitation were put into the framework of this little firm. When a man was hired, he was expected to do his job, apply himself, and get it done.

During the period from the beginning until late in 1959, Wakefield was a hand-to-mouth operation. Tom and Joe worked over all their contacts and tried hiring sales representatives to bring in job work. Tom made sales calls too, reluctantly. His strong suit was design engineering, tooling, and manufacturing. Time waiting in purchasing reception rooms could be spent on a drawing board, at a lathe searching for a new tooling concept or looking for a good buy on another machine tool. At one point, when the business for the machine shop ran dry, they made proposals and obtained work in the microwave and radio telescope power supply areas. Jane, Joe, and Tom all pitched in here, and they brought other engineering friends in to moonlight for them. Still the things weren't moving fast enough and their shop capabilities were limited.

What could be done next to move along faster? Develop a product? Nothing was in sight. How about an acquisition or a combine? Where? Why, right upstairs was Irving Burwen Company, a stamping and tooling job shop with whom they'd exchanged assistance from time to time. As it turned out, Irving Burwen had been in the business for some time, had a good firm and was interested in tying up with the young fellows downstairs. They decided to absorb Irving's firm into Wakefield Engineering, Inc., and double the depth of management as well as the number and types of machine tools. By mid-1959, the company could tackle just about any type of machining or stamping job, as well as tooling and electronic equipment design.

About that same time, the Air Force asked Wakefield to design and build a fancy power supply for a radio telescope and some scatter transmission test apparatus. With the help of "moonlight" engineering assistance, they designed and built the equipment satisfactorily. The power supply was a problem, but their outside consultant licked this and, more importantly, came up with a product possibility in so doing. Available semiconductors could not provide the power required without cooling and there wasn't a heat dissipator on the market that could do the cooling job. The semiconductor manufacturers were faced with the same problem and were designing their own dissipators for specific requirements.

Could this heat dissipator—or heat sink—be a potential product? Tom asked a friend in the marketing business. Together they made a market survey among semiconductor manufacturers and local firms that used rectifiers and diodes with heat-dissipating problems. Most of these firms were designing and making their own to the specific requirements because the few possible suppliers had very limited lines. It was decided that this was worth further investigation.

POWER OF THE PRESS

Again the lack of money came to the forefront. Every cent was being poured back into new equipment and personnel. Tom still wasn't taking anything out. So, it was decided that a publicity release would be made to the electronic trade press on Tom's design for a forced convection heat sink as a product line. Tom was warned that this would be dangerous because the interest potential was there. He would have to have something ready in printed form to answer inquiries from readers of these publications. So, again with limited funds, Tom set up a crude test stand to get data and he enticed Jane in to record data for months.

No one was ready for the way the publications picked up the release. Almost every magazine editor to whom it was sent used the item. No one could have predicted the interest. The first publication in which it appeared was the January, 1960, issue of *Electrical Equipment*. On January 3, the telephone started to ring, telegrams were delivered and letters began arriving later that week. The next week saw a flood of inquiries, as the publicity broke in other publications. Clearly, they had struck a rich, interested market. Instead of putting out a simple bulletin on the limited line, it was decided to hold up on answering the inquiries for three weeks while additional models were designed, tested, and recorded. The scramble to build other-sized prototypes and test them was on.

In the meantime, letters and calls were coming in following up the original inquiries that could not be answered properly. It was decided that Tom would get on a plane and call on those who yelled loudest. By the end of January, there were over four thousand inquiries of all types, some companies getting impatient at the lack of response. In early February, a simple, inexpensive four-page brochure was sent to all inquirers.

Between the inquiries and the calls Tom was making, it was obvious that some kind of market existed. The job shop was rolling pretty well. The production of those first heat sinks would not interfere with shopwork. It was mainly a simple "cutoff" operation with milling of slots in the copper base. Then stamped fins were set in the slots, strands of solder were laid between the fins after fluxing and the assembly finished up by placing it on a hotplate.

The product looked good, but time was a big factor. It was known that the average length of time that it took to sell an electronic component in quantity was about two years after a prototype was produced. In other words, at least eighteen months must pass before getting production orders on sample prototypes. For example, the first call Tom made was on Westinghouse Electric Corp., in Youngwood, Pennsylvania. It was nearly one year and six months to the day from their purchase of a prototype that Westinghouse made a major purchase.

A MAJOR DECISION—"WE'LL GO PUBLIC"

By the time that Wakefield's first line of heat sinks was in production, the need for other types, mainly natural convection standardized units, became clear. This meant more money and more time. But mostly money was needed for test apparatus, and more production equipment to put out new types of heat sinks that their equipment at hand could not produce. They also needed a sales manager, without any sales likely to come in for possibly over a year. The type of man they needed would run well into a five-figure salary. Now, Wakefield's management quartet was convinced that the product was right and the market was there. The decision was made to go public. An editor from the *Boston Globe* was invited to hear of the unusual response to the publicity. He wrote up an interesting report, and after it appeared in the local press, the stock was all absorbed. Now there was cash for development work on new lines and as means to survive the many months before substantial purchase orders would start to arrive.

Tom and his group decided that the offices of their job shop in the old building and their new heat sink engineering, test, and sales offices should be separated. Office space was rented on the second floor over some retail stores in the center of town. This was within walking distance of the house Tom and Jane had moved into after their marriage. The proximity of the home to the office was important because they all were putting in long hours. Early in 1961, this became even more important when a son was born to the Coes.

Young David did not see much of his mother his first six months. Jane was needed in the laboratory and she worked there for six months taking the needed data for design and quality control. A full-time nursemaid took David over for a while.

Early in their efforts to start selling the Series 500 heat sinks, Tom decided that if this product line was good, they ought to take a close look at pricing. It was decided that since they had a jump on the market, they would discourage competition by keeping their prices as low as possible. This policy worked, and explains the strong position the company has in the market place.

To be able to concentrate on design and to improve production procedures, Tom hired a sales manager. The purpose was to obtain sales representatives; then to build up an electronic distributor network. Both of these were difficult tasks because the sales representatives and distributor work entirely on a percentage of sales. There wasn't much to sell and there would not be much for a couple of years. However, with diligent effort, Wakefield obtained the services of some representatives. As the product lines grew and were standardized, the company had something to discuss with potential distributors.

By the end of 1961, a small but steady amount of heat sink business was coming in. Most of this business was on special jobs. This indicated that they really would need two marketing projects: first would be their line of standard heat sinks and the second would be adapting their standards to large, engineered forced convection packages that could be sold direct through the representatives. Also, since many new lines were utilizing aluminum extrusions, they could sell lengths of raw extrusions to firms wanting to build prototypes to their own requirements. Wakefield offered engineering assistance as well.

Then, late in 1963, Tom had to take over as sales manager, but under protest, because he believed that his biggest contribution could be made in engineering. As new product lines came out, he issued a brochure describing the units and providing technical data and had small advertising-publicity budget appropriated. Most effort was on continued publicity, both on new products and new literature. A couple of trade shows also were attended. The various types of promotion, literature, and the building of the sales representative and distributor organizations proved effective. Wakefield management realized that a sale is the result of accumulated effort, so they poured it on from as many directions as possible. The result: a surge in sales from 1963 through 1965.

Tom Coe is continuing his effort to keep abreast of new product design in the heat sink field. Also, his influence continues to be felt in machine tool procurement and tooling. The basic philosophy of hiring good men and giving them leeway to do their jobs has not changed and Wakefield's work force has nearly doubled from 1964 to 1965. The investment that Tom Coe made in time and hard work—for which there are no substitutes—is paying a dividend in company growth. He also continues to warrant the support of an interested wife and many friends. At one time, they were in so deep they could only go ahead for survival. Now, long-range planning is going into every contemplated step. Tom Coe is still working hard because he enjoys it.

BEHIND THE THOMAS D. COE STORY

"Formative years" is a persuasive phrase. It suggests that an individual's interest in activities in the early years will be logically followed by interest in activities in maturity. Clearly, this isn't necessarily so. The element of a sound motivation has converted many a dull David into an eager beaver. And many a lively and curious youngster beaten down by failures and repressive circumstances has ended up a repressed and unadventurous adult. Tom Coe's childhood is an interesting example of truly formative years. His somewhat lonely rural life somehow led naturally into the individualistic life and interest of the engineer. The behavior patterns of the youth on his own in a rural countryside form a pattern that is similar to the requirements of a creative engineer: independence of thought, willingness to act, a firm sense of the realities of things.

Tom Coe's biography reveals these further key elements:

Master of His Fate. In William Ernest Henley's celebrated *Invictus,* we are reminded that the individual, despite the strains and failures of everyday life, may still have the fortitude and the sense of command to be the "master of his fate" and "the captain of his soul." As pointed out in other biographies—for example, those of Owen K. Murphy and Mildred Custin—the successful individual is willing to take on an awesome responsibility: he is willing to seize the reins of his destiny and attempt to guide it to some self-designated end. Tom Coe showed this tendency when he enlisted in the U. S. Air Force, and of course, still more so when he decided to go into business for himself.

A Learning Milieu. Many people are aware in their own lives of an experience that has had a great influence on their development. For some it may be a college or university. In other instances, it may be a first job which provides a strong platform on which to build a subsequent career. For Tom Coe, the learning milieu that created such a strong and advantageous learning situation was the modern laboratory he found at the Air Force Cambridge Research Center. The interesting fact is that for some foresighted individuals, a conscious effort is made to seek out such a meaningful experience. This is the case, for example, when a man says, "I will take that assignment in marketing, although I know production is my field. That way I will round out my experience. . . ."

Allies. "Behind every successful man," goes the old saying, "stands a woman." For Tom Coe, this woman was not merely a helpmate in the ordinary sense, but also an aider and abettor of his business career. And in Joseph Bianco, Tom Coe found that other frequent ingredient of the success formula, a partner capable of sharing the burdens of entrepreneurship and supplying some of the experience and capabilities required to make a business go.

The importance of enthusiasm in an individual's success has been related time and time again from Charles Schwab to Dale Carnegie. The country's outstandingly successful people have emphasized the need to be enthusiastic. But the problem is obvious: How does one generate enthusiasm? It is clearly related to personality, and some individuals have considerable difficulty in generating an enthusiastic attitude. Tom Coe's biography provides one helpful answer. The triumvirate of Tom Coe, Jane Shriver and Joseph Bianco succeeded in reinforcing each other's enthusiasm in their projected enterprise. Once again we see the effectiveness of a partnership. Each member benefited from the interest and support of the others. Where an individual on his own might be hamstrung by problems and difficulties, the involvement of two or three people make it possible to keep enthusiasm high and to achieve great success.

11 { Amelia Lobsenz –
FROM WRITER'S STUDY TO
EXECUTIVE SUITE

How does a woman fare in a man's world? The Amelia Lobsenz story provides specific insights as to how a woman can proceed to score in a tough, competitive, generally masculine field. The Lobsenz biography also is an interesting example of an important transition in the world of enterprise, that of an individual trained in a professional field—in this case, writing—who makes the transformation to successful businesswoman.

*   *   *

"As I see it," said the smartly dressed lady wearing the John Fredericks hat, "the problem is not to publicize the foundation itself, but to make people more aware of the national importance of the service that the program is providing. Now here are a few things I would like to suggest. To begin with . . ."

The man sitting opposite the speaker was president of the foundation to which she referred, but the lady might as easily have been talking to a ranking officer of a large insurance company, a major pharmaceutical firm, one of several service businesses, or a nationwide professional organization. These all have one thing in common: a need for the counsel and services of the Lobsenz Public Relations Company, of which the lady is president and owner. Amelia Freitag Lobsenz has traveled a long road in a short time. She started her own public relations business in three rooms of her New York apartment in 1956. When she decided to leave the well-established public relations firm for which she had been working and go into business for herself, she had only three accounts: a pharmaceutical company and two "personalities." She had one part-time editorial-PR aide, who is still with the company, a secretary and a maid who doubled as a messenger.

Each of those first three accounts brought in between eight hundred and nine hundred dollars a month, which is peanuts in a business where monthly telephone and postage bills alone can easily eat up one thousand to two thousand dollars. Miss Lobsenz bridged the initial gap between company income and company expenses by plying her original trade—writing magazine articles—at night, acting as consultant to the firm where she was formerly employed, and working hard to get new clients. Determined, as she had been all her life, to make it on her own, she never borrowed money from anyone— friends, relatives or banks—to help float the new venture.

Of the hundreds of articles she has written, she is perhaps most proud of two she wrote during this period of getting her own business under way. One, titled "My Teacher Is Three Feet High" and printed in *This Week* in 1956, was based on her experiences in raising the Lobsenz oldest child, Michael, and offered an eye-opening lesson in how and what parents can learn from their children. The second, printed in *Parents' Magazine,* posed the question "Should Women with Heart Disease Have Children?" Reprints of this article were used widely by doctors.

With the sustaining help of financial water wings like these, in four months the new public relations business was brisk enough to merit moving its headquarters out of the apartment. The Lobsenz Public Relations Company rented its first modest office space in the Squibb Building, on Fifth Avenue just above 57th Street. There have been three moves within the same building since, each time to offices offering three or four times as much space. There are now twenty-five people employed in the Lobsenz "shop." These moves are an indication of how Miss Lobsenz's business has grown in the few years since she set out on her own. Another indication of growth lies in the changed character and size of the accounts she brought into the fold or, in some cases, that landed on her doorstep. Today the company has ten major corporate and philanthropic accounts, representing a cross section of the American economy and American society. They include the Travelers Insurance Companies, largest multiple-line insurance company in the world; the Schering Corporation, leading pharmaceutical company and maker of Coricidin; Kelly Girl Service, Inc., one of the world's largest employers of women "office temporaries"; The Rockefeller Public Service Awards (administered by Princeton University); and others of equal distinction.

A "YL" HAM

Amelia grew up in Atlanta, Georgia, where a number of her friends were radio hams, which led eventually to her own activity as one of the relatively few "YL" (for young lady) radio operators in the country. She passed her FCC test and received her license in 1941. As a practicing "ham" Amelia developed a speaking acquaintance with dozens of other hams throughout the country, and later got to know many of them personally in the course of research and magazine and book-writing trips that took her to practically every state in the Union and to many foreign countries.

Amelia Lobsenz's experience with radio and as a writer came together fortuitously during World War II, when she did public relations writing for an electronics firm and also taught Morse code to civil defense groups. As with most learning experiences she's had, the ham radio experience was grist for her mill as a professional writer. Amelia wrote extensively on the amateur-radio-operator subject for national magazines, and put her technical and practical knowledge of the field to effective use in each of two books she wrote for teen-agers. Both sold well. One, *Kay Everett Calls CQ,* was a junior Literary Guild selection in 1951.

THE "SPONGE" TECHNIQUE

She calls her ability to absorb information on any subject and then use it in some specific project, "the sponge technique." She began to practice this technique unconsciously when she was a young girl listening to the grown-ups talk at dinner or a party in her parents' house in Atlanta. She asked a guest questions that often seemed strange coming from a young "Southern lady": How did his business run? Did he have employee problems? What about his customers' preferences? Why was his product any better than anyone else's?

"I remember one guest of my father's who ran an unusual send-out food business in Chicago," Miss Lobsenz said. "After spending what my parents considered too much time quizzing him, I spent half the night thinking up story lines that could be developed about his business—unusual angles that might interest readers. By that time—I was still in high school—I already considered myself a writer. And I had no doubt at all that I would be a *professional* writer."

For someone living in the polite Southern society into which Amelia was born, life in Atlanta during her formative years could have been an unending social whirl, despite the depression and its lean aftermath. For many girls of her age, as in past generations in the South, life was *only* a gay whirl, fenced in on all sides by the proper schools, the proper training to produce a proper young lady, the proper tennis court and ballroom, and—as the proper goal—the proper marriage. Yet someone with creative energy and individualism could vary the theme. Amelia did grow up with and travel with her "set." But from an early age she thought there must be something more to life than just going to dancing school and preparing to be a "Southern lady," as her female ancestors had been. She did not object to being a Southern lady, she says now, but she wanted to be that *plus* something more—a lot more. In that ambition she had the early encouragement of many who recognized her writing and other abilities.

THE TWO R'S COME EARLY

When Amelia was only two she was dressed in one of her prettiest frocks one spring afternoon and taken by her mother to see an exhibit of drawings at the local public library. Amelia doesn't remember anything about the exhibit today, but she does recall that this was the first of what turned out to be a continuous round of exposures to "cultural" events and institutions, in the company of her mother. Possibly the most important of these exposures was to books. Her mother taught her to read long before she started school. Young Amelia became an avid reader of everything she could lay her hands on. Almost as soon as she learned to read she began to write.

Her mother listened to an excited daughter one morning as the child, green eyes shining, read a poem from the pad she held. "It's good," her mother finally pronounced. "Let's try to have it published." And so Amelia broke into print. A national magazine paid her five dollars for her first poem. Thus it was that at the age of five, with the encouragement and guidance of an understanding mother, Amelia was launched on a professional writing career.

Encouragement in her literary ambitions came from outside her family too. Many of her teachers in the Atlanta public elementary and high schools spurred her on. One of them was also responsible for introducing her to the business side of publications. Amelia was an editor of her high-school newspaper and interested only in writing when the English teacher in charge of the paper asked her to take over the usually thankless job of business manager. She insisted that Amelia had the ability to "sell." The idea terrified the aesthetically-minded girl, but the survival of the school paper was apparently at stake: the publication had to be self-supporting, and it was getting "in the red." Amelia agreed to become its business manager. For the next two years she bicycled around the neighborhood after school, selling enough ads to local businessmen to keep the paper afloat. And she learned that her teacher had been right: she had the ability to sell.

While still a high-school student Amelia worked summers on a local newspaper, the *Atlanta Georgian*. Those were years when most of her friends in Atlanta were spending their vacation time improving their tennis or just loafing. The experience she then gained as a "professional" newspaperwoman was a continuous thrill—and later of practical use in her career. After her graduation from Girls High, she attended Agnes Scott College, in Decatur, Georgia. Her next move, in the early forties, was to the mecca of practically every young American writer with ambition: New York City.

THE WORLD OF THE FREE-LANCE WRITER

Speaking frankly about herself, Amelia Lobsenz says she never had considered herself a "great" writer. On the other hand, she is equally direct in stating that as a writer she has an ability lacking in many who do consider themselves "superior" writers: the ability to sell what she writes. In the highly competitive magazine and book-writing field this is a mighty important attribute. Yet Amelia Lobsenz was a salable writer almost from the beginning. With New York and its magazine market as her home base, she traveled around the country almost constantly for about two years, working on article assignments she or her agent secured from such publications as *Coronet* (the first national magazine to which she sold steadily), *Today's Woman, Better Living, Woman's Home Companion, This Week, Collier's,* and *Nation's Business.*

During the early years and later, she wrote many articles about business throughout the country, specializing in stories about men who had "made good." That experience made her begin to realize that if *they* could do it, so could she, in a business of her own. During the course of her business research she picked up and stored away a good many pointers about running a business, and came to see that there are many common denominators, in administration and practical techniques, in running any business successfully, whether it is U. S. Steel or a public relations firm. The experience was to yield fruit later on.

Amelia worked hard and ceaselessly at her writing during those years. When she started to write for *Today's Woman,* for example, she worked with the editors so intensively that they published eight of her by-lined articles within twelve months, setting a record matched by few other free-lance writers. Similarly, in fourteen months she did ten articles for *Better Living*.

Like many another writer, Amelia Lobsenz lived through a period when many national magazines were dying: *Liberty, Collier's, Woman's Home Companion, Better Living, Today's Woman, Everywoman's, Coronet*. All of them had been major sources of income for her. But like many other free-lancers confronted with a shrinking market, by dint of hard work she survived. "Don't misunderstand," she says in recalling those years. "I was saddened and even frightened at the death of each of the magazines. It was not only a matter of losing a source of personal revenue. From the standpoint of public information and education, the death of many of those magazines was a national loss. Every time I learn of the demise of a magazine or newspaper that had been serving a good purpose as a medium of communication," she concluded, "I cry a little. In a sense, it's a reflection of my long-standing love affair with the written word—one of the safest kinds of love affair to have, by the way. In any case, mine led me to become a writer, which in turn gave me the experience I was able to put to use in my present field."

The intensity with which she tackles any professional objective was evident in her response to the attrition of the magazine world: every time one magazine outlet closed, she looked around until she found another that she could interest in her article ideas. As a result, after she had made her mark as an established pro—which she dates from about 1946—there never was a time when she was not working on one or more assignments—and earning a comfortable living as a professional writer.

Amelia Lobsenz is proud of that fact. She has little patience with writers who complain about the shrunken market, yet do more hand-sitting than new-door-opening. Her attitude on the subject was summed up recently in her pointed advice to one such young writer who came to her office. "If you have the proper tools and know how to use them," she said to him, "there is a market for what you can produce. It is simply up to you to find the market."

NEW HORIZONS

In discussing the circumstances that caused her to switch from a successful writing career to the public relations field, and then to her own public relations business, Miss Lobsenz notes that each change had something of a challenge behind it. As far as professional writing was concerned, she felt she had mastered the techniques—in her own words, "not like Tolstoy, but like Amelia Lobsenz." She wanted something more challenging, though she was not sure what. She also had discovered what every writer comes to know: writing is basically a lonely job, with an untold number of solitary hours spent staring out the window or down at the typewriter, figuring out the next sentence or paragraph. And she liked people and enjoyed being with them.

So she was more ready for a change of profession than she herself realized when, at a dinner party, a close friend and her friend's editor-husband suggested that she consider entering the public relations field. A few days later, while she was working on a book in the special writers' room in the New York Public Library, the editor phoned her a list of PR agencies where she could use him as a reference. She phoned the one that happened to be nearest the library and talked to the executive vice-president, who knew her by reputation as a writer. Fifteen minutes later she was in his office. It was her first—and to this date only—job interview.

That was on a Friday. On Monday she went to work for the firm, beginning a mutually beneficial association that lasted seven years, continuing through the first year after she started her own business in 1956. It was only much later that she learned that the agency did not actually have a spot for her when she was interviewed: they hired her first, then found a spot for her afterward.

PR, SELF-TAUGHT

Amelia was not without qualms about the move to a field entirely new to her. But if it was challenge she wanted, it was challenge she certainly got. "Those early days were quite remarkable, in retrospect," she recalls. "The first night I took home fifty releases on fifty different accounts and analyzed them. I had never written a release before, but the next day I knew how to write a release. The second night I took home the same number of radio fillers— and so on, straight through what you might call a self-taught public relations course. I worked until midnight or one o'clock every night during that first six months, but after that I felt I knew the various public relations techniques, and could use them effectively. And of course I read every book on public relations that I could lay my hands on."

Exactly six weeks after Amelia Lobsenz started at the agency, she was asked to run a major account singlehanded while her boss was on a leave of absence. She assumed a responsibility that generally presupposes years of public relations experience. A few months later she was named director of the agency's magazine department, working on all accounts. In that post she began to develop the special techniques for magazine placement for which she is now so well known.

From the very beginning Amelia Lobsenz found public relations a fascinating field. For her it combined the creativity of writing with the opportunity to work in depth, developing and carrying out constructive programs for the agency's—and later her own—varied clients. She was proud of her new profession, and recognized it as one that could open the door to a wider development of her potential. Very soon she was helping in every aspect of the big agency's work—getting new business, seeing new clients, making new business presentations, getting familiar with and working on every account in the office.

"I certainly was not consciously trying to learn everything about everything," she remarks. "But it was always exciting to learn new things—and I was willing. I'm an 'absorber' from way back. In any case, I learned a great deal about the public relations business during those years, both from my colleagues and from the work itself, just as I had learned a lot from some of the wonderful editors I worked with as a writer. Those exciting years at the agency gave me the solid background I needed and desired."

By the mid fifties, starting her own business had become a fixed goal for Amelia Lobsenz, and the public relations field was her chosen field. When that first client approached her as an individual PR practitioner, she decided the time was right: another new mountain, another new challenge.

A BUSINESS IS BORN—IN AN APARTMENT HOUSE

Amelia Lobsenz had no illusions about the demands of entrepreneurship. She says, "It's extremely difficult to own a business. You must want it badly enough to put up with long hours, great effort, and personal sacrifice." She wanted it badly enough. The attractions: the challenge and excitement of running the show. She admits, "I like to follow my own instructions."

The name, "Lobsenz Public Relations," was decided on because her name was well-known in the magazine field. She started working out of her Park Avenue apartment. Although she had ten rooms, the flood of business communication marking her initial success— phone calls, messengers, office equipment—soon made the arrangement untenable. She moved into Squibb Building at 57th Street and Fifth Avenue, enlarging her quarters in succeeding months. Financing had been comparatively easy. In addition to her clients, she was able to support the enterprise by her free-lance writings that continued in the starting phases of Lobsenz Public Relations.

Quickly she built the nucleus of a staff—two account executives and two secretaries. She interviewed twenty-five people to select one. What did she look for? "I tried to hire people with the capacity not only to do the work, but with the interest to want to do it well."

She states, "I've almost never had to solicit clients. Satisfied clients have recommended others. The best way to get new business is to do well by the old." And in developing a new client, she would do a comprehensive research job, not only on the company, but on the industry as a whole. "I try to analyze the prospect's public relations situation," she says, "so that I understand its need better than the company does itself."

The major portion of Amelia Lobsenz's working time goes into personal supervision and nourishment of the business she launched in 1956. The fact that she often puts seventy or more hours a week into the job is another example of the intensity that characterizes her approach to everything in which she is interested.

Is it worth it? Amelia Lobsenz says it is. Her own experience has proved to her that anyone who wants to go into business for himself, with no backlog of capital, must want it badly; otherwise he is likely to go out of business scarcely before he has begun. In her case, she was willing to work any number of hours during the crucial early period when the firm needed help if it were to survive. Hence the magazine writing at night, the consultant work. Yet even so, there were many times in the first two years that she wondered if she really wanted her own business that badly: she could always go back to writing, or to work for another PR agency, and let someone else have the management and financial headaches.

As it turned out, she stayed with her new business. Today, looking backward, she believes one reason for her determination in that respect is that she actually likes *work* for its own sake, as well as for the sense of professional achievement it brings, through having an article in a national magazine, a well-handled account, pleased clients, continued renewals.

A WOMAN ON "WOMEN IN BUSINESS"

The biological fact of being a woman in what is still chiefly a man's business, has meant some plusses and a very few minusses to Amelia Lobsenz. When she founded her own company many friends and advisers warned her that she was automatically at a disadvantage since she had no intention of concentrating on typically "feminine" types of accounts such as food and fashion. Her goal was to develop a general agency, handling all kinds of accounts. As it turned out, she found that being a woman proved to be more of an advantage than a handicap. But like other successful business-women, Amelia Lobsenz believes that a major problem of many women in business is that their emotions influence their business relationships. Objectivity is something women cultivate—often consciously—if they are to compete successfully as entrepreneurs and as employers.

Cultivating objectivity does not necessarily mean putting femininity in a bottom desk drawer, according to Miss Lobsenz. Far from it. A pretty hat and an attractive smile can be a definite asset: it is more difficult for an editor to say no. "At the same time, a woman who thinks that beauty or charm or femininity can substitute for hard work or creative skill is absolutely wrong."

Amelia Lobsenz is equally firm in her conviction on another subject often raised about women—their role as employers of men. She herself has had no difficulty in getting good men to work with her, perhaps because she acts on the principle that a good business executive, male or female, treats every employee alike, regardless of sex. Personally, she believes that the idea of men being hesitant about working for "a lady boss" is an old-fashioned notion that is now in its death throes. Her point of view stems from what she has described as her "horizontal view" of people in general: she sees them not as inferior or superior, as male or female per se, but as individual human beings, each with his or her own personality.

One definite danger Amelia Lobsenz believes *does* exist for many women in business is the possibility of becoming overtense and even hard. This must be guarded against. "Perhaps many of them feel that they must be 'tough' in order to compete in the business world, and especially with men," she remarks. "I've never felt that. I do think one must be smart and capable, but I don't feel that I as a businesswoman am in competition with men as men. If I compete at all it must be with other public relations firms. But frankly, I think there is room for us all. In fact, industry has a far greater need for good public relations people than has been filled to date, since the profession is still relatively young."

And what of the "minus" factor mentioned earlier in connection with Amelia Lobsenz running her own business, as a woman? She admits it could be a little awkward to take a male client or editor to lunch or dinner and reach for the tab. She has solved the problem by having her secretary make advance reservations and ask that the bill bypass the table and be sent directly to the office. On balance, it seems a minor disadvantage of being a successful woman in public relations. She also works to overcome a personality trait that is very little in evidence today. An apparently outgoing personality, her friends and associates would be incredulous if they were told that the young woman from Atlanta had ever been shy about meeting or talking to people. Yet shyness was one of her early problems. She originally had to force herself to go to an editor with an idea or make a pitch to a client or get up and talk before a convention. Force herself she did, however, with a success that is self-evident. But the problem has not disappeared entirely. "I don't think I have overcome my shyness 100 per cent," she confesses. "But it's my secret now."

BEHIND THE AMELIA LOBSENZ STORY

Amelia Lobsenz's story follows the classic pattern of the proficient professional who switches to business. In the biography of Sol Dutka we have another example—the statistician turned businessman; J. J. Mascuch exemplifies the inventor-engineer who breaks out into the business field. Amelia Lobsenz is the successful writer turned entrepreneur.

Sponge Technique. Amelia Lobsenz calls her practice of absorbing information to be stored and later put to practical use, the sponge technique. It is of enormous value in many situations. The sponge technique need not be passive. Really effective use of the method involves asking questions, often framed in the key words "How?" "What?" "Why?" "When?"

Communications Skills. Many successful people add another sizable dimension to their capability when they master the ability to speak in public, or the ability to communicate by means of the written word. We all tend to be impressed by the man with a keen mind, but when he can get up on his two feet and communicate with large groups of people, he multiplies his effectiveness. The same is true of the businessman whose writing ability has become a potent tool. In Amelia Lobsenz's case, her writing ability is undoubtedly an advantage in working with clients, both in the presentation of ideas and in their development. However, even for the businessman who is not in what's generally described as the "communications industry," the ability to write effective reports, letters, memos and articles that appear in business or trade journals, can be a vital adjunct to his business capability.

Learning the Business Game. The same point emerges in several of the biographies appearing in this book: The successful individual, at some point, develops a "core" education; he learns the basics of business from a source that imprints the lessons indelibly on his mind. Amelia Lobsenz got her pointers in the course of doing business research. Donald M. Kendall of Pepsi-Cola acquired his basic business understanding from the customers he sold and from his boss, Al Steele. The opportunity occasionally presents itself for this type of practical education. Learning the core lessons about business in hard, realistic terms can make all the difference in the way a man operates and in how successful he will be.

The Good Angel. It was a friend at a dinner party who first suggested to Miss Lobsenz that she consider entering the public relations field. Also, in the career of Donald Kendall, it was suggested to him by a friend that he take a job with the Pepsi-Cola Company. Helpful friends can be a huge help indeed. Yet they can also recommend courses of action that prove disastrous. It's up to the individual to take an objective position on the suggestions of friends, relatives, and well-intentioned acquaintances; separate the good ideas from the poor ones.

Self-Development. After years of observation, the executives in charge of General Electric's vast management development program came up with a basic finding: "The only real development is self-development." What they mean is that an individual can be presented with all the knowledge in the world and subjected to every possible teaching technique, but the training only "takes" if the student acts on his own initiative and uses the tools to develop himself.

Amelia Lobsenz provides a good example of self-development. She taught herself public relations by taking home various kinds of material—news releases, radio fillers, etc. She studied and analyzed them by herself until she came up with principles of how to plan and develop these PR implements.

Apprenticeship. Amelia Lobsenz's description of her start in public relations underlines an important note for the would-be entrepreneur. Since eventually she started her own PR firm, what she learned as an employee in the PR field represented a kind of apprenticeship, a relatively inexpensive way of learning what she had to know in order to succeed on her own. The day of the apprentice in the ordinary craft sense is almost over. But for the individual interested in getting to the top, or starting his own business, the concept of apprenticeship can be valuable. It suggests that one can learn important lessons. And if failure is involved, the cost need not be personally shattering.

Finally, Miss Lobsenz's comments, spoken by a woman on the subject of women in business, are revealing: "A pretty hat and an attractive smile can be a definite asset," she asserts. Then comes the realistic reminder: "You've got to have a sound idea under that hat, however. Any woman who thinks that beauty or charm can substitute for her work or creative skill is wrong."

John M. Fox –

$400,000,000 FRUIT CUP

The United Fruit Company is three organizations in one. First is the growing operation, the raising and harvesting of fruit, much of it in South America. Second is the marine operation, the fleet of freighters that make up the transportation arm of the company. Sales, marketing, and distribution makes up the third segment. It is this triple empire, with annual gross sales of $400,000,000, that John M. Fox directs, as president of the company. This position was won after years of success with other organizations. What does it take to win the presidency of a vast business enterprise like United Fruit? John M. Fox's story provides an unusual inside view of the top-level marketing and financing operations of a corporation trying to make it big in the food field. You'll be drinking your morning orange juice with respect, as well as relish, after learning the ups and downs of Fox's personal breakthrough.

*   *   *

Raised in Atlantic City, where his father worked as a commercial artist, Fox had early come to the conclusion that education was a prime requisite for success. But by the time he graduated from high school in 1930, the great depression had gotten under way. In view of the family's rather modest circumstances, his chances of getting a higher education were thin. He didn't want to burden his parents by asking their help in financing a college education, so he chose to apply for entrance to the U. S. Naval Academy. He had always loved the sea, and Annapolis would keep him from being a parental liability. He was selected as first alternate, but the principal passed his examinations and was appointed. Rather than wait a year to enter Annapolis, Fox decided to try to go through college on his own. He chose Colgate.

When he graduated four years later, his business experience had included a stint as a gas station attendant, shoe salesman, insurance agent, and bill collector for the Atlantic City sewer department. All of this was in addition to waiting on tables for his bed and board. This regimen left little time for extracurricular activities, except for track. Fox was a three-letter man and captained the track team in his senior year. His specialty was the 440-yard and mile relays, and during his college career he set the Colgate quarter-mile track record. Fox says, "College was somewhat of a grind. I didn't like it much at the time, but I now realize that my college education was worth more to me as a result."

BIRTH OF A SALESMAN

In 1934, his senior year, jobs in business and industry were scarce and hard to come by. His roommate's father, a bank director, arranged an interview for him with a New York bank during the spring vacation. The day before he left for his appointment, he casually wandered into the Atlantic City boardwalk exhibition of International Business Machines and chatted with the manager. Fox was intrigued with the IBM products—punch card equipment—and their technical capabilities. His father's friend suggested that he drop by IBM's New York office for a job interview.

After his interview at the bank, where he was assured that a job would be waiting for him after graduation, Fox went to IBM headquarters. He received a cordial reception, went through several interviews in depth, and was invited to join the company's training program at five dollars per week, plus expenses. If he survived the rigorous course, he was promised a job at sixty-five dollars per week and no expenses. Though this was far short of what the bank had offered, Jack Fox felt that the long-term potential of IBM was greater. He accepted. After passing the IBM course in October, he was assigned to the St. Louis office for sales training. After a year in St. Louis he was given his first sales territory, in Providence, Rhode Island. Fox didn't quite realize the sad plight of this economically depressed region.

He spent six futile months trudging between Fall River, New Bedford, and Taunton, Massachusetts, without being able to make one single sale, not even a punch card. But Fox was not alone in this experience. At the end of six months, IBM transferred the local branch manager. Fox, though he didn't know it at the time, was on the top of the deposed manager's list to be fired. Fortunately, the new manager decided that his predecessor had made such a mess of things that from now on he would do just the opposite. This reverse line of reasoning was lucky for Fox. He became a top prospect rather than a candidate for dismissal. As Fox tells it, he was still in the position of bringing problems to the sales manager, rather than solutions. "The new manager, Laurence Flick, hammered some good common sense into me, made me a tolerably good salesman, and was instrumental in securing my first advancement in IBM."

Fox sold his first installation of tabulating equipment shortly after the new manager took over. This first sale gave him insight into the workings of the subconscious mind. In his enthusiasm he had oversold the customer. As the machines were being installed he realized, with a sinking sensation, that he had promised results the machines couldn't produce. Several days elapsed as Fox wracked his brain trying to find an answer. After spending one long final evening in reviewing his problem, Fox went to bed exhausted.

The next morning in the bathtub the answers he was seeking started to come to him. Jumping out of the tub like a latter-day Archimedes, he hastily wrote down the procedure that came to his mind. Rushing down to the plant, he punched up the necessary cards for the test program. They worked exactly as he had visualized, and produced the information his customer wanted. "Many years later I learned that this was a demonstration of the subconscious mind at work. I now know that it is best to feed the elements of a problem to your mind just before you go to bed. After a night or two of this procedure, the answers seem to come to you like the remembering of a forgotten name. Furthermore, the answers are more logical and lucid than those produced by conscious mental effort." Out of this and similar experiences, Fox has come to believe that the ability to think creatively can be developed, and that one of the greatest aids to an executive is the use of the subconscious mind. He points out, "There are many misconceptions about the ability to have ideas. The brain not only never tires, but becomes even more productive and efficient with use."

With the confidence gained from his first sale, and the steady, guiding hand of the new branch manager, Fox began to make solid progress with IBM, advancing to become branch manager of the Worcester, Massachusetts, branch office. Worcester had a broad spectrum of business and industry, and Fox was exposed to a variety of problems. "I got into the guts of a lot of businesses—banks, insurance, machine tools—gaining an insight into the manifold problems of business management. More important, I gained experience through the sheer necessity of being required to come up with solutions to problems in many areas."

Fox probably would have remained with IBM, moving up the ladder as time went on, except for the outbreak of World War II. As more and more of the young trainees that Fox had been nursing along to positions as responsible salesmen left to join the armed forces, he became more and more restless. And as IBM products began to be channeled into military use, he realized that his position was becoming a "holding operation" for the duration of the war.

A STRATEGIC SWITCH

His first idea was to give way to his love of the sea and to apply for a naval officer's commission. While awaiting action on his commission, another opportunity intrigued him. The National Research Corporation, at Cambridge, Massachusetts, was engaged in a broad area of war work. National facilities overflowed with scientists and technicians, but sales skills were lacking. Fox's background met the requirements of sales leadership. He had sold highly specialized equipment calling for substantial investment on the part of corporations. He had dealt with top-caliber management people. National's scientific work also had great appeal for Fox, who was a technical buff at heart. It seemed to be a perfect match of talents and job requirements. Fox also learned that when his naval commission went through, he was slated to take charge of a tabulating section staffed by Waves. Sure in his own mind he could make a greater contribution to the war effort with National Research, Fox joined the company in 1943, shortly after becoming vice-president in charge of sales, finance, and administration.

Among the military projects that National Research was engaged in was the preservation of heat-sensitive materials. The company had developed high-vacuum processes for dehydrating penicillin and blood plasma. National Research scientists had found that flavor, as well as nutritional content, could be preserved by applying the same high-vacuum process to form orange powder. The Army was anxious to provide orange juice in some form to troops out of reach of ordinary means of supply. And it was ready to purchase 500,000 pounds of orange powder from anyone who could fill the bill. National Research's laboratory samples met the Quartermaster's specifications. The big question was whether it could produce the powder in quantity and at low cost.

A PERIOD OF TRIAL AND ERROR

National Research decided to go ahead with the proposed project. "I was given the job," Fox recalls, "because I was the one who urged National to develop the product with its research department. After it was developed, I led the drive to exploit the process in the formation of a company. I suppose part of the reason was that I wanted to head the operation, and I guess they couldn't think of anyone else to suggest."

The first task was the construction of a pilot plant at Plymouth, Florida, in conjunction with the Plymouth Citrus Growers Association. After this plant was built, there was a period of experimentation before a powder was produced which met the Quartermaster's specifications. Finally the contract was awarded, with one reservation. National Research had to raise the capital to build its own plant. National Research decided to go to the public with an offer of approximately three million dollars in securities in a new enterprise called Florida Foods, Inc. National Research organized Florida Foods first as a wholly owned subsidiary. As the processes were developed and capital needs mounted, shares of the company were sold to the public, with National retaining 25 per cent of the common stock equity. Later National disposed of its equity share to keep Florida Foods afloat.

The Army contract was the key factor for Florida Foods, which had begun to manufacture a product that had never before been produced commercially. At this critical juncture, the new venture's problems began to multiply. In the spring of 1945, with the end of the war in sight, the Army suddenly canceled the contract. The securities underwriters promptly suspended their activities; unless the Army order was reinstated, there would be no basis for the offering.

This cancellation came shortly before the offering was scheduled. In a state of shock, Fox caught a plane for the Chicago headquarters of the Quartermaster Corps, determined to get a reinstatement of the contract. On arrival he found that he was just one of hundreds of frantic businessmen whose orders had been canceled.

"Forget it," he was advised, time and time again. But Fox was not the forgetting type. He would "hang on." Learning that the only man who could countermand the Chicago office's order was a general in Washington, D.C., Fox flew there. He soon found himself treading a well-beaten path up and down the chain of command. He bounced from lieutenant to major to colonel and back down the line again, seeking a review hearing from the general. Turned down time and time again by the staff, including one particularly obdurate colonel, Fox's persistence finally wore the Army brass down. He obtained a hearing from the general in an atmosphere of reluctance and even antagonism. Fox presented his case. He argued that the company had spent tens of thousands of its own money developing the product at the request of the armed forces. He pointed out that the company had been promised that if it were successful in producing a satisfactory product the Quartermaster Corps would buy it in large quantities. He said that the company was not asking for funds to be used to construct the plant, but would accomplish capital formation for these purposes with private sources.

"We had the encouragement of the procurement officers in the Army to proceed with our plans right up to the arrangement for the financing which had been done at considerable expense to National Research," Fox remembers telling the general, "and it was necessary for the Army order that was involved to be reinstated if the financing was to be consummated. Finally, I pointed out that the quantities of orange juice powder in the initial order were relatively small in relation to the needs of the base hospitals where the product was destined to be used." His final argument was that the orange juice powder was for use in base hospitals that would continue to care for the sick and injured after the armistice. The contract was reinstated and the Florida Foods stock issue was underwritten.

There was another close call for Fox. Under wartime regulations War Bond drives took precedence over all other types of security offerings. The company succeeded eventually in getting its securities sold only by placing them in between these drives, raising a total of $2,650,000.

The day that Fox received the check from the public underwriting, the A-bomb was dropped. This really signaled the end of the war, and the Army order for powder was again canceled. However, by that time the new company had its capital and, of even greater importance, it also had priorities for obtaining essential, but hard-to-get, materials and equipment to build the plant and get into production.

THE MOMENT OF TRUTH

Florida Foods was officially launched and Fox (now thirty-three years old) was named president. The plant was completed in March, 1946, and in April the first carload of the product was shipped. This was a concentrate, destined for the institutional trade. Arrangements were made with a new organization, Snow Crop, for distribution of the frozen concentrate. There was no relationship between Snow Crop and National Research or Florida Foods except as that of a sales agent. Florida Foods packed the juice under the Snow Crop label but maintained title to the product until it was sold.

During the summer the company (which had changed its name to Vacuum Foods) had planned to produce orange powder from concentrate produced in the five-month growing season and frozen and stored in drums for year-round production of powder. But problems easily solved in a pilot plant assumed enormous proportions when it came to large-volume production. Figuring out how to produce large amounts of powder at a reasonable cost was such a difficult problem that Fox decided to tackle first the problem of marketing the frozen concentrate.

The company showed a loss of nearly $80,000 (including $30,000 for cost of organizing) for the year ending July 31, 1946. Sales amounted to $375,000. About ninety thousand gallons of concentrate were produced. During the summer the concentrate started to sell well in institutional test markets, and Fox began to think about expansion of productive facilities. However, during the early fall, sales problems loomed as market conditions began to change. In November, before the product really had a chance to prove itself, citrus prices crashed, bringing down all citrus products.

Fresh oranges, four dollars per box at the end of the 1945–1946 season, plummeted to fifty cents a box at the start of the new one. Warehouses and shelves were loaded with single-strength juice. Packed fruit costs were high and this glut had to be sold at a loss, if at all. Distress pricing destroyed normal marketing patterns and, as panic spread among canners, single-strength citrus also took a nose dive. The embryonic frozen juice business crashed.

This was the beginning of John Fox's ride on the nightmare chariot as his company started its second packing season under the worst of conditions. That season, 360,000 gallons were produced.

As wholesalers went broke in droves, Snow Crop's distributing system, which had expanded to take on the retail sale of concentrate along with a complete line of frozen fruits and vegetables, fell apart and the company sold out to Clinton Foods in early 1947, leaving Fox with the task of finding other distribution outlets. In addition to being faced with a loss of $371,000 on sales of $454,000 in 1946–1947, Vacuum Foods had an inventory of over half a million dollars tied up in retail-size packages carrying the Snow Crop label.

In order to market the product the company needed sufficient funds to pay for advertising and sales promotion and for daily operating costs. Bankers, when approached, shrugged off requests for funds by pointing to their own heavy losses on frozen-food inventories. Did Fox really have a product that consumers wanted? At this stage, he decided to determine the potential demand from customers for frozen orange juice. If he could prove he had a product which was in demand, it might be easier to get the money he so badly needed.

Fox proceeded to demonstrate the validity of this theory at Hingham, Massachusetts, where he was then living. Loaded with concentrate he went from door to door, giving a can of juice to housewives and leaving the names of local grocery stores where it could be bought. The resulting demand cleaned out the stocks of the local stores and proved to Fox that he had the right product. But it did not convince the bankers.

At his annual meeting of stockholders that year, Fox faced an experience that comes to only a few chief executives—and then to fully seasoned ones. He and his management were attacked by a dissident stockholder group organized by one of his own directors. This issue was so close that the deciding votes were in the hands of the stockholders attending the meeting. Fox addressed the stockholders, but credits H. Struve Hensel, the company's lawyer, with doing "a magnificent job" of presenting management's side of the picture. Hensel, incidentally, later became Assistant Secretary of Defense. Fox and his group barely squeaked through. As he recalls it, "it did have me waking up a little earlier than usual every morning."

A CHANGE IN FORTUNE

At this crucial moment, Fox received what he calls "a lucky break." William A. Coolidge, board chairman of National Research, loaned fifty thousand dollars to tide the company over until new financing could be arranged. Not stopping there, Coolidge was also instrumental in getting John Hay (Jock) Whitney interested in the struggling company. The latter, after an intensive investigation which included all aspects of the business from production through marketing and finances, joined Coolidge in putting up nearly eight hundred thousand dollars of additional money. This infusion of capital enabled Fox to move ahead with his initial sales and advertising programs, and to finance a new season of packing operations.

Fox relates an interesting story in connection with Whitney's investigation. The special investigator Whitney used turned out to be the same Army colonel who had put so many roadblocks in Fox's way when he had gone to Washington to plead for reinstatement of the canceled contract. The ex-colonel grinned as he met Fox and said, "I bet you wish I had been successful in turning you down the first time. Then you wouldn't be in this mess." The colonel—Laurence Giles—in civilian life was a vice-president of the Safeway chain, and was brought in to appraise the product and its future potential in retail chain outlets. Fox was relieved that the colonel bore no grudges and gave technical approval to the investment.

The third season opened in December, 1947, and production ended in June, with more than one-and-a-quarter million gallons of concentrate processed. A tough, hard selling effort by a vastly expanded distributing organization netted sales of three million dollars. "We had to engage in every device and strategy we could think of to get the product placed in stores," Fox remembers. "Up to this point, few stores had heard of it and frozen orange juice was simply unknown to the public." The company realized its first profits, proudly reporting in its annual report for the year ending July 31, 1948, a net of $149,566. This was in contrast to the disastrous showing in the previous year when losses totaled more than $300,-000.

The tide had apparently turned. The frozen-food field showed signs of revival. The success of frozen orange juice spearheaded this revitalization of a sadly disorganized industry. Word-of-mouth advertising supplemented a well-rounded publicity and advertising program.

And in succeeding months two things happened which Fox feels were extremely important in the development of the company. First, singer Bing Crosby became a stockholder, on the recommendation of the Whitney organization. "Actually, we exchanged the stock in return for Bing Crosby's entertainment services," Fox disclosed. "We gave him twenty thousand shares of stock for a fifteen-minute-per-day, five-day-a-week radio show. It worked out well. Bing was a very enthusiastic stockholder and took every opportunity to promote the welfare of the company." Secondly, a *Reader's Digest* article in June, 1949, drew widespread attention to frozen juice concentrates and sent interest in the new product soaring.

AN ERROR RECTIFIED

On September 1, 1953, Minute Maid (the name adopted in October, 1949) paid its first common-stock dividend. Sales that year ran over $36,000,000 and net amounted to more than $1,000,000. It was then that Fox decided to expand activities through broad diversification. The following year, Minute Maid purchased the Snow Crop division of Clinton Foods for about $40,000,000. This acquisition added a complete line of frozen fruits, vegetables, fish, poultry, and various prepared foods plus Snow Crop's concentrates. At the time, Minute Maid with Snow Crop was doing an annual volume of about $100,000,000.

Minute Maid had a complete line, now. But this move was eventually to cost it dearly. It also forced Fox to coin another maxim. Looking back on this episode, he sadly admits that "we learn far more by our errors than our successes." The purchase of Snow Crop also pointed up the important factor of "timing," already a key word with Fox. For when Minute Maid took over Snow Crop, it entered the vegetable field at a time when private label competition was becoming stronger every day. Minute Maid made money on its Snow Crop fruit and vegetable lines the first year, lost money thereafter until disposal of it to Seabrook Farms. This was in 1957. Fox had decided for the moment to get back into the business of processing juices exclusively, where his specialized production and marketing techniques could best be put to use.

Fox's timing was better and more successful a couple of years later. He acquired Tenco, the nation's largest maker of instant coffee and tea, which gave Minute Maid a solid and widely-accepted product line. Tenco produced instant coffee for ten large regional coffee companies and several major chains. Minute Maid thought that Tenco's sales pattern would help to smooth out the seasonal ups and downs of the juice business.

Meantime, Fox continued to cope with the up-and-down cycle of citrus prices. His ingenuity was taxed to develop new marketing techniques and to make innovations in fruit procurement practices to offset the swings in the business, which could be tremendous. For example, in one year the company had a loss of $6,000,000; the next year it had a $9,000,000 profit before taxes. This swing of $15,000,000 was considerable for a company of Minute Maid's size.

"Perhaps the most important innovation to counter the cycling effect of the citrus industry was the development of our grower participation plans and, finally, our grower cooperative," Fox says. "From the beginning we were short of fruit supplies to keep our plants running and frequently found ourselves out of phase with the raw fruit market as concerns prices. To remedy this and be sure of constant supply of high-quality fruit, we devised methods whereby growers could participate in the prices of the concentrate when it was sold at retail. Another helpful innovation at the time, during a freeze crisis, was our work in proving that you could successfully concentrate the juice of oranges that had been frozen on the tree by the weather. Up until then, it was thought that frost-damaged fruit was absolutely unusable. We proved otherwise, and won our point with the citrus authorities."

Once Minute Maid had progressed to the point where profits had achieved some consistency, Fox set to thinking about seeking a strong, well-financed partner who could see it through future difficulties. This search culminated in the purchase of Minute Maid by the Coca-Cola Company at the end of 1960. Minute Maid had just put three good years of earnings end to end, and had boosted its sales to around $140,000,000 annually.

Fox feels that this was a fine move for the company, its stockholders, and its employees. Minute Maid had taken a giant step forward; its financial worries were over. It had now become part of a strong, well-financed organization with recognized merchandising know-how. Fox was all set to go along with Minute Maid in the merger, continuing to head the company when it became part of Coca-Cola.

A NEW CHAPTER

Among the companies that Fox had approached in his search for a partner was the United Fruit Company, which had displayed some interest. At the time, however, the Coca-Cola arrangement seemed best for Minute Maid and its shareholders. Shortly thereafter, United Fruit Company approached Fox, offering him a position at a top management level. The company was going through a transitional phase. It was looking for a man with marketing know-how, and management thought that Fox could not only provide the direction needed in this field, but also would bring to the company mature and broadly diversified management qualifications.

After careful consideration, Fox accepted the offer, joining the United Fruit organization in February, 1961, as executive vice-president. He became president in 1964 and chief executive officer in March, 1965. In a sense, the skills called for represented the culmination of his varied experiences since leaving college. His years with International Business Machines, National Research Corporation, and Minute Maid had served as the crucible. He had met the test and was ready to assume new responsibilities.

Business is a matter of taking risks, he points out. The magnitude of the risk is a measure of the possible loss or gain. Fox says, "In nearly every business someone must have the courage to take positive action without having in hand all the facts and data that may make the decision risk-free. A manager can never abdicate this responsibility."

BEHIND THE JOHN M. FOX STORY

John M. Fox's biographical sketch is really three stories in one. First, it's the personal narrative of a man who made his way up the business ladder from salesman to president, after some preliminary stops as shoe salesman, insurance agent, and bill collector of the Atlantic City sewer department. Second, in the course of the narrative, the problems of bringing a new product to market—in this case, frozen orange juice concentrate—are described. And third, Fox's story reveals some of the conflict and crises that arise in the corporate enterprise. The attack of a dissident stockholder group was just one of the battles that had to be fought on the way to the top.

Fox's breakthrough is marked by these factors:

Idea Production. Every successful man shows himself to be capable of producing ideas; not ideas in the abstract, but those needed to solve a problem, or to provide a plan for action. Fox describes a situation he'd gotten himself into: selling a customer some IBM equipment that apparently wasn't going to be able to produce the results needed, and tells how he dealt with the difficulty.

The entire area of creative thinking is, paradoxically, a foggy area that even our best minds have been unable to clarify to any great degree. One engineering professor, a woman giving courses requiring considerable creativity, remarked: "One of the problems with creative thinking is that it seems to be a groping, kind of zigzag process." United Fruit's president developed his own personal method for producing ideas, by "feeding" his unconscious with the raw materials required to construct the desired product. The individual who is aware of how he gets his ideas, can usually systematize them. Eventually, this is what Fox did, making his production of ideas more effective.

Failure Rejection. At several points, John M. Fox demonstrates that he considers failure to be temporary. Once this point of view is developed, it becomes possible to withstand the worst aspect of failure—the sense of defeat that lowers effort and self-confidence. The six months spent in vain attempts to sell IBM machines in the Fall River area during the depression—one of several of Fox's "failures"—might have dented a lesser man. He persisted. The conviction that failure is a passing thing kept him going. Generally, it's the secret that has kept many successful people from being crippled by sagging fortunes. The man who is thrown by failure and can't shake off its effects often may find this one inability a major reason for lack of achievement. Fox's experience makes it clear that he possessed the ability to ride out the unpleasant consequences of failure, and to prepare for continuing achievement.

Core Training. Many successful businessmen describe a period in their lives when they had the opportunity to learn about business in a direct, realistic and memorable manner. This type of practical education also came to John M. Fox. As he says, "I got into the guts of a lot of business—banks, insurance, machine tools—gaining an insight into the manifold problems of business management." His exposure came about as a result of analyzing company operations as a preliminary to the installation of IBM equipment. Donald Kendall, of Pepsi-Cola, got similar valuable training by long conversations with the businessmen he called on while out in the field selling soft-drink installations.

No matter what the particular source or method of this type of brass-tacks business insights, it provides a strong platform for the career-minded. And, of course, if it doesn't just "happen to happen." One can make it happen by figuring out where the knowledge exists, and exposing one's self to it—whether it be by going to school, or taking a job as a salesman, a shipping clerk, or a third assistant purchasing agent.

The Riposte Reflex. The trip up the ladder is seldom an unimpeded journey. A special difficulty: the antagonism of a competitor or rival, who for one reason or another has the knife out with intent to commit mayhem. The individual intent on advancing in the world of business need not adopt the popular "jungle" concept of the milieu. But he would be unrealistic not to expect attack, and to be prepared to cope with it.

Fox and his management group were put on the spot by a number of stockholders, organized by one of the directors of the Vacuum Foods Company. His ability to fend off the attack made it possible to go on to the next phase, the financing of the cash-short firm.

Grass-Roots Action. A major problem for many top executives: inefficiencies and difficulties of serious enough nature to threaten the entire organization originate at the outer limits of the company. In one case, it might be a festering employee problem, arising from an unwise company policy. In Fox's case, somewhere along the line during the marketing of concentrated orange juice, there was doubt as to exactly how the consumer felt about the new product. Fox might have hired market research people to learn the answer. Instead, he went out on the firing line himself. He went out into the streets of Hingham, Massachusetts, and distributed cans of juice door to door, talking to housewives and getting their reactions to the new food product.

The willingness to go the grass roots of a problem, instead of handling it remotely, gives the individual the firsthand information and "feel" of a situation that can make all the difference in how he proceeds. Fox learned what he had to know.

The Premonition of Success. "Grasp opportunity by the forelock," counsels the old proverb. It's a fine directive. But major trouble lies in recognizing the old gentleman in the dim light in which he is usually seen.

Yet, one sees repeatedly that the successful individual is able to spot a situation—or even an object, as in the case of Owen K. Murphy's exercise chair—that is immediately seen not in its present status, but in the light of its potential.

In reviewing John M. Fox's career, one of its major keys is

certainly his quick recognition of the possibilities of orange-juice concentrate. The strong stand he took in urging his company to develop the product is an outstanding example of a man's ability to look into the future—and risk his personal fortunes on the vision he has seen.

13 { Rex Wood —
SHOWROOM IN THE PARLOR

The door-to-door salesman is a basic and essential part of the American marketing scene. He literally beats a path to the consumer's door. By the time a door-to-door salesman leaves many houses, whether he was selling cosmetics and perfumes, brushes or vacuum cleaners, housewives often end up wondering how in the world they'd been able to do without their new purchase.

Sarah Coventry, Incorporated, has still further advanced the art of selling the housewife on her own grounds. The organization sells jewelry—specially designed and presented with almost irresistible appeal. Rex Wood is the man who played a major part in building the organization, and training the people who make it effective. He became a salesman for the company as the result of a chance encounter, ended up as head of the organization some fifteen years later. The story of his breakthrough affords a fascinating view of the challenging art/science of personal selling.

*   *   *

As great black clouds swirled from under the hood, the driver of the brand-new Ford jumped out of his car, ran over to the filling-station owner and spluttered: "What kind of a mechanic *are* you? Look at this thing!" The mechanic, Rex Wood, lifted the hood and his heart sank. He tried to keep the quaver out of his voice as he said, "Let's see if it's anything serious." One glance was all he needed to tell that the worst had happened. He had serviced the car only a couple of hours earlier, but, he now realized with horror, he had forgotten to refill the drained crankcase with fresh oil. The engine was ruined.

The year was 1935; Wood, the filling-station owner, was nineteen; and the price of a new engine was $125, which came directly out of his pocket. Recalling the episode not long ago, Rex Wood said, "That catastrophe impressed me with the need to double-check every job, to take nothing for granted. In business, particularly at the executive level, you have to act with the same care you'd exert if you were planning a military campaign."

A TWENTY-TWO-THOUSAND-MAN ARMY—ALL WOMEN

Wood does operate rather like a skilled general. His troops consist of ladies—some twenty-two thousand of them—who each year march daily to the homes of half a million other ladies, where some four million *other* ladies have gathered to buy eight million necklaces, pendants, earrings, pins, bracelets, rings, chains, tie bars, tie tacks, and cuff links worth twenty-five million dollars. All this feminine hurly-burly is performed on behalf of Sarah Coventry, Inc., the world's largest direct-selling costume jewelry company, of which Wood was named president in 1964. Today, Wood, whose boyhood ambition was to make forty dollars a week, makes many times that amount every day.

In direct selling, the manufacturer's salesmen go directly to the consumer, bypassing wholesalers and retailers. The most common method of direct selling, of course, is through the door-to-door salesman. Wood's ladies engage in a variation of this technique; each of his sales representatives persuades an acquaintance to invite several friends into her home for a couple of hours, during which the representative exhibits the jewelry and usually stimulates the guests to buy some of the merchandise.

A general directing twenty-two thousand men in battle has a difficult job on his hands. Directing twenty-two thousand women in business is of a different order of magnitude; few military men would welcome the task. Yet Wood, who resembles a slimmed-down and somewhat cherubic Jackie Gleason, flourishes on his assignment.

AN EARLY LESSON—PATIENCE BRINGS FIFTY CENTS MORE APIECE

Wood came from an impoverished and broken home, and his memories of early hard times undoubtedly played a role in his drive to success. Following the tested pattern, he demonstrated good business sense as a youngster. While other boys in Frankfort, New York, would capture muskrats during the winter and sell them immediately for fifty cents apiece, Wood kept his until the spring, when the traveling muskrat buyer came through town and offered a dollar apiece for them. Patience, he learned, has a price that can frequently be measured in hard coin.

Upon graduating from high school, where he captured most of the athletic and scholastic honors that were offered, Wood found himself one more poor boy among the millions that abounded during the Great Depression and he took a job at a local filling station. A year later he persuaded a group of local businessmen to sell him a run-down gas station on the outskirts of town. He paid five hundred dollars—his entire savings from his job. The auto-repair and gasoline business prospered; further, the local customers took enough of an interest in the punchboard in Wood's office to enable him to pay his brother's salary as an assistant. Whatever success Wood achieved as an entrepreneur was due largely to two qualities: his persistence in asking neighbors to patronize him, and an inherent streak of business wisdom.

For example, a local trucker once asked him for credit on tires. Upon checking the man's references, Wood found that his finances were even shakier than Wood's own. No other supplier in town would touch him. However, Wood also discovered that the man had a contract with Railway Express, and that every month the company sent him a check for the deliveries he'd made. Wood visited the man's office, and said, "I think maybe we can make an agreement."

"You mean you'll give me the credit?"

"Yes," said Wood, "if you'll sign your Express check over to me every month. That way, I'll be sure that your bill is paid, and you'll get the tires you need." So, by ignoring his customer's reputation and concentrating on his income, Wood picked up a regular piece of business where others had feared to tread.

FREE EDUCATION—AT ALMOST ANY PRICE

Within two years, Wood managed to put aside three thousand dollars. He sold the gas station and lit out for Cornell University's School of Agriculture. Not that he had any interest in becoming a farmer. His reasons were more basic. New York State paid the tuition for residents who wanted to attend an agricultural college, and Wood, eager for a degree, was in no position to argue about the kind of institution he was attending as long as it was free.

Graduating in 1941, Wood spent most of the next eight years trying to rise upward from agriculture, and in the process, he picked up a couple of useful pointers for his later career. Perhaps the most valuable lesson he learned was from his first employer, Sears, Roebuck: quit when the kick is gone. He had been with the firm six years and had risen to the position of assistant merchandising manager of the Rochester, New York, store, when, one afternoon, feeling rather restless, he asked his boss: "Frank, am I getting anywhere?"

Frank looked him squarely in the eye, and answered, "Rex, when you reach the point where you feel you're not getting anywhere, it's time to pick up your hat and say 'so long.'"

The following day, Wood picked up his hat and said, "So long."

On his next job, as a salesman for a life insurance company, he improved his score enormously. He became fed up in only two years —when he began to feel that he was selling some products his customers didn't really need. Until that feeling overcame him, however, he had been one of the top salesmen in the company, and had learned several lessons which were tremendously pertinent to his later business success.

"IF YOU ASSUME HE'LL BUY, HE'LL BUY"

He had come across two partners in a fuel-oil business who were interested in a policy that would provide money for the survivor to buy out the other's share in the event that one should die. Having concentrated on the selling of life insurance, he wasn't too sure of the details of the policy, and he asked his boss to come along and help. Wood explained the coverage and the costs, and when the partners agreed that this was what they wanted, the boss took over. "Would you prefer to pay the first year's premium now by check," he asked blandly, "or with cash?"

The men looked at each other, and the older one said, "Well, I don't think there'll be enough money left in the safe if we pay you in cash, so we'll make out a check."

Wood looked on with amazement as the man wrote a check for the entire year's premium. "It would never have occurred to me then to ask for more than a couple of months' premium," he says. "He taught me that if you assume a person will buy, the chances increase that he will buy. We've used the principle consistently in selling Sarah Coventry jewelry, and it works."

Wood also learned not to assume that he knew the customer's wants better than the customer. He visited a prospect one time who said, "I'm primarily interested in an endowment for my young son." Wood remembered that standard insurance practice was to sell a man a policy on his own life first, then to offer him additional coverage. Wood pointed out to the prospect that the man needed a policy on himself first; the son's turn came later.

The prospect listened politely and replied, "Well, you've got a good point. Let me think about it and call me next week." Pleased with himself for operating according to Hoyle, Wood called the man the next week. His heart sank as he heard, "Oh, I'm sorry, but I've spoken to another man and he's sold me the endowment I wanted."

One rule overrides another. Wood says now, "I should have

listened to him. That's one of the greatest weaknesses a salesman can suffer—to talk when he should listen."

After two years, Wood realized that he did not want to talk about insurance, and he moved his young family to a farm he had bought with his savings. But small-time farming in 1949 was no more lucrative than it is today, and Wood soon began scanning the help-wanted columns again.

THE RIGHT AND WRONG WAY TO HIRE A MAN

Responding to an ad placed by Commercial Enterprises (now C. H. Stuart Co.), a nursery company which sold trees door-to-door, he scored high in a psychological test given to all applicants, and was immediately accorded a warm reception. "The sales manager gave me one of the most strenuous pep talks I've ever had," says Wood, "telling me what a terrific company it was, and how sure he was that I'd be a phenomenal success. He assured me it was an opportunity I couldn't afford to miss."

To his own astonishment as well as the sales manager's, Wood said no. Why? "He oversold me. I had the uncomfortable feeling that he was being too enthusiastic. I decided that if ever I were in a position to hire anyone, I'd make him reach for the job. And I've always done it that way. When I interview a man, I tell him, 'This is a responsible position. Do you think you can qualify for it?'—and then I let him do the talking."

C. H. Stuart Company, formerly Commercial Enterprises, was—and is—a family-owned concern with headquarters in Newark, New York. It was started some 165 years ago by an ingenious farmer, an ancestral Stuart, who planted the seeds of the business by peddling trees and shrubs to his neighbors. The nursery business is still a substantial contributor to the family revenues, but succeeding generations carried the door-to-door principle into other fields, including cosmetics, silverware, china, and crystal. The current head of C. H. Stuart Co. is the founder's great-grandson, C. W. (Bill) Stuart, a tall, slender, perceptive gentleman who, after seeing

Wood's test scores, realized that he was losing a potentially excellent salesman. He had seen Wood in town occasionally and knew him slightly.

Soon after Wood refused to be overwhelmed into the nursery business, Stuart bumped into him on the street and invited him to discuss a new proposal. Commercial Enterprises was going into the jewelry business, using the home-party technique, then a relatively new development in direct selling. Would Rex like to try his hand at it as the first salesman for Sarah Coventry, which was to be the new company?

WILKES BARRE, AT THE POINT OF A PIN

Wood had sold jewelry at Sears and had enjoyed it. He thought that the home-party technique might have interesting possibilities, and he wanted a job. The two men shook hands on it. Then Stuart, eyes closed, picked up a pin and stuck it into a map of the United States. Wilkes-Barre, Pennsylvania, was punctured. "That," said Stuart, "is your territory. Good luck."

A few days later, Wood arrived in the Pennsylvania coal town with a satchel full of jewelry. It was the fall of 1949, and Wood, then thirty-three, was bursting with the innocent enthusiasm of the recruit about to save his country from the enemy. He stepped off the train and turning to the first man he saw, asked, "How's business here?"

"Terrible," came the answer. "Nineteen thousand people unemployed."

"Wonderful," said Wood. "That means people need jobs, and that's what I'm here for."

He marched off to find his first target—any Wilkes-Barre lady who would agree to invite her friends to a home demonstration. Wood, not knowing any better, decided to try a frontal attack. He walked up to a couple of likely-looking prospects, two women who were looking into a jewelry shop window. Smiling in his most ingratiating manner, Wood asked, "Excuse me, but would you ladies like to have a party?" The older one stared at him coldly, spat out, "Masher!" grabbed her companion, and stalked off indignantly. Bruised by his first encounter, Wood realized that this was not the right way to win the war. But by the week's end, he had developed a much more effective approach, based on the make-'em-reach strategy.

He approached a lady who was sweeping her sidewalk and said, "You're doing a good job. The place looks beautiful."

Intrigued, but still suspicious, the housewife asked, "What are you selling?"

"Nothing. I'm giving something away."

"What is it—where's the catch?"

"Let's sit down and talk about it. Frankly, the catch is that I'm new in town and I need your help."

As Wood has since remarked, asking for help is one of the strongest appeals a salesman can make. On the steps, Wood explained how the house-party plan worked. The sales representative earned a commission on every piece sold, and the hostess who gathered her friends in her home received commissions in the form of jewelry.

Innocently he asked, "Do you know anyone who needs part-time work, or who could use a little extra money?"

"Let me see the jewelry," said the lady. "Maybe I'd be interested in buying some now."

"You can't. As I told you, I'm not selling it." He made her reach, and she agreed to be a hostess. After the first party, Wood signed up several guests as representatives and future hostesses. He had survived his first encounter and, in the process, had promoted himself to corporal with a handful of new recruits who would form the nucleus of his army.

In the succeeding months as he traveled through Pennsylvania, Wood became expert at dealing with the ladies. On more than one occasion, when he was visiting a home where the ladies had gathered for a demonstration, Wood went through a ritual: he stopped before the house, put his cigarette on the ground, stepped on it, and toed it into the gutter. Then he strode toward the door, stepped carelessly on the lawn, jumped back, kneeled down, and patted the grass smooth. Finally, he walked up the path and rang the bell.

Upon opening the door, the hostess encountered Wood's back. He turned, smiled and said, "Hello. I'm Rex Wood. I was just admiring the neighborhood, but I think you have the nicest home on the block."

To those who ask for an explanation of the ritual, Wood explains: "I knew the women would be watching from behind the draperies, and their first impression of me would be important. Pushing the butt into the gutter indicated that I was considerate—no sidewalk litterer. The lawn business was a bit of comedy, but it indicated I knew my manners. Presenting my back when the hostess opened the door was a way to surprise her. She'd be expecting an aggressive salesman. I turned away as if getting in the door were the farthest thought from my mind. And then, my first words were flattering ones, not selling ones. Everything was designed to persuade her to accept me, personally. After that, it was simply a matter of showing my product to a favorably disposed group."

Indians used to paint their bodies luridly before battle. Modern soldiers are taught to scream ferociously as they attack with bayonets. Their aim is to enhance the drama of the act, to persuade the enemy that resistance is futile. Similarly, Wood learned to enhance the drama of his presentations with a variety of stratagems. He wrapped each piece of jewelry in a gauzy, delicate kerchief, rather than simply pulling it willy-nilly from the case. Result: the jewelry took on an aura of luxury. He handled each piece gently, showing it on the back of his hand first, and speaking about it as if it were Tiffany's best: "You've seen all kinds of jewelry," his voice hushed with wonder and pride, "but you've never seen anything like these Sarah Coventry brooches." Result: the prospective customers tended to look at the brooch as if it were some rare piece.

At the beginning of a demonstration, he gave one piece to each guest to model for the others. As a result, the ladies became involved in that piece of jewelry, tended to think of it as their own, and were more likely to buy it. He distributed compliments with the liberality of a conquering general distributing loot to his followers. An excellent, all-purpose compliment, as effective as it was vague, was: "This necklace would look especially beautiful on you because you have the kind of neck that looks especially handsome with necklaces."

When he used pressure to overcome resistance, it was as invisible and as strong as the pins that secured his brooches. If a lady hesitated to buy a piece which Wood thought she ought to have, he reassured her, "All right, I'll put it aside for you and we'll come back to it later." Then he went to one of her friends and said, "Jane, Mary's just tried on a bracelet that looks lovely on her. She really ought to get it. Come, help me out." Bringing the friend to Mary, he said, "Now, doesn't Mary look superb in this?" Since the two girls were friends, what else could Jane say but "Yes, it looks wonderful."

Wood's comprehension of feminine thinking extends considerably beyond the sales pitch. He persuaded the company to change the term from "party" to "fashion show" because he had discovered that hostesses were more successful in inducing friends to visit them when they asked, "Will you come to a Sarah Coventry fashion show at my house? I'd especially like you to model some of the jewelry."

"NICE" AND "PRETTY" ARE OUT

A preoccupation with words has been characteristic of Wood ever since adolescence, when he walked off with the state, county, and city championships for public speaking in his junior year of high school. It manifested itself in two striking ways during the early years with Sarah Coventry.

One was his insistence that new recruits avoid the overworked words "nice" and "pretty" in describing the jewelry. "There are so many dramatic words that will do a better job," he has said. "Elegant, charming, handsome, delicate, eye-catching, scintillating. Who needs 'nice' or 'pretty?' "

The other was to give the jewelry names that were elegant, charming, handsome, delicate, eye-catching, and scintillating. Golden Cascade, Starburst, Sun Flower, Radiance, and Galaxy, he believes, have added much to the sales appeal of the items to which they were attached. On the other hand, some names have come a cropper. One piece, christened Cobra, was rapidly eliminated after women reacted with, "Ugh! I wouldn't want a snake on me."

In 1958, the Stuart family recognized that Wood was now their most seasoned veteran. He had been responsible for training an army of nearly nine thousand and was obviously ripe for a promotion. They made him vice-president of sales.

Wood realized that motivation is vital to any business which depends on temporary workers. Either commissions or promise of permanent associations with Sarah Coventry must be sufficiently rewarding to draw forth the best efforts of the salespeople. Those who elected to stay with Sarah Coventry he rewarded well with excellent pay. Many women who joined intending to earn twenty dollars to thirty dollars a week selling jewelry temporarily, have stayed on permanently to earn from ten thousand to forty thousand dollars a year.

At a sales convention in St. Louis recently, Sarah Coventry's top field personnel, both men and women, were asked to tell what they had earned the last two years before coming to Sarah Coventry; then what they had made the previous year with the company. Thirty-one top managers reported the following: average annual income for the two years before joining Sarah was $9738; average income with Sarah the previous year $19,337. Forty-two top women managers, before joining Sarah, earned $3481; average income the previous year with Sarah was $15,789. Wood likes to tell the story about one "temporary" saleslady who joined Sarah so she could afford a sewing machine. She bought the machine with her initial earnings, then became so busy on a full-time basis that she hasn't had time to sew. She looks better in the Dior creations she can now afford anyhow, says Rex.

LICKING AN ORGANIZATIONAL PROBLEM

Between 1949 and 1955, sales had gone from nothing to about four million dollars. In the next five years, they skyrocketed to nearly twenty-five million dollars. It was the same story with personnel. In 1955, the company had about three thousand people. Three years later, the number was nine thousand. It was not surprising that there were weaknesses in the organization's structure, and it was to those weaknesses that Wood first addressed himself, concentrating on the lower levels, where the greatest problems seemed to lie.

At the time, the first three ranks looked like this:

> Division manager
> District manager
> Fashion show director

A sales person started as a fashion show director, rose to district manager, supervising a number of fashion show directors, and then went up to division manager, supervising a group of district managers. Compensation increased at each level, for each manager received a share of all sales under her jurisdiction. A major problem lay with the district managers. This was the first supervisory job for many of them, and they were not especially well-trained in supervisory or administrative work. It was difficult for them to conduct their own shows, train new salespeople, and handle the necessary administration, all at the same time and all by themselves.

The problem was particularly difficult because, as Wood noted, "In this business, where we're dealing with part-time people, many will start off enthusiastically in order to earn a few extra dollars. But once they've made it, they may slack off unless they're constantly inspired." The district managers simply didn't have the time or training to give the inspiration on top of their own duties.

Wood's solution was to create a new position—unit manager—between district manager and fashion show director. The unit manager would be responsible for fewer salespeople than the district manager, and would also act as an administrative assistant to the district manager. This would give her additional training, so that she would be readier to assume the responsibilities of district manager. At the same time, he realigned the superstructure, replacing the title of district manager with that of branch manager. The old and new alignments looked like this:

OLD STRUCTURE	NEW STRUCTURE
Division manager	Division manager
District manager	Branch manager
Fashion show director	Unit manager
	Fashion show director

"In order to make the system work," Wood said not long ago, "we had to persuade our division managers to take what looked like a step down, to the newly created position of branch manager. While the title wasn't as high, I honestly felt that they could make more money because their groups would be more effective."

How did Wood persuade a good executive to accept a demotion in the interest of the company? He went to a lady who had been an excellent district manager, but who, as a division manager, had failed to increase sales proportionately. He told her, "I'm quite sure that it isn't your fault. It's the fault of the system, and I want to improve the system so that your earnings will come up to your abilities. I'm pretty sure I can guarantee you an increased income, if you'll take the step down in title."

Wood was sufficiently astute to approach a woman who had implicit faith in his sincerity. She accepted the suggestion on a trial basis. It worked. "Where she had never been able to crack ten thousand dollars a year before," Wood said, "at the end of her first year as a branch manager, she made nineteen thousand dollars. After that, we had no trouble getting the rest of the division managers to go along."

Sales shot up, and in 1960, Wood became executive vice-president for company operations east of the Mississippi. In this job, he repeated his revamping on a much higher level, creating a new layer of area managers just below the vice-presidents. This posed several delicate problems in executive generalship, however, and it was here that Wood began to show his potential ability to lead a large company.

"When you introduce changes," he said, "all kinds of unexpected headaches are going to pop. If you're not right on top of them, the whole house can go up in smoke." One of the more difficult problems he faced was this: how much can an upper-echelon executive interfere in the field operations when he sees something going wrong?

Wood recalled, "I had seen one home-office executive bypass his field subordinates and go directly to the lower echelons. The subordinate became resentful and the lower echelons became uncertain. This sort of thing can wreak havoc with an organization. And I saw another situation where the subordinate didn't resent the intrusion, but he became dependent on the interfering boss. When the boss returned to the home office, the subordinate panicked because he had no one to lean on. Either way, it's a losing proposition."

Wood learned the lesson. "In the field," he said, "I almost invariably worked through the top man in the area. Even if I had questions about the man's performance, in public I built him up, and I expected him to build me up. Once we were alone, then I criticized."

Notice Wood's qualifying word, "almost." He admits that there are special occasions when prudence calls for bypassing a subordinate. "For example," he said, "you face this problem when morale is sinking because an executive isn't doing his job properly in all respects. He may be a good producer, but he may not yet know how to deal understandingly with his subordinates. They may let top management know they're unhappy, and there may be a real threat of their leaving the company if something isn't done to ease the friction between them and their immediate boss. What can top management do in this situation?"

Wood's solution, when he faced the problem, was both hard-headed and effective. "The executive in question was a top-notch producer," Wood recalled, "but we were faced with the threat of wholesale quittings which would have crippled us seriously. Essentially, the solution was to make the subordinates more aware that they were working not just for this man, but for the whole company."

At conventions, Wood went out of his way to talk to the employees and show them that the company was interested in them. After a visit to their area, he sent them letters, telling them what an excellent job they were doing, and indicating on the bottom of the letter that a copy was being sent to the president. On their birthdays, they received friendly notes from him. It was inevitable that they should begin to think warmly of Sarah Coventry—so warmly, in fact, that the division subsequently turned in a record sales performance.

This episode raises one interesting question: Why wasn't the troublesome executive discharged? The answer: good men are hard to find, and if an executive is doing a superior job in most respects, it's the better part of wisdom to avoid firing him as long as he's contributing to the company's growth in sales and profit—particularly if, as in this case, a little diplomacy lets you side-step the problem.

But side-stepping isn't always possible. When faced with a situation where a man's performance is causing substantial harm, and it looks as if he'll have to be fired, Wood has worked out a three-step set of principles to guide him.

"First," he said, "I never tell a man, 'If you don't shape up, you'll lose your job.' This type of threat doesn't work very well; on the contrary, it's likely to cause resentment. I prefer to approach it as if it were a problem facing both of us. I'll tell the man, 'Joe, you don't seem to be making the progress that we expected from you. The difficulties seem to be A, B and C. Now, I'd like to help you; let's talk about these problems.'"

Second, if after the first warning, the man still hasn't shaped up, Wood feels that it's important for the boss to make up his mind firmly that the man has to be fired. "Once you've made up your mind," he said, "stick to it; if you vacillate, you'll hurt the company, the man, his subordinates, and your own reputation as a good executive."

Third, try to make the parting as amicable as possible. Said Wood, "I've tried to help the men into some other company, and I've seen to it that they've received everything that's coming to them in the way of compensation."

Why this solicitude? "Because I want to maintain the company's reputation," Wood explained. "Any executive has a lot of contacts, and if the word gets around that we're unfair, we're going to have trouble recruiting other top people." Enlightened self-interest, in other words, dictates a policy of firmness coupled with decency.

Terminating a valued employee is, of course, a last resort, and Wood, as executive vice-president, went out of his way to avoid it. "For example," he recalled, "we had a situation where two good field executives simply weren't able to work together. Basically, it was due to deep-seated personality differences, and all the judicious counseling in the world couldn't have got them to work together. In these circumstances, there's no solution that works every time, but one course I've found to be effective is to move one of the men to a different area—someplace else in the company, or someplace else in the country. Of course, this takes patience—we've waited as much as two or three years."

CARROT VERSUS STICK—THE CARROT USUALLY WINS

"When I was faced with this situation with my two men, I began taking one of them with me on trips to another part of the country where we needed his special skills for short periods. Gradually, he learned to like that part of the country so much that eventually he voluntarily made the switch. I think it would have been impossible two years earlier to force him to make that move."

Like many other top executives, Wood learned that the carrot is often mightier than the stick. And even when he did use a stick, it was wielded with minimal force. "In one field office," he reminisced, "we had an executive who wasn't performing up to par. He was dissatisfied with his salary. But we felt we couldn't pay him more because he wasn't worth more. So we decided to see if the application of some gentle pressure would work.

"We brought a man into his area who was on the same level, but in another department. The two of them did different work, but they had to consult together frequently. The first man began to wonder if the new fellow was being considered as his replacement, though actually he wasn't; we needed him too badly in the job he was doing. Suddenly, he began shaping up and doing a first-class job, and our problem was solved."

Because he solved so many of these problems effectively, Wood was promoted to the presidency of Sarah Coventry in 1964. Recently, when an acquaintance asked him to identify the personal traits which he felt had contributed to his rise, he gave this reply:

"First, there's been the need for recognition—the desire to be recognized as someone in my own company, my own town, and in my country. I know I'm a good worker, and I like the satisfaction of having people recognize it. Second, I have to enjoy what I'm doing. At Sarah Coventry, the enjoyment stems partly from knowing that I'm helping to give lucrative work to thousands of people. And partly, it stems from the pure pleasures of being able to see broader horizons. Third, there's a need for security. No matter how high you go, you're always gambling—and the higher you go, the bigger the stakes. So you might say there's an increasing insecurity, and an increasing drive to be more secure. In a way, you create your own tensions, and you grow to meet them."

Wood admits that the tensions have occasionally caused him some loss of sleep. "The other night," he said, "I woke up around one o'clock in the morning and found myself thinking about the business. I went into the living room and picked up a newspaper. I started reading about de Gaulle, how he was trying to juggle between China and Russia and Germany and the United States. And I thought to myself, 'Boy, you think *you* have problems?' And then I felt better."

It was a sincere tribute from one skilled general to another.

BEHIND THE REX WOOD STORY

Rex Wood's success is due essentially to the symbiotic growth of a man and an organization. Coming into Sarah Coventry, Inc., on the ground floor, he was in a position to develop and build the organization from scratch. The compatibility between what he had to offer and what the organization needed accounts to a large degree for the successful expansion that followed. His two outstanding feats were the development of an approach to the housewife in the form of the "house party" or "fashion show" and the organization of an effective sales force. In addition, there are some other factors in Wood's success that can be isolated.

The Employee-Boss Gambit. Again and again, the careers of successful people reveal a learning period on which achievement was subsequently based. Rex Wood's first enterprise was his own gas station. But he learned this business by working for somebody else. This may not always be possible, of course, nor is it necessarily the best way to rise in business. There are some individuals who learn a business from the bottom up yet can never grow away from a bottom-of-the-ladder orientation. In other words, the views and concerns of the business as seen from the lower echelons, while of some value at the top, may prove limiting. Nevertheless it can be an inexpensive and practical education in certain types of business.

The "Business Deal." One hears a great deal about the ingenuity of the successful businessman. Rex Wood provides an interesting example of this in the way he arranged to extend credit to a customer who was actually a bad credit risk. At the heart of the "ingenious business deal" is often an idea that accomplishes a single objective. It makes it possible to take a desirable action and eliminate an obstacle or minimize a risk. Rex Wood was able to get a profitable but risky account and hedge against the chance of nonpayment by getting the trucker to sign over one of his income checks in a kind of informal factoring arrangement.

Dead-End Avoidance. In somewhat humorous fashion, Rex Wood makes clear his early aversion to jobs in which he was going nowhere. First with Sears, Roebuck, then as a salesman with a life insurance company, he became "fed up" and left the premises. The ability to know when to get out as well as when to get in is clearly an important factor in achievement.

Handling People. One of the outstanding elements in Rex Wood's biographical sketch is the detailed description of his ability to understand and motivate people. Call it human relations, leadership or what you will, the successful individual must learn how, in ex-President Eisenhower's words, to "get people to do what you want them to do because they want to do it." There are technical aspects to almost every business and every executive function. In the case of the sales function, the presentation of a product or an idea to a potential customer is one of the important tools of the trade. One of the secrets of Sarah Coventry's and Rex Wood's success was the creation of a system of presenting jewelry to the housewife. This was no mean feat. It represented a one-man penetration of a tough market. Wood showed his keen understanding of the feminine heart and mind and was able to convert this understanding into an effective selling technique.

William Russell Kelly—

14 THE MAN WITH
EIGHTY THOUSAND SECRETARIES

Say the phrase "service industry" to a stock-market analyst and even the most vinegary will break into a smile. Once a minor segment of the economy, the service industries began to burgeon after World War II and have continued growing until now they outstrip manufacturing in their rate of growth.

William Russell Kelly's story shows the birth and progress of one "service firm," highly specialized, but significant of the revolution in business methods taking place in the United States after World War II. The firm—Kelly Girl Service, Inc.—is also an interesting example of how an idea developed into a fifty-million-dollar-a-year enterprise. Today, Chairman of the Board of Kelly Girl Service, Inc., William Russell Kelly (he prefers to be called Russ or Russell) is a man who has made a full-time career out of part-time work. In less than two decades he has developed a small temporary-help service for local business and industry into a national organization with eighty thousand employees working out of 183 Kelly Girl Service offices from coast to coast, including San Juan, Anchorage, and Honolulu, and serving 100,000 customers.

*   *   *

Russell Kelly was born November 21, 1905, in the village of Koksilah, Vancouver Island, British Columbia, on a 150-acre virgin-land farm site adjacent to the Koksilah River. James Watson Kelly, his father and an internationally known developer of oil fields, was living in Canada at the time, in between a gold-mining venture in Alaska and further oil explorations. The elder Kelly was one of the oil pioneers at the turn of the century, and gained and lost fortunes in France, Spain, South America, Canada, and the United States.

To a certain extent, the James Kelly ménage—Russell was one of seven children—led a feast-or-famine existence. Russell recalls wryly that he was the only undergraduate at the University of Pittsburgh who went home to a hilltop castle in France for summer vacations. On the other hand, James Kelly's financial reserves left the family in straitened circumstances when he died a few years later. The willingness to try for major stakes evidently passed from father to son. For Russell Kelly gambled—and came perilously near to losing—when he went into business for himself.

As a teen-ager, Russell Kelly more closely resembled the prototype of the rich man's spoiled son than the man he was to become. After attending Riverside and Gulfcoast Military Academies, Russell matriculated at Vanderbilt University when he was only sixteen. Transferring to the University of Pittsburgh as a student of business administration, he began to neglect his studies: he was a good-looking young man, out to have a good time. At one point even the indulgent father elected to drive home a lesson the son was never to forget.

Chiding by the dean failed to rouse him to thoughts of a career or to pursuit of study, but a letter from his father, who was in France on an oil project for the French government, made a lasting impression on him. Wrote the senior Kelly:

> You must learn to make sufficient effort in anything you undertake. You certainly will have to earn a living and you have only two ways of doing it. One, by using your head—and you haven't yet educated or equipped it for the task—so there is no other way except working with your hands. . . . Make no mistake, you surely will have to work either with your hands or your head to support yourself and, if you don't realize it, I want to tell you emphatically that you haven't many more years to waste in the matter of education.
>
> If you work faithfully at hard physical work of some kind for a year, it will teach you the value of money, the value of an

education—which you are still young enough to get—and I hope change your views and habits so that you will not be satisfied to remain an educational hobo, as your dean calls you. . . . What you have been trying to do is not work, but find ways to escape it.

The father closed by reminding his son that he had tried his best to make him understand the importance of exerting himself; from there on it was up to Russell himself. And up to Russell it was indeed. When his father died in 1928, he left no appreciable estate. Kelly, who had had to leave college two years earlier for economic reasons, became an automobile salesman in an effort to support himself and help support the rest of the family. From then on, he was motivated by better-than-average effort in everything he did.

THE FALLOW YEARS

Selling automobiles was not the surest way of earning a living at that time, even for a determined young man. At the suggestion of Leland Frantz, a fraternity brother, Kelly went to Altoona, Pennsylvania, where Frantz introduced him to Edward M. Muldoon, Division Auditor and Assistant Treasurer of the Central Division of the Great Atlantic & Pacific Tea Company.

"My friend Leland Frantz came to me," Muldoon recalled recently, "with the story that a girl he was dating had a sister who was dating a very nice fellow—no business experience, but a fine chap who needed a chance to get started. I said I'd see what I could do."

Muldoon hired Kelly on condition that he spend extra hours on his own learning the business and learning auditing. This was in 1928, at a time when Muldoon's office was brand-new and beginning its first big use of business machines. Kelly saw the challenge as a wide open door to a future with unlimited possibilities for advancement. He worked nights and weekends to master the intricacies of auditing and other aspects of business as part of his job as staff accountant with the big food-store chain.

His early days with A. & P. were characterized by frequent moves, mostly lateral. During one year, he recalls, he worked under five different managers but his status remained unchanged. Recognition was still lacking. He became determined to move up in the executive hierarchy, and when promotions and raises didn't keep pace with his own plan for advancement, he made it known that he was dissatisfied. Between 1928 and 1938 his salary was increased from thirty-five to fifty-five dollars a week—perhaps a small measure of his value to the company in that depressed era, but a larger measure of the personal frustration of the ambitious young man seeking to show his mettle.

On his tenth anniversary with the company, the "young man in a hurry," was summoned to his supervisor's office. He was prepared to receive a promotion, a raise, or at least a note of recognition from management. What awaited him instead was a dismissal notice. The fact was that A. & P. had started a decentralization program which changed many jobs and eliminated others. Kelly had read about the transition in *Fortune* the previous week but really wasn't concerned about his job: the article described the pains management was taking to move round pegs from square holes into round holes, and he thought he was one of those round pegs. His career with A. & P. ended abruptly.

After the initial shock had passed, Russell Kelly appraised his accomplishments. He seemed further than ever from finding the proper outlet for his talents. What he didn't appreciate at the time was that the decade with A. & P. would eventually prove to be valuable in many ways. His job had sparked his natural inquisitiveness, giving him the desire to learn everything about any operation with which he was connected. Again, the fact that he had lost out by trying to move faster than the company was ready to let him, made him sensitive to the frustration of people associated with him. Through this awareness, he developed the ability to delegate authority; he encouraged initiative and the exercise of judgment among all employees. It was a quality that paid off when he started his own organization.

Unable to afford going into business for himself, he nevertheless wanted to be his own boss. He thought he saw the right opening in the widespread interest in training for jobs opening up in the expanding economy. Drawing on his sales and systems background with A. & P., he took a job selling home-study courses with the International Accountants' Society. Although he soon learned that demand for training was highly overrated, he managed to join the elite "Five-a-Week Club," whose members sold five or more courses a week. An associate recalls that "his graciousness and infinite patience with members of the opposite sex" were apparent. "He was never a ladies' man, but always a gentleman." These were characteristics that undoubtedly helped him sell more courses to females than anyone else on the sales force. Women liked and trusted him because he respected them and "appreciated their abilities as individuals." Little did anyone dream that someday this quality would shine—that he would eventually employ more than eighty thousand women.

CAREER TESTING

Ever impatient with the progress he was making as a salesman, he welcomed an opportunity to "get off the street" and put his knowledge of organization and systems to work with the Frontier Fuel Company of Buffalo. It did not take long for him to realize, however, that here too his pace was not synchronized with that of his employer. This time he decided not to wait for the company to find it out! He left in favor of a Buffalo trucking company—Pacific Transport.

Kelly had developed a keen interest in trucking during his association with A. & P. suppliers. He could look at a stack of orders or a warehouse full of produce and know exactly how many trucks, drivers, and helpers were needed to get the job done with a minimum amount of spoilage and downtime of men and equipment. His knowledge, plus his "get the job done" attitude, got him into trouble more than once in the trucking business. Once, when he noticed that a shipment was slow in getting off the shipping dock, for example, he loaded it himself—and got a severe reprimand for his trouble. It was a good lesson in the touchy union jurisdiction area. Kelly had his troubles with temperamental associates, too. Drivers were happy in their work as long as he assigned them to the shiny new "Whites," but there was dissension in the ranks when they were assigned to haul a load in one of the company's old "junks," as they were called. From problems such as these Kelly learned much about dealing with people.

While Russell Kelly was with Pacific Transport, an SOS went out from military procurement centers for specialists who could "get the job done" as civilian employees of the Army's Quartermaster Corps. Duplication, red tape, and inexperienced administrators were strangling efforts to build military establishments. The Army and Navy established joint centers to procure perishables, and called on the largest buying organizations in the world—including A. & P. —to help staff the centers. Russell Kelly learned of the need through friends still with A. & P., and joined a group of chain-store buyers and "fast paper men" in the Marketing Center in Chicago. At that time, it was customary for suppliers to wait sixty and ninety days for payment of their invoices, which caused long delays in deliveries. Kelly and others on the young team of auditors and expeditors gained a national reputation for getting the job done when they established a centralized system that assured payment within eight days of deliveries made anywhere in the country.

The drive and the ingenuity Kelly brought to his wartime job were obvious to those who worked with him. Said one of his associates of those years: "Russ pushed that food the way General Patton rolled his tanks." Gone was the youth the dean had called an educational hobo. In his place was a man of trained analytical and organizational skills and the determination to develop them still further. During those years, Kelly became a master of office procedures. He also gained a healthy respect for the new business machines developed to meet the manifold office needs of the wartime emergency. And as he looked ahead, he realized that the office needs in postwar America, as well, would be enormous.

Thus it was that he decided to put his knowledge to work for himself, after the war, by opening a general office service bureau in Detroit. This was the opportunity for which he had been working and training so hard: the chance to own and run his own business.

THE "KELLY GIRL" IN INFANCY

Russell Kelly chose Detroit as his headquarters because he believed the nation's automotive manufacturing center, sure to be bursting with activity to catch up with postwar demands, was ripe for the office services he planned to offer. His experience in cities in various parts of the country enabled him to analyze the potential in terms of the few office service organizations that already existed. On that basis, Detroit won over Chicago and other cities he considered. This familiarity with trucking, coupled with the fact that he had made many friends in that business, made Detroit an even more logical choice.

With his small accumulation of cash and war bonds—about ten thousand dollars in all—he got his Russell Kelly Office Service off the ground in the fall of 1946. He rented modest office space in the city and equipped it with the latest kinds of business machines. With a staff of only two girls, whom he hired and trained himself, he worked tirelessly to solicit jobs from Detroit firms—typing, duplicating, inventory calculating, addressing, almost any kind of office service needed.

Behind him were almost twenty years of hard-won knowledge of office practices and needs, of auditing and other business systems, of the potentialities and the limitations of office machines. Helpful, too, were lessons he had learned about dealing effectively with people as employees and as customers, about bringing his sharpened powers of careful analysis to bear on any and all problems, about curbing his impatience so that it did not defeat his primary purpose:

to build and expand a successful business. Prospects looked good for the Russell Kelly Office Service. His business flourished, and he made a host of friends as well as customers in Michigan. But while the view was bright, the future was clouding over.

THE BUSINESS OF A BUSINESS MAY CHANGE

In discussing the transformation of his small company into the major temporary-help organization it has become, Kelly emphasizes the changes that appeared on the horizon almost as soon as he opened his doors—and what they taught him about the *un*changing need for flexibility. As he recalls, "in the mid-forties, mature business organizations initiated unprecedented expansion plans while less seasoned companies were vying for top production quotas in the midst of giant-sized growing pains. Added to this were the thousands of products, nonexistent in prewar days, that were being turned out by companies never heard of before.

"Manufacturing facilities could not keep pace with pent-up consumer demand for refrigerators, stoves, radio sets, and automobiles, to name just a few products. And the logjam that was occurring backstage on the production lines was reflected in the front offices as well.

"It was from these offices, after all, that thousands of letters had to be written to confirm orders, to arrange for shipments, to make revisions—letters requiring skilled secretaries, stenographers, and typists. Bills, invoices, and payments required trained fingers at scores of tabulating, accounting, and bookkeeping machines. Moreover, new office equipment was being introduced at a rapid rate and it was being bought by companies anxious to serve their customers more efficiently. In short, more and more companies were buying the new equipment, hoping to perform the very same services our company was selling. Then came a startling realization. The equipment was outstanding, these customers said, but where in the world could they find the personnel trained to use these new fangled business machines? Lack of trained white-collar women office workers became one of industry's biggest bottlenecks."

Kelly changed his impending failure into a multimillion-dollar business by a major adjustment—he offered to send his personnel to those companies who needed their services. Important, too, he would assign his employees on an "as-needed" basis, freeing large and small companies from the burden of paying workers for periods in which they were nonproductive. This concept was, and still is, enthusiastically endorsed by management. From this basic idea—the willingness and ability to provide customers with experienced personnel during emergency situations—Kelly Girl Service, Inc., came into being.

A firm believer in the philosophy, "A satisfied customer is always a customer," Russell Kelly guaranteed at the very start the services of his temporary employees. For whatever reason, if a customer was dissatisfied, a bill was not rendered. This policy has prevailed since the company began operations in one small office in 1946.

THE KELLY GIRL'S GROWING PAINS

Russell Kelly's employees at the end of the first year numbered under one hundred. During the first two years, when the concept of temporary service was not completely known or accepted by the business community, there was no shortage of trained temporary personnel. As the idea caught on, however, and the phrase, "Get me a Kelly Girl," came into popular usage throughout the Detroit business community, Russell Kelly faced another crisis: how to find more and more experienced white collar workers. "With people our most important asset," he states, "I had two choices. I could lower the standards or make a concentrated effort to find the additional quality personnel needed."

Kelly chose the latter course, and exerted himself mightily to make it work, since the amount of money he could afford to put into want ads was extremely limited at the time. His first source of qualified referrals, as it had been from the beginning, was his own employees: they acted voluntarily as person-to-person recruiting agents among their friends and acquaintances.

Kelly himself talked to women's organizations—to the PTA—

to civic groups—to any group he thought might furnish even one potential worker of the caliber he sought. He discovered that many women whose children were in school and who had had previous office experience, were interested in part-time employment because their home schedules did not make full-time jobs feasible. He also assiduously cultivated the market of trained older women, who often faced employer prejudice when they wanted to change jobs or re-enter the business world.

A systematic search began for trained white-collar women, of all ages. It extended into suburban areas—into supermarkets, even into laundromats and other stores. With a trailer remodeled into an office, temporary workers were recruited and tested. Fringe benefits such as car pools to transport new employees from the suburbs, and the reputation which Kelly Girl Service, Inc., had already won, contributed greatly to the success of these recruitment drives.

All these efforts bore fruit, but even so, Kelly sometimes found that his supply of temporary office workers could not keep up with the demand. There were many times, in fact, when he had to send his own much-needed secretary to fill an emergency need in the offices of a customer.

Both business and personal standards played, as they still do, a part in Russell Kelly's selection system. In addition to a high degree of skill, Kelly consciously looked for the qualities which many people now accept as "typical" of Kelly Girls: the ability to adapt to changing business environments and sometimes pressured offices, willingness to work at maximum efficiency on whatever task was at hand, whether it was routine typewriting or a complex machine operation. Neat grooming and a wholesome personality were equally essential.

THE KELLY GIRL GROWS UP

The Kelly Girl organization is one in which nepotism is practiced judiciously, and seems to work. A number of friends, associates, and family members have earned important positions in the company. There is, for example, Russell's brother, Richard, whom he persuaded to join him as executive vice-president during the 1950s. A graduate of the University of North Carolina, Richard H. Kelly brought to the company years of business experience gained on the accounting staff of A. & P.—the same company, of course, that had once fired his older brother.

With Richard's help, things boomed faster than ever. Russell Kelly's sales during his first full year of operation had totaled $92,000. By 1954 they had climbed to $1,500,000, by far the bulk of them made in the temporary-help field. "If we can do this in Detroit," the brothers reasoned, "why not in other cities?"

In 1955 they began a tentative program of expansion, opening offices in several other large metropolitan areas across the country. How well the test worked is illustrated by the fact that a decade later Kelly Girl Service, Inc., had branch offices in 183 cities. Richard became president in 1965 and Russell moved up to board chairman.

Another key man is Terence E. Adderley, Russell's stepson, who is now executive vice-president of the company. Adderley is a graduate of the University of Michigan and received his M.B.A. in finance from the university's School of Business in 1956. He joined the organization after a grounding in finance with a major oil company.

When Kelly had his first visions of expansion, he resolved to have sufficient able executives—and a clear division of responsibilities. Not only did his ability to delegate help his people and his company grow; it also made it possible for him to stay closely associated with a highly detailed business without getting mired in detail himself.

Long before he considered expanding from a local service to a national service, he built an executive cadre capable of running a business several times its size. Kelly had a sharp eye for a likely comer. Early in his new venture he met Tom K. Graham, a salesman who stopped in to sell him office equipment. Kelly bought, and made a mental note that he liked the way the young man handled himself. He made a similar notation on Burton Schuster and John Brandt—and when the way seemed clear, he brought all three into the organization *on the same day*. Each is still with the organization. Each is an officer.

THE KELLY GIRL'S SECRET

There are currently some fifteen million persons in U.S. business who work on a temporary or part-time basis. This is in contrast to the ten million temporary workers in 1955. By 1970, temporary personnel are expected to number seventeen million. Richard Kelly attributes the rise to the new concentration on controlling costs. "In management's search for better productivity," he notes, "the spotlight has been turned on heavy 'waiting-in-line' costs: typists waiting for something to type, machines waiting for something to make, warehouses waiting for something to house. Leasing equipment, renting space, and purchasing temporary services are answers management has found to reduce this high cost of unproductive time."

From management's viewpoint, employing a temporary-help service means savings in time and money because management pays only for the actual hours worked. Over the years, employers have also discovered the advantage of being able to call for temporary personnel to fill in during vacation and illness periods as well as during production and conversion periods without becoming involved in recruiting, termination, and withholding and other taxes. Kelly Girl Service, Inc., as the employer, assumes responsibility for all payroll deductions.

When a Detroit automotive manufacturer bought a group insurance plan, the insurance company had to type 330,000 policy certificates. How could any insurance company afford to draw upon hundreds of its own personnel to complete the job within the required period? Instead, an order was put through the local Kelly Girl office for some hundred top-flight typists, who completed the mammoth assignment in fifteen days. Fringe benefits and overtime costs were eliminated and the normal work flow continued without interruption.

Another manufacturer has a standard order for 150 Kelly Girls for one weekend each month to map out parts scheduling. Overtime costs of seventy-five thousand dollars a year are saved.

According to Executive Vice-President Adderley, "In early 1962 we were a company organized to distribute one product—temporary white-collar services. In order to grow, we had to expand." The services of men predominate in two new divisions: Kelly Technical Services and Labor-Aides. Through the former, all types of technical personnel are available for limited or extensive assignments. They are mainly men who, because of age, have been forced to retire from permanent employment, or graduate students involved in fellowships or advanced educational programs, or professionals who prefer the mobility permitted by temporary assignments. In contrast, the Labor-Aides Division permits business and government to contract for unskilled and semiskilled maintenance service, materials handling, and light productive work, all on a temporary basis.

As a recent complement to the Kelly Girl Division, the company has initiated a bank teller training program. This is a new concept in which temporary bank tellers are screened, tested, trained, and bonded by Kelly Girl Service, Inc., for banking institutions throughout the country. Up until now, banks have conducted their own training programs, convinced that their own special training requirements could not be accomplished effectively and economically by an outside organization. However, the Kelly bank teller training program has met every bank standard. Through it, potential candidates for Kelly bank teller assignments are recruited, screened, tested, and sent to the company's schools that have been set up in major cities. Since the program went into operation in January, 1965, banks from New York to Little Rock, Arkansas, to Los Angeles have accepted it. Training programs are currently under way or have been completed in scores of other cities across the nation. Expansion plans are expected eventually to reach out to the international market.

BEHIND THE WILLIAM RUSSELL KELLY STORY

Kelly's rise is a prime example of a success built around a single idea. It has been pointed out that an idea, although originating in the abstract realm of the mind, often becomes a solid platform for concrete activity. In short, an idea is actually a plan for action. The development of the Kelly Girl Service shows how an idea came into being, survived unexpected obstacles, and finally emerged clear and incisive—a potent blueprint for a business breakthrough. If an idea such as Kelly's is to succeed, however, two developments must take place:

First, the idea itself must be made clear and explicit. The trouble with many business ideas is that they remain mere glimmerings, half-baked products that have neither the virtues of dough nor of bread. The office services concept, as Kelly's biography shows, did not spring full-grown into the world; it emerged as a short-term expedient. But once the concept began functioning, Kelly clarified it, along with a few other entrepreneurs in the field, and immediately realized its potential.

The second phase begins once the basic concept has been refined to the point where it can serve as a plan of action. This is the exploitation phase. There is considerable argument as to which of the two aspects of the idea is the more important. Some people say, "Ideas are cheap—it's knowing how to use them that counts." Others feel that the idea is the thing. If it is original, clear, and practical, implementation is a simple, almost mechanical development. In the Russell Kelly story, we see both the development of the concept and the company he built to apply it.

Need Spotting. Behind Russell Kelly's successful exploitation of the temporary-help idea was the recognition of a need. Even while he was still in the Army, he came to realize the tremendous office services needs of postwar America. Some authorities have constructed an interesting success formulation out of the identification of unsatisfied needs on the part of the public, the business community, and so on. Stated in a sentence, the formula runs: find a need and develop a profitable way of satisfying it. There's no question that part of the success scored by Kelly's firm grew from his awareness of the growing importance of clerical operations on the business scene.

We all have some ability to anticipate future events. Many of us can look at the storm clouds and predict rain. A smaller percentage of us can read the news and predict the gyrations of the stock market. A small but potent minority can analyze one situation and apply the results of the analysis to a parallel field, developing as a result a kind of model of the shape of events to come. This special kind of business clairvoyance is a common stock in trade for the successful man. It is not a mystic tool but in all cases the result of observation, comprehension, and the ability to project from present facts into the future. Russell Kelly, once he had been exposed to clerical procedures on the vast scale required by wartime Army operations, observed and understood the white-collar revolution business would be undergoing when the war was over. He projected this situation in terms of postwar America resuming its business growth. This foresight put him in the office services business. Kelly Girl Service was a natural development from this point.

Snowballing. Several examples of this success factor have already been described—in the cases of Owen K. Murphy, Joseph Katz, and so on. Kelly's version of snowballing took place early in the development of the Kelly Girl Service organization. He had started with the common categories—typists, stenographers, file clerks. He spread the availability of this type of help—from 1 to 183 locations. In addition, somewhere along the way he began getting demands for different categories, more specialized types of help. He made the decision to expand his operations by offering these specialized services to his clients.

Apprenticeship. Like many successful individuals, Kelly's rise was preceded by a period of intensive learning. In his case, Kelly's wartime experience as a management analyst for the Army's Quartermaster Corps gave him the background and training in office procedures that made the development of Kelly Girl Service possible. So much for the "wasted years" label too often pinned to an individual's army training or service.

Ally Selection. Making an organization grow is often a direct function of the quality and skills of the people that are brought in to man it. Russell Kelly used the rather unusual approach of bringing into the organization friends and relatives. In his case, nepotism was no detriment because, in every case, the men brought in apparently were of high caliber.

Ideas for Tomorrow. One of the important aspects of the Kelly story is that it provides a model for tomorrow's services. Everything that grows changes. And certainly the business world under the hammer strokes of automation, computerization, new products and materials, will be very different tomorrow from what it is today. Accordingly, needs for new services will arise. In that world of tomorrow, Russell Kelly's ingenuity may very well be duplicated by another individual with the same ability to anticipate a need and satisfy it.

15 { Solomon Dutka–
PROFITS FROM PROPHECY

From the fourteenth floor of One Park Avenue, New York City, Solomon Dutka directs the domestic and international activities of Audits & Surveys, Inc., the company which he founded in a one-room office in 1953. Today, his firm does an annual volume approaching ten million dollars. It is the second largest marketing research organization in the country, employs a headquarters staff of four hundred, an available field force of five thousand interviewers and auditors, and serves many of the nation's largest corporations, including A.T. & T., DuPont, General Electric, General Foods, General Motors, and Procter & Gamble. Here is the story of a man who scored a breakthrough in an unusual type of business.

* * *

Entering Solomon Dutka's office through a maze of hallways, the subdued hum of electronic data processing in the background, a visitor finds Dutka working in his shirt-sleeves at a massive, leather-topped desk. Behind him are rows of well-thumbed books and folders of notes, to the side, a built-in blackboard for chalk-talk meetings. The setting reminds one more of a student's room than a corporation president's bailiwick. But this is the clearest clue to Sol Dutka's character; he has never stopped being a student.

The first spurs to success for Sol came very early in life. His parents, both European immigrants, placed great stress on the success of their sons. "But earning a lot of money was not their criterion—it was education," Sol remembers.

The senior Dutkas had little formal education but became

thoroughly involved in the schoolwork of their two sons. Sol's father ran a small tailor shop and his mother worked in the needle trades. "We always had food on the table so I don't think you can classify us as poverty-stricken; I remember that my first pair of long pants was a hand-me-down from my older brother, however, and I didn't get those until my senior year in high school."

The family emphasis on education began to pay off early in Sol's life. He entered the College of the City of New York when he was fifteen years old after having been skipped several grades in the public school system because of his excellent scholastic record.

"ALWAYS THERE WAS SCHOOL WORK"

"My inclination had always been toward the sciences. Between my brother and teachers such as John Firestone, the brilliant statistics professor I studied under at CCNY, I was gradually influenced toward statistics."

During his college years, Sol worked as an usher in a movie theater nights and over the weekends. During the summers, he held jobs in a bakery, caddied at a golf course, and worked as an assistant to a traveling salesman, setting up displays. But always there was the schoolwork. While his dominant interest was in science, Sol also was attracted to literature and philosophy. A source of pride from his undergraduate days is his translation, in meter, of Goethe's *Faust,* Part One, from the original German into English.

"In 1942, the big trend among college students was to go into government work—because of the security civil service offered. And I joined the bandwagon. The summer between my junior and senior years at CCNY, I worked for the New York State Insurance Fund where I helped process workman's compensation applications." This stint provided some valuable experiences for Sol. With his school background in statistics, he was able to work out a multiple correlation technique for estimating the number and types of claims to be processed. This technique saved the office days of work. Dutka thinks it may still be in use. But his government career came to a quick end.

"One day during a lull," he relates, "the supervisor came by my desk and saw me looking into a statistics book. He told me to put it away and look busy, even if I had to string paper clips. This incident marked the end of my desire for a government career."

In his senior year at CCNY, Sol was taken on by the War Research Division of Columbia University as a "machine jockey." "These were the pre-computer days, and 'automation' meant a desk-top calculator. With my courses in statistics, I had used almost every type of calculator in existence, from the old crank models to the new electric ones. Maybe this is why they asked me to join them at Columbia—I knew how to work all the machines."

In 1943, at the age of nineteen, Sol graduated from CCNY and was inducted into the Army. After the usual basic training, Sol was assigned to an infantry battalion, but he never stopped studying. "The back pocket of the fatigue uniform the Army used in those days was precisely the right size for carrying a paperbound book," says Sol, "and mine was never flat."

CARTOGRAPHER AND SOFTBALL CAPTAIN

To this day Sol contends that no knowledge is ever wasted; to prove his point, he tells about his infantry days at Fort Hood. "It was during the Sicilian campaign and our headquarters wanted three-dimensional maps of that area in a hurry. I had taken a course in cartography in school—a marginal subject for a statistician. But I knew the technique of making three-dimensional maps based on two-dimensional, printed maps. We were able to supply headquarters with sand table maps of Sicily without waiting for specially trained technicians to be brought in." This episode, Sol recalls, didn't hurt his prestige at headquarters. But he remembers that he derived more personal pleasure from being named captain of his unit's softball team, which won the battalion championship.

Sol was then transferred to the Army Specialized Training Program at the University of Illinois, where he took a course in advanced civil engineering. "I had no engineering background so I really had to apply myself to these courses. However, the math connected with the subject was very easy for me. My first taste of 'profit from knowledge' came from my standing offer to the men in my barracks to do their math homework. My fee per assignment was one hamburger and a Coke. I put on a great deal of weight in those days."

NEW ASSIGNMENT—THE MANHATTAN PROJECT

At the end of the engineering course at Illinois, some six men, Sol among them, were shipped out at night . . . destination unknown. They wound up at Oak Ridge, Tennessee, where Sol was put to work developing wage-scale systems and job classifications for the Manhattan Project. He also developed statistical techniques for measuring radiation exposure, based on blood count and other physical data. As the scientific work gained momentum, he was transferred to the laboratory, where he performed sequential analyses of samplings of uranium hexafluoride.

After Oak Ridge he was sent to a theoretical research center at Union Carbide where he had an opportunity to read and study the current secret papers on nuclear physics connected with the project. Then he was transferred to Columbia University, where he plunged deeper into the Manhattan Project's top-secret work that led to the development of the first atomic bomb. It was during this period that he married.

"These are what I would call the most satisfying and exciting years of my life," Sol says. "The work I was doing was secret and very urgent." As a sergeant, he was assigned to a physics lab where he devoted his time to developing methods for counting alpha particles. By the end of his stay there, he was in charge of that laboratory. "We would very often work around the clock, catching catnaps on a cot in the office. When the first atomic bomb was set off at Alamogordo, New Mexico, it was our job to test samples of fused sand from the blast site. We had to send out an urgent call to retrieve all samples of the fused sand that were picked up as souvenirs. We found they were still highly radioactive."

At the end of his work at Columbia, Sol Dutka, age twenty-one, was cited by the Secretary of War for his contribution to the atomic research program. "Those days demanded creativity. They were urgent and tremendously exciting. And they taught me a valuable lesson. With a great deal at stake, individual initiative was stressed at all times. We were given the ball and told to run with it. And we did."

Sol relates that it was during those Army years that he first realized the importance of effective personal communications. "I was no longer in the somewhat cloistered academic world of the statistician where one could talk in technical terms and be understood. I met many diverse people, trained in many diverse disciplines, and I had to discover the method of effective communications so we could work together most productively. I also learned the value of diplomacy in such relations. The Navy at that time was giving a commission to its scientific personnel. Many such officers were working in the laboratory for which I was responsible as a sergeant. A noncom walks a thin line when he has to bawl out an officer and still maintain military courtesy."

At the end of the war, he was faced with the decision of making his career either in atomic energy research or in statistics. The Army wanted him at Bikini as an observer and several private companies engaged in atomic research offered him staff posts. "I chose civilian work in statistics because, I guess, I just didn't want to go to Bikini. I wanted to spend a little time with my wife. Also, I think I was tired of making bombs."

GOLD MINE BETWEEN COVERS

Sol's first job in civilian life was as a college statistics instructor. He taught the intersession course in statistics at Columbia Graduate

School and then taught a summer term at his alma mater, CCNY. "Despite the war and the responsibility thrust on me during the Manhattan Project, I was still a young man—still trying to decide the course of my future. During the six-week course I taught at Columbia, I was allowed to use the office of the head of the department. This office was lined from floor to ceiling with books on statistics and I set myself the task of systematically going through every book to study areas in statistics that were new to me. This gave me a great sense of accomplishment and I felt a growing pride in my ability as a statistician. This was perhaps where and when I achieved the confidence to seek a career in this field."

In the next three years, Sol taught at CCNY. In 1947, he co-authored a paper on statistical analysis of some psychological sampling. It was published in the *Journal of Applied Psychology*. This article brought him to the attention of Dr. Raymond Franzen, a leading business statistician who acted as a consultant to many of the marketing research firms of that day.

Sol, forever the student, prevailed on Dr. Franzen to let him work in his office . . . for no pay. "I remember that my mother didn't understand. She was shocked at the idea of so much work for no salary. But I had lived my life up to that point in the world of theoretical statistics. Now I wanted to learn applied statistics. Looking back, those jobs I did for nothing—including some consulting work I did while teaching—have been the ones that paid off most handsomely in the long run." Dr. Franzen, by the way, is now a consultant to Sol's firm.

Among Dr. Franzen's clients was the Elmo Roper organization. For years Sol had resisted the thought of leaving teaching to go into business. But at that time, staff instructors at CCNY without tenure were treated rather shabbily, he felt. "We sometimes wouldn't know until a few days before the term began whether or not we had a job," Sol remembers. Elmo Roper was looking around for a sampling statistician. Franzen recommended Sol. Sol admitted that he knew little about the then relatively new area of survey sampling, but in the summer of 1948 he took the job. "Elmo and I hit it off fine from the beginning. We argued. I told him that if I didn't like the job I would quit by the end of summer. He said, 'I may kick you out before then.'"

THE TRANSITION STARTS

When Sol joined Roper's staff, he entered upon a new phase of his life: the gradual change from statistician to businessman.

Elmo Roper and Sol Dutka worked together very well. "Elmo is one of the finest people I have ever met. In addition to being a brilliant marketing researcher, he is an astute businessman. He possessed all of the qualities which the successful head of a research business should have. Today, consciously or unconsciously, I don't know which, I find myself trying to do many of the things Elmo did and taking the same approach to a problem as he did.

"These early years in business taught me that a man shouldn't be any different during business hours than he is in his private life and that a business can be run successfully without compromising personal convictions. Elmo, for instance, is a nice guy twenty-four hours a day. He was a good boss to work with, and to learn from. Everyone who worked for him admired and respected him."

Sol stresses that one of the most important things he learned then was that a boss must take the initiative. He must lead and lead strongly if the organization is to succeed. "Memos and directives are fine and necessary but a boss must lead by example. And he must be the type of person that encourages people to follow that example."

With the Roper organization, Sol got his first depth experience in the application and the business of statistics. His education was furthered a few years later when he took over the post of chief statistician at Dun & Bradstreet. Again Sol found himself in an area where he had to become a student. Dun & Bradstreet was the place where he learned retail establishment sampling. "This was also my first heavy experience in writing and making proposals and in meeting clients. Again I must hark back to the importance of personal communication in business. Communication is the crux of client relations. At D. & B. I had to learn that the client was not some kind of enemy but a man who needs and is asking for help. My experience there taught me to see the problem from the client's viewpoint as well as my own. Once his frame of reference is understood, then communication becomes easier."

It was at Dun & Bradstreet that some of the ideas that were to underlie the formation of Audits & Surveys began to take shape. One of D. & B.'s market research clients was Mars Inc., the candy manufacturer. A representative of Mars told Sol that they were having a difficult time in gathering complete and meaningful marketing data on retail sales of their candy products. Mars subscribed to retail audits of food and drug outlets—the only ones available at that time—but they sold much more candy than the audits indicated and they wanted to know where and how much. Mars wanted to cover all the retail outlets which carried its products.

Sol applied himself to the solution of the problem. He started by defining the study not by types of stores but in terms of total retail population. This concept, plus the practical mechanics of the project which Sol worked out, became a new service of D. & B. "Once the preliminary work was started, the people who were working it out (myself, two assistants, and a secretary) were treated like lepers. Almost everyone ignored us, I suppose, because they wanted to stand clear if we fell on our faces. Then the first data began to come in and they checked out perfectly. Suddenly, we had partners."

The new service began to gather momentum. Several manufacturers exposed to the idea liked it and contracts were signed. At that point, Arthur D. Whiteside, then D. & B.'s president, stepped in and reviewed the entire program. He invited the team that worked on the project plus several executives from the division out to dinner at a private club. "I remember that he congratulated us roundly and then dropped the bombshell. The service was canceled. He said that he felt it was not consistent with the firm's operations and tradition. Whatever the factors affecting his decision were, I will probably never know. I just sat there stunned, watching several months' work go down the drain."

However, the effort was not wasted. Sol's pioneering work in developing a new technique for measuring the total retail market of a product and the extent of its distribution is used today as the core of Audits & Surveys' unique national total-market audit.

Sol left Dun & Bradstreet to help organize and direct the Medimetric Institute, Inc., a firm devoted to marketing research in the medical and pharmaceutical fields. He wanted to do more than his job at D. & B. allowed him. Medimetric was an exciting challenge. As chief executive officer of the firm, Sol had his first experience with complete control of the reins of a business.

BOOST FROM A FRIEND

In 1953, he relates that he was approached with an offer of a partnership in an existing marketing research organization. Sol turned to his friend and business mentor Elmo Roper for advice. "Elmo sat and listened to the various aspects of the partnership which I was offered. Then he turned and said, 'That's very interesting. How about going into business for yourself?'"

Roper, Sol recalls, had a history of helping young men get started in business. A number of firms owe their birth to the impetus supplied in some degree by Elmo Roper. "Elmo believes in people. He often said, in effect, that if he finds a guy with a vision and the capacity for work, he will invest." And that is just what he did with Sol. In 1953, Audits & Surveys was founded. Sol borrowed money on his own to get it going and Roper put money into the business as an investment. "Every cent was paid back and, I am happy to say, Elmo realized a nice profit on his investment." Today, Elmo Roper is a member of the board of directors of Audits & Surveys.

DESIGN OF AN ENTERPRISE

The basic concept of Audits & Surveys Services is indicated by
its name. "The marketing research industry was evolving into a
field of specialists. Auditors, the count-and-tally people, walked one
side of the street. Survey specialists, those who measured attitudes,
walked the other side. For the most part, research firms stayed
on either one side or the other."

Sol believed that a need existed for a complete research service
which could bridge this gap and meet all of a client's requirements,
be they auditing, product concept testing, test marketing, media
analysis, consumer surveys, etc. Hence, from its inception Audits &
Surveys has deliberately traveled both sides of the street.

"The company was born in a highly competitive atmosphere. But
this worked in our favor. Management was gaining a growing awareness of the value of marketing research. The market for business
data was ready for sophisticated innovation. The unique set of services which Audits & Surveys developed was well received and we
were launched. Besides, we did not have to cope with so many of
the trail-blazing problems which confronted the earlier marketing
research organizations. The path through the woods was already
there, so to speak. All we had to do was pave it."

Among the innovations initiated by Audits & Surveys is Sol's
basic approach to problem solving. "We try to remain oriented to
a client's problem, not to an existing technique. It had been common practice in the industry for a client's problem to be applied
to a set of existing services, whether it fit or not. Our approach
always has been to develop a technique to answer the problem,
not twist the problem to fit an existing technique."

Hanging up a shingle and printing stationery is not the point at
which success is achieved, however. "We started in a cramped
one-room office, myself and a secretary, and we built from there,"
Sol says. He recalls that six months later he brought in his first
associate. To allow privacy during client meetings, Sol hit upon

the idea of a movable partition. This enabled either man to receive a visitor in a fair-sized "private" office while the other two members of the firm labored on the other side of the partition, cramped for space.

"One of our first major problems was getting an effective field force to collect the data we needed to service our clients adequately. We initially solved the problem by hiring the Roper field force. We paid the full fee and received no special treatment. Very soon, as our demands on the Roper field organization grew heavier, conflicts arose in scheduling. It was at this point that we decided to organize our own field staff."

Very early in the company's life, Sol realized that he had to stop trying to wear two hats: he had to choose between the role of the statistician and that of the businessman. "Obviously the measure of a business' success is profit. This is the only true measure of success unless you are running a philanthrophic enterprise, which Audits & Surveys is not. In the beginning, however, we tended to be satisfied with our efforts as long as the data we were supplying our clients were good, pertinent, and useful. The clients were happy with our service and so were we . . . until we looked at the P. and L. statement. We just were not making a profit on the work we did."

Sol knew it was increasingly imperative that he make the transition to businessman if the company was to become a success. "At the firm's beginning I was 90 per cent statistician and 10 per cent businessman, but this had to change. It was a very frightening transition. There is a certain security inherent in science. You deal with exact knowledge and values, progressing to a logical conclusion. As a businessman, you are more insecure. The information you work with is less exact and it often deals with vague probabilities instead of certainties. I had to turn away from the security of statistics and accept the responsibilities of running a business with all its diverse and often diffuse problems. But I still keep my finger in the pie. Today, you could say I'm 80 per cent businessman and 20 per cent statistician."

TO FIND THE NEEDLE—DIMINISH THE HAYSTACK

Ironically, he found many of the answers he needed to operate a business successfully in the discipline he had learned as a statistician. "Finding data to answer a problem is very much like looking for a needle in a haystack. The needle is hard to find because there is so much hay. If the needle, or business goal, is not found readily, some people have the tendency to collect more hay on the theory that 'there must be a needle in there someplace.' A good statistician takes the opposite tack. Cut down the hay—or extraneous data— define the needle precisely, and the needle becomes easier to find. We tightened our business operation, using the same approach. We cut out all the profit-wasting extras and set goals for our research projects so that the object could be accomplished with a minimum of extra time and effort.

"It was, in a way, fortunate that we started this way. I firmly believe that if I had thought in terms of profit alone at the beginning, the company would not have succeeded. Because we thought primarily in terms of service, the business was initially successful. It endured because we managed to make it profitable."

Beginning with his first job at Roper, each experience brought him new insights into the workings of a business enterprise. The supreme importance of salesmanship and client relations, for instance, was impressed on Sol during his days at D. & B. While he was developing the total-market audit concept, he often went out with the salesmen of the new service in order to field any technical questions that might arise.

"Most of the time I would sit quietly at the meetings and let the professional salesmen make the presentation. However, good salesmanship is not a passive art. New ideas, I learned, are not absorbed by osmosis. They have to be logically and forcefully presented in the context of the client's needs. I realized this the day we were making a presentation to Johnson & Johnson. Robert Johnson, then executive vice-president of the company, was sitting in on the meeting. Unfortunately, some of the critical points in the service were not being presented clearly and he was getting the wrong slant on it. As a result, he was asking some very pointed questions based on an incorrect premise. I decided then and there that I had better get up and open my mouth. The questions he raised were quickly covered to his satisfaction and the misunderstandings were clarified. We got the contract that day.

"In addition to the insight I gained here into the art of salesmanship, I noticed something which I was to experience again and again in later years. It is that top executives are open-minded and receptive to new ideas when they are presented logically and forthrightly. With very few exceptions, they are not afraid of losing face by changing their minds."

Sol believes that complete understanding between himself and the client is absolutely essential before a job begins. This is the keystone of any service business. After entering into a contract with a client, Sol feels his firm becomes, to a degree, that client's partner, sharing many of the burdens of the problems it has been asked to solve. "Although we immerse ourselves in these problems, we try never to lose the objectivity which is so necessary to coming up with effective solutions." This attitude is one of the keys to the success of the operation, he says.

LOOKING BACKWARD

The three positions which Sol held in the business world before establishing his own company are likened by him to the three legs of a tripod which support him today.

"If a person must grow, it is essential that he never lose the ability to learn. A successful person, in my estimation, is forever a student. For instance, in my journey from statistician to businessman, I learned from the good and the bad examples of other people, and I learned from the situations forced on me by circumstance. From Roper, I observed many of the personal qualities necessary for success; from Dun & Bradstreet, I learned many of the practical aspects of client contact and the techniques of making meaningful proposals; and from Medimetrics, I achieved good basic experience in the day-to-day operation of a business organization. And it was when I formed Audits & Surveys that I received the impetus to draw on all this experience and finally make the transition away from science and into business."

The transition was a difficult one for Sol to make and he would be the last person to minimize the difficulties. But he relates that there was one point at which he knew he had turned the corner successfully: "We were making a proposal to DuPont on our audit services. I delivered the sales presentation, which was well received. Afterward, one of the DuPont executives came to me and said that they were probably going to buy the service but first he wanted to talk to one of our technical experts. At first, I resented the inference. After all, I was the one who developed and set up the entire service. However, it showed me that I was the president of the company and accepted as such . . . and not solely a statistician."

Another lesson which Sol says that he had to learn the hard way was that the company president is at one time the most powerful and the weakest person in the organization. "As president, you must weigh each word and remember always that when the president sneezes, it may be a thunderclap heard throughout the company. For instance, several years ago, a client called me and said that they were having a meeting the next day and needed such-and-such information. Could we get it for them? I had my own ideas on how the problem should be approached and where the information was available. However, I decided to approach the problem in the 'best' executive manner. I called in several people concerned with the problem, asked them to work it out, and told them the deadline was the next day. I reasoned they would be happier and more efficient working it out themselves rather than just following my instructions. A few hours later, my controller called me and asked if I had authorized eight thousand dollars to strip the computer of what it was working on and program a problem which was needed for the next day. Sometimes the price of experience is high indeed."

CLIMATE FOR INNOVATION

Even today Sol claims that he never stops learning. His company, as large as it is, maintains an atmosphere in which "disagreement" flourishes. "Without disagreement, there can be no climate for innovation. This company was started with an innovative idea and I don't want that tradition to stop. This is why I never hire people in my own image. A staff of four hundred people cast in the mold of Sol Dutka would not lend itself to invention . . . but four hundred diverse individuals do stimulate each other and produce a better product for us to offer."

The hiring policy of Audits & Surveys reflects this approach. "We don't hire by defining an executive hole and then finding a peg to fit into it. It is our philosophy to build the job around the capabilities of the individual—we fit the structure to the person, not vice versa."

As the company grew it became necessary to delegate much of the hiring responsibility. Of course, Sol still insists on personally interviewing all candidates for executive posts. "Naturally, we seek to employ people to compensate for our weaknesses. But we also have learned the value of strengthening our strength. A good example is when we got Les Frankel to join us. One of the best statisticians in the business, Les enhanced our already fine reputation for statistical excellence."

Sol runs his company on a first-name basis. "I'm never remote from the people who work with me." He prides himself on the fact that he never loses his temper even when provoked. "You can't run a company based on fear. I don't want my staff wasting their energy on trivialities, hesitating, and bumbling, trying to guess whether

or not something will please me. I never liked being in that position
and I won't impose it on others."

A very important aspect of Sol's approach to the marketing research business is the concept of "professionalism." "I refer to this
company as a 'professional service business.'" All three words in
that phrase are important. Maintaining professional standards gives
people a pride in their work; service is the nature of our business,
and we must never forget it; and it is a business, run in a business-
like manner to show a profit."

BEHIND THE SOLOMON DUTKA STORY

A recent issue of *Personnel* featured an article, "The Troublesome Transition from Scientist to Manager." Its authors, Professor Robert E. Bailey of Purdue University and Barry T. Jensen, Administrator of Manager Development at Atomics International, point out that there are several reasons for the difficulty of making a transition from technical man to executive:

- The specialist must move away from the area of his competence to one in which he's had comparatively little training.
- The average professional exercises direct control over his work. As a manager, he must work through others. He is, therefore, presented with an entirely unfamiliar set of problems—the problems relating to directing and motivating people.
- For the individual who has had a real feeling for his professional calling, its abandonment for the new world of management sometimes suggests, "I have sold my birthright for a mess of pottage."
- The complexities of management resemble an art rather than a science. For the average scientist or engineer accustomed to working with natural laws, the vagueness of many areas of management is a trying departure.

Solomon Dutka, however, successfully made the change from statistician to successful entrepreneur. Dutka was fortunate in meeting, at a critical point in his career, a man who facilitated the transition. When Dutka met Elmo Roper, Dutka found someone whom he admired, and who had made a similar transition himself —from market researcher to businessman. Somewhere along the road, an executive must develop skill in leading people. Solomon Dutka learned a great deal by observing Roper at work. For example, he learned that a leader must take the initiative, lead by example, and at the same time encourage his subordinates to follow.

As is true of many successful businessmen, Dutka gained clear and practical insights into business operations by working in a job that exposed him to new knowledge and experiences. It was at Dun & Bradstreet that he learned about client relations and gained the experience that made it possible for him to attract and serve client companies when he started his own firm.

Idea Application. There are many instances of ideas that fall flat in one application and succeed gloriously in another. It's possible that the man who invented the wheel was considered a failure, or at most given credit for devising a child's plaything. It was not until a fellow inventor showed up later with the axle that the idea of the wheel really paid off. In the same way, the new service Dutka developed for Dun & Bradstreet was first rejected by management as being inconsistent with the firm's operations. Later on, Sol developed his own application of it, and his original idea paid off as a successful Audits & Surveys' market technique. In short, one man's poison can be another man's meat.

Advice Selection. Says a character in a modern novel, "Advice-givers surround one like vultures. . . ." Ambitious, able young men are especially prone to be targets of advice; they attract all kinds of well-meaning suggestions from their admiring friends, family, and acquaintances. The trick the successful person learns, however, is to take the right kind of advice and to let the wrong kind go. At one critical point in his career, Dutka had to decide whether or not he should go into partnership with another individual. His friend and mentor Elmo Roper suggested: "How about going into business for yourself?"

Why not, indeed? As far as Dutka was concerned, the answer was clear-cut. He had great admiration and respect for Roper. The fact that Roper was willing to put money into the business was further assurance that the advice had been carefully thought out in advance.

A Philosophy of Business. Like Russell Kelly, Sol Dutka developed a basic business philosophy that gave his company constructive approach to its customers and its markets. In his own words, "Our approach has been to develop a technique to answer the problem, not to twist the problem to fit an existing technique." Dutka's business philosophy was an action concept, a basis for service to the customer that had a strong likelihood of paying off.

Direct Action. From time to time, one sees how the successful businessman learned important lessons by taking grass-roots action. John Fox of United Fruit peddled his orange concentrate to the housewife in order to find out how the new product would be received. Dutka's version of grass-roots action stemmed from his desire to understand, firsthand, a crucial business area—selling. By making sales presentations to prospective customers, he learned, for himself, what selling was all about. In the process, he added a few more percentage points to his businessman rating.

Power Assessment. One of the final lessons that Dutka learned in his slow and painful education was to take an objective look at his own strengths and weaknesses. "The company president is at one time the most powerful and the weakest person in the organization," he says. "No individual can be effective in a top position without a realistic view of himself, an awareness of what he can and can't do, what he should and shouldn't do."

Mildred Custin of Bonwit Teller also realized the importance of assessing one's power capability. She knew she had authority, but she also felt that in the long run she could work with her subordinates successfully only by enlisting their cooperation. Whether in government, business, or the family context, it is not the quantity of power available that determines effectiveness, but the wisdom of its use. Dutka understood this subtle principle very well—and this was perhaps his greatest strength. By using his power wisely, he was able to mobilize the efforts and capabilities of his people—an essential for the effectiveness of any organization.

16 BIG COMPANY VERSUS SMALL COMPANY – ARE OPPORTUNITIES EQUAL?

"A large firm is just like a small one," wrote an economics student, "only bigger." For simplicity's sake, it would be nice if this naïve thought were true. It isn't. There are qualitative differences between big and small companies. There are structural differences. There are even differences in profitability. Together, these differences spell contrasting worlds for those who seek success within them.

Offhand, one might think there would be no difficulty in pinning down something as tangible as company size. Yet, for years, economists have struggled with the question, "What measure shall be used?"

Number of Employees? Some industries, like chemicals, utilities, and oil, produce their products almost entirely by automatic equipment: they have a low labor ratio. A typical oil refinery, for example, may have acres of equipment tended by a mere handful of men. A construction crew, covering the same area in the course of erecting a highway bridge or office building, might number in the hundreds. Which is the "bigger" operation?

Capital Investment? Service industries, such as advertising agencies, often have a very small amount of capital in fixed assets. Essentially, they are "brain factories." Yet many agencies have annual billings that run high in the millions. (In 1965, J. Walter Thompson did $530.1 million worth of business, for example. Young & Rubicam's sales totaled $372.7 million.)

Gross Sales? This is the most commonly accepted measure of size. It's the one that *Fortune* uses annually in ranking its list, "The

500 Largest Industrial Corporations." But there are many companies that wouldn't come within smelling distance of *Fortune*'s 500, that could still describe themselves as "the largest in the industry." A firm might specialize in a single product—one entrepreneur, for example, is widely known as the "artichoke king." The largest producers of special electronic parts may be "small companies"— measured by number of employees, or gross sales.

In the following discussion, however, the terms "large" and "small" business will be based on a loose combination of the several commonly used measures of size. For ordinary purposes, there need be no serious problem. No one will argue with the designation of General Motors, Standard Oil Company, or General Electric as "large," and the corner restaurant or service station as "small" business.

PLACE IN THE SUN

It's generally accepted that the United States is the land of "big business." Although the fact may be true in one sense, it certainly is untrue in another. According to the Small Business Administration, of the nearly five million enterprises that made up "the business establishment" in 1965, 95 per cent are small enterprises. These small firms account for 40 per cent of the business activity in terms of sales, and employ over thirty million people.

The distribution of large and small firms is not the same within all industries. Certain types of business tend to attract large-company operations: steel, oil, chemicals, and automobiles are prime examples. In other areas, small businesses flourish, notably textiles and clothing, retailing, wholesaling, plastics, machine shops, metalworking, and foundries.

Another common notion is that big companies are better places to work because they promise more security. Comparatively, the small company carries a rather shaky image. This idea is indeed confirmed by key indicators. The rate of small-business failures compared to that for large companies is about ten to one. Or, as a

1964 figure shows: small-company failures—91 per cent of total failures; large-company—9 per cent. Small companies (those with assets under one million dollars) show a net profit after taxes of 2.3 per cent (of sales). Large companies: 5.7 per cent. The same basic differences are reflected in other figures such as the average life of small and big businesses, large companies having a substantially longer life.

LOG CABIN VERSUS SKYSCRAPER

In building a log cabin, one can be casual about structural details. As long as the design satisfies the need to withstand the elements, a few feet more or less in one dimension or another, will probably make little difference. The architect designing a skyscraper can't be as arbitrary. Everything from zoning restrictions to structural strength must be carefully calculated and applied to his design. In somewhat the same way, a small company needn't pay too much attention to its organization, as such. As long as there are people around to touch all the bases, the business "structure" seldom gets further attention. The large company is quite different. Organization charts may be sweated over at great length in an attempt to make the organization more "logical."

Accordingly, a small company tends to be less rigidly structured. This single factor has several implications for the executive. For one thing, his area of responsibility is generally broader in a small organization than in the large company, where functions are often divided into specialized subareas. For example, a small company may have a single financial executive. In a big company, the same function may be split up among several specialists: a tax expert, an authority on investments, an economist who understands the mysteries of cash flow, and so on.

As a result, the executive operating in the small company often has much greater freedom to exercise imagination and creativity. There are no colleagues to hem him in, no board of directors watching with a critical eye to see how he handles the ebb and flow of the company's cash. At the same time, he's more exposed. Any sheeplike tendency to huddle among one's peers is doomed to failure. There aren't any to huddle among.

Believing that the small company offers greater emotional satisfaction for its executives, a group of Harvard graduate students set up an employment bureau to improve liaison between Harvard graduates and smaller companies. As the Harvard group sees it: "The small firm offers a greater challenge, an earlier opportunity for contribution, and a correspondingly greater personal opportunity than do some large corporations. The interest in the smaller business stems from the realization that significant participation and resulting contribution are more readily available to the employee within a firm having a small management group."

Here are additional points of difference:

Job Control. The small-company executive tends to have a greater control of his job. Says Dr. Louis Hackemann, president of Hackemann & Associates, San Francisco and New York management counselors: "In the small company, the individual executive can make things happen. Results are what count. Authority with a small company may be greater, and the opportunity to be in closer contact with the board of directors, the owners, or the president. The small-company executive's personal goals also lend themselves to creating, inventing, and considering new ideas."

For the individual who likes to "know the score," who likes to see what's ahead and know where he's going, the small company is a more graspable and visible entity. A larger company necessarily has a more elaborate organizational structure, and these organizational differences go beyond mere bulk. Larger firms develop many more staff and service elements. The sheer complexity, the existence of divisions, departments, and affiliates necessarily outside the ken of all but those at the very top, can leave many executives of the middle echelons in larger companies with a feeling of incompleteness.

One businessman sums up the difficulty this way: "The man in business for himself sometimes doesn't know where his next meal is coming from. The executive in a big company very often doesn't know where his next promotion is coming from."

Work Methods. Large companies by their very nature tend to be more tradition-ridden. In comparison, the small company swings more freely. There are no company manuals with voluminous pages that regulate everything from the way a requisition must be made out to what a department head is expected to do when one of his employees dies.

In large companies, too, there may be so many echelons of command that performance does not follow policy. Decision-making, the key to organizational effectiveness, may suffer in the large firm, because of "slippage" between organizational tiers.

Says Paul H. Kiernan of Kiernan & Company, executive recruiters: "There is a major difference between a large and small company in the way decisions are made. In the small company, the decision-maker decides on the basis of personal knowledge. In the large company, the decision-maker often makes his decision on the basis of facts, figures—and sometimes the recommendations—supplied to him by others."

Mr. Kiernan observes that "an executive moving from a small company to a large one often faces difficulties. Many a fine performer in the small firm flounders and can't seem to mesh in a big organization. On the other hand, many men who grow up in small companies may reach a point where their experience, maturity, and desire to grow give them the basis for success in a larger company. It depends on the individual, his personality and adaptability."

PRESSURE OR BOONDOGGLE

"Frankly, I'm frightened," says an up-and-coming young assistant personnel director in a large food company. "I find myself taking four hours to do something I can do in an hour's time. This is no way to work. I want a job that stimulates me, not one that puts me to sleep. But the terrible thing is, the company *expects* the assignment to take four hours."

"I'm looking for a new job," says the production manager of a small chemical company. "Between the two partners making conflicting demands on me, and the size of the work load, the pressure is driving me batty."

These are two extreme cases, of course, and the trend in large companies *is* increasingly toward encouraging initiative among their people. Yet, many big organizations *say* they set great store by the original thinker and the maverick, while in actual practice they promote him out of the way (or out of the organization) if his efforts don't happen to jibe with operating policy, or prove "embarrassing" to the company image.

The free-swinging approach of James Connaughton of Wheelabrator Corporation, a Geneen and a Howard Hughes, would seem to contradict the idea that the big-company executive is less a free agent than his small-company opposite number. But executives like these are exceptional. Generally it is true—and for perfectly sound reasons—that the executive in the large company is less free to act. "Neck-consciousness is a prevailing way of life," as one executive puts it. More policies exist that limit what the big-company manager can do. He's more firmly hemmed in by the areas of responsibility of other executives.

And as for the pressure on executives in small companies to produce, the figures speak for themselves. The narrow profit margins, the high failure rate, means the small-company executive must exert himself more to stay above water.

Certainly, in the case history of Thomas Coe of the Wakefield Engineering Corporation, one sees the personal sacrifice and effort that the entrepreneur of a small, self-financed company must make. Yet, for the individual who wants to "run things," who savors the sense of personal power and accomplishment that comes from owning a company, the small company has a distinct appeal.

Says one businessman in explaining his preference for small business: "It's the difference between hunting in a jungle and visiting the zoo. Life in the small-business jungle is dangerous, but it's exciting and its triumphs are glorious. Big-company life is interesting, perhaps, but it's tamer, with many of the challenges and hazards of business life neatly walled out by an elaborate system of checks and balances."

THE BIG-COMPANY APPEAL

Obviously, individuals find offsetting compensations and attractions in working for the large corporation. For one thing, although it may seem to be the same game, the stakes are far higher. The smaller company deals in thousands, the big company in millions or even billions. To the individual attracted by power, there is an almost monarchical feeling in being the top executive in a large company. His moves can change the destinies of towns, cities, even countries.

Psychologists are not alone in their view of business activity being essentially a kind of game for grownups. For that matter, the phrase "business game" exists in our everyday speech. And if it's a game one wants, the big business, more than the small, is the place to find "the action." The rules are more highly codified, there are more players. Competition within the organization for advancement and promotions, is more keen, making for sharper rivalry. There are more prizes, but also more competitors.

There has always been a certain amount of interchange among large-company and small-company top personnel. But in recent years the flow has been increasing in the direction of the large company, and slowing down toward the small. The reason: increased demand for executive talent on the part of big business.

The larger a company becomes, the smaller becomes the potential group of people with the vision and executive ability to manage it at the top echelons. Thousands of people have the capability of running a service station or a local real-estate firm. A mere handful of men have the background and orientation to guide the destinies of a G.M., G.E., or I.B.M. Out of this situation of scarcity, the demand increases and with it the material rewards. Accordingly, no matter how content a capable executive may be to play the big frog in the small pond, if he is spotted as a man with big-company potential, the resulting outside offers of high salary and substantial fringe benefits become almost irresistible.

This process—the attracting of outstanding executive talent through the promise of greater responsibility and fatter fringes—has been assisted by the rapidly expanding operation known as executive recruiting. Two-hundred-and-fifty-odd companies are at present engaged in providing for business—usually big business—the top executive talent it must have to operate efficiently. Generally, the executive recruiter operates as a transmission belt in one direction, from the smaller company to the larger.

Robert E. Sibson, President of Sibson & Company, a New York management consultant specializing in employee-employer relations, asked one thousand job seekers this question: "If you had your choice, would you prefer to work for a large company, or a small company?" The tally—five hundred and sixty preferred large companies, four hundred and twelve preferred small. (Those polled represented a cross section of ages and types of management job being sought.)

In Sibson's opinion, those who chose the large company did so because they saw a greater opportunity in the sheer number of management jobs existing in the larger firm. (Apparently, the fact that there would also be more competitors was given less weight.) The factor of job security, of working for a more stable enterprise, less susceptible to the whim or fortunes of a single man, was another attraction.

On the other hand, those preferring the smaller company seemed to feel they could find more personal satisfaction in direct accomplishment, since assignments are less often fragmented. There was a strong appeal in the greater diversity of assignments or responsibilities—the "generalist" appeal versus the specialist appeal of the large firm. And finally, many preferred the idea of being a more important factor in a small firm—the big frog in the small pond.

Sums up Robert E. Sibson: "The key seems to be the desire to tie in with a growing company, one that's going places and that would take the man along with it."

The advantage of the large company as a starting point is also stressed by Rawle Deland, of Thorndike Deland Associates, executive recruiting consultants. "A big company is generally a better training ground for a young man aspiring to top executive ranks. Their training programs are more refined and more reliable, and there are simply more opportunities, statistically speaking. Too, if you do hit a roadblock, you've got the big name to sell. How much better to say you were with Procter & Gamble, for example, rather than ABC Soap Company."

In many cases, the beginner eyes the lower rungs of the business ladder with a certain amount of honest avarice in his heart. His question: "How about the relative pay between big and small?" The answer is rather surprising. According to Herman Scott, president of H. H. Scott, hi-fi equipment manufacturer of Maynard, Massachusetts: "Despite assumptions to the contrary, there's not much difference between large and small firms. Obviously, top salaries in the largest corporations are far higher than any small company can pay. But actually, there are few such jobs. I would even go so far as to say that after the first couple of years, the average income for small-company executives tends to be higher than for larger companies."

POSITION'S THE POINT

With the small company, a good deal depends on *where* the individual enters the organization. If he is the founder or the owner, his career is obviously bound to what he achieves with his firm. It becomes the vehicle of his success.

On the other hand, many people who enter small firms as second-level executives, as V.P. in charge of marketing or production, for example, suffer a frustrating experience. No matter how well they perform, they find themselves up against a roadblock to advancement. The ownership of the company—whether it's an individual, a family, or a small group—has no intention of letting an "outsider" cut in. Many an executive has had the unhappy experience of having a youngster brought in over his head—a relative of the owner.

Although nepotism is not unknown in large firms, it is generally frowned upon. And after all, in most cases, public ownership means that the ruling dynasty, no matter how firmly entrenched, can be called to account by the stockholders. Nepotism means vulnerability for a big company: a group of discontented stockholders can too easily use it as a rallying point for discontent with earnings or growth.

BOOK III

J. J. Mascuch –
SPARK-PLUG TAMER
EXTRAORDINARY

There are more than a few little millionaires with enormous egos. J. J. Mascuch is not of this group. People meeting him are reminded of that charming member of Philadelphia's Biddle clan whom Walter Pidgeon portrayed on Broadway in "The Happiest Millionaire." One of his close associates says, "J.J. is a truly happy man, and it's almost impossible to make him unhappy—for more than a minute or two."

Mascuch grew up in Newark, New Jersey, and in the 1920s was a friend and neighbor of Thomas Edison. He knew, as did everyone else, that Edison's inventions included the incandescent lamp, the electric induction motor, the dynamo, the phonograph, the dictating machine, and the motion picture machine. What Mascuch also knew was that Edison had made millions—but only for other people. "The butcher and the grocer sometimes had trouble collecting from the Edison family," Mascuch observes sadly. "Mr. Edison simply was no businessman." Of course, the Edisons were only relatively poor. Thomas Edison did leave a business to his family, and his son, Charles, became Assistant Secretary of the Navy and Governor of New Jersey. But to youthful Joe Mascuch, also destined to be an inventor, Edison was as much a negative example as an admired hero. He tried to emulate the virtues and avoid the weaknesses of the great man. At least in some degree, he seems to have succeeded.

J. J. Mascuch is founder and president of Breeze Corporations in Union, New Jersey, and Victory Engineering in Springfield, New Jersey. He has many financial interests—based on over 150 patents he holds in the automotive, aeronautical, and aero-space fields. Mascuch lives in an Italian-style villa on a steep ridge in the foothills of the Ramapo Mountains at Millburn, New Jersey. He goes on safari for big game in Africa every few years, fishes in Canada and Florida, and is an expert movie cameraman. A few years ago, he acquired a very expensive Rolls Royce. He decided it was incomplete, however, and sent it over to Italy for a new body, a television set and a toilet in the back seat.

Mascuch's Breeze Corporations is a company that makes most of the rescue and cargo-lifting hoists and winches used on big aircraft and helicopters as well as a variety of other industrial and defense products. Breeze winches are used, for example, to retrieve astronauts from the sea after their orbital flights. J.J.'s Victory Engineering Corporation at nearby Springfield, New Jersey, makes delicate sensing instruments for medicine, scientific laboratories, and industry.

Mascuch's inventions have earned him a lot of money and made him well known in the industrial world. While most Americans haven't heard of Joe Mascuch, your present automobile radio was influenced by him, as were police radio patrol systems and radios in military and civil aircraft. Back in the 1920s, Mascuch invented the ignition shielding that enables the gasoline engine and radio to work together. He personally installed the shielding on the Wright Whirlwind engine of *The Spirit of St. Louis,* the Ryan monoplane that carried Charles Lindbergh on his historic flight to Paris. His road to the top takes in some of the milestones of contemporary industrial history.

*   *   *

Mascuch (pronounced Ma-shoo) is of Slovakian origin and the Mascuch clan is numerous in New Jersey. Joe Mascuch was born June 2, 1896, in Newark, New Jersey, on Montgomery Street opposite Kruger's Bakery, still a most important and delightful enterprise to New Jersey folks. "Our neighborhood was populated by Irish, Germans, and Jews, many of them immigrants," Mascuch explains. "My father was born in Slovakia and my mother is Bo-hemian. They had ten children. Only one brother survives with me and like me, he is an engineer.

"We lived in a decent, working-class neighborhood. Most of the families were very religious and most of them had a lot of mouths to feed, so they had to be frugal with money. But my parents never stinted on real necessities and comforts in the home. Even as a child I learned to value good and comfortable living and what is more, I think I learned, before I was six, that to be comfortable in this world you had to work hard and be what the grownups called a success."

J.J. says his father had the talent to be a success but was en-slaved by his Old World class psychology. "Father tried to accept American idealism and egalitarianism wholeheartedly, but the Eu-ropean class system was so ingrained in him that he could never comprehend the degree to which he was being exploited by his employers, and that it was his own fault for letting them do so."

The older Mascuch was a patternmaker and an expert designer of lock components. "He specialized in designing extremely strong locks for prisons. Some of his designs were so ingenious they were bought by foreign governments. He also designed special locks for the railways and for oil companies." But although Mascuch, senior, supported his family adequately, he never grasped the real oppor-tunities open to the man with talent and industry in America. He never dreamed of cutting loose from employers, and striking out to garner all the fruits of his talents for himself and his children.

Young Joe started his mechanical training at an early age by following the European custom and going to the factory to serve as helper to his father after school and on Saturdays. There he learned the principles of machine-shop practice plus ancient moti-vating principles. "If I made a mistake while working for my father, I got a belting," he recalls without a trace of rancor.

But the elder Mascuch didn't make the mistake of keeping his sons under too close rein. They were encouraged to get out and work for other people, make friends and learn what the world was really like. Joe soon found a part-time job with a butcher. In these days few people had telephones and the butcher's boy made the rounds of the homes of the regular delivery customers, taking down their orders, learning a bit about salesmanship in the process, and then, as often as not, accompanied the horse-drawn cart delivering the orders he had taken.

THE CAREER, HOOK GETS BAITED

But the butcher business was only a source of income to young Joe. He preferred machines to animals, alive or dead. This was the age when the automobile was new and held the imagination of boys the way interplanetary exploration does now. In his free time, Joe quite naturally hung around the garages of the community. He watched the mechanics clean and adjust spark plugs, grind valves and lubricate the chassis of cars. Although he was only thirteen, he was sometimes allowed to help out. In no time, he had conceived his first creative project. He was going to build an automobile.

The idea came to him when he found several old motorcycle engines lying unused in the garage and persuaded the owner to let him have one. He tuned it up and got it running, scrounged four spare cycle wheels and some oak timber for a frame (in 1909 even some full-sized cars had wood frames) and some short steel strips.

"It took me nearly a year but I fashioned a small car complete with springs, a friction clutch that gave me a variable speed and a pulley reverse action," he remembers. "At that time I was a skinny, rather timid kid, too bashful to ask all the questions I needed to; so I made a lot of mistakes. Then I had to ask the questions of the garagemen and, somewhat to my surprise, I found they were eager to help me. In those days, a garageman had to know how to cut a casting or forging from metal stock in an emergency and they helped me design and cut some of the special parts."

Joe could make about fifteen miles an hour in his little car but almost at once a cop stopped him and told him he couldn't drive it on the streets, so he had to pick his time and drive on the sidewalks.

The skinny kid soon got another important idea. He had to go to college. In 1913 this was still a rather radical idea in a working-class family. With so many children to care for, his father wasn't able to help much. Fortunately, Newark Engineering College offered night courses. It is a school well known in the engineering world but not famous outside of it. Joe enrolled, realizing it would take him five years to get his degree. He got a daytime job as a draftsman in a tool shop at nine dollars a week—for a six-day week —and went to school five nights a week. Because he had, and still has, an extremely rugged constitution, he didn't miss a class in five years at Newark Engineering.

"MR. SLOAN LIKED ME"

Very soon, Joe graduated from the tool shop in Newark to the designing department of the Hyatt Roller Bearing Company at Harrison, just across the Passaic River from Newark. He started at twice the wages he'd made in the tool shop and worked up to $150 a month, a respectable salary for a lad of nineteen in 1915. He didn't have his engineering degree yet but he was classed as a design engineer by his boss and was put to work designing journal boxes for railroad cars, a rather routine job but one that had to be done carefully. His boss was a demanding chap named Alfred P. Sloan.

"Mr. Sloan took a liking to me. I think it was because I never watched the clock." Sloan would send Mascuch out on service calls as a trouble shooter, giving him valuable chances to meet a variety of people and to learn about their problems and personalities.

Sloan, of course, later became head of General Motors. Having succeeded in making a friend of Mr. Sloan, young Joe realized that he could make a friend of anyone he wished if he tried honestly to do so. He also realized right then and there, he says, that "a young man ought to try constantly to associate himself with people who are bigger than he is and people who are genuine. I don't mean he should kiss the boss's tail or be a social climber, but he should try always to get as close as he decently can to the man from whom he can learn the important things about life and business."

THE INVISIBLE PANCHO VILLA

The next year, Joe got a once-in-a-lifetime opportunity to do just that—to "learn the important things about life and business." The New Jersey National Guard unit to which he belonged was called out and sent to the Mexican border. A colorful character named Pancho Villa, part bandit, part clown, part patriot and one of the great guerrilla leaders of all time, was annoying the Wilson administration no end by riding hell-for-leather across the border into Texas or New Mexico whenever the Mexican army cavalry got too hot on his trail. Before going back to Mexico, the Villistas would usually shoot up some town on our side of the border, rob the local bank, saloons, general store, and livestock corrals. Since the Mexican government obviously couldn't stop Villa, President Wilson sent General John J. Pershing with a mixed column of regulars and National Guard to try to catch him. It was a fool's errand; Pershing and his men rode for hundreds of miles through the deserts and mountains on the Mexican side of the border without ever catching a glimpse of Villa.

But for Corporal Joe Mascuch, the Mexican border expedition opened up a vista. By this time he was an extremely capable motor mechanic and driver. He applied for a transfer to Pershing's headquarters as a courier and got it; there weren't too many men in the brigade who could keep a car or motorcycle going on the abominable Mexican mountain roads.

"Black Jack" Pershing didn't take to people easily; indeed, most officers in his command were scared to death of him. But he noticed the tall, good-looking kid from New Jersey who could be depended on to get dispatches through. (Field radio was just starting to be used in the war in Europe.)

The farcical pursuit of Villa soon became too embarrassing and President Wilson called it off. Joe came back to Newark, his designing board at Hyatt, and night classes at the engineering college.

GENERAL MOTORS AT THIRTY-SEVEN CENTS A SHARE

Then one day he heard that General Motors, which in those days played a rather muted second fiddle to Henry Ford in the auto world, was going to buy Hyatt. By that time he had six hundred dollars in the bank. He drew it out and asked Sloan for some advice about how to buy Hyatt stock. Sloan told him to put five hundred of the money back in the bank and get a broker to sell him shares on 10 per cent margin. He bought a thousand shares of Hyatt at a dollar a share that way. His information was correct. In less than a year, G.M. did buy Hyatt, giving him two thousand shares of General Motors for his thousand shares of Hyatt.

"I figure I actually paid about thirty-seven cents a share cash for my original two thousand shares of G.M. It has been split many, many times and I never have sold a penny's worth of it," he explains.

On Sloan's advice, he made another purchase, again on 10 per cent margin. For six hundred dollars down he got title to ten shares of Christiana Securities Corporation at six hundred dollars a share. His father lent him the six hundred so he wouldn't have to sell any of his General Motors stock. Christiana, of course, is the DuPont family holding company that held so much General Motors stock for so many years. Mascuch still has his Christiana shares, which were split eighty-five for one a few years ago and now are worth around a hundred and seventy-five thousand dollars.

FLYING, WORLD WAR I STYLE

His education was interrupted again by the outbreak of World War I. His National Guard unit was one of the first sent to France, but young Lieutenant Mascuch had his heart set on getting in the Aero Section of the Signal Corps, as the infant Air Corps was known.

The acquaintances Joe Mascuch had made on the Mexican border got him the transfer and he landed in the famous 91st Squadron, whose pilots included several men destined for fame. During his service in the 91st, he met Eddie Rickenbacker, who became his partner in an automobile speedway venture in Pennsylvania. Another famous pilot he met in France was Wiley Post, who later would girdle the globe—partly bankrolled by Joe Mascuch.

At the front, Lieutenant Mascuch flew in Spads, frail little wood-and-doped-canvas box kites powered by a 180-horsepower Hispano-Suiza engine. He was wounded in the back of the neck in a dogfight early one morning when "a German pilot dove at me from out of the sun and I lost him like an outfielder loses a fly ball." Mascuch returned to the airdrome, got his wound dressed and was back in the air in two and a half hours.

He conceived two ideas while flying the Spad. (They took him years to develop, but ultimately were rewarding.) First, he saw the need for some way to provide cockpit armor for fighter planes. "We used to steal stove lids and steel plates off French cars and sit on them while flying to get some protection," he chuckles. Eventually, Mascuch designed the first successful cockpit armor for military planes after pondering the problem for years.

The other idea was radio shielding. During the last year of the war, the Germans and the Allies both were trying to use radio, crude radio, in fighter planes and bombers. "The range was so short it might have worked if it hadn't been for the interference caused by the ignition on the engine," he explained. "But the only way you could hear anything was to cut the motor—then pray it would start again so your plane wouldn't stall and crash." The obstacles to shielding the ignition system of a gas engine were so formidable, however, that nothing was done about it then. And it wasn't until 1924, when he already was a successful industrialist, that Joe Mascuch proved the feasibility of ignition shielding by successfully using it with a radio receiver in a Lincoln touring car. Even then, the market for it was tiny. Police and other civil transport radio still was several years in the future.

When the war ended, Lieutenant Mascuch was faced with the decision of whether to come back home at once and take his engineering degree or see more of the world. He chose to see the world. As the product of a multilingual family and a polyglot neighborhood, he had spoken German and Czech fluently from childhood and could "get by" in Polish, Hungarian, and Russian. Because he had an aptitude for languages, he had made high marks in French in high school, so he applied for a post as a translator with the military section of President Wilson's peace mission. For the next two years Lieutenant Mascuch was shunted around Europe, serving as a translator for VIPs and technical experts. "I even roomed with Herbert Hoover for a few days in Warsaw," he recalls.

Finally, at twenty-three, Mascuch returned to Newark to take his last few courses at engineering school. But he didn't go back to Hyatt. He now had several thousand dollars in cash, and his General Motors and Christiana stock had appreciated to the point where he had the necessary credit to go in business for himself. He determined he would not let others reap the lion's share of the fruits of his toil, as his father always had.

AUTOS—HOW THEY USED TO MAKE THEM

He decided to open an engineering laboratory to design better parts for automobiles and devices for automobile maintenance. It was still the heyday of the "assembled car." Every month a new auto company went into business and nearly every month one went broke. There were between forty and fifty companies making cars. Only Ford was making an integrated car; everyone else, even General Motors, was buying parts and whole assemblies from suppliers. Any small manufacturer or engineering laboratory that could come up with a better spark plug, a better bumper, a better transmission assembly, or radiator had a huge market to sell. Each car maker was eager to buy some improvement that would give him a slight edge over his rivals that he could trumpet in full-page ads in the *Saturday Evening Post*.

The market for maintenance equipment was practically virgin territory for an enterprising chap like Mascuch. He and his mechanics made spark-plug cleaners, improved transmission parts, and radiator caps and the hammered piston ring, which was harder and clung to the wall of the cylinder better than the ordinary piston ring.

"We made the prototypes of these things in our laboratory at night so I could get out in the daytime and sell them to automobile manufacturers and parts jobbers," he recalls. "I didn't have enough capital to go into manufacturing at once, so I had to sell licenses under my patents. I was accumulating patents fast. Many were mere design patents, important improvements but not involving anything basic. But some of my ideas were original—a bumper design, for example, that was both rustproof and gave better shock protection. Although the auto makers were eager for better parts, they weren't willing to come looking for them. As often as not, it was the replacement parts dealers, called accessory dealers in those days, who were more progressive. They would buy an improved part or accessory from a small manufacturer and sell it to motorists who would put it on their cars and throw away the original factory part. I put a pair of new bumpers I designed on my car and made a sales trip to Boston. I sold $600,000 worth of the bumpers on that trip alone and found a manufacturer to make them for me under license."

What Mascuch was doing was, from a business point of view, very simple. He was finding merchandisable opportunities and taking advantage of them, the same thing successful businessmen do today.

"It didn't require genius; it required hard work," he says. "Automobiles came from the factories with certain shortcomings, either in performance or appearance. Hundreds of design engineers like me were out to capitalize on these shortcomings. For example, the L-head engines of those days and the low octane fuels produced a hell of a lot of carbon. The head had to be taken off the engine and the valves ground every couple of months. So we all tried to make and sell intensified spark plugs that would burn more of the fuel and leave less carbon. I made such spark plugs at night and hawked them from garage to garage by day."

HOW TO LEARN THE ROPES

To conceive a product and design it so it could be sold to a manufacturer was not easy. The designer had to be able to show the manufacturer exactly how to make it and how to sell it. Mascuch also had to learn to finance his own operations, meet his payroll, avoid tying up too much of his capital, get the banks to extend him a maximum line of credit and impress his suppliers and customers so that they would do business with him on the most favorable possible terms.

"Actually these things are far more important than having ideas," he insists. "They are what makes the successful businessman and they are open to every young person of reasonable intelligence. I'm told that today you can find all these procedures described in great detail in textbooks and taught in business colleges. But in my day, we had to learn it all firsthand and the best way to do it was to make people like you well enough so they would go out of their way to show you the ropes instead of taking advantage of you. I'm sure things are much the same today."

How did he raise the money to finance an enterprise that made him successful and fixed for life before he was thirty?

"A key principle I learned is that it is vastly easier to raise fifty thousand dollars than fifty or five hundred," he explained. "If you go to a banker or a manufacturer with a piddling deal that obviously can't amount to anything, he will put you down as a fool and won't waste his time on you. But if you come to him with a sizable proposition, he will at least listen.

"The second thing to learn is to be precise and practical. To ask for five hundred thousand when fifty thousand is adequate is just as silly as asking for five hundred. The businessman must learn at a very early age to calculate the financial possibilities of his ideas with reasonable accuracy, making due allowance for the operations of a competitive market and other hazards. The bankers and other businessmen whose cooperation he is seeking all want to make a profit. If he can convince them he can make a profit for them and that he is honest and reasonably intelligent, they will gamble on him."

In his early contacts, Joe Mascuch kept meeting more and more people who were genuinely wise in the ways of business. These men gave Mascuch more good advice about investments. He learned that speculating in good stocks was foolish; the thing to do was to buy as much as he could reasonably hope to pay for on margin, and put them away in a safe-deposit box. "I became a confirmed bull on stocks," he recalls, "and later I was to pay the full price for that. But I don't regret it, for in the light of half a century of investing, I learned the bulls are on the right track for the long pull."

THE MASCUCH ENTERPRISES

By the middle of the 1920s, Mascuch had enough capital and reserve to go into manufacturing on his own. His brother, John, who had a good business mind, was working with him. There's more money, obviously, in manufacturing your own products than in licensing others to make them.

Mascuch had realized the need to organize his own manufacturing enterprise as early as 1921. "My first one was a little corporation called Duro Company, which made my intensified spark plugs. We also made some hammered piston rings. It cost almost nothing to get going and the profits were big enough so that two years later I was able to buy Provident Machine Company of Philadelphia, which made a machine for installing brake linings. I paid ninety thousand dollars for it, putting up eighteen thousand dollars in cash from savings and notes for the rest. We moved the business to Newark and designed an improved machine called the Lewis brake-lining machine that was to be standard equipment in better garages for many years. A modern variation of this machine is in use today, although I don't make it. We did so well with the brake-lining machine that we paid off the notes for the purchase of Provident in less than three years."

His next production venture was with his rustproof bumpers, which he had been licensing to other manufacturers. "In the very early 1920s autos came from the factory without bumpers; the motorist bought them and put 'em on. The cheap ones rusted quickly. We developed a method of electroplating heavy steel bumpers with a double layer of nickel directly on the steel—no copper underplating and no grinding. This was a ten-strike. We formed a little company in Newark called Cox Corporation to make bumpers. For this venture, I borrowed heavily for the first time—half a million dollars from banks and friends.

"We started out as the fifty-first company in the business of making bumpers. Three years later we were number two in the industry. We had two plants, one in Newark and one at Wilkes-Barre, Pennsylvania. Then we got a handsome offer for a controlling interest in the bumper business and sold it at a $500,000 profit. But we kept the Cox Corporation and continued to make some bumpers for years."

The notes for financing Cox were paid off rapidly and by now Mascuch was working intermittently on the problem of radio ignition shielding. "I needed a flexible metal hose for this to carry the wiring and I heard about a company called Breeze Metal Hose & Manufacturing Co. in Newark. Their main business was making carburetors for Model T Ford cars. They weren't doing too well and didn't seem to realize how valuable their metal hose was. We bought Breeze Metal Hose for about $200,000, paying all cash; it was a bargain. We sloughed off the carburetor business and began developing markets for the flexible hose. We made many varieties of the hose for use in machine tools, power tools, automobiles, for gasoline lines, and other uses."

The decision to merge the three small enterprises into one company was made for two reasons—"economy and the need for a plant big enough to handle ignition shielding." In 1926, the Mascuch brothers put Breeze Corporations together by merging their engineering laboratory with two small auto parts manufacturing firms. When the lawyer's stenographer typed the charter, she spelled it "corporations" instead of "corporation." "Let's keep it that way," Joe told his brother, "it's eye-catching."

On the day in 1927 when he made the trip to the airfield in New York to install the ignition shielding in Lindbergh's monoplane, Joe Mascuch was worth several million dollars. Radio ignition shielding was Breeze's first sophisticated product but Mascuch said he realized rather early that the market in bumpers and other automotive parts was not going to keep on being a gravy train. "We were going to have to become a company well ahead of our competitors and even ahead of our time if we were to do well," he explains.

The second group of Breeze products included multi-lectric connectors. These little devices were used in radio equipment of all kinds, particularly for radio in aircraft. Breeze began making them in the late 1920s and found them very profitable. Later, Breeze became a leading producer of a descendant of these little connectors, the electrical slip ring, which sells for as much as twenty thousand dollars per unit.

A STRONG BREEZE SPRINGS UP

By 1928, Mascuch realized that he had to keep abreast of technological advances in other countries if he was to succeed in his goal of making Breeze one of the country's most sophisticated engineering companies. He began going abroad every year, studying German and British engineering, particularly. He established a plant in Britain in the mid-1930s to make ignition shielding; it was sold to British interests at a good profit in 1942.

The next Breeze products were explosive cartridge starters for piston aircraft engines, and aircraft cockpit armor. "We found a market for the cartridge starters wherever aircraft had to be started in extremely cold weather. The batteries of those days simply wouldn't turn the engines over fast enough. The military was a good customer for cartridge starters as well as for ignition shielding," he explains.

Mascuch, who still remembered that he had to sit on stove plates to protect his rump from German bullets as a World War I pilot, next spent $150,000 on a prototype of a laminated steel cockpit armor. In 1938 the War Department wouldn't take it. "In 1940, they came to us to turn it out in quantity in a hurry."

A little earlier, Mascuch and his engineers produced a series of stainless steel doors and hatches for naval craft that were corrosion-resistant and only one-third the weight of ordinary steel doors and hatches. These included ammunition hatches, personnel hatches, and watertight bulkhead doors for destroyers and cruisers. The company made these for nine years.

Along the way, Mascuch and his brother bought Federal Laboratories at Saltsburg, Pennsylvania, the world's leading maker of tear gas and other police supplies.

THE BRAVE BUT BLOODY—BULLS

The 1929 crash in Wall Street hit him hard, as it did most of the devout bulls. Overnight the value of his stocks fell from between six and seven million dollars to one million—but by that time he had very little on margin. The inflated prices of his stocks were wiped out but he still owned most of them free and clear and although he couldn't know it for certain then, most of them would in time go much higher than they had been in the summer of 1929.

And, fortunately for Mascuch, President Hoover began encouraging the production of both civil and military aircraft. While progress in aviation was not rapid, it finally opened up the market for radio ignition shielding. The nation's police forces, highway patrols and fire departments also began buying Breeze ignition shielding for radio in automobiles. In later years, Mascuch's personal fortune pyramided. During World War II, Breeze had many military contracts and a sales volume of around forty million dollars a year.

The corporation's sales volume is now around twelve million dollars a year.

Joe Mascuch is a happy man. And even though he has the reputation of being a strict taskmaster, he makes people who work around him feel that they are in a happy environment. How he accomplishes this isn't always clear except that he seems to be genuinely interested in people—literally in everyone he meets—and his own range of interests varies widely.

BEHIND THE J. J. MASCUCH STORY

Important people—men with a permanent place in the business history of our times—played a part in shaping Joe Mascuch's outlook on life and his own career. Edison, Alfred P. Sloan, General John J. Pershing, Eddie Rickenbacker, and top executives in the automobile industry formed a kind of counseling panel for the Mascuch career. But others have made friends, even close friends of prominent men, without benefiting from the association. To discover what was specifically responsible for J. J. Mascuch's winning pattern we must look at other factors:

Career Sights. The goals individuals set for themselves often are created within the family circle. In most cases, the process is unconscious. A young man, mulling over career possibilities, sometimes finds he has an "instinctive ambition" to study law, or engineering, or archaeology. Such seemingly spontaneous career objectives are often not spontaneous at all. They stem from ideas and attitudes that existed within the group mind of the family. These impulses are described by sociologist David Riesman as "tradition-directed" aspirations.

J. J. Mascuch absorbed specific values and aspirations in his early youth. He quickly decided that he had to pin his hopes on a combined concept: work *and* achievement. Proof that hard work, even inspired work, does not necessarily lead to affluence lay before his eyes in the example of Thomas Edison and his own father. With these two harsh reminders at the forefront of his conscience, he set himself the double goal of work *and* achievement, with a strong emphasis on the latter. And there was no doubt that achievement meant *material* results, *profitable* enterprise.

Career Take-Off. With a regularity that defies coincidence, people seek their fortunes in fields they've been familiar with in their childhood or early youth. For example, it's no coincidence that a writer's children become interested in writing or a lockmaker's son becomes interested in things mechanical.

Hollywood movies have perpetuated the myth that stern parental pressure forces the young hero to follow in Daddy's footsteps. In real life, Poppa often doesn't have to raise a finger—or even his voice. More often, the youngster, absorbed and impressed by the activities that are obviously important to his father, unconsciously seeks to emulate him. This element of the career pattern explains young Mascuch's interest in mechanical innovation. And, as a logical sequel, ingenuity is where the heart is.

Action-Seeking. Like a gambler, a businessman must "go where the action is." The wheels of Mascuch's business career started to turn at a critical and important period in America: the early beginnings of mass automobile production. And in the evolving and many-faceted situation that existed in the early days of the auto, Mascuch found several chances to get a good thing going—his special bumpers, for example. In Mascuch's own phrase, what he sought was "merchandisable opportunities." It's the hunt for and the development of such situations in which the successful man excels. And it was this element in Mascuch's pattern that explains both the number and variety of ways in which he was able to make money.

Learning the Business of Business. Mascuch states, "In my day, we had to learn [business methods] by the hard school of experience, and the best way to do it was to make people like you well enough so they would go out of their way to show you the ropes instead of taking advantage of you."

Just as in the careers of Donald Kendall, Thomas Coe, and Solomon Dutka, Mascuch illustrates the seminal importance of developing a tough and realistic understanding of the hard core facts of business—everything from financing his operations to getting the most favorable terms when dealing with suppliers and customers.

Money-Raising. It's true in every type of enterprise, of course: cold cash is the hot lifeblood of business. Mascuch offers an interesting, provocative, and helpful idea when he states, "It's vastly easier to raise fifty thousand dollars than fifty and five hundred dollars." Regardless of the nature of an individual's job or the company he works for, an understanding of the financial aspects of what he's doing must precede his rise to the top. Particularly these days, the financial function in business is becoming more and more complex. The good old simple days where a single executive could handle all the financial affairs of an organization are gone forever. New concepts and practices of financial operations have become superspecialized. Everything from cash flow to tax considerations require the control of a knowledgeable specialist. The man at the top must know the facts of money manipulation himself or must quickly secure the services of an assistant or counselor who can back him up in this critical area.

Company-Building. One of the notable aspects of J. J. Mascuch's upward march: he set up companies the way a kid at the beach makes mud pies. Viable business ideas quickly became a base around which he constructed a corporation. Mascuch's approach suggests that this "another idea, another company" pattern is a way of scattering one's bets. The approach presupposes one condition. The entrepreneur must get good people to watch over each of his interests.

Working for the Pay-Off. Remembering his father and Thomas Edison, J.J. decided that he would not be a hard-working fool *for somebody else.* Aware that ingenuity, hard work, and dedication were nonetheless necessary, Mascuch became an early, if unconscious, advocate of the idea of "managing by result." By a continuing insistence that he be a major beneficiary of his own efforts, he was able to achieve the pay-offs toward which he pressed his energies.

18 { Patricia Murphy—
SUCCESS BY CANDLELIGHT

During the Great Depression of the thirties, a spunky wisp of a girl came to New York from the tiny town of Placentia, Newfoundland. Her name was Patricia Murphy and her intention was to study music. Instead, she invested her sixty-dollar return carfare in a hex-ridden tearoom—and eventually became owner of the internationally known Candlelight Restaurants. Patricia Murphy is also a prize-winning horticulturist, operating eight technically perfect greenhouses with twenty full-time gardeners. She is a perfumer, author, and much-traveled collector of art and craft objects. She clocked 180,000 miles in a recent year while furthering this interest. Her most recent business venture combines her love of travel and good eating: she initiated a twenty-one-day escorted "Patricia Murphy Gourmet Tour of Europe."

Thousands of ambitious and intelligent women throughout the U.S. have opened tearooms. The number who have been successful can be counted on the fingers of one hand. Here is the story of one who made it to the top.

* * *

Pat's childhood memories of Newfoundland are of gently rolling slopes where ice-sculptured valleys often left residents community-bound for five months of the year. The family meat supplies (including caribou, moose, black bear, and hares) were hung outside their back door. Chops and steaks were cut from hard-frozen steers as needed. Her father, a vigorous man, Captain Francis Murphy, was one of the most respected figures in town, for he ran the general store ("Everything from a Needle to an Anchor"). He was publisher of *Murphy's Good Things* (no crime or *bad* things reported), a four-page weekly which was distributed free. Since the export of fish was a primary industry in Newfoundland, Captain Murphy, who at one time commanded a large schooner, dabbled in boat building and was a fish merchant besides.

When Pat was eight years old she was granted access to the kitchen to experiment with an apple butter recipe she saw in an American magazine. "It came out looking like Newfoundland slush and tasted like codfish soup," she says, but it did whet her interest in the preparation of food. To this day, she loves to try intriguing suggestions from gourmet periodicals.

Patricia Murphy, like many of the Irish, French, and English girls who made up the Newfoundland populace, attended strict parochial schools. The curriculum at boarding school included Classical Piano and Home Economics in addition to the usual academic subjects. "I don't think I excelled at neatening up," Miss Murphy confesses now. "I distinctly remember having to be told one sweeps stairs from the top down." Nevertheless, the discipline made her aware of housekeeping principles that later proved invaluable in running a restaurant.

Pat was just a schoolgirl when her family installed the first telephone in their community. Her love affair with the instrument has never ended. She once said her greatest personal thrill was seeing her name listed in the Brooklyn phone directory. Almost every photograph published of her shows a phone in her hand—she utilizes it day and night to keep close tabs on her complex operations.

When Patricia returned home from boarding school for vacations, she loved to help out in the store. She learned to take inventory, do elementary bookkeeping, wait on customers, and patiently listen to their troubles. She also wrote obituaries for the local paper with all the tender flourish she could muster. "I pored over the dictionary trying to find meaningful words so that each demise was reported in a special way. My father pretended to be amused but I think he was pleased."

AT SEVENTEEN, NEW YORK BECKONS

During the last year of Pat's schooling, an examiner came to Newfoundland from Trinity Music College in London and reported she showed exceptional musical talent. Patricia and her teacher convinced her parents that she needed to further her studies in New York. So, at the age of seventeen, with her father's blessing and three hundred dollars, Patricia Murphy migrated to New York City.

The Staten Island relatives with whom her father had arranged for her to stay appeared to be "unkindred" spirits. When she said that she wanted a fine New York hat, they introduced her to bargain stores on 14th Street; but Patricia had always loved good things and she knew the city must have better merchandise to offer. By nightfall of her first day in New York, she began to feel uncomfortable with her relatives, who were actually strangers to her. Nothing was as she imagined it would be, and her dreams of an exciting life in New York seemed doomed to failure. The next morning she gingerly counted her money and made an announcement to the startled relatives. She was moving bag and baggage to "the city."

She had to ask a million questions to get there. As Patricia Murphy says now, "Some strangers come to town and hesitate to ask directions for fear of being put down as an out-of-towner. I have to know the whys and wherefores of everything. With my insatiable curiosity about people, places, and things, I've managed to ask my way out of most 'mysteries.' "

Her ferry-and-subway trip to New York City seemed to take hours but she finally arrived, unexpected, at the West 52nd Street home of her mother's former guardian, a general practitioner named Dr. Bagg. He was startled when Patricia requested nighttime refuge in his examining room "until other arrangements could be made." Reluctantly, he consented. But he didn't need to worry about a lengthy visit from his guest. As she tossed about on a narrow, makeshift bed, huge glassy-eyed animal heads glared down upon her, and the moaning echoes of sick people haunted her. Before the week was up, she had decided on a proper place for an unchaperoned young lady to live. For eight dollars a week, she took a room at the Three Arts Club, and said good-bye to the doctor. Next Pat looked up a home-town girl who was studying at Columbia University. Through her Miss Murphy located a more economical room (four dollars a week) and a temporary job playing classical piano compositions at a nearby students' restaurant-cafeteria in return for lunch ("I ate enough to last the entire day").

Pat was told to report at noon each day, but she decided she could earn and learn more by appearing on the scene earlier. Soon she began arriving at 6 A.M., filling in for help who failed to show up. Even to this day, she's at her home desk working on detailed reports and correspondence before 7 A.M. "You miss so much in life when you don't get up early," she insists. And anyone who has ever dealt with the indefatigable lady realizes she's a stickler for punctuality, a woman who utilizes every waking moment to the fullest extent. Her work at the restaurant included getting behind the counter and dishing out blue-plate specials. At the same time she was learning what customers liked and what they spurned. ("Color is most important in meal planning. To be appetizing, the platter should have at least three attractively blended colors. There should be a harmonious taste and sight theme to every meal.") Her restaurant serving proved an interesting sidelight to her musical participation and she enjoyed it as long as it lasted.

By the fall of 1929, Patricia Murphy, like millions of others, was discovering that job-hunting was a discouraging grind. The alarmed girl saw prominent businessmen reduced to peddling apples on street corners, and skilled technical people jobless, pacing the pavements. The beginning of the depression was undoubtedly the blackest period in our entire economic history, and young Pat Murphy needed a job. One of the first help-wanted ads she answered was for a "Young Girl Bookkeeper." To save the nickel subway fare, she walked to the plush Riverside Drive address. A suave, middle-aged man greeted her and with exceptional cordiality escorted her to his comfortable, paneled den. "Yes," he cooed after a long appraisal, she was *just* the type he was looking for. "Only it's not for *bookkeeping*," she decided, bolting out the front door. Jobs weren't *that* hard to get!

Reasoning that restaurant workers seldom starved, Patricia Murphy found a cashier's position. Her employers, a Mr. and Mrs. Foster, owned two charming mid-town eating places. She made a whopping eighteen-dollars-a-week salary and lasted several weeks, replaced only because of misplaced zeal. The owners had received complaints that Patricia pushed chewing gum, chocolate bars, and Sweet Caporal cigarettes just a bit too strongly on departing customers. She also supplemented her income by hand-painting postcards for three dollars a hundred. In time, she playfully changed the designs but no one seemed to notice. The creative urge was always there waiting to be developed.

Meanwhile, she found a more adequate furnished room across the East River in Brooklyn Heights. Many evenings Pat skipped a meal and dined on raisins and water to purchase fresh daffodils which would brighten her little "snuggery." Flowers have always meant a great deal to the girl from rocky Newfoundland. Her mother had been something of a miracle gardener, raising flowers in the acid soil on Placentia Bay. If Patricia Murphy lives by any particular adage it's "waste not, want not," a carry-over from those early days when frugality meant survival. Seemingly, she is incapable of squandering money foolishly, yet she was to spend thousands every year on the exotic floral paradises that have become her trademark.

ONE HEXED RESTAURANT FOR TWENTY-FIVE DOLLARS

Most evenings, Patricia dined at an inexpensive Italian restaurant near her residence. One night she was crushed to discover a sudden "Out of Business" sign tacked upon its front door. Inquiries revealed that people thought there was a hex on the place—three sets of owners had failed in one year. The owners were willing to turn over the restaurant to anyone who'd pay $25 a week, including equipment. Why, she asked herself, shouldn't it be Patricia Murphy? When told about her plans, the previous owner sighed and shrugged. "I hope you have a secret, Miss Patricia." In a way she did. She was not afraid of work, she genuinely loved doing things that brought pleasure to others, and she didn't believe in hexes. Her restuarant experience had convinced her this was a challenging field in which she could be quite happy. On January 3, 1930, with the sixty dollars return carfare she had prudently stashed away in case New York didn't work out, the nineteen-year-old Miss plunged headlong into the restaurant business in a basement at 114 Henry Street, Brooklyn Heights.

Pat had definite ideas from the start. Her initial project was to eliminate the naked overhead electric bulbs, and install flattering candlelight, which produced a happy, party-like atmosphere. Also, most important: it was less expensive. As she scurried around, her mind was actively seeking the perfect name for the place. Several were considered but the word "Candlelight" seemed to convey the mood she hoped to achieve. "Patricia Murphy's Candlelight Restaurant." There was a ring about it which she liked and she adopted it immediately.

Eating-out money was scarce during these desperate times. She realized that unless she could produce an abundance of good, graciously served food that would make customers temporarily forget the horrors of the depression, the breadwinner would take his hard-earned money elsewhere. By a careful study of the shopping habits of neighborhood housewives, Patricia knew that by buying wholesale, she could serve substantial meals as cheaply as they could at home. This meant forty-five-cent lunches, and sixty-five-cent or eighty-five-cent dinners. People, she felt, enjoyed the added luxury of ordering somebody else around, so that was another plus in her favor. If initial financial calculations were correct, serving one hundred meals a day, with a dime profit on each, meant a return of seventy dollars a week. This would cover the rent, groceries and more. It was worth the try.

"Our now-famous popovers," she says, "did not occur to me in a blinding flash. I studied dozens of cookbooks, anxious to find a delectable hot bread people weren't likely to have at home. Popovers were the logical choice, for they were tasty, slightly exotic— and not too difficult to make."

Fortunately, Patricia Murphy has always exuded a sincere enthusiasm that is contagious. At Columbia she found student friends who were willing to work for half-priced meals plus tips. An experienced cook agreed to hold off a week or so on salary. An architect friend joined others willing to occasionally plunge into tubs of dirty dishes. On the first night in business, Mr. Anthony, the previous owner, was so impressed with her ingenuity that he surprised her by setting up all the tables while Pat was nervously attending to other duties. "I was so touched," she says, "that I have always folded my linen napkins Italian style in every restaurant I've owned since."

There was one job Patricia deliciously reserved for herself because no one would give it to her in other places she had worked. She longed to be a hostess. For the opening of her own establishment, she donned the one special long gown that the family had bought for concert appearances. There was no higher authority now to scoff that this five-foot tower of strength was simply too tiny to be directing traffic. Her gracious welcome to guests and her alertness to their needs were far more important requisites for a hostess than great stature. Among the opening night perplexities was how to juggle twenty cups and saucers among thirty-six diners at a time. Fortunately, none of the eighty-four treasured guests served during the evening voiced any complaints on that score. How did they manage? "We prayed a lot," she says. And, of course, supplemented prayer with a constant watch at every table.

It was during these days that Patricia Murphy's ever-roving eyes helped develop a talent which astounds her employees and guests even today. With a sweeping glance over several large dining rooms, she can "count the house" and at the same time report which customer in the far corner needs seconds on butter. She insists it is this painstaking attention to details that has made her successful.

Patricia Murphy admits now that if the dime-a-meal profit hadn't been realized the first night, there wouldn't have been a second. There was total chaos when someone misplaced a twenty-dollar bill. A cash register was financially out of the question so money was cached under a display of pots, pans, and crockery which had been decoratively iced to resemble party cakes.

It was fully a month before the Candlelight's financial situation was ascertained. All she knew was that guests were coming in and she was able to pay each bill in cash. One evening when the dishes were finished, her architect friend, Harry Weston, explained the facts of business life to her. Counting cash on hand and in the hidden "register," and subtracting rent, food, and service bills, she found a five-hundred-dollar profit—and lost a voluntary dishwasher. "You can afford a pro now," he announced, hanging up his wrap-around apron.

Before long, her promotional campaign was in full swing. Eager students were hired to distribute attractive hand-painted menus with samples of cookies to residents from nearby hotels. She was convinced if they tried her Candlelight once, they'd join the regulars. Even today, Patricia Murphy seldom advertises, believing the word-of-mouth method more satisfactory. In her country restaurants where leisurely dining prevails, colorful postcards are offered to guests and mailed free. Postage bills usually top twenty-five thousand dollars a year but she feels this is an honest endorsement to her business, and the most valued kind.

Patricia Murphy started each day at the Wallabout Market. She found they sold excellent produce at good prices and sometimes took pity on the little girl who looked as if she might be collecting for the Sisters of Charity, by throwing in extra celery, lettuce, or whatever they had in surplus. "When it came to meat, I never stinted on quality, however. You can't cut corners on the mainstay of a meal and expect to survive."

EXPANDING THE BUSINESS

Soon Patricia Murphy found it necessary to break through neighboring walls to expand the Candlelight operation. Then she added a garden where additional customers could be served during the warm weather. ("Having experienced loneliness myself, I feel customers appreciate the warmth and friendliness that flowers and plants provide.") Her friend Jack Lynas, a painter and interior decorator, helped paint trees on the walls, construct a pretty fountain, and design a terrace. Shortly after the renovation, she was serving 350 customers a day.

It's human nature to enjoy something for nothing. In those early days, Patricia Murphy borrowed a punch bowl from the Presbyterian minister next door, filled it with iced fruit punch, and kept guests happy while they were waiting for a table. This proved a very successful gesture that in time was extended to include complimentary shrimp and hors d'oeuvres to cocktail lounge patrons who were waiting to be served dinners, and after-dinner candies for all departing guests.

During the early days of Operation Candlelight, Pat's eyes were opened to a totally unexpected element of business life. When the linen supply company brought shabby, undesirable goods, she blithely changed companies. Soon a stocky, glowering man paid her a visit, assuring her that people who wanted to stay in business didn't cancel with them. In her blissful naïveté, she ushered him out with a broom. She realized later, she was too insignificant to carry out threats of reprisals. Nevertheless, she and the stray German shepherd dog who had come to share her room suffered some uncomfortable weeks.

Within two years of that first opening, Patricia Murphy—always on the alert for desirable new innovations—installed one of the first air-conditioning systems in the country. Elderly guests complained she was trying to give them rheumatism, but enough people flocked there to make the $1400 investment worthwhile. She had accepted the unit at cost with the understanding that the York Ice Company salesmen could bring in prospective customers for demonstration purposes. Since their clients frequently became her customers, it was a wise decision with dual benefits.

Next she branched out into the catering business, supplying breakfasts at a riding academy, and luncheons to the Brooklyn Union Gas Company and nearby schools. Miss Murphy claims to be the only restaurateur in the city at that time who dared to offer lobsters. She imported them from her home town in Newfoundland and served them on the twenty-five-cent table d'hôte luncheon. She also persuaded a concessionaire at Jones Beach to purchase lobsters, which she precooked in Brooklyn. But finally the sheer exhaustion of a grueling fifty-mile drive to Long Island plus her primary restaurant duties proved too taxing and she abandoned the lobster project entirely.

In 1938, she was realizing a tidy fifty-dollar-a-day profit in Brooklyn, and she looked with interest at the booming restaurant potential of an area she thought destined to be the new center of Manhattan activity, Park Avenue and 57th Street. Her motto: Always Think Big—and Hope for the Best. An appointment was arranged with the building's rental supervisor for "Pat Murphy." When the diminutive young woman introduced herself, the agent burst into unrestrained laughter. The Pat Murphy he apparently envisioned was a burly Jack Dempsey-type restaurant man, and he simply refused to consider her offer seriously. "I was furious to be discriminated against before we had an opportunity to even discuss the rent. In fact, from that day on I've championed scores of other ambitious girls who were rebuffed in the career world. Actually, though"—she smiles rather contentedly—"we've proved ourselves so capable, the problem hardly exists today." Then she adds thoughtfully, "I must say, many people took a paternal interest in my career and helped me immeasurably along the way."

CHALLENGE ON 60TH STREET

With typical "I'll show him" Irish aplomb, Patricia Murphy signed a lease on the Betty Barclay Tea Room at 60th Street, east of Madison Avenue. The location was just as desirable as the 57th Street spot. With a two-hundred-customer capacity, it was seating half that number although the somewhat lackadaisical owner admitted an ambitious and energetic proprietor might do a three-hundred-dollar-a-day business. That was all the venturesome girl had to hear. The only time she admitted insecurity was when she requested permission to keep the tearoom's old name for a few months until her reputation was established. Aside from the financial jitters such an undertaking creates (eight hundred dollars a month rent!), there was a culinary challenge, too.

In Brooklyn Heights the customers wanted simple, "meat-and-potatoes" meals. In Manhattan, her restaurant was frequented by New York's old-guard socialites, as well as professional and business people. Their tastes were inclined toward fancy salads and constantly changing menus. If she was to capture some of this business, it was necessary to introduce light yet tasty and nutritionally adequate platters with a daily element of surprise. Again, she delved into the more advanced gourmet guides, anxious to please an entirely new set of customers. The glowing candlelight, towering baskets of hot popovers, and a profusion of flowers on white cloths remained, for these had become her hallmark of gracious dining. Timidly, Pat initiated what she considered an exorbitantly-priced lamb-chop luncheon—seventy-five cents! In the beginning her orders at the wholesale butcher were so conservative one or another of the help was frequently seen dashing to a high-priced Madison Avenue butcher for eight chops. Often, by the time he arrived a phone message would "make it a dozen," or even two dozen.

During these busy days, well-dressed, very feminine Patricia Murphy was a standout among the burly men at the produce, meat, and fish markets downtown. She did all the buying herself, and personally delivered foodstuffs to the 60th Street kitchen where every item was carefully reweighed. "When you're working so close to cost, every penny counts. I couldn't afford to be cheated and if I was, they heard about it!"

That first summer on 60th Street, July business was so poor and the premises so hot, it was not worthwhile to stay open. Although it was unheard-of at the time, she gave her help vacations with pay, for she wanted them to come back. Then she arranged to expand into the adjoining building before the reopening. Next year air conditioning would save the day.

Pat's friend Jack Lynas came to the rescue again. There wasn't too much extra money to work with but they made do with second-hand furniture in some areas, used large mirrors to cover ugly walls, added a profusion of flowers to brighten dark corners and produced the right aura once again. The Candlelight had not only bucked the summer slump, but used the time for improvements. Pat spent the first part of her half-vacation sitting in a small Italian restaurant across the street from her 60th Street place, watching people pass by, apparently disappointed at her shutdown. She studied them as they bypassed several restaurants, then flocked to another. What made one place more successful than the other? She went in and saw for herself, making a series of mental notes on the *do's* and *don'ts* of pleasing customers.

Although the bar business at any Candlelight restaurant is a secondary accommodation, Miss Murphy was anxious to install a cocktail lounge at her more sophisticated Manhattan restaurant. The "cocktail hour" was becoming popular and all her elegant competitors had lounges catering to the after-business socializers. She had a problem, however. An old statute on the New York legal books forbids the sale of alcoholic beverages in a building where an employment agency is housed. Unfortunately, there was such a business in the offices above the Candlelight. Besides, the landlord was a devout Christian Scientist who frowned upon liquor being served on the premises. It remained a sticky situation for several years. Finally, Pat and her real-estate man found new headquarters for the employment agency and she bought the original building for $105,000—without the help of bankers. Eventually she purchased the property next door as well, for the same amount. The little girl from Newfoundland had crashed the big time.

By now World War II was on. With restaurant owners and housewives alike, she faced the ration coupon crisis. "It was reasonably easy for anyone in-the-know to buy coupons, but I just couldn't do it," she says. "Too many people I knew and loved were involved in the war effort. Naturally, no one in business wants to lose money, but I had to make some concession, so luncheon service in Brooklyn was curtailed." Again it was a matter of those customers requiring scarce meat coupon dishes while the Madison Avenue people happily settled for crabmeat, shrimp, and fruit salads. "At least when the war was over I could look at myself in the mirror and know I had acted in good conscience," she says of her refusal to participate in black-market deals.

During the memorable big snow on New Year's Eve, 1947, Patricia Murphy discovered there are more rewarding facets to life than being a successful businesswoman. Unannounced, friends brought along a brilliant, ruddy-complexioned naval architect to her town house on Cranberry Street. Captain James E. Kiernan (Annapolis and M.I.T.) proved the perfect aid to the harried hostess when he suggested the instant-chilling of champagne in the snowbanks for a midnight toast. During the following months, she realized that the Captain's placid manner offered the perfect complement to her own excitable nature. He could make her laugh at personal idiosyncrasies, and he succeeded in arousing her enthusiasm about various phases of New York's social life. The two were married the following July 12, to enjoy "ten of the happiest years a wife has ever known."

MANHASSET, HERE SHE COMES

Before long the Kiernans were thinking about a retreat away from the bustling city. Patricia Kiernan sensed from conversations with customers that the trend was definitely toward suburban living.

Among the Candlelight regulars, a congenial group of dentists and other professional people frequently stayed on past closing time to engage in topical discussions that kept Pat well abreast of important news, trends, and ideas. In 1950 the Kiernans discovered a deserted clubhouse with adjoining house, garden, and garage, set back on a main artery in Manhasset, Long Island. It was a choice spot for a country restaurant!

Alert to customer inconveniences, Miss Murphy had often thought restaurants made parking facilities needlessly irksome by hiding them to the rear. At Manhasset she revised that idea and put the gigantic, easily accessible expanse in front of elaborately landscaped grounds. After the main buildings were completed, Miss Murphy decided she wanted a gift shop where guests could browse while waiting for tables. The Newfoundland store of her girlhood had fond memories, and she traveled extensively to find unusual items for her own shop. To her absolute amazement, of the $1,500,000 grossed the first year, $60,000 came from the small gift "box."

When floodwaters threatened their restaurant during the initial season, Captain Kiernan (whose experience included duty in the Philippines and battleship designing) devised a pumping system that experts said defied the law of gravity—but it worked. In addition, he handled their accounts so effortlessly that a bank president, not knowing his connection with Patricia Murphy's, offered him a position!

In Florida, finally getting a much-needed rest, the Kiernans found a tremendous estate which they envisioned as their eventual retirement home. Completely renovated, "Kinsale" (named for a favorite harbor town in Ireland) now boasts a gigantic swimming pool beside fully equipped marble cabanas, a lagoon, and forty-eight acres of land under cultivation. The garden products are used at their restaurants. Over the past fifteen years, thousands of flower enthusiasts and world-famed botanists have stopped to admire the many varieties of orchids which Miss Murphy grows there in temperature-controlled greenhouses. Like any subject which interests her, orchid growing has become almost an obsession and she has virtually memorized an encyclopedia of information on that delicate flower and others.

THE PERFECT CANDLELIGHT—OR MURPHY'S FOLLY?

By 1955, business was booming in all three restaurants, but their unique problems and diverse tastes left little time for anything but work. Finally, the Kiernans decided to sell all three and concentrate on one "perfect" Candlelight, incorporating all they had learned from past experience.

This had to be a restaurant totally of their own design from beginning to end. The location they chose was twelve acres of field and swampland on Central Park Avenue, Yonkers, that showed so little promise people referred to it as "Murphy's Folly." By the time it was transformed into a showplace setting, $169,000 had gone into landscaping alone. (Captain Kiernan looked over the bills and said, "Let's forget the grass and paint the ground green.") The total cost of the sprawling restaurant with sloping gardens, and a bridge over a man-made lake, hit one million dollars. Townspeople fought the building at first, and new building codes were suddenly initiated to halt a project that all banks considered a very risky proposition. But the Kiernans won out. The restaurant became the largest in the East, serving as many as ten thousand meals on a single holiday. In five years, the owners were offered five times the original cost.

They succeeded immediately for a simple reason. From her previous experience in Manhasset, Patricia knew that people who drove to outlying areas sought a relaxed afternoon or evening in the country. Many times "dinner out" was a family's big event of the week and she was determined to make her meals a memorable occasion. She revived holidays in the old-fashioned traditional way with decorations, costumes, and gifts. She didn't bar or discourage youngsters, as many competitors did, but encouraged their business with niceties that made parents relax with a feeling of genuine welcome. At

Christmas there was a nativity scene with real animals grazing out-side. A huge merry-go-round with Santa and his reindeers were added to the front lawn; it drew visitors from all neighboring states. Other holidays are similarly festive. She introduced colorful, sea-sonal costumes for the employees at her dream restaurant as well. Once again, the Candlelight was made up primarily of young, edu-cated people, many trained for other fields but preferring the op-portunities and atmosphere in a congenial organization. Miss Mur-phy is especially pleased when second-generation workers come to stay. She calls herself a "frustrated housemother," doling out aid and advice when it's asked for. When employees have weathered an especially hectic period, there are parties or personal gifts. She takes an interest in the families, believing a happy wife at home sends a contented man off to work. She has added medical benefits and kept pace with larger organizations. She claims to be a "brain picker," rewarding employees who come up with worthwhile sug-gestions for improvement. Advancement is always from within the ranks.

In 1957, the bubble burst for Patricia Murphy personally when a heart attack killed her husband as they returned from a vacation abroad. Friends feared for her life. She admits she didn't want to get out of bed mornings and face another day alone. Gradually, she realized the wisdom of employees and friends who prodded her into activity again, and she began to be active in business once more.

Captain Kiernan had wished for her to publish the story of her life. For over a year she worked diligently on the book, *Glow of Candlelight,* which not only proved excellent therapy, but has en-joyed continuing success since. On publication day her autograph party at Macy's broke all records reported in *Publishers' Weekly.* Advance mail orders in that one store amounted to 950 copies and in two hours she personally greeted the buyers of 1500 additional books! "I think people were surprised to discover there really is a Patricia Murphy," was her way of summing up the excitement she generated.

"U.S.S. CONCRETE" IS LAUNCHED

In a continuing effort to regain her zest for living, Patricia Murphy next decided to take flying lessons. There seemed to be a wonderful consolation and rebuilding of self-confidence aloft in the clouds in her own twin-engined plane. Since then her plane, christened "Miss Tango," has taxied personnel, food, flowers, and gifts between the restaurants and proved a most practical investment.

On a trip to Florida in 1959, Miss Murphy saw a shuttered restaurant on the site of the Bahia Mar Yachting Center. Three previous owners had met financial disaster during these years. For sentimental reasons, mostly, she decided to accept the challenge it presented. She dubbed it the "U.S.S. Concrete," denoting its total lack of charm or landscaping. Leaving only the shell of the building, she had the entire interior restyled. The flat area outside was transformed into Oriental gardens with one-hundred-foot-tall palm trees. Not only did the Candlelight become a vacationists' mecca and yachtsmen's haven bettering $1,250,000 in receipts the first year, but there was a complete rejuvenation of the whole region.

In time, Miss Murphy acquired the lease to run the entire yacht basin. Then, wishing to utilize space on either side of a causeway leading to it, she spent thousands of dollars on fill which increased the land area by eight and a half acres and made it a more workable piece of property. Ultimately, a hotel and theater complex will be erected on the site.

During these years, Patricia Murphy also branched out in other fields. Plunging into the perfume business, she spent considerable time with chemists to create an imaginary scent for her favorite flower, the green orchid, which has none of its own. She has her own private stock in alcoholic beverages now, too. And there are jams, jellies, and party goods packaged under her label.

In 1964, Miss Murphy was approached about taking over two insolvent mid-Manhattan restaurants in a popular chain. One was at 38th Street and Madison Avenue, the other on East 49th Street, a few doors off Fifth Avenue. She agreed. Again, she changed the entire façade and culinary offerings and within eight days of opening (sans advertisements of any kind), there were lines waiting to get in. To a woman gambling a fortune on her reputation, there is no prettier scene.

In the years since 1930 when Patricia Murphy first went into business, literally thousands of other ambitious women have opened tearooms in New York. The number remaining today can be counted on the fingers of one hand. None, certainly, has achieved the success enjoyed by the brilliant and progress-minded woman who seldom has time to analyze why it happened to her. "Perhaps," she muses, "there has to be an inborn fear of failure that makes a person persevere as I have." Then she adds, "The business is my life. I thoroughly enjoy people and am grateful to have been blessed with an instinctive knowledge of what it takes to make them happy."

BEHIND THE PATRICIA MURPHY STORY

Patricia Murphy's success started at the age of nineteen, when she opened her first Candlelight Restaurant. Her story is an interesting example of the "single enterprise" career. She pyramided one success onto another in the same type of business. After she'd brought her first restaurant in Brooklyn up to a point of profit, she went on to Manhattan. This type of leapfrogging is particularly common in retail businesses. One store's success is used as a steppingstone for the launching of a second, and so on. That's how many chains are built.

But the question is, How is the initial success accomplished? In Patricia Murphy's case it was achieved by a set of operating practices—unconsciously but nevertheless precisely developed—that built a clientele, despite tough competition, and despite the shortage of cash that kept many would-be diners home during the Great Depression. Essentially, Patricia Murphy's formula was to offer good meals at a reasonable price, in gracious surroundings. Her customers enjoyed an aura of good living—candlelight, flowers, pleasant decor.

Being a woman plainly had as many advantages as drawbacks. True, when "Pat" Murphy turned out to be a diminutive young woman, a renting agent turned down her offer on a desirable restaurant site. On the other hand, she didn't lack male help in starting her original enterprise. Male gallantry saved the day. Everyone from dishwashers to decorators turned up to help this courageous young lady.

Patricia Murphy's breakthrough can be pinpointed almost exactly: it was the moment when she opened her first restaurant, removed the naked overhead electric bulbs and replaced them with candlelight. These candles became her business trademark. But more than that, they symbolized her understanding of what the "diner-out," particularly of the less monied classes, sought: a feeling of intimacy, warmth, and an *unhomelike* atmosphere. Patricia Murphy's other innovations all stem from a basic understanding of her potential customers. Her ideas were all variations on a theme— glamour and beauty at a reasonable price. Her energy and ingenuity in developing this approach accounted for the success of her first restaurant and all the others to come.

In addition, several other approaches helped swing the balance in her favor:

Quality Appeal. In an interesting way, Patricia Murphy's personal problem with hats was transferred to her approach in running a restaurant. As the episode in the 14th Street apparel store showed, she was very much aware of the difference between first and second rate. In running her restaurants, she transferred her personal good taste to her potential customers and catered to it to the best of her ability.

Adaptability. Miss Murphy clearly believed in free enterprise. However, in her case the phrase refers to her ability to move about the map freely. If she ever suffered from homesickness or pined for the comforts of home, her story doesn't reveal the fact. She traveled from Placentia to New York, from Staten Island to Manhattan, without any signs of awkwardness or inhibition. She was, one might say, "at home in the world." Certainly for a woman this feeling of personal freedom is unusual. It obviously played a part in her progress.

Opportunity Creation. Symbolized by her first big move, from Newfoundland to New York, Patricia Murphy was constantly looking for ways to improve her situation. Notice, for example, her change in rooms to gain the advantage of lower rents. Or her resolve to show up early at the restaurant where she had the job of playing piano. In this case, "early" meant 6 A.M., to give her the opportunity of filling in for restaurant help who failed to show up. This practice not only enlarged her income but also her experience.

Basic Calculation. One approach of Patricia Murphy's shows up repeatedly in the lives of successful people. They make an assessment of basic factors to check how they're doing or what they must do to make out. Patricia Murphy did this when she opened her first eating place. She studied the shopping and eating habits of neighborhood housewives and decided that she could serve substantial meals as cheaply as they could at home. She then figured if she made only a dime profit on a hundred meals a day, she could clear seventy dollars a week, a satisfactory return. It's what the metal tycoon does when he prices his product a few cents a pound under the prevailing market, in hopes of gaining through volume more profit than he loses in margin. Nowhere did Patricia Murphy put the idea in words, yet she worked on the principle of the "slight edge." She aimed to develop an edge over the competition, the slight margin that would make customers come to her restaurant in preference to others in the neighborhood. By the use of candlelight, popovers, and personal attention, she built that intangible slight edge into a million-dollar business.

Entangling Alliances. Many a successful businessman can look back to a critical period when the very life of his enterprise hung in the balance. The one factor that made the difference was the help of a friend or family member. This help may have been in the form of actual participation or the investment of money. However the assistance was offered, it was enough to save the day. In Patricia Murphy's case, the help she got from friends—Jack Lynas and Harry Weston, Mr. Anthony, the previous restaurant owner, her student friends who served as waitresses in return for half-priced meals and tips—turned the tables in her favor.

Attention to Detail. The ability to handle details has a yes-and-no position in the stories of successful people. In some cases it is the ability to stay *away* from detail and concentrate on the broad issues that accounts for results. In Patricia Murphy's case, however, it was the ability to *concentrate* on details—everything from decor to free hors d'oeuvres and air conditioning—that gave her restaurants customer appeal.

Success Pyramid. Pat Murphy's pattern of progress is the classic case of stepping from one success to another. Another individual in her position might have been content to rest on the laurels and profits of her first enterprise. After all, even the fifty-dollar-a-day profit she eventually made in Brooklyn was not large enough to automatically suggest expansion. But she was convinced that, with some tailoring, the ideas that had worked successfully in Brooklyn would also pay dividends in Manhattan. She was willing to take the next forward step despite its risks—and she won.

"Make Do." There is a kind of fascinating paradox in Miss Murphy's approach to running an enterprise. She wanted her restaurant to be "different," that is, "superior," and she was able to accomplish this with a minimum of resources. This ability showed itself when she demonstrated that she could keep thirty-six diners happy with only twenty cups and saucers. In the decorating of her 60th Street restaurant, by the judicious use of secondhand furniture, large mirrors, and a profusion of flowers, she was able to create an atmosphere that attracted and pleased "the Manhattan crowd." It took both courage and the ability to juggle, to put lamb chops on the menu with only a few in the refrigerator. Backed up by a fleet-footed assistant who could make it to the butcher shop in jig time when additional orders came into the kitchen, she was able to keep up with the demand.

The ability to scrimp and scrounge isn't the only way to score. Actually, the opposite approach has been the path other successful people have taken—that is, they "do it right." They make sure that they have at hand all the resources they need before they start an enterprise. Patricia Murphy is an interesting example of the viability of the other approach. Her creation of a successful enterprise is also marked by her ability to modify her style to the need. Each restaurant she opened developed its own character and appeal for the type of customers available to it.

There is an interesting choice and emphasis on a major principle here. It might be said that Patricia Murphy applied two principles in her Brooklyn restaurant: the candlelight appeal that keynoted emphasis on warmth, intimacy, and hospitality; the other was that of low cost that would make eating out compare favorably with dining at home. It's a key to her subsequent success that Miss Murphy put major emphasis on the first principle rather than on the cost appeal in her later enterprises. It is this flexibility coupled with her understanding of the particular groups making up her potential customers that explain her continuing success in the enterprises she started.

19 { Jeno Paulucci—
HE BRINGS EXOTIC FOODS TO
AMERICA'S TABLES

Probably no other nation could produce the combination of culture
and temperament that has shaped the life and career of Jeno F.
Paulucci. His story couldn't be more American: A poor boy, the
son of Italian immigrants, becomes a millionaire by making and
selling Chinese food—and he does it all in the Viking country of
northern Minnesota. At forty-eight, he is the president and sole
owner of the Chun King Corporation, of Duluth, a company that
sells two out of every three cans and frozen packages of Chinese
food all over the world, and has annual sales of over fifty-five
million dollars. He remains a driving, intense, imaginative, frequently controversial business and public figure. Economically, he
fits the Horatio Alger image as few men do. But in his style and
drive, Jeno Paulucci is not much like the bland heroes of the Alger
novels.

* * *

He recalls his early poverty in matter-of-fact fashion. He has
never tried to capitalize on it, but he hasn't tried to forget it, either.
Having insisted on remaining in the same rather remote part of the
country where he was born, he can still look out from his cherry-
paneled office to some ramshackle buildings that "remind me
every damn day."

He was born in a town called Aurora, in the heart of the Mesabi
Range of northern Minnesota—an area that had already used
up most of one great natural resource—timber—and was fast running out of another—iron. The date was July 7, 1918, and here on
the edge of the wilderness, the hard times, which weren't to afflict

the rest of the country for another decade, had already struck. His father, Ettore, was a miner. In the late twenties and early thirties, he was unable to get work more often than one week out of six— for which he was paid twenty-five dollars. His mother, Michelina, was an immensely practical and industrious woman.

The family moved to the town of Hibbing with no improvement in their fortunes. Jeno (his name was Luigino, but everybody called him Jeno from the start and everybody still does today, including his employees) went on nightly foraging expeditions for coal, to fuel the family stove. He would pull a homemade wagon along the tracks leading to the mine faces, looking for chunks that might have fallen from the cars. If he didn't find any, he would turn to the abandoned streets of the area and help himself to any tar blocks he could move. There were quite a few such roadways, because the entire town of Hibbing had been moved two miles south some years before, when iron deposits had been discovered under the town.

WHEELER-DEALER IN KNEE PANTS

Some people have a natural gift for commerce, and Jeno, at the age of seven, was one of these. He noticed that during the brief summers, tourists often came to see the great but inactive mines. He decided to start a guide service. For a time Jeno had a busy enterprise in guiding tourists along the more accessible shafts, and in selling them souvenir ore he had packed in glass bottles.

At eleven, he turned to washing cars for fifty cents each, which was good money—but there weren't enough cars around. At twelve, the hundred-pound Jeno was working after school in a lumberyard, unloading thirty-ton boxcars of coal for fifty cents each, plus a few sacks to take home. Sometimes he unloaded boxcars of watermelons—for the same fifty cents plus a melon or two that had been spoiled on one end. On Saturdays he had another job—selling horse manure as fertilizer. The family was never on charity.

At the age of fourteen Jeno went to work as a handyman in the Downtown Daylight Market and got his first contact with the food business. His hours were from six to seven-thirty each morning, then from four to ten each night. On Saturday he worked from 5 A.M. to midnight. For this fifty-six-hour week he was paid in food to take home—bread that was not very stale, lettuce only slightly wilted, fruit only a little speckled. Later Jeno asked for cash payments and received $2.50 a week, but he did so well that he got a raise to $5.00.

Two years later, the boy journeyed to the lake port of Duluth, some seventy-five miles away, to take a summer job of another sort, but still in the food trade. He became a sort of barker for an outdoor fruit stand. At sixteen, he was earning sixteen dollars a week through good Italian lung power. Jeno's employer was an independent operator. His neighborhood competitor, a chain-owned fruit stand, brought in the best of local talent to out-holler Jeno, and the battle continued for two and a half months. Then the professional people in the surrounding buildings—doctors, dentists, lawyers—circulated a petition, and the city passed a law against fruit-stand barking. In a way, it was an ordinance against Jeno. It was also the beginning of a stormy love affair between Paulucci and the city of Duluth—an affair that has been going on more than thirty years.

At the time, however, Jeno returned to Hibbing, where great things were stirring for his family. A mining company decided to clear a section of old company houses—little four-room clapboard boxes. They were offered for sale at $125 each to anyone who would move them, the assumption being that they would be cut up for firewood. But the Pauluccis had other plans.

They had never owned a home of their own. They had found a vacant lot they could get for $100. There followed a tense family council, during which each member of the family emptied his pockets into a big glass bowl. At last a decision was reached—they would buy the house, have it moved to the lot and make it livable, putting in all the electric wiring themselves, and even some of the plumbing.

The foundation turned out to be the hardest part. Suitable material was hard to find, so Jeno and his mother began to drive along in their battered Ford behind telephone company trucks, waiting for them to replace poles. When the crew would knock down a pole fifty or seventy-five feet long, mother and son would put a rope around it, tie one end of the rope to the axle of the Ford and drag it down the street to their homesite to be used as part of their new home's foundation.

At last all the fixtures were in, the last door had been planed to fit and the paint was drying on the newly completed back porch. Now Jeno had an idea: "Let's open a store—a grocery store."

It seemed a logical move to him. After all, people still bought food no matter how hard times became. And a business of their own would give the hard-pressed little family a place in the world. Hadn't his mother already been packing spaghetti for sale around town—with Jeno acting as salesman? The family was swept away by the teen-ager's enthusiasm, and the front room became a grocery store, with a small assortment of canned goods, a few sacks of potatoes, and some produce. In 1933, with bread lines forming all over the United States, the Paulucci family business was born. Looking back on it now, Paulucci believes that was the turning point in his life. "For the first time, I began to appreciate the unlimited opportunities open to a determined, hard-working person. This was the capitalistic system. This business enterprise could grow, I could put my energy into it. The idea was tremendously exciting!"

The little business didn't do badly at all. Now Jeno began to think of education. He entered Hibbing Junior College with the idea of becoming a lawyer, and stayed there a year and a half until a further tightening of the family belt forced him to leave school, for good. He got a full-time job with a grocery chain, turning over the operation of the family store entirely to his mother. Michelina worked just as hard at the enterprise as her son, long after he became a millionaire, in fact. She couldn't be persuaded to give it up entirely until 1955, when she agreed to retire and move to Florida.

"FIVE-FEET-FIVE OF DRIVING FURY"

But in his first job, the nineteen-year-old Jeno quickly grew restive. There wasn't much chance for advancement in the chain. He could probably get a better job in the big cities to the south, but he loved his bleak northern homeland. Finally he made a characteristic decision: He told a big wholesale grocery concern in southern Minnesota that he would open up the northern market for them by increasing their sales to retailers—but strictly on commission. And he wanted a healthy percentage of the profits. Sixty per cent for Jeno and 40 per cent for the wholesaler. Were they interested? They were.

Now Jeno Paulucci became five-feet-five inches of driving fury. He traveled throughout northern Minnesota, and parts of Wisconsin and North Dakota, sleeping in his car, shaving in filling stations, eating his various samples of canned meats, salmon, sardines plus bread he'd buy while driving the vast reaches of his territory.

The trouble, he decided, was that most retailers bought too little at a time, five- or ten-case lots to be dribbled out. Why not make it worthwhile for the retailers to buy by the carload? In the middle of the Great Depression, the idea was obviously preposterous—but it worked. Jeno got his company to sell straight carloads pooled among the various retail customers at a discount; then he worked closely with grocers in every town across the north to help them stage "buy-by-the-case" promotions. Jeno's commission grew, and so did his confidence.

He began to get the idea that he was going to be a success. He was supporting his family, paying his sister's way through the University of Minnesota . . . but then the wholesaler wanted to put Jeno on a salary like their other salesmen instead of Jeno's lucrative commission, which they claimed was more than the wholesaler's president was earning. Maybe it was time for Jeno to go into business for himself.

A PAINFUL FAILURE

He began to watch for opportunities, looking for some new idea in the food business that he could make something of. Then a friend talked to him about the potential demand for garlic—packaged, dehydrated garlic. Dehydration was a new field, full of possibilities. Jeno invested his savings of several thousand dollars in the venture. It failed. He was not wise in the choice of a business or in the handling of it, and years later he was still paying off his share of a judgment against the defunct firm. Considerably chastened, but still boiling with determination to get ahead, Jeno looked for new ventures.

World War II was coming to its climax. A bad knee, and his family's dependence on him, had kept Jeno out of the service and so nights he worked in shipyards. But he also was aware that the travels of American soldiers and sailors all over the world had permanently broadened the horizons of the people. Oriental foods, for instance. Tens of thousands of servicemen had sampled them and were coming home with a newly found appetite for them. Besides the popularity of Chinese restaurants, housewives were beginning to make Americanized Oriental dishes such as chop suey or chow mein. Yet Chinese foods were hardly merchandised at all in supermarkets.

PULL OF THE EXOTIC

Paulucci sensed another opportunity, this time to enter the exotic-food business. He read up on the subject, talked to experts, and became intensely interested in bean sprouts. The sprouts, important ingredients in Oriental dishes and readily adaptable to other kinds of foods, were grown indoors from mung beans, without soil, which means they were especially appealing in a climate where outdoor farming conditions were harsh. For centuries the Chinese had grown their bean sprouts in crocks of water. But Jeno got six aluminum trays, 24 inches deep, added hormone fertilizer to the mixture, and waited to see what would happen. In five days the sprouts grew four inches. He decided to raise and pack bean sprouts.

It was early 1947. His thirtieth birthday was still several months ahead. Paulucci borrowed $2500 and rented a quonset hut (formerly a rutabaga cannery) in Grand Rapids, Minnesota, a town near Hibbing. Here he set up his "hydroponic garden" to grow the sprouts, and his packing operation. He hired a staff of twenty. He started packing a prepared chicken chow mein in cans, seasoned as he learned how to season foods watching his mother cook in past years. He also proposed marriage. Now that he was entering business again, he felt the time had come. He and Lois Mae Trepanier were married about the time of the birth of the Chun King Corporation. The name for the business, he simply pulled out of the air.

At first, there was every chance that Paulucci's new business would fail. The growth from bean to sprout is only a matter of hours; there is a new harvest every day and one can prosper, or go broke, in a hurry. Paulucci assigned the sales job to himself, taking off every four weeks for a missionary tour of supermarkets. He gave demonstrations of his new prepared canned chow mein, sold and sold hard. In a few weeks he was selling three hundred cases of chicken chow mein a day to retailers in various parts of the country. Often enough, he came home from a sales trip and loaded shipments in trucks and cars himself, whenever he got a rush order.

Paulucci decided to go into the canning business in a big way, but his quonset hut was too small. So he moved down to Duluth, where Chun King has been located ever since. The company quickly outgrew its first plant there, and in 1951 moved into a huge plant of two million cubic feet of production and storage space. Paulucci planned to grow.

Duluth seemed the least likely place in the world for a manufacturer of Oriental food to set up operations. Paulucci could get celery from nearby Michigan only part of the year; the rest of the time he had to buy from Florida and California. Water chestnuts and bamboo shoots were imported from the Orient, shrimp from the Gulf of Mexico. The list of food supplies that had to be hauled long distances grew as Chun King added more items to its line.

But Paulucci had faith in his part of the country, and he insists that if he had it to do all over again, he would stay in Duluth. The very obstacles the company faced, he believes, made for a tougher, stronger organization. Very early in the game, Paulucci realized that he was too far away from the communication centers of the country to get much in the way of merchandising attention. He began to spend some 10 per cent of his total sales for advertising (4.1 per cent is the average for the food industry these days).

Paulucci perhaps could be called a successful businessman at this point, but his company was to struggle for several years, and a considerable amount of turmoil lay ahead. As a matter of fact, he has never stopped "running," and there is some question whether he will ever consider himself so successful that he can let up.

ENTERPRISE ON THE RAMPAGE

In those early years, Paulucci borrowed $200,000 from the Iron Range Resource and Rehabilitation Commission, a state agency, and set out to solve some of his problems. First he turned his attention to farming. He was anxious to assure sources of supply for Chun King, but at the same time he wanted to get his beloved northeastern Minnesota out of its prolonged depression. Perhaps the cut-over timberlands could become productive farms.

He organized a subsidiary called Wilderness Valley Farms and bought five thousand acres of tax-forfeited land in the shadow of the iron dumps. Here he would grow his own celery. And he had plans for potatoes, the rebirth of a Christmas tree industry, and for other crops that might thrive in the northland.

To his indoor bean sprout industry, he added mushrooms. He hired a staff of experts to develop a special indoor soil. When he found that the soil could be used for only one crop of mushrooms, but that it remained highly valuable for other purposes, he began to package the excess potting soil and sell it under the brand name, Living Earth.

At the same time, Paulucci tried to encourage the growing of fruits and berries. He had formed another subsidiary, Northland Foods, Inc., to market a line of (non-Oriental) pie fillings and related products. The blueberries were all imported from Canada, and Paulucci saw no reason for this. "You have some of the best blueberry land in the world," he preached to the sturdy Scandinavian farmers of Minnesota. "Use it. I guarantee to buy your crop —your whole crop." And so he did—at guaranteed prices.

For years Paulucci devoted time and money to an almost obsessive search for ways to increase the yield of Northern farms. He flew to South America and elsewhere, conferring with agriculturists who reported methods of speeding up the growth of certain plants, the better to raise them where the season is short. He was willing to try anything. For a time he even considered harvesting cattails, a weed common to the Northern lakes that was being used in high-temperature insulation, such as in jet aircraft.

One of Paulucci's early food diversification ventures was into the packaging of wild rice. Here, he was sure, was a food that could be successfully produced at home. The rice grew in the remote lake regions and by law could be harvested only by Chippewa Indians, during a certain period in late summer. The Indians moved along in boats, harvesting the rice with flails, in fields that had once been battlegrounds of Sioux and Algonquins. Wild-rice buyers, such as Paulucci, would fly into the region and bid on the crop, with a U.S. ranger acting as supervisor. Then the rice would be trucked to the city under armed guard. Wild rice was an expensive delicacy, and hijackers were fairly thick in those deep woods. Paulucci tried to expand the rice industry in several ways. For a time he airlifted Chippewas to the larger fields of Manitoba. Finally he invested in a modern rice-processing plant in the Minnesota wilderness, to be operated by Chippewas. This gave him a ready source of supply, but the crop was often hit by "rust," leading to substantial losses.

Most of Paulucci's farming ventures were less than completely successful. The early frosts and uncertain precipitation of the country were too much for many of them. But he still believes firmly that northeastern Minnesota can be made to bloom, and he is still ready to do his part. With his company's continual demand for raw ingredients, however, he has had to turn to major commercial sources for his needs.

PROBLEMS AT RETAIL

Paulucci also was struggling with problems at the retail level. One thing that bothered him was that a housewife who wanted to prepare a Chinese meal had to look for soy sauce in the condiment department, Chinese vegetables among the other canned goods, noodles on the macaroni shelf, etc. He sent his salesmen out to promote the idea of a Magic-Menu Bazaar, in which all "American-Oriental" foods would be grouped together.

And to give his line more impact, he threw out the red labels he had been using and switched to a family of white labels, each one clearly picturing the product inside, yet keeping the over-all Chun King family appearance.

He also invented and patented the divider pack, a simple but effective merchandising device. A can of chow mein sauce was taped to a can of vegetables, thus keeping the product crisp, and the two were sold as a unit called "Divider-Pak." This was an important step for Chinese food because of the difficulty of combining all the ingredients of a meal in one container.

In the early fifties, Chun King added a big frozen food line and many other Oriental and non-Oriental items. Already Chun King was developing its distinctive "image" through advertising and promotion. Always willing to take a chance, Paulucci staged a variety of "money-back" and discount coupon promotions, at one point offering to present an extra frozen tray dinner—of any brand—to anyone who would try a Chun King dinner.

Paulucci favored humor in advertising, but never could find an agency that quite satisfied him. He switched his account from one large agency because he felt they were satisfied with only a 10 per cent sales increase a year. "I think we should do twice that amount," brooded Paulucci. Finally Paulucci settled on the madcap advertising approach of humorist Stan Freberg ("Nine out of ten doctors recommend Chun King chow mein," a TV commercial announced some years back; then the camera panned in on ten doctors to discover that nine of them were Chinese), and that has been the Chun King approach since—to put fun in its advertising.

MEANWHILE, BACK AT THE DESK . . .

By 1960, the company's sales had grown to $26,000,000, from $400,000 in 1947. Restless, quiet-spoken but a compulsive worker, Jeno Paulucci stalked through his two plants in Duluth, his plant in Jackson, Ohio, and smaller Chun King operations around the country. He continued to get up at 4:30 every morning, drive through the chill Duluth dawn to the post office, where he picked up the company mail by 5:30. Then he would go on to the office where he would have hours to dictate into his machine or scribble memos before anyone else arrived. Often his executives would find new ideas, suggestions, or directives waiting for them on their desks. During the long day, Paulucci would frequently take time out to personally taste the products in the kitchens.

Paulucci kept this Spartan schedule for a decade, without the comfort of either tobacco or alcohol. In the past couple of years, he has hunted and fished in remote Canada with friends drawn from all levels of his plant and community. He is out of town more often, attending to business in the more widely dispersed company operations.

On the advice of friends, he took up golf as a method of relaxing. He has bought four sets of clubs and joined three different country clubs (two in Duluth, one in Florida). At this writing he has but two sets of clubs and has made the decision to quit the game—again. His pro noted that he always kept several reserve sets of clubs for Jeno and after each time Jeno played, restocked his golf bag with the various clubs that Jeno had either thrown away or broken. (He addresses the ball with the same competitive determination as he has with his business.)

In the mid-fifties Paulucci came to feel that he was watching things too closely, that his operational and marketing managers should be given more responsibility for daily decisions. Accordingly he began to exile himself for part of the first six months of every year. "I wanted to change the idea that this was a one-man organization," he says. "It was composed of hard-working young people with fine capabilities, who operate as a group. A one-man operation is fine to build up an organization, but not so good for continued operation." So Jeno spent more time in his vacation home at Sanford, Florida, and the Chun King team grew more effective. "To hell with committees," reads a sign he put up at the home office. "Think, act, expedite, and push it through yourself."

By 1965, Chun King had sales of some fifty million dollars and was by far the most widely known name in prepared Oriental foods, selling about two out of every three cans and frozen packages of Chinese food all over the world. Chun King has seven plants: three in Duluth, Minn., and one each in Jackson, Ohio; Cambridge, Maryland; Windsor, Ontario, Canada; and Compton, California. The fifty-million-dollar sales complex now owned by Paulucci includes the Chun King Corporation of the U.S.A., the Chun King Corporation of Canada, Ltd., Northland Foods, Inc., Etor Realty Corporation in Duluth and Chop Chop Corporation. Chun King's product lines include canned and frozen Chinese food, Wong's Frozen Foods (West Coast), Dragon Frozen Food (Canada), Jeno's Italian Foods, Wilderness Fruit Fillings, cake and pastry fillings, cream pies, and cakes and Wilderness Wild Rice products. On the "drawing boards" are Polynesian and Mexican lines. The company's Chun King Inn was one of the most popular pavilions at the New York World's Fair and the Brass Rail restaurants at the Fair had been persuaded, by Paulucci, to sell his products to all its stands. Paulucci now is full of plans to build a string of take-home food centers, called Chop Chops, across the country.

"But the amount of money one accumulates is no measure of success," says Paulucci. "Unless the success is collective, among the individuals participating in a venture, and unless the growth that results contributes to the general economy, no man can claim success."

Never really at home among the wealthy, Paulucci once complained: "I still see myself as a miner's son. I know Rome wasn't built in a day, but I look out my window and I see people living in houses like the one I used to live in."

At 6 A.M. one Thanksgiving morning, Paulucci landed at the Duluth airport, hurrying home from a business trip to spend the holiday with his family. The terminal was almost deserted, but he noticed one small shoeshine boy, there ready for any customers who might happen by. Congratulating him on his enterprise, Jeno offered him a future job with Chun King. But he doesn't believe in overprotection, or anything that might destroy initiative. He has the courage of his convictions, too. Not long ago he withdrew support from the city's Junior Achievement program because he felt it made the youngsters too inclined to do business in groups, instead of striking out on their own.

When Jeno fails at anything, it boils around inside him and continues to do so until he can straighten it out. Some things take years or a lifetime. For example, Paulucci probably would have preferred at the beginning to produce Italian foods, but the field was overcrowded. When Chun King was well established, however, he brought out a line of Italian foods, including pizzas, lovingly prepared according to recipes that had been in his own family. The project, however, was not as successful as Jeno had hoped. But he refused to let a temporary marketing mishap be turned into a merchandising malady. The program was indeed expensive—but in the end it turned out to be a profitable experience.

THE "FAILURE TABLE"

Characteristically, Paulucci takes occasion to remind himself of his mistakes. For years he kept a table near his desk for the purpose of displaying mementos of past miscalculations. Included were his "$100,000 Hat," a handsome Italian model that he once allowed himself to use as the basis of a food promotion. His intuition told him it would be a mistake—and it was. Also on the table was his "$85,000 Gavel," the instrument that a judge had banged down after a decision that set damages against Paulucci in a long-forgotten court case—a case he stubbornly fought, at one point refusing to agree to a compromise sum of $25,000. Then there was a very ornate coat hanger, to remind Paulucci of the time some business associates talked him into investing in the production of these high-style hangers, a venture that cost him $2500. Paulucci looks on the hanger as a reminder to stick to the business he knows: food.

BEHIND THE JENO PAULUCCI STORY

Paulucci's career was sparked by two factors that are common in American success stories: low-level economic background, which gave him compelling reasons to pull himself out of the mire of poverty, and the social and economic mobility of our culture that makes it possible for a person to "graduate" to upper socioeconomic levels.

Opportunity Awareness. Well before his teens, Jeno demonstrated that he was able to see a situation in profit-producing terms. He noticed that tourists were interested in the abandoned mines near his home town of Hibbing. The sight of tourists wandering around, looking for shafts and other mine workings (as familiar to him as his own face) might have been taken for granted. But Jeno put together the sight-seers' needs with his capabilities. Up came the idea of a tourist guide service. He was not content to stop there, however. The tourists were interested in souvenirs, and Jeno obliged. He put bits of ore into glass bottles and they sold like hot cakes.

Trigger. "That's when it all started," a successful man often reminisces. There is actually an event, a point in time, which serves to catapult the individual into the series of moves culminating in his arrival at the top. In Jeno Paulucci's case, this moment occurred when the family put together their first home. To Jeno, the physical building represented more than a place for sleeping and eating. In his subconscious, apparently, there lay the idea of an enterprise and this idea was suddenly brought to the conscious level by the sight of the one thing that could give it substance—a building. Said Jeno, as the family stood back to admire their newly completed home, "Let's open a store—a grocery store."

Foundation Strengthening. Talk to the average person about his career and chances are that somewhere in the course of the conversation he'll say, "I didn't have enough . . ." The words that follow may refer to anything from education to finances. By contrast, the successful person always seems to be able to obtain what he needs to operate. If he needs financing, he is somehow able to develop it. If he feels the need for additional education, he will expend the time and energy necessary to get it. Paulucci failed to go further in college. After a year and a half he had to leave school because of economic pressures. But the indication is that he had probably satisfied his feeling of need for an education even though he didn't complete the prescribed courses leading to a degree. However, in other areas—finances, personnel—he seldom stopped short of getting what was needed.

The Unexpected Solution. A successful man will often strike off in a completely unexpected direction in order to gain his ends. Jeno Paulucci demonstrated this when he was working for the wholesale grocery concern in southern Minnesota. In the middle of the Great Depression, when deals were small, enterprise hesitant and business imagination at a low ebb, Jeno Paulucci decided to peddle cases of food stuffs—not in five- or ten-case loads, but by the carload. And once having gotten this masterly concept, he *made it work*. He gave his retail grocer customers quantity discounts and helped them stage "buy-by-the-case" promotions. This particular operation of Paulucci's dramatizes in simple terms a strong point of many successful people. First they develop a good idea. Then they follow up with practical steps that will assure an advantageous outcome.

"Good Isn't Good Enough." There is an interesting difference between the dissatisfactions of the persnickety perfectionist and the dissatisfaction with mediocre results typical of the successful man. Paulucci demonstrates the latter situation dramatically. A large advertising agency had his Chun King account, and was able to produce a 10 per cent sales increase annually. By ordinary measures, the showing might be considered satisfactory. To Paulucci, unwilling to accept "ordinary measures," the increase was insufficient. "I think we should do twice as well," he said, and switched

agencies. He didn't accept "ordinary measures" for his own performance. He saw no reason to use them for appraising the performance of those on whom he depended for assistance. Setting a high standard is often a sure way of getting better-than-average results—from one's self, or others.

Maturity and Easing Up. Many successful businessmen have difficulty in handing over the reins to logical successors. They even find it difficult to delegate tasks to subordinates, in order to lighten their own work load. It's unfortunate, because it suggests strain, an inability to let go, rather than a healthy desire to want to run things. Jeno Paulucci, despite his strong energy drive, was able to ease off when he reached his middle forties. Note that in his case, it did not mean retirement from battle. He eventually was able to give his subordinates the responsibility of running his organization. But this became a constructive step up instead of a step down, because he then went on to apply himself to broader-gauge activity.

20 { Stanley Arnold –
IDEA MAN, INCORPORATED

Stanley Arnold has narrow shoulders, modest limbs, and an average voice. His graying hair lies on top of his ears with a senatorial curve, large horn-rimmed glasses magnify the twinkle in his eyes, and prominent teeth dominate his face. The total effect sometimes causes people to wonder, "Could *this* be Stanley Arnold?" It is, and people soon learn he's not a man to be trifled with. Arnold's physical presence is disarming, as are his ideas and words. His entire life has been committed to finding answers that are audacious, exciting, and uncluttered. In this lifelong pursuit, he has enlisted all the resources of personality and intuition. Arnold stands virtually alone as a creative spirit who is also a commercial success. Sought out by businesses of every variety, he has built his stream of promotion ideas into a million-dollar business.

During an average week, Stanley Arnold is said to meet with more presidents and board chairmen of blue-chip American corporations than any private man in business today. On a Monday, for example, he may be on United Air Lines 8 A.M. jet flight 294 to Chicago, to see United's president George Keck about a plan to increase traffic between New York and Los Angeles. On Tuesday, Stanley Arnold may have lunch with Barney Walker, the board chairman of the American Tobacco Company, a long-term client. Walker thinks that Arnold might be able to apply his talents toward the growth of an appliance manufacturer in the same way that he has contributed so many profitable ideas to American Tobacco. Walker has arranged for the president of the appliance company to meet Stanley Arnold at lunch that day. On Wednesday, Arnold might be presenting a new promotion to Jack Straus, board chairman of Macy's, the world's largest store. One day in 1964, after Jack Straus had said, "You work so hard for us you'd think Macy's was your middle name," Arnold had his middle name legally changed from Norman to Macy's; the public notice appeared on the front page of the *New York Times*.

Here's how the man sometimes called America's number one idea man has converted a stream of ideas into a million-dollar enterprise.

* * *

Stanley Arnold, thirteen years old, leaned against a back-yard tree and brooded about the fact that he was probably the worst broad jumper in the entire Cleveland school system. "If I'm so bad at jumping forward," he thought, "maybe I could learn to jump backward." Stanley stood up, hopped back, and tumbled down on the lawn. He tried it again, and this time, didn't stumble. Before long he was able to jump backward several feet, with even a measure of grace.

When he told the gym teacher about it, and suggested that the class might have a backward-jumping contest, the man looked at his spindly pupil and said, "Perhaps; it might be fun." At the next gym class, the coach announced, "Now we'll try a standing back jump." An excited buzz went through the crowd of boys. What, they wondered, was this new competition? The teacher explained that it was like a regular broad jump, except that the contestants would be measured on the basis of how far back they could go.

One by one, the class's top athletes took their positions, flung themselves backward, and landed a few inches away, flat on their rumps. When Stan's turn came, the others leaned forward, expecting the usual clownish performance. He bent low, and then, unwinding like a coiled spring, flew gracefully in reverse, landing neatly on his feet. Unquestionably, the school had not only a new and exciting event, but the world's first champion backward broad jumper.

BRAINSTORMS TO ORDER

Since that time, Stanley Arnold has jumped on to considerably greater things, invariably creating the same sort of excitement for his clients that he created as a youngster for his schoolmates. Today, he is president of Stanley Arnold & Associates, Inc., an organization whose sole function is to contrive novel ways for companies to increase the sales of their products. It may be a "Win a Share of America" contest, like the one he devised for Remington Rand, in which the winners received a share of every company listed on the New York Stock Exchange. It may be a "Treasure Island" contest, like the one he thought up for Piel's Beer; the winner received a Caribbean island. Or it may involve sending a rose every Monday morning for a year to the secretaries of a thousand presidents of New York companies—an idea which so increased travel volume for United Airlines that the company happily and hastily extended the practice to San Francisco, Los Angeles, and Chicago.

In short, Arnold's business is to spend other people's money—profitably. In the nine years since he started his firm with no clients and one secretary, he has helped American industry to dispense more than $75,000,000. In return, those companies have benefited by sales increases of hundreds of millions of dollars. It is no wonder then, that clients such as Ford, American Express, Goodyear Tire and Rubber, and American Tobacco regard him with awe. The profits that have flowed from Stanley's apparently inexhaustible imagination have endeared him to the corporate giants who must sell steadily larger quantities of their products in order to survive in mass consumption.

Stanley has benefited handsomely in the process. His company now earns about one million dollars a year. Stanley himself is a friend of many of the most famous people in America, has been the subject of a lengthy *New Yorker* profile, and has a handsome office in a prestigious glass-and-steel tower in Manhattan, an elegant Park Avenue home whose walls are enhanced with Dufys, Roualts, and Picassos, and a country place where he can get away from it all with his wife and his teen-aged daughter.

THE "TYPHOID MARY OF CLEVELAND"

It is a far cry from the beginning in Cleveland, Ohio, where he was born on May 26, 1915. While Arnold's childhood was not the most wretched ever suffered by an American youngster, it was also not the happiest.

His father owned a small creamery. "What I remember most clearly about him," Arnold recalls, "is that he kept both feet firmly on the ground. He worked hard—so hard that he rarely had time to relax. He had little interest in books or music or the theater." But Arnold was never able to follow his father's routine of long hours and little relaxation. He once confessed to an acquaintance: "A lesson I learned early is that if you apply yourself to business with all your might, you can learn to hate it damn quickly."

Arnold's mother was a gentle woman. She sang, played the piano, and must have done more than the ordinary amount of worrying about what would become of her only son, for Stanley was, to put it kindly, a difficult boy.

In the first place, he was frequently ill. "I was the Typhoid Mary of Cleveland," he has said. Whatever diseases were to be had, he had virulently. And he apparently had them more frequently than anyone else. One result was a monumental absence record in school, which did nothing to help his scholastic achievements. In fact, he now claims with what may be a measure of exaggeration, that in his first nine years of school, he racked up more failing grades than anyone had achieved in the history of the Cleveland schools. "I remember childhood," he recalls, "as running, running, always running to make up the time I'd lost away from school."

In the second place, he was, to use his own words, "a bad, bad boy." Undoubtedly, some of his malfeasance came from his attempts to find a better way of winning. One of these attempts, stemming from his desire to win a Boy Scout merit badge in camping, led to the near-incineration of wealthy Cleveland Heights. His assignment was to start a fire by rubbing two sticks together, and then to extinguish it. Practicing one dry summer in an open field, he found that rub though he did, the only thing that heated up was himself. In desperation, he decided to forego the first part of the assignment, and try his skill at fire extinguishing. He lit a match to the dry grass, and the flames immediately leaped across the field. "I remember the man who lived next to the field running out, and standing there with his little hose trying to put it out. It was useless. Before they got that fire under control, they had to call twelve fire trucks."

Is a difficult childhood a spur to adult success? Arnold thinks so. "It's hard on the parents," he has said, "but it's good for the kid. Successful youngsters can't understand this; but those of us who've been intimate with failure never stop running when we grow up."

SOME INFLUENTIAL FRIENDS

Like most youngsters, he was an avid baseball fan, and collected autographed baseballs from visiting teams. Gradually he began to garner autographs from other well-known people. He wrote one letter to Harold Burton, the Mayor of Cleveland, asking for his signature. Burton sent back a brief, kindly reply, and Arnold answered it, thanking him and telling the official a bit about himself. Soon, a steady stream of correspondence ensued. Burton left Cleveland for the Senate a few years later, and eventually became a Supreme Court Justice. By this time, a warm friendship had sprung up between the two men—so warm, that when Arnold's daughter, Jennifer, had her tenth birthday a few years ago, Burton insisted on celebrating it by acting as the guide on a tour of the Supreme Court.

Arnold's initial letter to Burton was an act typical of any youngster who hungers for a ray of reflected glory. But there was more to it

than that. He had sensed that an excellent way to broaden one's
horizons is to approach those who have already achieved breadth.

He made one of his most valuable friendships shortly after being
graduated from the Wharton School of Business and Finance, when
he returned to Cleveland and began working in the family business.
Once, during a vacation in Mexico in the early 1940s, he left his
hotel and climbed into a sight-seeing limousine. A gentleman in the
back introduced himself as George Z. Medalie. As they chatted
about stateside affairs, Medalie said, "It's a shame that Dewey
lost the nomination to Willkie last year."

"Dewey made a mistake right at the beginning," said Arnold.
"I went to school in Philadelphia, and I know that his convention
headquarters was in one of the second-class hotels. How could he
expect to impress people?"

"Where would you have had him stay?" Medalie asked.

"In a top hotel, like the Belleview Stratford."

"But Willkie had already reserved that."

"If I'd been running his campaign, I'd have reserved it months
ahead of Willkie."

"How could you know?" Medalie countered. "The nominees
didn't know where the convention would be held that far in advance."

Arnold pondered a moment, thought big, and answered, "If I'd
been running his campaign, I'd have reserved a suite in the best
hotel in each of the ten biggest cities in America. Then, when the
site was announced, I'd have canceled the other nine."

Medalie looked at him. "I never thought of that," he mused
aloud.

"What do you mean?" Arnold asked.

"You see," said Medalie, "I was his campaign manager."

After that, the two men became fast friends. Medalie invited
Arnold to many parties in New York, most of them attended by
high-ranking politicians, top-echelon executives, and recognized artists. "If Justice Burton kindled the flame of ambition in me," Arnold
said recently, "George Medalie put more fuel on the fire."

THE ZEN METHOD OF PROBLEM SOLVING

It is one of Arnold's peculiar characteristics that he does not strain systematically for ideas. Rather, he looks at a problem and lets it, in effect, tell him how it should be solved. He once stopped at the desk of an associate who had been struggling for days to think up suitable prizes for a contest that a carpet company was sponsoring for its salesmen and dealers. Arnold simply looked at the client's product and said, "Carpet—car . . . pet; why don't we suggest that the prizes be cars and pets? Everyone wants them, and it'll be a natural tie-in with the firm's products."

It is this ability to look at problems in a simple, direct, analytical way that has attracted the attention of businessmen yearning for solutions to their marketing problems. Recently, he described his approach in these words: "I let a current catch me. I may have some goal in mind, but I don't consciously figure out how I'm going to achieve it. I let *it* figure out how it's going to achieve itself, and then I act accordingly. In a way, it's like the Japanese philosophy of Zen. There's a Zen book on archery, and one of its basic principles is that you undermine yourself if you strain too hard. So, they say, to hit the target, don't aim."

Back in the depths of the depression, when he was still in college, his father put him to work during the summers supervising the dairy route salesmen. "Every night," he said not long ago, "they'd come in and tell me how rotten business was. I was convinced that this was largely a state of mind; that they could do better if they tried. But I didn't know what to do about it, at first. I suppose, if I'd been a direct, no-nonsense guy, I could have fired the nonproducers; or maybe I could have gone out on the routes with them. But somehow, this wasn't my way of doing things; as I say, I like to let ideas take hold of me.

"One day it occurred to me that maybe some sort of contest would get them to sell better. So I went to an aquarium and had them make up a fish tank about six feet wide and sixteen feet long, with

six troughs running the length of the box, each trough divided
into several removable compartments. I got six different-colored
fish and put one in the end compartment of each trough. I assigned
a fish to each man, and then marked his trough with a crayon. As
he passed a certain point, we'd pull out the compartment so that the
fish could advance. The last compartment was marked with a figure
10 per cent above the man's previous sales for that month a year
ago. Then we had a race to see whose fish reached the end first.

"Believe it or not, every one of those men raised his sales by 10
per cent. And this, in spite of their *still* coming in every night and
telling me how bad business was. It taught me several lessons.

"First, to get people to produce, you don't have to harangue or
threaten to fire them. Second, people can do better than they think—
if they're properly motivated.

"Third, you don't necessarily have to offer them expensive prizes
—what they want in their lives is excitement."

The public's need for excitement is something that Arnold has
exploited consistently throughout his career. His supermarket experience is an excellent case in point.

CONTACTING THE PUBLIC MIND

During his college years, Arnold had visited California and was
tremendously impressed with the then-new concept of the supermarket. Returning home after earning his degree, he urged his father to open one. Despite the older man's doubts—he reminded
Arnold that Cleveland was already dominated by one giant grocery
firm—he finally agreed to gamble. "As for the competition," said
Arnold, "I don't think they paid too much attention to us. They
must have figured we were so small and they were so big that if
they closed their eyes, we'd disappear."

The supermarket did not disappear; in fact, it thrived, and soon
after, the family opened a second. It was at this point that Arnold
systematically began to put excitement to work for him. "I would

walk down the street and watch people's faces," he now says. "I'd see they were mostly bored or sad, and I wanted to do something to make them happy."

One of his first attempts to bring joy to his customers resulted in an astounding success. He had read in the newspapers that the father of Bebe Shopp, the girl who was then Miss America, was an officer of the Cream of Wheat Co. Calling her at home in Minneapolis one evening, he asked if she would cut the ribbon at the opening of a new store. Before Miss Shopp could think about it, he added that if she agreed, he would put large ads in the papers, announcing a special promotion of her father's cereal. The appeal was direct and irresistible. She agreed.

Arnold was true to his word; the ads featured Cream of Wheat, and they were promoted throughout the store. And, of course, the advertising also proclaimed that Miss America was opening the new market. The crowds came in droves, and while they bought great gobs of cereal, that wasn't their major reason for appearing. They had come to see Miss America, and in the process, they gave the new store a tremendous send-off.

Subsequent promotions were bigger still. In one instance, Arnold wrote a letter to Hawaii, to Duke Kahanamoku, a former Olympic swimming champion, the sheriff of Honolulu, and one of the last survivors of the Hawaiian royal family. The gist of his message was: "Come visit our store. In your honor, we'll have a hoop-de-doo promotion for Hawaiian products." The Duke accepted, and his visit generated reams of newspaper stories and priceless publicity for the Arnolds' Pick-N-Pay chain, and for his "Hono-lulu of a Sale."

Arnold now did some personal stocktaking. He could excite Cleveland shoppers, but what about shoppers in the rest of the country? If he stayed with Pick-N-Pay, he would be secure, but security was not his aim. He wanted to test himself against bigger challenges—but was he ready? He had discovered the value of talking to successful men, and now he turned to one at the very top, Bernard Baruch. "It had been my experience," Arnold has said, "that the more successful a man was, the more approachable he was. I wrote him, explaining that I was in the grocery business, and that I was thinking about moving to Manhattan to try for bigger stakes. Would he spare me a few minutes to give me his thoughts?

"He gave me an appointment for 11 A.M. at his home in Manhattan. I got there a few minutes early, and a servant led me into Baruch's study. Against one wall stood a grandfather clock. At 11:00, it began striking, and precisely on the last stroke, Mr. Baruch walked through the doorway, erect, distinguished, forceful."

Baruch listened quietly while Arnold explained that he was not sure whether he should take a chance on leaving a good-paying, executive position for the hazards of the big city. In spite of his present rewards, he said, he still felt dissatisfied. Although the appointment was scheduled to last for twenty minutes, Baruch and Arnold talked for an hour and a half, and at the end, the older man said, "You know, Stanley, when you're riding a horse, you just give him his head until you're sure which way you want to go. Then you lap rein him—you tell him which way *you* want to go."

Baruch suggested that Arnold was probably ready to lap rein himself into New York.

APPRENTICESHIP FOR THE TOP

Returning to Cleveland, Arnold wrote to William Weintraub, head of a large New York advertising agency. "The firm," Arnold recalled, "was one of the hottest in the business, and I wanted to go with the best there was." Weintraub was intrigued with Arnold's supermarket success, and after a couple of interviews, asked him to join the agency, where his job would be to think up promotional ideas for clients' products. And so, in 1951, Arnold took his great leap forward.

In New York, he began refining his skill in the art of rising to the top. He learned, for example, how to block the idea-stealer. At a conference one day, he had tossed off an idea for a special client promotion. The suggestion was well received, but nothing further was done with it. Soon after, one of his colleagues submitted a full-scale report on how the idea might be developed for the client. The colleague took full credit for originating and exploiting the proposal.

Arnold was chagrined, but bided his time. A couple of days later, one of his bosses asked him for some suggestions on a related promotion. "Why don't you ask Jim about it?" Arnold suggested, referring to the colleague. "He's more familiar with it than I am." Soon after, the boss returned and said, "I'm afraid Jim can't help us out on this. He just doesn't seem to have the feel for it." Only then did Arnold propose a solution. In other words, instead of sulking because an idea had been stolen, he bided his time, knowing that the company would sooner or later have to come back for more.

Idea-stealing, in fact, is one of the things that bothers him least. "There's no point in hoarding ideas," he once told a friend, "because if you have them and they're any good, you're the only one who can carry them out. When my wife and I go into a restaurant and I discuss some idea I've had, she often warns me to lower my voice. And I tell her, 'I'll bet I could take this fork and bang on my glass for attention. Then, when everyone was looking at me, I could get up on the table, describe my idea, and tell them exactly how I planned to carry it out. And do you think anyone could do anything about it? Not a chance in a million.' "

After a year and a half with the Weintraub agency, Arnold moved on to another one, the giant Young & Rubicam, where he continued his apprenticeship for the top. One of the more important rules he learned was to stand his ground when he believed in something. A marketing man, a specialist of high repute, had developed a plan for selling a well-known cake mix. He had submitted the plan to Sam Cherr, one of Young & Rubicam's founders, and had had it circulated through the organization. A most impressive report, it was documented with complicated charts and dizzying lists of figures.

Arnold read it through and then went to see Cherr. "I've just read Harrison's report," said Arnold.

"And?" said Cherr.

"It's all wrong."

"All?"

"From beginning to end."

"He has a lot of facts to document his pitch. Where are your facts?"

"I don't have any facts, yet, I've been in the grocery business most of my life, and this simply isn't the way you're going to sell this stuff in supermarkets."

"Well," said Cherr, "if you're right, Harrison's wrong."

"That's right," said Arnold. "I *am* right, and he *is* wrong."

"If you're that sure, we'll take a closer look at it. And send me your own proposal."

Arnold did submit his own plan, and eventually saw it accepted. "I suppose I could have kept my mouth shut, or weaseled about the report," he says, "but I felt that I had to stand on my own feet. That's what they were paying me for, and that's what they had a right to expect from me."

CALL FROM CLEVELAND

Arnold's abilities were starting to earn him the recognition he craved, and he might have moved steadily ahead in the agency had not an urgent call come from Cleveland. The Pick-N-Pay chain had grown phenomenally under the supervision of the senior and junior Arnolds—so phenomenally that it was now the largest in the city. But Arnold senior was growing older, and Arnold junior had left town, and the family had decided to sell out. Now, the new owners were in trouble. Sales were sagging, morale had slumped. They sent a call to Arnold: would he return and try to rejuvenate the business? They would make it well worth his while.

The offer was too attractive to reject. Certainly, the money was part of the attraction, but, given Arnold's temperament, the challenge was equally alluring. On at least one occasion, he has admitted, "I think I go through life making unhappy people happy." No one who makes such a statement can be devoid of vanity, and Arnold has his share of it. But it is a vanity directed toward constructive ends, and he returned to Cleveland to see what he could construct.

He quickly realized that he'd have to do two things to get the chain back on its feet. Somehow, he'd have to convince the employees that the company cared about them and their future. And somehow, he'd have to bring the customers back, so that the employees *would* have a future. It was an almost instinctive act on his part to conclude that what was needed was some excitement. And he began to stir up his prescription.

George Belle was the beginning. George had been with the company twenty-five years, starting as supervisor of the first Pick-N-Pay. Now he was general superintendent of all the stores—and he was tired. Arnold recalled: "If George wasn't enthusiastic, then the employees under him couldn't be enthusiastic. I felt that we had to get him revved up again, and this would be a start on making the whole chain perk up."

Arnold's method was simple and unabashedly sentimental, but it was remarkably effective. He announced a sales meeting for the executives and the heads of all the food departments—some 150 people. It was a dress-up evening affair, and when the moment came, Arnold turned to George, and to the supervisor's bafflement, said, "George, the real purpose of this evening is to honor you, the admiral of our fleet. You've been with us a quarter of a century, and you've made this team into what it is today. Now, we want to recall those twenty-five years with you. . . . This, George, is your life."

From behind a curtain, one by one, came the members of George's family, many of whom he hadn't seen for years, and whom Arnold had imported from all over the country. There was much hugging and gasping, of tears and laughter, and it was difficult to tell who was the most euphoric: George, his family, the employees —or Stanley Arnold.

"From that time on," Arnold said recently, "George behaved as if he were ten years younger. The old zip returned; we'd excited him and he in turn became excited about his work. It spread to all the employees, too, because they all knew and loved George. In a way, it was as if in honoring him, we were honoring them."

At the same time, Arnold undertook a series of store promotions to bring excitement to the customers who had drifted away from Pick-N-Pay. In March of that year, for example, a terrific blizzard paralyzed Cleveland, leaving the stores deserted. Arnold realized that there was no point in keeping them open, but he wasn't about to chalk it off as a total loss. He sent out orders for the employees to lock up and go out and make snowballs. "We went out on the streets," he recalled, "and began packing them into empty grapefruit crates. That night, we had seventy-nine hundred snowballs, which we put into the frozen-food lockers. The staff had a wonderful time, but I know many of them wondered if I was cracking up."

Arnold wasn't. He was biding his time. He called the Cleveland Weather Bureau and learned that the middle of July was traditionally the hottest week of the year. Then he contacted the makers of Birds Eye frozen foods, and persuaded them to give away prizes in a special Pick-N-Pay sale that would spotlight their frozen products.

The heat wave came right on schedule, and Arnold was ready for it. He had packed the snowballs into insulated bags and allotted five hundred to each store. That week, he put on a five-day sale, advertised as a "Blizzard of Values." Every five minutes a bell rang, and the customer at the check-out counter received a bag of snowballs, plus a prize. By mid-afternoon, the mercury had climbed to 98 degrees, but the police had to be called to control the crowds trying to jam into Pick-N-Pay. Sales records fell by the wayside, and Pick-N-Pay commenced its climb out of the doldrums.

At the end of a year, Arnold had reversed the chain's slump. Young & Rubicam asked him to return and to work his magic on its clients. This time, he had little hesitation, and he was soon back prowling the executive suites of the country's largest corporations.

But success in this field was not always as easy to come by as it was in the supermarkets. As he has commented, "One of the drawbacks of my business is that I can't put my brain waves into immediate action, the way I could when I ran a chain of retail outlets. Now I have to sell my ideas twice over—first to the client, then to the general public. And no matter how earth-shaking a project may be, it won't get the chance to shake even a pebble unless I can persuade some business tycoon that it will be worth the often-considerable outlay involved."

This persuasion has taken many forms; but invariably, underlying all of them has been one attitude, the conviction that what Stanley Arnold wanted for the client was precisely what the client needed. "People are walking around all day," Arnold once said, "without any direction. If you tell them what to do, they'll usually be grateful to you."

"UNMAKE THE DECISION—OR I'LL UNMAKE YOU"

On occasion, "telling them what to do" has involved the daring use of pressure. Once, several years ago, Arnold interested a large cosmetics firm in a promotion based on a special phonograph record featuring several popular singers. He was given a deadline by which to negotiate contracts with all the singers. On deadline day, having signed up all but one, he visited the client's promotion manager and asked for a two-day extension. The man reluctantly agreed. But, two days later, Arnold still hadn't secured the contract, and it looked as if the six-figure deal was about to go down the drain. Arnold returned to the executive and asked for one more twenty-four-hour extension.

The man looked at him coldly, pursed his lips, and said, "Mr. Arnold, time's up. That's the end of it. The decision has been made."

Arnold stood up slowly, raised his fist, and brought it down on the desk. Coolly and distinctly, he said, "You're going to unmake that decision—or I'm going to unmake you."

The man stared back in astonishment, then mumbled, "Okay, but twenty-four hours is all you get. And that's final."

Arnold got the signature and closed his deal. Some time later, when he was recalling the episode, he said, "Frankly, I don't think I'd recommend anyone following my example. What I did was instinctive, although it was dangerous. My feeling at the time was that I had somehow to shock the man out of his negativism, and that was the only thing I could think of. Of course, if I hadn't delivered the goods the next day, I would have been finished forever."

On one occasion, for example, he found it useful to use a negative approach by warning clients of the catastrophes that would follow if they didn't adopt his ideas. When several members of the board of directors of a large food-processing firm hesitated to go along with a program his agency had worked out, he told them: "Gentlemen, I'm sorry, but we've created a monster, a Frankenstein. In working out the details of this program, naturally we've had to discuss it with a number of people. This idea now lives, and if you don't buy it, one of your competitors will."

He has since found this technique to be particularly useful when the client group is divided on the merits of a project. "It won't work if everybody thinks the idea is poor," he has said, "but when you have a slight majority in your favor, the negative approach can help bring over the others, who already feel uncertain because they're in the minority."

A BUSINESS BASED ON EXCITEMENT

In 1958, Arnold felt that he had mastered enough of the techniques of merchandising excitement to set up his own business. Although he had no clients, he was confident of his prospects, and signed a lease for an office in the most expensive building in New York—the Seagram Building—which was just being finished, and already being hailed as one of the most outstanding structures in

New York. "I wanted to be in that building," Arnold has said, "simply because it was the finest; I wanted everything in my company to be top-drawer."

Unfortunately, Arnold moved faster than the building, and he was ready to go into operation two months before his space was ready for occupancy. This fazed him not at all. He called on the chief executive of the Chemical Corn Exchange Bank—which has since become the Chemical Bank New York Trust Co.—at 55th Street and Park Avenue, and introduced himself. "I don't have an account with you now," he said, "but I'd like to rent your board room to use as an office for the next eight weeks. I'll be happy to pay you for the use of the space, and for telephone service; and if you agree, I'll promise to keep all of my accounts here in the future."

Whether the bank executive was bowled over by the novelty of the request, or whether he sensed that Arnold was a comer, will never be known. But he not only agreed to the proposal, he gave Arnold the space free. Arnold thinks that the bank may have acquiesced "because with my proposal, they were face to face with the free enterprise system, and they decided to participate. Generally, I find that business people are willing to help someone who asks for their help—it's simply part of our way of life."

With some astuteness, Arnold had the foresight to get the advice of a good lawyer right from the beginning. "George Medalie," he recalls, "had told me that if he weren't available, I should go to Orrin G. Judd, who had been the Solicitor General of New York State, and who was, in George's opinion, the ablest lawyer in the city. George passed away before I set up the business, and so I went to Orrin and told him about my new venture. Instead of asking him just to be my lawyer, I asked him to become an officer of the company." Arnold recalls no significant problems that needed major legal advice, but Judd's presence was undoubtedly of considerable psychological value. "With Orrin behind me," he once said, "I felt like the Rock of Gibraltar."

Because of his Wharton School training and his extensive experience at Pick-N-Pay, Arnold was able to act in the beginning as his own accountant. "However," he has said, "if I didn't have that background, I certainly would have hired one to help me out right at the start."

And, if a new business needs a good lawyer and a good accountant, it surely helps to have a good secretary. Arnold had won his ingeniously, six years before. The girl he chose was Rosemarie Giarrusso, a young lady in the Young & Rubicam typing pool who had occasionally acted as his girl Friday. During one of his first days at the agency, Stanley walked up to the woman in charge of the pool, with a large box of candy in one hand, and a small, plain box in the other. "If I give you what's in the large box," he said, "will you let me keep what's in the other?" The bewildered woman agreed, and Arnold then pulled from the small container a sprig of rosemary. A few days later, Rosemarie became Arnold's girl Friday.

From that start, with Rosemarie Giarrusso as the only employee, the firm has expanded to the point where it now has over thirty members. In hiring new people, Arnold has always looked for two things: creativity and relevant experience. "First," he says, "I look for the ability to think in an imaginative way. But imagination alone isn't enough. I want my people to come from successful advertising agencies and have a merchandising background, so that they'll know the difference between dreams and dollars."

Although the product he sells is rather unique—namely, promotion ideas—Arnold feels his success is that of a businessman rather than an idea man. "What I offer may not be tangible, but it produces tangible results. Like any other product, it must be produced, packaged so that it can be used effectively, and above all, it must be sold. Ideas, as such, are a dime a dozen. It's because the organization I've set up is an effective one, run on sound business principles, that it's worked as well as it has." Among his friends, it's his astuteness as an executive, his keen sense of where potential lies, that is given the most credit for his accomplishment.

PURPLE HORSES AND SEVEN-FOOT GIANTS

In building his business, Arnold followed a consistent method for obtaining new clients. Eschewing the standardized system of sending out broadsides about his services, he always has used a personal approach to the man he wanted to sell. "I'll usually write to the president of the company, because if he's the president, he's going to be bright enough to appreciate my ideas," Arnold has said. "If we don't know each other, I'll tell him who some of my clients are, and explain simply that I'd like an appointment because I have an idea that I think will make money for his company."

Having been given an opportunity to present his proposal, Arnold is likely to use some ingenious method to rivet attention on himself at the beginning of his talk. Once, he tinted a horse purple and displayed it to emphasize that his idea was a horse of another color. On another occasion, he walked into a board meeting with a seven-foot giant and told his listeners that his new idea was head and shoulders above anything they'd ever heard. He has donned boxing gloves and shadow boxed in front of one eminent board of directors, in order to remind them that they had to fight for business; and he has brought in a pair of shoes belonging to the owner of a large chain of retail stores, and asked his prospective clients—who sold their products to the man—to try them on and see how it felt to be in his shoes.

Arnold admits that these devices are simply gimmicks; that if he had nothing more to offer, he would have been out of business in very short order. But he obviously was able to duplicate the success of his earlier promotions, for inside of a year his clients included such corporate behemoths as Standard Oil of New Jersey, Lever Brothers, DuPont, and I.B.M. Since then, his firm has grown steadily and spectacularly.

When he is asked to summarize his approach to business, Arnold gives a rather original answer. "First, I think you have to be discontented—discontented with what and who you are, with what you have, with what you're doing. If you're smug or complacent about your position, you're dying. Superficially, I've reached the top of my business, but still I'm dissatisfied; I want broader horizons for myself, and I want to help other people to broaden their horizons.

"Second, I think you have to be curious. Walk the streets, look at people's faces, talk to strangers, read, know what's going on in the world around you. This is the way your mind gets fertilized; it's the way that you open up to fresh ideas, new ways of looking at life.

"Third, I think you should avoid having specific goals. You can want certain things for yourself, but if you tie yourself down too closely to your plans for achieving them, they become a strait jacket. Let yourself drift a little. Remember that life isn't tightly organized —so much depends on chance, on the turn of a card. Don't hand yourself a stacked deck."

It's a remarkably unorthodox set of suggestions for rising to the top. But for those who can take advantage of them as Stanley Arnold has, they work.

BEHIND THE STANLEY ARNOLD STORY

The novelty of Stanley Arnold's accomplishment lies in the nature of what he sells. The "idea merchant" is in a curiously weak position in our business society because he must sell his ideas rather than use them himself. He faces the continuing challenge of having to sell individuals (who may have considerably less imagination) on the value of an intangible. The ability to sell his ideas was one of Stanley Arnold's big strengths. This capability, too, showed up at an early age. It was startling enough that he thought up a "backward broad jump" to give him an athletic event in which he might be able to develop some prowess. But his real coup lay in selling the idea to his teacher. This capability is the second half of Arnold's stock-in-trade—creating *and selling* ideas in the market place.

Work Aversion. People of achievement are often quoted as admitting, "Basically I'm very lazy." This is by no means self-deprecation. Stanley Arnold said, "I learned early that if you apply yourself to business with all your might, you can learn to hate it damned quickly."

In Arnold's case, there's considerable revelation in this statement. What happens to the ambitious, creative man who's lazy? Exactly what happened to Arnold. He tends to turn away from the "perspiration aspects" of enterprise to the "inspiration" aspects. For Arnold, it was a lot easier and more profitable to *think* than to expend his energies in the more common kinds of business activity.

The Spur of Failure. "We who have been intimate with failure never stop running when we grow up," says Arnold. Psychologists have pointed out two possible reactions to failure. In one case the individual caves in. He accepts the failure as a sign of his inability. There follows a loss of self-esteem and the spark of motivation is extinguished. The other reaction to failure is the one exhibited by

Stanley Arnold. Not only didn't he cave in, but he viewed failure as a challenge. The result in his case was *increased* motivation, with its corresponding benefits.

Shoulder Climbing. "Most of us get where we are," said the late Bernard Baruch, "by climbing on the shoulders of others." Certainly, the ability to benefit from the examples, the accomplishments, or the direct help of others can make a material difference in an individual's achievement. Stanley Arnold, like J. J. Mascuch, benefited greatly by a host of valuable friendships formed early in life. Mayor Harold Burton of Cleveland, George Z. Medalie, and others provided the leg-up that advanced Stanley Arnold that much closer to the top.

Problem-Solving. Arnold developed a conscious approach to handling problems which he himself has likened to Zen. As he put it, "I let it [the goal] figure out how it's going to achieve itself, and then I act accordingly." Implicit in his statement is the idea that a problem contains within itself the seeds of its own solution. An illustration of this principle is contained in his description of how he thought up giveaway prizes for a carpet company. The word "carpet" itself suggested the answer—*cars* and *pets.*

One might say that high-school student Stanley Arnold foretold his later career when he hit upon the idea of mastering the broad jump—backward. This approach is sometimes described as "turning it upside down." The objective is to stimulate the mind to produce fresh and original ideas. An interesting example of the "upside-down" approach was provided during World War II. Our Air Force had trouble getting fighter planes out of the hangars and into the air in the shortest possible time. Many different types of hangar doors were developed but none were satisfactory. Then along came a bright engineer who said, "Perhaps the solution lies in turning the problem around. Instead of trying to get the planes out of the hangar, can we take the hangar away from the plane?" The idea was radical, but it worked. Hangars were built at the end of concrete runways. When a "scramble" was called, two-piece hangars would slide quickly away on tracks, exposing the planes, already on the runway, ready to take off. The "backward approach" is one of the important principles used by Arnold in developing his "brain storms to order." In addition, his "mind fertilizing" concept is stimulating. "Study the world around you," says Arnold, "to enrich the creative layers of your mind." This awareness breeds and stimulates ideas.

Motivation. Stanley Arnold's theory that excitement is an important key to motivation may not bring cries of approval from psychologists, but there's a kind of practical sense to it. Certainly his "fish race" spurred the dairy route salesmen to improve their selling performance. The real-estate pages of magazines and newspapers arc replete with examples of developers who sell their houses to a frantic buying public by making the sale something of a circus. Large signs, colored flags, hot jazz, a salesman proclaiming through a sound system the outstanding advantages of the property being sold—these are all aimed at creating the excitement that Arnold speaks of. The sales figures of the developers confirm Arnold's layman's psychology of motivation.

Customer Visualization. "I would walk down the street and watch people's faces," Stanley Arnold says. The person who sets out to sell anything must have some picture of his potential customers. Stanley Arnold developed his understanding of the consuming public by studying them up close. Patricia Murphy did the same thing. Whether the object to be sold is an idea, a meal, or savings bonds, the seller must understand the attitudes and values of the people to whom he sells. The study methods developed by Arnold were perhaps informal, but they were obviously effective.

Risk-Taking. There comes a time when the man journeying to the top must take a chance. He must gamble on his idea, on himself, or on his judgment of others. Stanley Arnold had to lay his career on the line when he was at Young & Rubicam. He had to assert his belief in his own idea, although it was directly contradicted by a colleague. Arnold said, "I could have kept my mouth shut, but I felt that I had to stand on my own feet." As things worked out, he won the gamble.

The Shock Approach. There may also come a time when a man's back is against the wall as he is confronted by a difficult situation. This happened to Arnold in trying to secure an important contract. Arnold, after a few false starts, had failed to secure it and had to ask for an extension. He was turned down cold. "Time's up," said the client. "That's the end of it."

At this juncture, Arnold might have just shrugged and admitted defeat, or he might have launched into a passionate plea for more time. He did neither. Coolly and defiantly he said, "You're going to unmake that decision, or I'm going to unmake you." The man stared back in astonishment. Then he mumbled his acceptance of Arnold's terms.

Arnold was well aware that the shock approach is sometimes the best course a person can take when any logical action seems impossible. For example, the *New York Daily News* recently described a scene in which a young man stopping in a bar for a glass of beer suddenly found himself confronted by a neighborhood tough advancing on him with a knife. "I don't like your looks," said the knife-wielder. "I'm going to carve you."

Paralysis had apparently seized the onlookers. No one made a move while the attacker advanced. The young man blurted, "I know you, I've seen you before." Then he pointed down to the man's shoes. "I know what those suede shoes mean. You know, too. You'd better watch out. We know what those suede shoes mean." The attacker hesitated, whipped his knife into his pocket and fled.

To a query by the bartender about the suede shoes, the frightened but relieved young man said, "I don't know anything about his suede shoes. It was the first thing that popped into my head." The value of the shock approach is that it reverses the seemingly irreversible. When there's nothing to lose and the situation seems hopeless, it can provide a solution to the unsolvable.

The "Why Not" Approach. Another one of the powerful weapons in Arnold's arsenal of ideas is illustrated by his solution to the problem of securing temporary office space. The office building into which he planned to move was not completed by his moving date. Into Arnold's head came the idea of a generally unused space, the board room of a bank. The average person would certainly hesitate to act on such an idea. Ask a bank officer to use his board room? Too unorthodox. How embarrassing to make such an offbeat proposal, particularly to an individual as staid as the average bank official. But Arnold's reaction was "Why not?" He had nothing to lose. The worst that could happen would be a turndown. Accordingly, he made his request to the Chemical Corn Exchange Bank on 55th Street and Park Avenue and—to his pleasure—he was given the space without charge.

A Philosophy of Success. Dr. Erwin S. Stanton, chief psychologist of the McMurry Company, points out that an individual who has suffered an insecure childhood is less likely to leave a steady job than the person whose upbringing has given him a sense of security. Stanley Arnold's early life gave him a comfortable feeling of security. Thus, he was able to leave a profitable family business as well as several other safe and secure jobs to seek the greater stimulation of the advertising business. Eventually he left this for the even greater gamble of heading his own firm. Great mental flamboyance was necessary to conceive and sell the startling ideas that marked Stanley Arnold's success—and this can only stem from a deep belief in one's own abilities.

William Rosenberg –

21 { DO NOT UNDERESTIMATE
THE DOUGHNUT

William Rosenberg's path to success led him into the mushrooming business of franchising. Franchising is not altogether new. It's been used by automotive and soft-drink firms for some time. But in recent years, the idea has gained wide acceptance and has been extended to many types of retail and service enterprises. At present growth rates, the United States will see one hundred new franchise outlets every day, joining the over 400,000 now in operation. Dollar figures are even more illuminating. Franchise outlets in 1965 represented a total volume of fifteen billion dollars, and accounted for 25 per cent of all retail sales.

At forty-nine, Rosenberg is the chairman of the board of Dunkin' Donuts of America, the world's largest and fastest-growing retail doughnut and coffee chain in one of America's fastest-growing industries. Dunkin' Donuts was started in 1955. Today, its two hundred shops dot the highways from coast to coast, and gross more than thirty million dollars per year.

While no two franchising systems are exactly alike, the basic principles are the same. The parent company (the franchiser) licenses an independent businessman to conduct the business along specific lines set by the company. The individual operator (the franchisee) pays a fee for the franchise, in addition to a specified investment in the business. A franchise operation imposes stringent demands on the entrepreneur, for he must have the ability to judge people and to develop quite sophisticated financial deals. Rosenberg makes no secret of the fact that his formal education ended at the eighth grade of grammar school, yet, he was able

to overcome this handicap and go on to master the complex operations required for success in the franchising field.

In franchising, the headman and his independent partners are
peculiarly and permanently dependent on each other. Without the
support of the franchiser, the shop owner would become just another
fringe small businessman with all the prospects for failure that that
implies. Without the support of the franchisee, the national franchiser
could not stay in business, let alone expand it. The relationship is,
admittedly, a paternalistic one, and here Rosenberg's own personality nicely fills the bill. With his buoyant spirits, his massive
build and direct manner, not to mention his occasional (sometimes
deliberate, one suspects) lapses from the king's English, he is far
from the polished gray-flannel organization man. But then, so are
most of his franchisees. In Rosenberg they are able to see a wholly
gratifying image of themselves. Or rather, themselves as they might
be some day, if they follow his words of wisdom.

*   *   *

Franchising, doughnut empires, indeed any sort of grand plan,
was far from Bill Rosenberg's mind when he began his climb to
success. At the start, it was the simplest but most compelling of
drives that motivated him: the desire to free himself and his family
from poverty. His story is the classic American one of the self-
made man: the son of a poor first-generation American, without
education or background, without everything except his own native
abilities, backed up by what he calls "a burning desire not to fail."

When Bill Rosenberg announced to his parents in June, 1930,
that he had decided not to continue high school, but to get a job,
their reaction was predictably negative. Then, as now, it seemed
clear that a high-school dropout could never succeed in a world
that was increasingly bounded by formally acquired skills and training. Besides, his father had himself to offer as an example. He was
a man of large ambition and dreams, but his own education had
ended in fourth grade. Since then, he had been in and out of all
kinds of ventures, only to fail at most of them, a man whom the
1929 depression had put out of work and on relief.

However, since Bill was not to be moved from his chosen path of starting from the bottom, the family yielded and let him go off to work as a Western Union messenger. There may be few who remember the once-mighty Postal Telegraph Company and its battle for supremacy with Western Union. And few in Western Union's management today would be willing to say that the fourteen-year-old Bill Rosenberg contributed to its triumph over the competition. The fact is that in his limited way, he did.

In Boston, during those years, the two big firms were competing for the telegram business of a prospect called Royal Arcanium, which was strategically located at a dead-center point between the two communications services. Whichever one delivered the telegrams fastest was promised the business. Rosenberg held the record for three years: twelve minutes by bike for a five-mile sprint. As a result he earned a grand total of eighteen dollars per week (salary plus commissions, minus two dollars which went back to the company to pay off his installment purchase of the bicycle).

In 1933, Rosenberg left Western Union for a more promising job selling ice cream from trucks. Here, earnings were based on commissions from sales. Who knew how much ice cream people might buy, if properly persuaded? His beginnings were again auspicious; a poor route in Jamaica Plains was turned within a few months into a successful one. The technique was simple; find the places where the kids play and the workers come out for lunch; haunt the night baseball games, and then use your personality to sell. In due time, he was promoted to "route builder," then to branch manager.

Enter a man named Harry Simberg. As head of the ice cream company and Rosenberg's boss, Simberg unknowingly contributed greatly to Rosenberg's future success by laying him off for the winter. Rosenberg had become dissatisfied by what he considered to be the gap between his salary (forty dollars per week) and his value to the company. Like Oliver Twist, his request for more money was viewed as a form of insubordination that required prompt retaliatory action. He was laid off.

"FOLLOW INSTRUCTIONS" AND "TELL THE TRUTH"

"Upset but not fearful," Rosenberg started the job hunt again. It was 1938 and times were really bad. All he could find was a job selling household items door to door for the Interstate Company. With that "burning desire" still intact, Rosenberg assessed his prospects. He knew nothing about the techniques of door-to-door selling, but reasoned that his employer did. From this evolved his first formula for success: "Study the instructions they give you." He also developed another conviction which stood him in good stead throughout his career. "There is nothing so believable as the truth. When I talked to these housewives about silverware, I told the truth." Net result from the success formula: $15 in commissions on the first day; after that, a daily average of from $11 to $28. These were princely sums for a door-to-door seller in the year 1938.

When Simberg approached him to return to the ice cream company and take over the regional sales for a new vending-machine operation, Rosenberg played it cool at first; then finally agreed to return at a twenty dollar weekly raise.

Now he was really on the road to success. The vending-machine operation turned out so well that Simberg offered Rosenberg a new position as national sales manager. At the same time, the American Brass Company (one of the vending-machine clients) offered him an opportunity to start an in-plant feeding operation there. The war intervened, however, and in 1942 he was back in Boston, working in the Hingham shipyard.

A WARTIME HIATUS: THE UNION LEADER

At Hingham, Rosenberg's urge toward achievement led him into the union movement. He was the first Jew ever to be elected to office in a heretofore closed, independent union. Characteristically, it was his idea that he run for office. His fellow Jewish workers were cynical about his chances for election. Yet in the end, it was the non-Jewish vote that put him over the top. (Incidentally, his hard-working campaign manager, Barney Ackman, eventually became his first Dunkin' Donuts franchise operator.)

As union delegate, it was Rosenberg's job to represent the workers in the complicated wartime wage-incentive system which had been set up under government aegis. Eventually, he became so knowledgeable in this area that the company asked him to take on the job of contract coordinator. He agreed, but not without first getting the consent of his fellow workers. Loyalty, whether to workers or management, has always been a Rosenberg characteristic.

Later, when the war ended, the company asked him to stay on, but the war had given him time to think and to plan. For the first time his ambitions began to assume a definite focus. All his jobs, good and bad, had added a priceless asset to his own native abilities: confidence in himself. Now the time had come to achieve "something big." He decided the way to do it was to go into business for himself. Why not take the corporate path?

"I knew my limitations," he says. "With my lack of education, no big company would hire me as an executive. And besides, I knew there were inefficiencies and politicking in big companies which I didn't like and didn't think were necessary."

He had a clear idea of what his path would be; he was looking for a new business and a new industry. Where else, he reasoned, could a young man with no schooling but a lot of business experience already behind him, find a better opportunity?

The industry he had in mind was prefabricated homes. This new field had received a great deal of glamorous publicity during the war, and impressed, he had read up on it. In 1944, he said good-bye to the shipyards, took a temporary job selling plastic floor sealing to support himself and his family, and, with $1500 in savings, began investigating prefab manufacturers. His idea was to set up a sales operation for one of them.

BACK TO THE TRUCKS

It took only a few visits to convince him that his grandiose ideas were impractical. The prefab manufacturers had not yet solved their production problems. Anyone attempting to put prefabs on the market would be headed for disaster; how can you sell something that you can't produce?

Accordingly, he took his $1500, borrowed another $1000 from his mother and went into partnership with two other entrepreneurs whom he describes as "delicatessen men from New York." The business they set up in Bridgeport, Connecticut, had a familiar ring. They were selling food from a truck, dispensing coffee and sandwiches to plant workers.

As it turned out, this *was* the new industry he had been looking for: factory catering. But Rosenberg's first venture was unsuccessful. Not because of the business itself—one year Rosenberg raised the annual gross from $50,000 to $500,000; the trouble was with his relations with the partners. They were good sandwich men, Rosenberg recalls, but they knew nothing and cared less about building a business. They took large bonuses for themselves, failed to pay their bills, refused to reinvest in the company. It was simply a matter of differing business philosophies. They lived for the moment; Rosenberg was interested in the future.

In 1946, Rosenberg decided he wanted out. Inevitably, however, the getting-out was attended by troubles. The partners refused to pay him anything beyond the $2500 he had originally put in the business. He had asked for another $1000 as well to get him and his family re-established in Boston. Either one of the sums would seem to be niggardly, but Rosenberg was in no mood for quarreling. "I never liked a fight," he says. "Usually, I would just rather give in and walk away." This is just what he did, taking with him a vastly enlarged sense of confidence, gained from his successes in Bridgeport, plus an invaluable knowledge of how to make coffee and sandwiches. "You have to say one thing about those New

York delicatessen boys," he admits freely. "They *were* good sandwich men."

Back in Boston, Rosenberg set up his own factory catering service, the Industrial Luncheon Service Company. His assets: $2500 from the Bridgeport venture, plus another $2500 (half of it borrowed; another half invested by a former associate in the ice-cream business); an old butcher shop rented at twenty-five dollars per month for use as a commissary; a secondhand but newly painted delivery truck; a set of handsome stainless steel coffee makers; and his brother Leon, equipped with a spanking new blue uniform. Looking back, however, he realizes that his best asset was neither financial nor material, but something more abstract; a clearly defined philosophy of how to do business.

First there was the product. "The key to success in the food business," he says, "is to get the product to the consumer as soon after it's made as is humanly possible." Second, the merchandising: "I was convinced we would be successful if we looked distinctive." Thus: the freshly painted truck, the stainless steel coffee makers, and the uniform for brother Leon. And finally, the *pièce de resistance:* the decision to sell a cup of coffee for ten cents, instead of the prevailing market price of a nickel.

"Everyone in the food business told me I couldn't do it," says Rosenberg. "But I had no choice. I couldn't make a go of it at a nickel. I figured that coffee would sell for a dime, if it was *good* coffee, that is to say the best coffee you could get."

BUILDING A BUSINESS

On the opening day, Rosenberg and his brother reviewed the route they had planned: one stop at each of several factories, strategically timed to catch the different shifts of workers going and coming. All that was needed to complete the route was an early morning stop for the 8 A.M. shift. It was a toss-up between two factories, the Gillette Razor Blade plant and the Boston Gear Works. Both were located at the right points along the route. Leon threw up a nickel, Bill yelled, "Heads it's Boston Gear, tails, Gillette." It came up heads.

At 7:45 sharp, the truck and its uniformed chauffeur rolled up outside Boston Gear Works on Hancock Street in Quincy, just as the men were entering the plant. The rest is history. When the truck rolled in at noon, it was mobbed. That best of advertising agents, word-of-mouth, had spread the message around the plant. Industrial Luncheon Service, the business which started with one truck, was on its way to expansion.

Now began the slow, steady, often heartbreaking growth period. There were many roadblocks. Small companies were fine customers for a start, but larger firms were needed if Industrial was to grow beyond a one-truck operation. Materials and equipment were hard to get; this was the postwar period when practically everything was in short supply. Even worse was the perennial problem of the entrepreneur: lack of skilled personnel.

The first problem was solved by a dogged selling campaign, the second by plain grubbing: scouting around to find a truck manufacturer who was sending out a large shipment of trucks and then trying to persuade him to allot one or two trucks to the Rosenbergs. The third and most difficult problem was resolved in Rosenberg's unique fashion—by using whatever people he already had. His father was made a food purchaser; his part-time accountant was persuaded to come in as a full-time inside man. ("I knew I had to make up for my own weaknesses; I needed opposites from myself to keep the business growing. Inside work bores me. My value was greater to the company if I concentrated on sales and implementing new ideas.")

In these days, Rosenberg worked a shift that began at 3 A.M., when the orders were put up, continued through the morning when supplies were purchased, went into the afternoon when he went out to canvass for more business, and ended at 11 P.M. after the drivers had come in and the planning for the next day was finished.

This was also the time of real personal sacrifice. Rosenberg's previous experience with his delicatessen-men partners had given him an almost compulsive respect for financial stability in business. While his new business boomed, he continued to draw a modest salary and live with his wife and three children in a small apartment. The rest of the profits went back into the business.

By 1949, the business was big business: over 140 trucks operating out of New England and upstate New York, plus twenty-five in-plant cafeterias and a staff of one hundred with headquarters in Quincy, Massachusetts. But the big success, the really grand foray into new business territory, was still to come. This time it was not to be built on the popular ham sandwich and a cup of coffee, but on a more unique item, the doughnut.

EVERYBODY LIKES DOUGHNUTS

Bill Rosenberg's love affair with the doughnut began when he hired a Swedish baker to add doughnuts to the menu he served from his trucks and cafeterias. He became impressed with a number of things about the doughnut operation. The doughnuts were extraordinarily good. ("Good doughnuts are much harder to make than most people think.") They sold extremely well, accounting for 40 per cent of his total volume. What's more, a look at the competition turned up the interesting information that doughnuts would sell even better in another sales environment, small specialty stores offering only coffee and doughnuts.

Rosenberg opened his first doughnut shop on Route 3 in Quincy, on a site where two other entrepreneurs, one a gas station operator and the other an awning salesman, had already failed. Nobody in Rosenberg's organization was very enthusiastic about his ability to change this pattern with a doughnut shop. Their reasons seemed logical. The business of Industrial Luncheon was factory catering, not food retailing. Coffee and doughnuts offered too narrow a menu —who would buy?

Rosenberg's was the larger vision. He saw that truck factory catering was doomed to a short life, with vending machines looming on the horizon. Expansion had to take place in a different area, requiring a different business concept altogether. And then there was the doughnut itself, about which Rosenberg waxed lyrical. "Everybody likes doughnuts," he said to his dubious colleagues. "When times are affluent, they'll eat them for dessert or as a snack. If we get a depression, they'll buy 'em in place of steak. Look at what they contain: eggs, sugar, shortening, everything. Why, they're the staff of life."

The cynics remained unconvinced, but Rosenberg's enthusiasm was strong enough to sell himself, which was the main thing. Following the success of the first store ($2500 sales per week within eighteen months), he opened a second one, which proved equally lucrative. Then he sat down and wrote a twenty-page memorandum to his management group. He was taking off on a cross-country trip, he told them. The object was not pleasure, but investigation. Of doughnuts, of course.

Back from the eight-week trip, Rosenberg could hardly contain himself as he drove down Route 3 into Quincy. He had seen small doughnut shops dotted across the country, none of them very grand, nowhere in great profusion, none of them using the merchandising techniques or national organization he could muster, but all of them doing very well. That was the point! "I became convinced the whole country was our oyster," he said. Or more accurately, our doughnut.

Rosenberg's grand design was a national chain of doughnut stores. Like many such ideas, however, there was a hitch: financing. The assets of the Industrial Luncheon operation could not possibly be stretched to fill this bill. Outside financing was possible, but not probable, for such a new venture, and certainly not in the large amounts of money that would be required.

A familiar name in the food business occurred to Rosenberg: Howard Johnson. Like Industrial Luncheon (now Universal Food Services), this great chain of roadside restaurants and motels had its headquarters in Quincy. "I was not personally acquainted with Howard Johnson," says Rosenberg, "but my proximity to the company had given me a knowledge and respect for its operations. It came to me, as I drove home, that this chain had been built through a method of retailing I hadn't thought about; franchising." And that proved to be the answer.

In the twelve years since Dunkin' Donuts of America began operations, the franchising industry has grown at an incredible rate to become one of the nation's largest, grossing some sixty billion dollars. But at that time, its development outside the traditional gasoline and automobile dealerships had been spotty. Know-how in the field was strictly confined to a few individuals. The books, articles, analyses, and market studies were yet to be written.

DUNKIN' DONUTS IS BORN

It is probably one of Rosenberg's greatest achievements that, despite this lack of market information, he was able to come up with a plan for the new franchise business within two days: a forty-page memorandum which contained in detailed form nearly all the elements of the franchising system under which Dunkin' Donuts now operates. Viewing the world in the mirror of his own aspirations, he reasoned that hardly an American lives who does not want to go into business for himself. Who would not leap at the chance to go into a business which promised a potential annual income of at least twenty-five thousand dollars, possibly much more; backed up by a national organization which aids in the financing, trains the operators, supplies the benefits of national advertising and a national name, provides the purchasing setup, maintains quality control, and selects the store site?

Before setting up the franchise system, Rosenberg's organization opened five doughnut stores which were operated under his personal supervision. During this trial period, he supervised the stores, selected the personnel, and worked out the complicated mechanics of site location, leasing agreements, supplier sources, financing.

Using his own stores as test laboratories, he ironed out all kinds of problems, and shaped the image of the Dunkin' Donuts chain that was to be. A set of firm regulations for site locations was determined. The decision to devote 2 per cent of each store's gross to advertising was made. The earlier name of the operation, "Open Kettle," was changed to the more jazzy "Dunkin' Donuts," and an appropriately flamboyant style of architecture was devised. The break-even point in daily doughnut production was established.

Finally, the merchandising possibilities of multiflavor doughnuts were exploited to the fullest extent. Without question one of the biggest sales builders for the Dunkin' Donut chain is that it offers fifty-two separate varieties of doughnuts, one of them equipped with an edible handle as a built-in dunker. Over the years well over one hundred types of fancy doughnuts have been developed, to satisfy the seemingly inexhaustible demand for a different doughnut.

It was American ingenuity—corny, flamboyant, but at its core, good business—and a quality product, straight on down the highways and across the country, that did the trick. Looking back, anyone can see that it was bound to be successful. But at the start, only Bill Rosenberg had the necessary faith in the power of the doughnut.

The first individual franchise was signed in 1955. It went to a partnership—Leo Bernstein, a former cab driver, and Bill Rosenberg's old friend and union campaign manager, Barney Ackman. They set up shop in Dedham, Massachusetts. Over the next few years, the list began to grow. There were some failures; they were greatly outnumbered by successes. The pattern was set; less than 3 per cent failures—as compared with 90 per cent failures for nonfranchised new small business in the nation.

Out of both the failures and the successes, Rosenberg developed a clear idea of the prototype of the successful Dunkin' Donut franchisee. He should be a mature man, regardless of his age. An immature man has not yet acquired either the financial or the personal assets for success in such a venture. He should be accustomed to hard work, and willing to put in the long hours that every new business demands of its manager. He should be married and his wife should be willing to help him in the business; the modern small food service franchise works best when it is a "Mom and Pop" operation. He should be community-minded, a member of his local religious or business associations; such a man takes pride in his store and looks on it as a community enterprise. And, of course, he should be ambitious and independent—but not a lone wolf; a nice blend of aggressiveness and cooperation.

Not all of the Dunkin' Donuts franchisees fit the pattern precisely, but a majority do. Among the early franchisees signed up by Rosenberg were a welder, a retired fireman, a previously unsuccessful restaurant owner, a dentist.

Early in the game, an unexpected obstacle appeared; another national doughnut franchise operation opened up. This, plus a steady increase in regional competition (inevitably, the success of the Dunkin' Donut stores inspired others to go out and do likewise) pressed the new company for a time. Within a few years, however, Rosenberg's chain had gained a comfortable lead, to become what it is today—the largest retail doughnut chain in the world.

"In the long run, I suppose that competition was good for me," says Rosenberg. "As I look back, I see that it generated faster movement on our part." All this time, Rosenberg was building his organization internally as well as externally, reasoning that he must find men *not* like himself, men who could handle details and administer the program, aiming first at a strong central organization; later, as the business expanded, at a strong decentralized one.

Today, Rosenberg is still the head man and sole owner of both Dunkin' Donuts and its parent corporation, Universal Food Systems. At the same time, he has succeeded in finding men who could help him build the operation. As of now, the organization is decentralized, with a group of vice-presidents who are in control of separate geographical and operational areas. Rosenberg's son, Robert, a Cornell and Harvard Business School graduate, is president, while Rosenberg senior is chairman of the board.

The idea is and always has been to build a viable organization which is capable of expansion, not only nationally, but internationally as well. Rosenberg's ultimate goal has yet fully to be realized: a vast international chain of doughnut shops stretching across Europe first, and then Asia, Africa, and Latin America. To those who express polite skepticism at the prospects of an industrial empire based on the lowly doughnut, Rosenberg has an inarguable comeback: "Of course the doughnut is only the vehicle. But just the same, don't make the mistake of selling the doughnut short. Who would have predicted fifty years ago that someone would build a billion-dollar business on a single carbonated beverage, cola drinks?"

BEHIND THE WILLIAM ROSENBERG STORY

William Rosenberg's career is marked by the fact that he was able to fill in, with native intelligence and enterprise, the gap left in a formal education that terminated at the eighth grade. Exactly how he succeeded in making up for this education gap is explained by the specific factors that emerge in his career pattern:

Enterprise Visualization. With a skill that an engineer or an artist might envy, William Rosenberg was able to "think big." Size or complexity seems to have been no deterrent to his thinking processes. On the contrary, he operated on the principle that "whatever you can do on a small scale, you can do even better on a large scale." His ability to think in broad and sweeping terms largely accounts for the growth of his early individual enterprises, and eventually made possible the string of Dunkin' Donuts enterprises across the nation.

People Utilization. Rosenberg's ideas for using people efficiently are decidedly different from the average. Usually an individual is put into a job for which he has particular talents and then is given the chance to exercise those talents. Rosenberg frequently took the opposite tack. In 1949, when Rosenberg was striving to expand his business of selling sandwiches and coffee from trucks to factory workers, what he needed, he knew, was to sell more of the larger plants in the outlying Boston areas. To get those as customers, he needed more salesmen besides himself.

"You've got to help me," he told his younger brother, Leon, then a branch manager for the business. Leon pointed out some indisputable facts about himself; he was not sales-minded; his talents lay in the management and supervisory end of the business. A shy, modest man, he couldn't see himself opening doors in the ebullient manner of his brother.

"It doesn't matter," said the older Rosenberg. "Just call on one different company, every day, four days a week, that's all. Just keep doing it." Leon obliged and started making calls.

Within two months, the non-sales-minded but loyal brother had opened the door to the biggest and best account to date, the Crompton-Knowles plant in Worcester, Massachusetts. Bill Rosenberg walked in the open door, closed the deal and embarked on an expansion program that established Industrial Luncheon Service branches throughout New England and upstate New York.

The story is well known among the group of corporate executives that Bill Rosenberg now heads. He never fails to tell it when someone complains that he hasn't got the proper personnel to do a job. "Give him more responsibility. Never mind if he doesn't have exceptional ability or training. You'd be surprised what the average person can do, if you give him a good reason to do it."

Dr. Bernice M. Gurvich of the Personnel Laboratory, in analyzing the methods of a man somewhat similar to William Rosenberg, points out: "He decides what he wants and then somehow makes the resources on hand fit those goals. He uses the people he has and does so in terms of his needs, not theirs. He is an extremely persuasive man—the kind who can charm the birds out of the trees. He certainly has been able to charm people into believing that what he wants of them is in their own interests as well as his own. However, it's important to emphasize that he doesn't in any way seem to be dishonest with these people. After all, they do receive credits and rewards for their efforts."

Rosenberg's approach to the utilization of people is almost the opposite of that of Solomon Dutka of Audits & Surveys. Dutka starts with the talents the man has and finds ways to make them fit the job. Rosenberg starts with the job to be done and helps the person fit the requirements as closely as possible.

Drop-Hammer Progress. Sometimes the stereotype of the executive shows him cutting large and flamboyant swathes through the jungle of problems that beset him. William Rosenberg shows a different pattern of behavior. Again and again, his progress has been achieved by persistent, unremitting plugging. He sets his goals and then heads toward them, inch by inch if need be. "As long as you keep inching along," he seems to say, "you will eventually cover the miles."

Rebellion Reaction. Analyze the patterns of many successful people and you will find that they have followed, more or less closely, the pattern of progress exhibited by a parent. However, in many cases, the pattern of achievement of an individual seems almost intentionally *opposed* to the parent's pattern.

Again Dr. Bernice M. Gurvich's analysis of an individual whose pattern is not dissimilar to William Rosenberg's sheds some light on the latter's behavior:

"One can speculate that the individual's persistence and consistency were at least in part a reaction against his father's lack of these qualities. It's also very likely that a good deal of his need to be the man on top stems from a reaction to a parent who was clearly the low man on the social and economic totem pole." This latter point applies to Rosenberg, and to J. J. Mascuch, to some extent.

Point Pressure. Women who wear high heels are outstanding examples of the tremendous pressure to be derived from a weight projected through a small surface. The spike heel imbeds in hot asphalt while heels of ordinary dimensions scarcely make an imprint; it demonstrates the capability of a sharp focus to transform an ordinary pressure into a piercing force.

Rosenberg's single-mindedness operated in this manner. All his energies were focused on the single goal of achievement in business. Imagination, resourcefulness, and good old-fashioned sweat figure in the career activity of many people. But Rosenberg's single-minded dedication to business achievement took this force and made it almost irresistible because of the sharp point into which it fed.

Business Know-How. There might be the tendency on the part of some educators to view Rosenberg's success with alarm. Certainly, he's no advertisement for advanced education. With only an eighth-grade formal education, his achievements seem to suggest that a college degree is likely to be a waste of time for the entrepreneur.

But the educators need not be misled, nor should anyone else. Rosenberg is no example of an uneducated person who achieved great things. Rather, he's an example of the self-educated person making up in native intelligence and informal education what he lacked in formal schooling. In his "off the truck" food service days he developed what he himself calls "a clearly defined philosophy of how to do business." It involved an understanding of product, of merchandising, and of consumer psychology. Educators will recognize in these concepts some of the curricula of their own advanced business courses.

Playing to Win. As the individual grows up, he's surrounded by rules, regulations, and restrictions. And the average person reaching maturity is often unconsciously inhibited by this thickly packed, layer-on-layer, swaddling of unconscious restrictions.

For William Rosenberg, arbitrary and traditional restrictions were to be examined and put aside if they existed only in the mind, rather than in fact. If one was to play to win, then false assumptions, as well as other people's ideas and practices unsuitable to his situation, all fell by the wayside.

Energy as a Replacement for Money. Rosenberg, like Thomas Coe, Patricia Murphy, and other "low budget" entrepreneurs, made up for a lack of cash by an investment of personal energy. The single-mindedness with which he pursued his objectives was matched by his determination. Neither hours of the days nor days of the week were a limitation. The supply of energy was available as needed, and was never exhausted.

Idea Refinement. "The world is full of people walking around with *half* of a good idea," says Stanley Arnold. Rosenberg's development of merchandising and franchising plans for the doughnut is a good example of an idea nursed from a glimmer to a workable program.

Many people have attempted to build a business around a product. The item may be anything from a recipe for preserves to a complicated electronic gadget. However, it's only when the individual can take the subsequent steps, everything from financing to merchandising, that an idea becomes refined to the point of practicality, and can be commercially exploited.

Grass-Roots Action. John Fox of United Fruit stuck his foot in housewives' doors to find out what the real potential was for his orange juice concentrate. William Rosenberg did somewhat the same for his doughnut. He too went out into the grass-roots world, took an eight-week trip to find out how people were responding to doughnuts. It was what he saw with his own eyes that gave him the information he needed to make a realistic appraisal. This willingness to go to the source, to face up to the basic realities of a situation, is a particularly important and typical element in those who succeed.

Organization Building. Some enterprises are described as a "one-man business." An enterprise often *is* the product of one man's thought and energies. But no matter what an individual's capabilities, there is always a need for people to reinforce the top man. He needs assistants and subordinates to whom he can delegate jobs, to supply additional ideas, or to fill the gaps of his experience and expertness.

A clever lawyer once tried to elicit from Henry Ford the admission that his technical knowledge was very limited. Ford readily admitted his ignorance. But he pointed out, "I could hire a man at one hundred dollars a week to tell me anything about a subject I wanted to know." Developing an effective back-up force was one of William Rosenberg's keys to success.

22 { Myra Janco—
PRESIDENT IN A
GRAY FLANNEL SKIRT

"When I was getting started in the advertising field," says Myra Janco, attractive young president of the Chicago advertising firm of Draper Daniels, Incorporated, "it wasn't uncommon for people to ask for *Mr.* Janco. They would get quite a shock when I walked in!"

Myra's boss, chairman of the board of Draper Daniels, describes his president in these terms: "Myra is not only one of the most attractive ways they've found to package brains, but she has a childlike idealism, an innate decency, and a sense of honesty that only the truly able can afford." Daniels might have added something else: Myra Janco is feminine without being cloying. She is realist enough to know that being a woman may get her an appointment with an unapproachable top executive curious to see a president in skirts. But she also knows that only a convincing presentation of the benefit of doing business with her firm will land the account.

As her personal story shows, two of her assets were a strong orientation to the academic world, and the ability to grasp a potential client's needs better than he understood them himself. The first factor was almost unbelievable for a hard-hitting field like advertising. The second is extremely rare. But they are an integral part of Myra Janco's breakthrough.

* * *

Dark eyes intent as her scissors flew, the four-year-old girl sat at a miniature desk in her grandmother's real-estate office cutting rolls of brightly colored crepe paper. She was trying to supplement her nickel-a-week allowance by making party favors to sell for a penny apiece. Two ledgers faced her; one marked "MAKE" in black crayon, the other marked "SPEND" in red. The little girl knew one business principle—the "MAKE" book had to show more money than the "SPEND." This was not a strictly independent project. Her family, doting but severe critics, had to approve her creations. "Why would anyone want to buy that?" was her father's constant question.

The diminutive Myra Janco didn't always have an answer, but she moved her merchandise and made a profit. To this day she remembers the heady feeling of success in that first venture. Since then, she has never been able to satisfy herself with less.

She also learned about failure at an early age. Some years later, after graduating with honors from Gary, Indiana's, Lew Wallace High School, Myra approached the editor of the local newspaper for a job. Clutching an envelope of her clippings, and dressed as the job-hunter's manual suggested, Myra was sure that he would jump at the chance to hire such a promising candidate. After all, she had won a county-wide award as an outstanding journalist on the high-school paper. She had also dared defend her ideas before an irate principal when called on the carpet for an outspoken editorial attacking racial discrimination in school sports events. Myra's approach to the bristling gentleman: "May I talk to you about this later—when you're not angry?" Her psychology worked, and Myra won her point.

Seated confidently before the hard-boiled editor in her first job interview, she watched as he scanned her prose. He shook his head, handed the clippings back to her. "Sorry," he said. "We need reporters who can write—not budding sob sisters." Stunned and stung by her failure to land the job, Myra remembered her father. For half her life Myra had seen his face in the mirror of an iron lung. Looking now for an example of courage to tide her over this rough spot, she remembered his whispered words when she had taken childhood discouragements to him. "Keep trying, honey. Hang on tight and don't give up."

A few weeks later, on a warm September day in 1943, Myra

Janco stepped off the bus in Terre Haute, Indiana. She had applied for—and won—a four-year scholarship to Indiana State Teachers College (now Indiana State University). Although she had only ten dollars in her purse, her self-confidence was high. Moments after her arrival, she was greeted by the president of the college, Ralph N. Tirey, who whisked the promising student off to lunch. It was the beginning of a rewarding association with an inspiring educator.

KEEPING THE HOME FIRES BURNING

Myra's first problem was the practical matter of living arrangements. She could count on little financial help from home. Her father had been a promoter and salesman, but years of illness had dissipated the family's savings and when Myra's father died, shortly before her high-school graduation, her mother began to sell insurance. Yet in spite of their limited financial means, Myra had been given piano and ballet lessons, and her family refused to consider itself poor.

As a result, Myra had been sheltered from such cares as housework, and she was apprehensive when Dean Charlotte Burford brought an offer from a schoolteacher willing to give her room and board in exchange for help with the housekeeping. "I hardly knew how to make a bed properly," she says. But she was willing to learn and the teacher was willing to give her a chance. The arrangement flourished so well that the teacher, Miss Goldie Kinder Hiatt, became her adopted "aunt." Long since retired, but no less active today, "Aunt Goldie" will soon be eighty. While managing the twelve-room home she and Myra now occupy in Evanston, Illinois, she finds time to write sketches and stories—and has had several published.

One of the first things Myra did after her arrival at the college was to submit samples of her writing to the faculty committee in charge of naming an editor for the *Statesman,* Indiana State's weekly newspaper. It had always been taken for granted that the job—which paid a token salary of five dollars a week—would go to a senior. Myra hadn't bothered to mention her class. When they had selected her work as best, and then learned she was only a freshman, they held to their choice, and Myra became the youngest editor of a college newspaper in the United States. When other students were attending football games or playing bridge in the Student Union, Myra was usually to be found working late in the basement office of the college paper. Sunday night was no exception. She was absorbed in her work and never measured the time.

Eager to test her talents further, Myra soon found a job at a Terre Haute radio station. There she got involved in everything from writing continuity and operating the switchboard to learning how to be a commentator. She appeared as panelist on a weekly radio show with the varsity debating team that twice won the Midwest College Tourney. In her sophomore year she won a medal as the outstanding campus speaker. Yet her college academic load, her campus editorship, and her radio work were not enough for Myra in Terre Haute. She surveyed the downtown shopping area to find something more to utilize her talents.

ON THE PAYROLL AT MEIS

She soon found what she was looking for. One of the leading department stores, Meis, needed an advertising copywriter and she was hired as their "advertising department" at $7.50 a week ($7.35 after deductions, Myra recalls).

After a few months at the store, Myra was installed as assistant to the president, Salo Levite. She proved to be highly successful as a store coordinator with her finger in many departments and Mr. Levite was pleased. She also learned an important lesson from her boss.

Myra suggested to the fashion buyers that polka-dot dresses would be big that year, and the store bought a large stock. Myra was sure she'd found a best seller. She admired the crisp frocks hanging on the racks—and racks—and racks. But they hung too long. None of the ads that she dreamed up seemed to lure the customers. Mr. Levite said nothing. Although she worried about her boss's reaction, she persisted and her spring fashion promotion at last emptied the racks. Then Mr. Levite sat back, took a puff on his cigar, and told a mortified Myra, "Don't take yourself too seriously. They were just polka-dot dresses."

In spite of her outside responsibilities, Myra maintained a straight A average and received her B.S. degree in 1948. She continued to set the same record on her way to a Master of Arts degree in Education.

WABASH ADVERTISING IS BORN

In 1950, the petite brunette with her Masters degree was looking for new worlds to conquer. She decided that Terre Haute was ripe for a new venture. With two hundred dollars in the bank and a confidence in herself that approached brashness, the twenty-four-year-old Myra Janco launched an advertising agency. Her staff consisted of herself as president, marketing director, head of research, copywriter, and janitor. Terre Haute's location on the banks of the famous river suggested the name: Wabash Advertising.

But in the preliminary stages, Myra did more than look at the Wabash. She pretested the need for marketing and advertising services by calling on a carefully selected dozen prospects. In each case she explained her services simply: "We're creative problem-solvers." Then she applied a technique that she has relied on ever since as the beginning of all analysis; she encouraged businessmen to talk about their problems. "Once the problem areas are identified, solutions to the problem unfold rapidly."

Most of the prospects she called on were highly doubtful that a "mere one-woman agency" could offer something that the Chicago and St. Louis agencies couldn't. Myra explained that it was the "size of the thinking and not the size of the agency" that really mattered. All she requested was the opportunity to explore their communications and marketing problems and suggest a solution—they could compare the results of her creative approach with that of any competitive agency. The majority of her prospects were polite but not encouraging. Myra felt, however, that the "market survey" was not conclusive and that the real test would come only after she'd opened shop. The more she thought about starting an agency, the more "right" the idea seemed. "It might be called bull-headedness," admits Myra.

Once the decision was made, Myra wasted no time. She marched down to the bank, asked for the president, whom she knew from her dealings at Meis, and outlined her plans. She pointed out that she had little to lose except the investment of her own time and energy. In typical Myra Janco fashion, she didn't ask for financial assistance, but probed the banker as to what she'd have to show if and when she needed a loan. The interview was highly successful. Myra realized from the president's attitude toward her that as funds were needed they would be available.

She read the *Wall Street Journal* to find local companies that might be in need of sales help. She looked up their Dun & Bradstreet ratings. She talked to their customers to get a feel for their markets. She studied their competition. And then she was ready to talk to a prospect.

At first, while she was planning and organizing, Myra conducted business from her home. Then her old firm, Meis, asked her to handle their advertising and she landed two national accounts. After three months, she was in a position to lease offices in a downtown office building.

"SEARCH OUT THE TRUTH"

From the first, Myra Janco surprised advertisers by supplying them with information they did not have about themselves and their competitors. Her credo for solving advertising and marketing problems was, and always has been, "Get the facts—search out the truth." She never hesitated to go out in the field with the sales personnel of a company to explore marketing problems. She structured questionnaires and tested them on friends. A dinner date with

Myra was an experience they remembered. A typical conversation opener: "Suppose you were a traffic manager of a food manufacturing company and you had a lot of LTL (less than truckload) shipments. How would you compare shipping firms?" Myra learned from everyone and her interest in solving problems left her unaware of the strain she frequently put on her friends.

Myra's first client was Walter Bledsoe and Company, operator of coal mines. She had read that industrial coal sales were slipping and, figuring out what the objectives of coal company advertising should be, she wangled an interview with the general manager. He listened attentively to the program she outlined and said, "No thanks."

Myra remembered her father's question, heard so often when she was making those party favors: "Why would anyone want to buy that?" Her years on high-school and college debating teams had taught her something else—the value of facts. She recalls reading every book about research methods that she could find in Terre Haute. "The library was forever calling the books back." Myra laughed. "I kept so many of them checked out! I even studied the graduate theses in the college library to learn how facts were organized and correlated."

Her knowledge of research methods paid off. She now developed a comparative profile of the Bledsoe Company based on depth interviews with their customers and prospects. It revealed that the coal company wasn't nearly as well known in the markets it was striving to reach as management believed. When Myra returned to Bledsoe and placed the cold facts in front of the general manager, he *was* impressed. This was information that could make sales, information the firm did not have. He took Myra to the board of directors and they were impressed in turn.

Next she evaluated the company's advertising in terms of its effectiveness. It was obvious Bledsoe needed a stronger voice and she proposed to supply it. She suggested a coordinated program of magazine, trade journal, and direct mail advertising, giving coal buyers the facts that would move them to select Bledsoe "quality" coal. Coals and Btu's were compared; mine locations were noted for transportation savings. Wabash Advertising got its first account, and the girl from Gary was off and running.

Working from fourteen to eighteen hours a day, Myra built up her agency in a year's time to a point where it had twelve accounts, was doing a million dollars' worth of business and employed ten full-time people.

Myra built her staff carefully, using what she called her "4-A method of hiring." Her selections were based on four tests of a candidate: aptitude, ability, attitude, and achievement. Her art director and creative head was a man whom she had once hired as advertising manager when she worked at Meis. Two others were copywriters who had worked for her. To complement the young and ambitious, Myra hired several retired "pros" who worked part-time and served clients and taught colleagues. (Myra admits she learned a great deal from her pros.)

In 1954 with Wabash Advertising continuing to thrive, Miss Janco might have been expected to take it easy. Instead she enrolled in the doctorate program in marketing at Indiana University and learned more about research techniques. (While there she studied with such experts as the late Alfred Kinsey.) Meanwhile she associated her agency with one in Cleveland and another in Chicago, and weekends usually found her in the air bound for one city or the other. One evening per week she drove to Terre Haute to teach a class in advertising.

The sixty miles between Bloomington and Terre Haute are lonely, the route is hilly and loaded with curves. Myra drove it alone week in and week out. Eager students often detained her after class at a campus coffee shop for extra counseling. "I didn't worry about those late and long drives," says Myra, "but luckily nothing ever went wrong. If I had gotten a flat tire, though, I had my mind made up to take off my high heels and walk!"

In 1956, she was named Associate Professor of Marketing in the School of Business at Indiana University, becoming the youngest in the school (and the only woman) to hold such a position.

There, besides teaching advertising, she was counselor for the under-graduate division, and first advertising director of the newly launched *Business Horizons,* the Business School's quarterly journal. Her home became a frequent gathering place for students from such faraway places as India, Thailand, and Germany.

BREAKING THE TABOOS

Myra's advertising career continued, guided by a concern that she has never been afraid to put into practice: "There is too much me-too-ism in advertising. Have we forgotten the adventure of being different?"

Meanwhile, Miss Janco continued to break taboos against women. She ventured into another field that was a long way from polka-dot dresses: trucking. She inaugurated an advertising campaign to help the Eastern Express Co. achieve wider recognition and was at least partly responsible for the ensuing ten-million-dollar increase in Eastern's business. Daring to be different, Myra was the first to use four-color advertising in trucking-industry ads and the first to use fine art in that field. Her campaigns for Eastern Express won from the American Trucking Associations a series of "best" awards in the late 1950s. The ATA also gave her promotions the "Best Over-All Advertising Campaign Award" from 1960 to 1962, a recognition never before awarded three years in a row to the same company.

Advertising is often associated with "the man in a gray flannel suit," but Myra points out, "I've never found any petticoat prejudice!" She says, "I'm not particularly creative but I think being a woman gives me an advantage in what I do best—digging out facts. Women don't mind working with details as much as men, and I think they're more detailed and orderly in the way they go about things."

Many people disagree with Myra's modest opinion of her creativity. Calling one of her ideas a "first," *Printer's Ink* magazine ran a series on a project she developed while teaching a marketing course at Indiana University. From about three hundred in the class, she selected twenty promising candidates and called them "advertising interns." In the role of teacher, but acting as advertising director of the University's *Business Horizons* magazine, she whirled the interns on an eight-week, eight-thousand-mile trip from coast to coast. She taught them how to sell advertising space in the new magazine, then sent them to prospective advertisers to apply their new knowledge. At her suggestion, the young men selected their own general manager and four district managers. They made their own slide and flip-chart presentations, did promotional advertising and image studies, and even worked out rate charges for the magazine. At the end of one quarter, the interns had not only paid all their own expenses and salaries but pulled in a profit of twenty-five thousand dollars on the space they sold!

Today, many of those interns are company presidents, product and sales managers, TV and radio station directors, public relations and advertising account executives. "One of the greatest rewards of my teaching life," Myra states, "is my continuing associations with former students. They frequently phone to report their progress or to ask for some advice and counseling."

For the first time, however, Myra found that even her well-run schedule was becoming crowded. She had once told an interviewer for the campus newspaper: "Planning your time is essential." Now she became aware that there was too much happening in the advertising world for her to remain on the sidelines. Yet the thought of leaving the rewarding work of teaching troubled her.

She was struggling to reach a decision when she received a valuable bit of advice from the Reverend Mr. Ernie Butler, a handyman at work in her home. With eight children to support on his preacher's salary from an all-Negro congregation in a poor section of town, Mr. Butler earned added income by washing cars, mowing lawns, and painting houses in the community. From atop his ladder, he reassured her: "Remember, a door never closes but another one opens."

The minister's words came true shortly thereafter. The American Trucking Associations called on Myra to solve a problem: how to swing business going to privately owned truck fleets back to the common carriers—regulated trucking firms which it represented. Tonnage of the former had increased more than five times as much as the tonnage hauled by common carriers. Myra remembered again her father's old question: "Why would anyone want to buy that?"

Her research discovered that the advantages of regulated highway common carriers outweighed the high cost of "do-it-yourself" trucking, and her campaign told the story to everyone in the country who might be affected. More than a thousand major companies decided to switch from private truckers to common carriers. Miss Janco became the first woman invited to membership in the Sales Council of the ATA. A sales manual she developed is regarded as a bible by the trucking industry. (She never became a really expert truck driver, however—her legs were too short.)

In 1963, a new advertising agency, Roche, Rickerd, Henri, Hurst, Inc., was formed by a merger of two old Chicago firms. Out of eighteen applicants and four competitors, management selected Myra Janco to be executive vice-president—an impressive title and a big job for the young lady from Indiana.

She ranked tops in management experience, having worked with the training of four hundred employees at Meis, and having directed Wabash Advertising. There was no doubt that she had practical experience in all phases of agency operations. "Everything was right but sex," one of the managers said. When he weighed her academic background in business management and market research and her willingness to take on the responsibilities that accompany leadership, however, he swung his vote for Myra. A final check with some outside management consultants confirmed that Myra was indeed the girl for the job.

Among her new duties was the unpleasant task of trimming staff and reshuffling personnel into a new organizational pattern. Myra went into action with a firm, fair hand. Within three months she had the research, media, creative, and production departments operating smoothly and the clients were "at home."

SOME WINNING CAMPAIGNS

One day a Chicago bakery, Burny Brothers, came to her with this proposal:

"As you know, Miss Janco, this is a highly competitive market. We want you to find out what Burny's status actually is, and what our future prospects look like."

Once more it was a call to research, Myra's specialty. And once again she moved into action. Market analysts were deployed to see what people really thought of Burny's products, copywriters and artists were put to work designing newspaper ads. Teams of technicians were assigned to produce television commercials and they developed a method that resulted in a 50 per cent saving over the normal cost, being pinpointed to reach the right audience.

An agency executive who worked on the campaign called Myra "the most relentless searcher for marketing facts I have been privileged to work with."

Her reputation for doing just that brought her still another task, a face-lifting operation for a hundred-year-old firm in Milwaukee— Holsum Foods. It was her kind of job: Myra masterminded package, label, image, product, and promotional studies. Then she sat down with Holsum's management and sales staff to interpret the findings. "It was one of my most delicious projects," declared Myra, "for it meant sampling the firm's syrups, pickles, preserves, salad dressings, and olives."

At the end of six months, Holsum could boast of a fresh and fetching package for its salad dressing. An added line of preserves appeared—complete with promotions to whet consumer appetites. The president of Holsum Foods declared they had achieved a "new old-fashioned, homemade look that sells."

"Moving products," says Myra, "means designing people-moving ads."

To do this, however, the creative people have to be working as a team, and there must be a meeting of the minds of both the creative and the marketing personnel. This has always been one of Myra's outstanding talents. As one of her colleagues says, "She delves deeply into the personal working relationship of one person to another. She realizes the strength of an organization can only be increased by a common and harmonious understanding. She has furthered an *esprit de corps* throughout the entire group."

DRAPER DANIELS PICKS A PRESIDENT

In 1965, Draper Daniels, the vigorous and opinionated creative man who had been chairman of the executive committee of Chicago's traditionally tough and masculine Leo Burnett Company, obtained a controlling interest in Roche, Rickerd, Henri, Hurst. Through a mutual acquaintance, Daniels met Myra and a serious exchange of marketing and creative philosophies took place. They talked about the type of agency each of them had always wanted to work for in terms of an "ideal agency." They discussed the ingredients that made an agency win the respect and accounts of advertisers—an agency built on professional competence and excellence.

Remembering Daniels, as the adman who originated the he-man Marlboro cigarette advertising campaign, gossips along Chicago's agency row predicted, "Daniels will never stand for a woman as executive vice-president." For once the gossips were right. She didn't last as executive vice-president. The day Daniels took over as chairman of the board and changed the company's name to his own, Myra moved in as president.

When the news spread around, there were many people who observed, "Daniels has holes in his head! Always a sucker for a pretty face." But others decided, "He's smarter than I thought."

One question keeps popping up: "How come a woman president?" (Myra is the only woman to head a major general advertising agency in the United States.) Daniels fields the question this way: "Just lucky, I guess!"

From party favors to president. She had started Wabash Advertising with a staff of one—herself. Now she guides a staff of fifty. Has her business life really changed? Not basically, Myra thinks. There are still plenty of facts to be found, many problems waiting to be solved.

At the beginning of her career, she had visions of reaching a summit of success represented by making ten thousand dollars a year. She has long since surpassed that goal and found it was not so important after all. What really counted was the challenge of the advertising profession. From that two-hundred-dollar shoestring back in Terre Haute, her striving to "be better" has brought her to the very top of her profession. She had barely settled into the president's chair at Draper Daniels when the Advertising Federation of America named her 1965's "National Advertising Woman of the Year." She is the youngest woman ever to be selected for the honor.

On a sunny Sunday in June, this pint-sized perfectionist received the award in Boston. In her acceptance speech she paid tribute to the people in her life who had made it possible: her father, who taught her never to stop trying; her first boss, from whom she learned not to take herself too seriously; the late Ralph N. Tirey, who inspired her to never stop learning; the Negro clergyman, who helped her overcome discouragement; and her beloved "Aunt Goldie."

In his speech of introduction, Draper Daniels said: "Myra is not only one of the most attractive ways they've found to package brains since man first knew enough to find a cave and come in out of the rain, but she has a childlike idealism, an innate sense of decency, and the true honesty that only the truly able can afford."

Turning to his petticoat president, he concluded, "Myra has a formidable will to win but she carries her ability without arrogance. I'm glad she's on my side!"

BEHIND THE MYRA JANCO STORY

There are three unusual aspects to Myra Janco's breakthrough into top executive ranks. The first and most obvious is her sex. There just aren't that many women of presidential rank. Yet, significantly, nowhere in her biography does she ascribe setbacks or hardships to the fact that she is a woman.

Certain incidents and references in her story suggest that the sailing was not completely smooth. But when one meets Miss Janco, one sees exactly how the hazard has been overcome. There's no question of her femininity. Her modish hair style, her chic clothes proclaim her good taste in feminine fashion. But at the same time her manner is direct and matter-of-fact. From her questions and responses it becomes quickly clear that a first-rate mind is at work.

The second dominant factor is her interest in things academic. First as a student, then as a teacher at various universities, Miss Janco showed that learning while working was intensely important to her. Interestingly enough, her academic interests acted to complement rather than hamper her progress in the world of business.

The third unusual element was her approach to problems. Invariably, her first move when confronted by a problem situation was to ask, "What are the facts?" Then she would proceed, systematically and energetically, to dig below the surface for the underlying truths that contained the key to the solution.

Besides these three major elements, these factors sparked her progress:

"Customer Appeal." In early childhood she learned an important lesson, summed up in her father's gentle question: "Why would anyone want to buy that?"

Thereafter, whether she was making party favors or was out in the business world trying to interest a client in her company's services, she knew she had to provide specific "reasons to buy," or in the parlance of selling, customer benefits. Myra Janco instinctively understood a principle that is drilled into every novice salesman: to win a customer, you've got to sell "benefits" to him.

Entrepreneur at Four. It's sometimes difficult to assess the influence of childhood experience. But in Myra Janco's case there seems little doubt that her "business experience" as a four-year-old "manufacturer" of party favors gave her an interest and a feeling for enterprise. A couple of decades and considerable education intervened between the four-year-old manufacturer and the young lady who started her own advertising agency. But Wabash Advertising was unquestionably the fruit of a seed planted when Myra was in rompers.

Testing. Like Owen Murphy and Rex Wood, Myra Janco tried her hand at various jobs; which might be viewed as an unconscious "testing program." She got into radio very much the way Leonard Reinsch did. She, too, learned the radio business across-the-board and did everything from script-writing to being a radio commentator. But while radio turned out to be Reinsch's cup of tea, for Myra it was just a way station on the road to other fields of endeavor. Nevertheless, it was a worthwhile experience: Learning what one *doesn't* like is often a vital step in career development.

Step-by-Step Advancement. Miss Janco really came to grips with the world of commerce with her job at the Meis Department Store. Here, too, as in her radio work, her experience exposed her to a broad spectrum of department-store activities. Starting as advertising copywriter, she went on to become assistant to the president and then advertising director. The importance of the Meis experience: It helped her understand the problems and situations that face an advertising agency from the *client's* viewpoint.

End Game. The manner in which Myra Janco started her first enterprise, Wabash Advertising, is important to note. Both what she did and what she didn't do are significant:

One might think that once she decided to start an advertising agency, she would make a study of how advertising agencies are run. But this approach was not for Myra. She was more concerned with the *basic objective* of agency advertising. She looked on agency operation as not so much what one did—that is, she didn't get lost in the mechanics—but rather as objectives to be achieved. Companies advertised to increase their business. Accordingly, she asked herself in effect, "What can my company do that would help an advertiser sell more?" Her answer: "Help them sell their marketing problems by finding out first what the problems are and then providing creative solutions."

It was because of her result-orientation that Myra could confidently tell a potential client that the smallness of her agency was no handicap, that it was "the size of the thinking and not the size of the agency that really mattered."

Overview. Miss Janco observed and analyzed a situation the way a field commander might survey an area before committing his troops. In order to get an accurate picture of the problems her clients faced, she began, in her own words, to "search out the truth." With the "truth" in her hand—that is, with all the pertinent and available facts collected and at her disposal—she then felt confident about making suggestions and recommendations to the client.

Reality Orientation. While Myra depended heavily on pinning down the "truth," to her the truth was not an abstraction. On the contrary, it was the hard reality of things. In committing her energies to fact-gathering, she went out into the field. She sought ideas and insights from friends and she went to that often-neglected source of knowledge, books. From these and as many other sources as she could make available, she undertook to develop a comprehensive picture of the reality of a situation. And with this reality in her grasp, she was then able to do the creative thinking and make the specific recommendations that won her account after account.

Opsimathy. The dictionary reveals that the Greeks had a word for "education late in life." The word was opsimathy. The habit was Myra's. Despite the success of her advertising agency and despite the drain that running it must have been on her energies, the youthful entrepreneur chose to seek an advanced degree in marketing at Indiana University. For Miss Janco there was no division between the academic and the business life. Each helped the other to the advantage of both.

Rut Busting. The least likely type that Myra Janco might be compared to is the Western gambler. Yet again and again in her career, she demonstrated the fact that she was not reluctant to take risks. In her own words she sought out "the adventure of being different." One incident that makes the point: Hers was the first agency to use four-color advertising and fine art in trucking-industry ads. Her novel approach not only proved to be good business but also won her an award for the best advertising campaign three years in a row—1960, 1961, and 1962.

Meeting of the Minds. To get into the big time, Myra Janco decided to give up Wabash and join the large Chicago-centered agency of Roche, Rickerd, Henri, Hurst, Inc. And then, having escalated her professional career in the big city arena, she had the opportunity to meet Draper Daniels, an outstanding and experienced professional. It is not surprising that she gleaned from the meeting new insights into the advertising business as viewed from the top. But implicit in her profile is the fact that Daniels found a great deal to admire and respect in Myra Janco's own ideas. From this mutual respect came the concept of an "ideal advertising agency" and the business arrangement that eventually won for Myra the accolade "National Advertising Woman of the Year." She became president of the newly organized Draper Daniels, Inc. and from her tough-minded boss, Draper Daniels, chairman of the board, she won the tribute, "I'm glad she's on my side!"

23 ⎰ Jay Van Andel and Richard De Vos—
PROSPECTING ON THE DOORSTEP

In 1959, two young men in their early thirties set up shop in the basement of their homes on the outskirts of Grand Rapids, Michigan. Their aim: to establish a national network of sales representatives who would sell, direct to the consumer, a line of home care and personal care products.

The men—Jay Van Andel and Richard De Vos—were starting on the traditional shoestring, with only a handful of salespeople and a small line of goods. Their "office" consisted of a couple of desks and file cabinets. That first year, gross sales totaled $500,000. But in 1964—only five years after their beginnings—Van Andel and De Vos were, respectively, chairman of the board and president of the privately owned Amway Corporation, grossing sales of over $38,000,000. Working for them were seventy-five thousand sales representatives. The Amway line of nearly one hundred household cleansers and personal care specialties was a well-known brand name across the country.

*　　*　　*

Jay Van Andel and Richard De Vos were born in Grand Rapids, Van Andel on June 3, 1924, and De Vos on March 4, 1926. Their families had come to Grand Rapids—a center of the Dutch settlements in western Michigan—from the Netherlands one or two generations earlier. The heritage of Dutch industriousness and self-reliance was a real-life thing for both men. Van Andel's father quickly established himself as an automobile dealer, and young Van Andel earned his spending money by working for him after school, in the process becoming an expert mechanic. De Vos, who is the sales spark plug of Amway, stems from a long line of "direct sellers."

"One of my grandfathers," De Vos says, "was a huckster. He peddled fruit and vegetables in the streets of Grand Rapids, first from a wagon and later from a Model T Ford truck. My other grandfather ran a grocery store, but did a lot of his business by means of direct deliveries from his horse and buggy. During the depression years, when I was a little boy, my dad worked in a grocery store, too. But later he trained himself to be an electrician, and eventually became a top salesman in the Michigan region for the General Electric Corp."

De Vos himself took to the salesman's life early—selling newspapers when he was still only nine years old. During his high-school days he manned pumps at gasoline stations and clerked in clothing stores. But what was to prove to be the most important event in the lives of both Van Andel and De Vos was their meeting in Grand Rapids Christian High School. In their first year, they lived at the same end of town—directly across town from the school—and Van Andel, the older boy, used to drive a Model A Ford to school every day.

"I paid Jay twenty-five cents a week to ride to school with him," remembers De Vos. "We gradually became good friends, and remained so through school and military service and, of course, our business life."

Although military service separated them for several years, the two youths managed to keep in constant touch by mail, and by timing their furloughs so that they were both able to go back home at the same time. Van Andel volunteered for the cadet program of the United States Air Force, attended Technical Officers School at Yale University and became an aircraft armament officer stationed at various Air Force training bases. De Vos enlisted just prior to his high-school graduation in the Air Force Cadet Program, and served as a flight line mechanic on the island of Tinian, in the Pacific.

DREAM OF TWO SOLDIERS

During the war, in their letters and visits, the two used to dream, like most servicemen, of what they would do when "this thing is all over." In all their talks they kept returning to the same theme: "Why don't we go into business together?"

It seemed to be a logical suggestion, because their natures and abilities complimented each other's. Says De Vos: "For some reason we had something deep in common . . . perhaps because we were actually so unlike. Jay was quiet, studious, always getting straight A's; I was more of an extrovert, always making a little more noise. But for some reason we just hit it off."

Their wartime dream of running a small business together came to early fruition. Van Andel, because he had enlisted earlier, was discharged first. He and De Vos, caught up by the promise of civilian aviation—it was a period when thousands of air-minded youngsters were dreaming of careers in the skies—decided to open a flying business. Van Andel reached an agreement with the operator of a small air service operation to run a flying school in connection with his airport.

Both men put in all the cash they had—seven hundred dollars apiece, enough to buy a Piper Cub two-seater plane on credit, and to fix up a whitewashed chicken coop as an office. At first there were only a few customers willing to risk their two dollars for a sight-seeing flight. Because the airport's runways were not yet finished, Van Andel and De Vos had come up with the idea of putting their plane on floats rather than wheels and making their landings and take-offs from a nearby river. With this innovation, their flights took on added excitement.

When the G. I. Bill of Rights became law, the federal government underwrote tuition fees for flight training and the character of the business changed. Van Andel and De Vos bought another airplane, hired pilot-instructors, and qualified under the name of Wolverine Flying Service as a flight training school.

"Interestingly enough," says Van Andel, "there were four other flight training schools operating in the region. Even though we were new in the business, we outstripped all of our competitors. And looking back, the reason probably was the oddest thing you could think of—the fact that neither Rich nor myself were able to fly!" The competitors were licensed instructors, and they would go up with a student, teach him a lesson, come back down and hope they had another student waiting. "Since we had to hire the pilots," observes Van Andel, "we could spend all of our time getting more students. In other words, we could concentrate on the selling and management aspects of the business instead of the routine flight training operation." Eventually, however, both men got their rating as private pilots.

As business prospered, the two young partners employed eight pilots, all ex-G.I.s, and had a fleet of about a dozen trainer planes. De Vos, the more outgoing member of the team, occupied himself largely with selling and public relations; Van Andel, the quieter one, handled the manifold administrative details of dealing with the government and the banks who were financing the business.

ALL THIS AND CLASSES TOO

Although neither Van Andel nor De Vos had a college degree, both did an enormous amount of self-training. They took correspondence courses in administration, and specialized training in public speaking and selling and sales management. At the same time they both attended business classes at nearby Calvin College. Van Andel had also attended Calvin College before World War II, and Yale University and Pratt Junior College while in the Air Force. Going to school and running a business simultaneously presented a time problem that the partners solved in their usual unconventional way. Says De Vos; "We had only one car between us. Jay would drop me off at the airport in the morning and then go on to school. Jay's classes ended at twelve. He'd run to the car, race out to the airport, and I would take the car and try to make it back to college in time for my first class, which began at twelve-twenty. I'd be in school for a few hours and then go back to work at the airport. This went on for about a year."

Early in 1947, De Vos and Van Andel decided to expand their business by opening a small restaurant on the airport site. They built one of the first real "drive-ins" in the Grand Rapids area. After running the flying service and school till dark, they would hurry over to the restaurant and work there until two o'clock every morning, grab a few hours' sleep, and get back in time to open the flight school again at sunup.

In an effort to save time and footsteps, De Vos and Van Andel (who built their 15-by-20 pre-fabricated restaurant structure themselves) originated one of the now-standard characteristics of almost all drive-ins. By every car stand they erected a post with a platform with a switch on it. On each post was a clipboard holding the menu. When a customer had filled out his order, he flipped the switch. One of the partners would rush out, grab the order form, and get right to work cooking it. "We'd alternate cooking," says Van Andel. "One night he'd ruin the hamburgers and the next night I would."

The drive-in proved quite successful. "We became famous for our 'Riverside Specials,'" De Vos remembers. "They were something my mother had always made; cheese with bacon on top of it. Much of the time we'd burn them, but the customers didn't seem to mind. We had a lot of fun." When they decided they could not continue both businesses, De Vos and Van Andel leased the drive-in and eventually sold it.

THE FOOT-LOOSE YACHT OWNERS

Meanwhile, the aviation business continued to boom until it reached the point where it was a going concern of considerable size. Then a yearning for adventure, perhaps a desire for a last fling before settling down, began to beckon the two friends. It started late in the winter of 1948, when they read a book by a man named Richard Bertram. Bertram was a yachtsman and a yacht broker. His book, *Caribbean Cruise,* intrigued De Vos and Van Andel. One night they decided they too would take a Caribbean cruise—despite the fact that neither one of them had ever been on a sailboat in his life!

Wasting no time, once a decision had been reached, the partners started searching for a likely boat. They found a thirty-eight-foot schooner—the "Elizabeth"—in a Connecticut boatyard, and bought it. They reconditioned it and put it in the water the day after Thanksgiving, 1948. Van Andel returned to Michigan to wind up the air service business; the partners had recognized that there was only a limited future for flight training under the waning G. I. Bill. De Vos, with a hired crew of two, sailed the boat to Wilmington, Delaware, by Christmas. Late in January both men returned to the East Coast to start their trip in earnest. They were completely out of business, had some cash in hand, and were foot-loose and fancy-free.

"With an instruction book in one hand and the tiller in the other, we left Wilmington for Miami, where we planned to outfit the craft for the Caribbean," says Van Andel. "We almost ran her aground the first day, but by the time we reached Florida we'd learned a few lessons about sailing." One of the major problems with the "Elizabeth" was that it was a "leaker." If you went to bed at night and forgot to turn on the bilge pumps, you'd be stepping in puddles by morning. Even though the vessel was repaired and completely recalked at least twice, water still seeped in—and this was to provide the dramatic climax of the cruise.

De Vos and Van Andel, heading for Puerto Rico, decided to go the hard way—via Key West to Cuba, and then a long beat into the wind along the north coast of Cuba. "About six o'clock one night, while we were headed out into the open ocean for the run to the Dominican Republic," says De Vos, "I checked below and noticed we had some water coming in. I didn't think too much about it because we had just been recalked in Cuba. I turned the bilge pumps on and went topside. Half an hour later I looked below again and found the water was deeper. I got Jay up, and we started pumping.

"There were no ports to pull into, remember. We were about ten miles out at sea, and it was getting pretty dark. The water was now coming in faster than we could pump it out with two hand pumps and one electric pump. We sent out an S O S on our radio-telephone. Along about midnight we sighted one ship and sent up a red flare. The ship signaled us in Morse code, but—amateurs that we were—we didn't know Morse. We sent an S O S on our flashlight, but the ship went on its way.

"Luckily, we were in the Old Bahama Channel, a deep-water trench about twenty miles wide between the southern edge of the Bahama Banks and the Cuban coast. That meant there was lots of shipping coming through the lane. About two in the morning we sighted another ship. They came alongside—and not any too soon, either. The captain said, 'Who are you?'

" 'The schooner "Elizabeth," out of Michigan,' I said.

" 'What in hell are you doing down here?' he said.

" 'We're sinking!' I said."

The rescue vessel tried to rig a "jumbo boom" and sling the schooner on deck. But it proved impossible. The captain gave the two men ten minutes to get their personal gear salvaged, and then ordered a hole chopped in the "Elizabeth."

"They cut her adrift just as dawn was breaking," recalls Van Andel. "The ship backed off a ways, put on speed, and smashed head-on into our boat. I was on the bridge and watched as the tip of her masts sank beneath the water. It was a sad moment—a necessary one, to remove the 'Elizabeth' as a floating derelict, a threat to the safety of other shipping—but sad just the same."

THE "CRAZY BOYS" DRIFT AND DREAM

That was the end of the Caribbean cruise—and everyone said, "Well, I suppose those crazy boys will come home now." But they didn't. Although the sinking ended the trip, it started something else. For now De Vos and Van Andel spent several months touring the Caribbean and South America, stopping here and there as fancy led them. "We never bought a ticket beyond the next destination, for we didn't know what we'd want to do next." And it was during this time—when there were days and nights of long talks and much thought about the future—that they laid the foundations of the business venture that was to bring them success.

"There was no question in our mind that we were going into business together," says De Vos. "In fact, one day on the beach at Rio de Janeiro we decided on the name of our company—Ja-Ri, for Jay and Rich, Corporation. We didn't quite know what kind of business the company would conduct, but it was good to have the name. It solidified the feeling we had both had, ever since our high-school friendship days, that we would be partners for the rest of our lives."

De Vos and Van Andel were not entirely relaxing on their trip. Whenever they saw a native product or handicraft they thought might be of interest in the U.S., they made a note, or actually arranged, to import it. One such example was Haitian mahogany items. Arriving back in Michigan, the young men began to make money again by selling these and similar goods to specialty shops and department stores.

DIRECT SELLING CASTS ITS SPELL

The turning point of their business career occurred, however, when the partners became interested in the direct-selling field. In August of 1949 the two men signed an agreement to distribute the products of a growing direct-sales company. De Vos was twenty-three, Van Andel was twenty-five.

The direct-selling business was a brand new experience to them. Yet direct selling—or "door-to-door selling," as it is sometimes called—is as old as the United States, for it is an outgrowth of the Yankee peddler of colonial days, who carried in a pack on his back the necessities and small luxuries of life to homesteads far from towns. Shortly after the Civil War, house-to-house salesmen carried Bibles and sewing machines to households across the country.

More than two billion dollars' worth of goods are sold each year by direct-selling methods today—nearly 3 per cent of the total retail trade of the nation. More than twenty-seven hundred companies are in the field, selling everything from books to food products, housewares to cosmetics, wearing apparel to costume jewelry. Direct selling has been a major factor in establishing new markets, and solid acceptance for new items. The door-to-door salesman, for example, pioneered original consumer interest in washing machines, vacuum cleaners, silk hosiery, sterling silver, tableware, aluminum cookware.

At first, De Vos and Van Andel went on the road themselves, selling their products door-to-door. Gradually, however, they began to recruit, train, and supervise other salesmen, and to build a distributorship for themselves. Eventually, they had thousands of distributors working with them, primarily in Michigan and Ohio. This was not quite as easy as it sounds. It came only after long, searching talks with each of the individuals who responded to their advertisements for salesmen. "We'd tell them about the business," says De Vos, "the product, the opportunity for personal advancement." Van Andel did the initial screening, and De Vos would follow up with a training program. As the years passed, the business prospered, the partners expanded into other states.

But by 1959 a major crisis was looming. The supplier and the manufacturer of food and cosmetic items began to feud between themselves. De Vos and Van Andel were concerned on two scores. One was the integrity of the products. The other was the faith and confidence of the thousands of sales representatives who were beginning to wonder what was happening. The partners decided that they had achieved too much merely to abandon what they had done and go into yet another venture. They decided they would take the organization they already had, and build something new with it. This was how Amway began.

Says Van Andel: "We started with one cleaning product, a liquid detergent. We told our people they could go on selling whatever else they liked, but we offered them our product as an extra line." It was a new kind of liquid detergent—made from a coconut oil base instead of petroleum derivatives, it was bio-degradable—that is, did not pollute water supplies, rivers and streams.

The response from the sales representatives—who had by this time come to trust De Vos and Van Andel—was such that Amway (a telescoped contraction of the phrase "American Way") was soon able to add other products as manufacturers submitted them. The partners insisted, however, that each new product have a unique feature of value to the consumer, and that it also fall within their general structure of personal care and household care items.

Another thing the partners insisted upon was that the direct sellers themselves have a voice in the conduct of the business. This was in line with their belief that no business venture can function successfully for long without mutual faith among all those involved in its operation. Van Andel and De Vos thereupon set up the American Way Association, to which all Amway distributors belong, and in which the top field management people, called direct distributors, were given the opportunity to elect representatives to a board which would help select products, and be consulted on sales policies. In other words, while the Amway Corporation handled manufacturing and distribution, the Board of the American Way Association would protect the rights of the salespeople ("distributors") in the Amway sales organization. This organizational structure, unusual even for the forward-looking direct-selling field, went a long way toward building the kind of morale that was necessary to sustain Amway in its first years. With this loyal nucleus of people, the young men were able to strike out on their own.

The second crisis for the new company centered on the product line. By the end of the first year of operation, Amway was distributing five items, two provided by one manufacturer, three by another. When one of these suppliers began to prove unreliable, De Vos and Van Andel started to find an alternate source. But it soon became evident that if they were ever going to be able to provide security for the distributors of their products, and retain their faith in Van Andel and De Vos, the manufacturing process itself was going to have to be under Amway control. By stretching their credit resources, De Vos and Van Andel bought a 50 per cent interest in the manufacturing company owned by a second supplier.

Up to now, the entire operation had been run out of the basement of Van Andel's home in Ada, a suburb of Grand Rapids. (Both men had gotten married, bought some land alongside the Thornapple River in Ada, and built homes for themselves side by side.) Now, faced with the necessity of integrating the manufacturing setup into the Ada organization, the partners rented a warehouse in Ada. ("If someone came to Ada to pick up an order," explains De Vos, "I'd go to the basement office, check the order, run down to the warehouse, fill the order, and place it in the fellow's automobile truck!") They also bought their first building, on a plot of land 200 by 200 feet, near Ada. This became the manufacturing plant for their first two products.

MONSANTO TO THE RESCUE

"We were scratching awful hard for capital in those days. We had already borrowed heavily on our personal credit," De Vos recalls. "Practically everything we owned—and everything we could borrow—we plowed into the company."

"The important and beautiful thing that happened, at this point, was that we discovered the great faith that large American corporations have in small ones. For example, we needed to buy most of our raw materials for manufacturing on credit. And even when we would open our books to them, they would support us. I think of Monsanto Chemical Corp. as a prime example. Their regional sales manager came to see us. We told him of our small progress, of our hopes for the future, and of our lack of ready cash. But he must have thought we could make it, for he agreed to sell us all we needed, giving us sixty days from delivery to pay.

"One day their credit manager came down to look us over and

after we had stalled for a whole year on giving Monsanto a profit statement. We didn't have much to show, and rather than show them what we considered a pretty poor statement, we showed them nothing! But the credit manager twisted our arm, and we gave him our statement. It showed a net worth of ten thousand dollars.

"Yet only a few months ago," Van Andel remembers, "that same man came up to Ada to give us an award for buying over one million pounds of raw material from them in a month's time. He asked us if we recalled the day we gave him that first statement. We did, of course. 'When I saw what your net worth was, and thought of what you owed us—sixty thousand dollars—I never thought I'd see *this* day!'"

Recently Amway completed its twenty-first, and largest, plant expansion when it dedicated its $250,000 office building. The company's total space now exceeds 120,000 square feet, on a 250-acre site. Nearly 450 employees, working two shifts a day, turn out a line of nearly one hundred products which, transported by a fleet of twenty-seven trailer trucks to twenty major warehouses across the nation, enable seventy-five thousand direct-sales representatives to total up more than thirty-eight million dollars a year in gross volume. All of this makes Amway one of the largest direct-selling companies in the world—and only six years after it started.

Questioned as to the secret of Amway's success, De Vos says: "There's no secret. We work through individual people who tell an honest story to a friend or a neighbor, and who offer a product of quality at a fair price. But personal selling is still the key to this business. The people who sell our products have faith in their goods, in their organization, in themselves." Behind all this, however, is the relationship between Van Andel and De Vos—it forms the basis of the "faith" and "confidence" which permeates their company. According to the partners, the people who worked for and with them felt that the closeness between them would always be reflected in company policy. To a large extent this faith in Van Andel and De Vos is the core of the organization.

"Our representatives," says Van Andel, "came to know that we were willing to give them more of a voice in the company—and therefore more security—than anyone else in the direct-selling industry. No other company in the industry gives its distributors such a voice in sales management [through the American Way Association]; no other company gives its top distributors a share in the profits.

"This Association Board—there are nine representatives from the field, while Rich and I represent the company—is consulted on any changes in sales policy. So it isn't something where a couple of guys up here are going to pull all the strings and change the deal after everyone else has put forth all their efforts to build the company. We set this board up as a force against ourselves, so to speak, to make sure the field people are treated fairly and squarely."

This has built a feeling of oneness in the organization which is an incalculable factor in its progress. The product line and the sales plan really work because the direct-sales representatives have faith in their future.

A JOB? WHAT'S THAT?

"What inspired us?" De Vos asks. "In my life the major influence was my father, who would never let up on little things which eventually became a part of one's thought pattern. He would never accept 'I can't.' There was no such word for him as 'can't.' Also he would always tell me: 'If there's anything you must remember, it's this: get in business for yourself.' It was so important to him, and he said it so often to me, that I never thought of a job. There was no point at which I ever wondered who I'd work for. It was always, 'I've got to get into a business of some kind, a business of my own.'"

The early habit patterns instilled in De Vos by his father also held true for Van Andel. His father had always been in business for himself, and there was never any thought in the youngster's mind of working for anyone else except himself. The idea of a "job" never entered his mind.

Along with faith in themselves, plus the habit patterns of hard and responsible work, went a deep commitment to each other. Once Van Andel and De Vos decided they would build their careers together, obstacles seemed less difficult to surmount. For one thing, their closeness enabled them to communicate openly, to "lay our business problems on the table, kick them around, and come up with a solution acceptable to both of us." There has never been a serious difference of opinion between the partners—a truly remarkable achievement. Part of this is due to the long periods of discussion on their South American trip—sessions which both men feel went a long way toward eliminating any potentially strong differences in their philosophy of business and of life.

"If one of us feels strongly about some particular point," says Van Andel, "he says so, and the other agrees to go along. Even *this* situation has occurred only once or twice as far as I can remember."

Perhaps the relationship of the men can best be summed up in an explanation of how Van Andel came to be chairman of the board of Amway, and De Vos the president. "We used to alternate the positions," says De Vos, "until our employees and our attorneys became hopelessly confused. The latter asked us please to straighten out the matter, so one day I said, 'Jay, you're older than I am, so you be chairman of the board.' And that's the way it's been."

BEHIND THE JAY VAN ANDEL – RICHARD DE VOS STORY

Several other profiles in this book describe individuals whose rise to the top was aided by a partner or business associate. For example, Solomon Dutka acknowledges the help he received from friend, colleague, and mentor Elmo Roper. In the biography of Charles Berns of "21" Brands, the mutual-assistance team of Jack and Charlie is clearly portrayed. However, Jay Van Andel and Richard De Vos represent a team combination of unusual achievement. They attained financial success, yet their profile clearly suggests that business considerations played second fiddle to friendship. They offer a strong contradiction to the idea that "good guys finish last."

In the working relationship between Van Andel and De Vos, one sees the strength of the team approach. They reinforced one another in thinking, planning, and in action. There's no indication that their strong friendship and deep rapport was ever anything other than a strong assist.

It's not often in the telling of success stories that one can point to the enjoyment of business activity by the entrepreneur. More typical are the stories of painful sacrifices and distressing setbacks. Van Andel and De Vos make it clear that in part, at least, business life *can* be beer and skittles. Despite the fact that they were driving themselves hard to keep their enterprise going, they could say, "We had a lot of fun." Certainly fun is a desirable fringe benefit in any career.

In addition to this dominant factor in their success pattern, these significant elements also explain their breakthrough:

The Gamble. Van Andel and De Vos understood at the outset that business requires a willingness to put the chips on the table and take a chance. Coming out of service after World War II, they consolidated all their respective savings—seven hundred dollars apiece—and started their airborne sight-seeing service. Their subsequent adventures also demonstrated their understanding of a basic business fact: enterprise means taking a chance.

Business Training. Very often people have the impression that the only place to learn about business is in the market place. These two entrepreneurs had a taste of business when they started their own airplane sight-seeing tours. But then they decided that they needed to know more about the "business of business." Accordingly, they enrolled in courses at Calvin College. Their subsequent success should prove encouraging to two groups of people: business educators and business students.

Bet Doubling. Knowing how and when to expand an enterprise is a crucial factor in business success. This duo made its bid for increased profit by opening a small restaurant near their airport. Apparently their judgment was good. The restaurant succeeded, in a traditional pattern of the snowballing of an enterprise.

Money Substitute. This factor, the pouring in of personal efforts because of a lack of cash to hire, is true of many other successful people. Van Andel and De Vos had to hustle and wear many hats to keep their planes flying and their restaurant in operation. Their willingness to make this expenditure and their ability to sustain the effort is an ever present factor in the pattern of the underfinanced entrepreneur.

Operation "Spread." When the business pair began their door-to-door enterprise, they eventually faced the problem of growth. The way in which they went about their expansion is noteworthy. They showed a willingness to depend on others, to pick a man and to be willing to ride on the validity of their judgment and the man's capabilities. The method of profit-sharing used by Amway's founders probably would be viewed with bewilderment by some businessmen. On the scale that the two young executives did it, it seemed perhaps like an overly generous gesture. Even more unprecedented was the willingness to share control of the enterprise, to give the individual salesmen some feeling of partnership. But the interesting thing about the Van Andel–De Vos approach to profit-sharing is that it "worked"—that is, proved productive—by getting the interest and involvement of the salesmen, which, in turn, meant more business for the company.

It would be difficult to say whether the arrangements the executive team made with their people represented open-handed philanthropy or hard-headed calculation. The point is, it served to make Amway a thriving organization because of the strong motivation it provided for the men on the firing line, the door-to-door salesmen.

24 { INVOLVEMENT AND MOTIVATION – THE DYNAMOS OF ACCOMPLISHMENT

"The people in your book have one thing in common," observed the secretary typing the manuscript. "They are certainly highly motivated." The secretary's observation, of course, is true. And it raises an interesting question: Are the people described in this volume all motivated by the same factors? To one extent, the answer is Yes, for each one is highly involved in his professional activities. But what lies behind this involvement? What is its nature and its development?

WHAT DOES INVOLVEMENT MEAN?

"There's no better example of involvement," says Dr. Erwin S. Stanton of the McMurry Company, management consultants, "than a man fleeing from a charging bull." Dr. Stanton's example clarifies a key element in involvement. The man racing away from the bull devotes every ounce of energy and effort to what he's doing because his survival is at stake.

The executive or entrepreneur deeply engaged in running a business may not think in terms of physical survival, after his early years, but he certainly sees his activities as essential to the achievement of his dearest personal goals—be they money, power, status, or building an organization of his own.

The degree of involvement can be startling: "He's killing himself," asserts the wife of a hard-driving printing firm president. "The doctors have told him to ease up, but he won't." This president has a lot of company. The dedication of such men to their business enterprises, misguided or exaggerated though it may be, nevertheless transcends concern with self.

Says Dr. Mortimer Feinberg of BFS Psychological Associates, "The concern of the successful businessman is seldom with his own personal welfare. President Lyndon B. Johnson is an extreme example of the type. He rarely goes to bed before 1 A.M. or gets up after daybreak. Yet, despite such grueling hours, hard-driving executives often have few psychosomatic complaints. On the contrary, they may be buoyantly energetic."

Dr. Feinberg stresses the involvement factor in achievement: "No executive rises to the top without total personal commitment to the company." Apparently many executives make this commitment at the expense of personal relationships, for Feinberg also reports: "Most top executives find their careers more exciting than their wives, especially after twenty or thirty years of marriage."

One of the case histories from Feinberg's files contains this telling exchange between the president of a large building-materials company and his wife. The wife complains about their not spending more time together at the country club to which they belong. Replies the husband: "My dear, I can either run a successful business and make lots of money, or we can go to the club and do the social whirl. I don't have time for both. Maybe next year, when things ease up, we can spend more time with your friends but not now." Explains the wife sadly, "That was four years ago and he hasn't taken me to the club yet."

OTHER FOES OF INVOLVEMENT

The family has often been played up as an obstacle to the "marriage" between a man and his company. But the family is by no means the only interfering factor. Perhaps the single greatest obstacle arises from the individual's personal sense of what's important. From time to time, a high-powered executive or entrepreneur takes a long, hard look at himself and disapproves of what he sees. For example, he may realize that his life has become narrow, unrelieved. Of course, these days, sophisticated management often encourages top executives to take time off and develop nonbusiness interests. And many top men don't need to be pushed. The brilliant hummingbird photographs of DuPont Chairman Crawford H. Greenewalt, the African safaris of J. J. Mascuch, the dozen-and-one travels, hobbies, and sport activities of other successful executives are common proof.

Nevertheless, there are many individuals who can't let down, who are so totally absorbed in their business and career interests that even a temporary relaxation of the reins gives them the fidgets. The comedian at the resort who pokes fun at the non-laughing member of his audience by remarking, "He must own his own company," has probably hit the nail on the head.

Instances of self-doubt among people at the top are exceedingly rare. As a matter of fact, it is the lack of any doubt, the certainty of an individual that he's doing what he wants to do and that it really matters, that is one of the key factors in total involvement.

A study of executives whose achievements were only moderate compared to their potential was made by this author recently.* A single case illustrates the problem:

"Mr. X," a career counselor says, "you've had considerable experience in two areas, as a salesman and as a sales manager. You've described how, in your last job, you actually started from scratch and organized a fifty-man group of salesmen for a textile-products company that was entering a new field. Now, in your next job, would you like to continue as a sales manager, or get back into selling?"

The sales manager thought for a moment, then said: "Neither."

"But if you could have any job you wanted . . ."

"I just don't know," was the reply.

This man, at forty, still had not come to grips with a basic career question: "What do I *really* want to do?"

---

* See *The Executive Job Market* by Auren Uris, McGraw-Hill, 1965.

Clearly, any doubt in the mind of an individual that he is *not* in the job he wants to be, in the business he wants to be, headed in the direction he wants to go, is bound to weaken his sense of involvement, and accordingly, his motivation.

INVOLVEMENT OR COMPULSION?

Overintensive preoccupation with the world of work can, of course, represent a psychological imbalance. And the successful business executive has been accused of feeding his career at the expense of other values and human relationships. Some observers go even further. The energy that the highly involved businessman pours into his job, they say, is actually an attempt to make up for dissatisfactions and lack of interests in other quarters of his life. "The demands of business success," warns one authority, "sap the juice from a man's personal life."

A psychiatrist, working with highly involved business executives, says, "The men rarely will accept treatment. But I see their wives and their children, suffering from the effects of the husband's or father's failure to provide the warmth of personal relationships required for a normal family life." He also sees the businessman's intense preoccupation as a "flight into work," an attempt to compensate for anxieties and inadequacies in more personal areas.

But perhaps, just as to the cobbler the world seems to be made up of dilapidated shoes, the psychiatrist's view is colored by his professional vantage point. To those willing to accept the sexual area as an indicator of health and emotional well-being, the words of another authority are pertinent: "Sex is not a subject of special concern among executives." So states Dr. Harry Johnson, whose affiliation with Life Extension Examiners makes him one of the country's acknowledged experts on executive health. Based on an examination of over twenty thousand business executives annually, Dr. Johnson observes, "Of the thousands of executives I see in a year, not over fifty men ever indicate that sex is a problem."

Perhaps the question of one-sidedness is beside the point—to everyone but the individual executive. After all, the choice is his. And why should one deplore involvement by the business executive? Other professionals—scientists, doctors, lawyers, artists—likewise harbor in their ranks those whose involvement in their craft cuts them off from other areas of experience. And yet, seldom does one hear a voice raised in criticism here.

THE ROAD AND THE SUMMIT

The poets and philosophers agree: life is a journey. For the successful businessman, the road is the direction in which he works, the goal a peak of achievement that yields the kind of rewards that are meaningful to him—a profitable company, a top position in a large enterprise, the respect and admiration of his peers, and so on.

The journey of the success-seeker is somewhat different from that of the average individual. Consider the careers of the people described in this volume. In some few cases, early periods were marked by indecision and groping. But once the "right road" was found, there was no question of direction, or the will to press on to the road's summit. It is the forthright acceptance of the road, the certainty that he's going where he wants to go and that the distant summit is worth his efforts, that makes the journey of the business success relatively direct and uncluttered.

This is not to say that he won't face difficult choices, conflicting loyalties, along the way. Many a top executive has had to fight the battle between his professional and his personal interest. A favored potential mate may have been set aside because, desirable though she was, "she would have been a handicap to me in my career." Friends, social relationships that may have meant a great deal, are sometimes permitted to pass outside a man's ken, under the press of the demands of business: "We must see each other more often, Tom," a financier tells an old and valued friend feelingly. "Let's get together real soon." The months become years, and the meeting never occurs. But the successful man takes the bumps and obstacles in stride. In the journey which is his life, he knows he's on the right road, and he is willing to do whatever is necessary to get to the goal.

There are a number of other characteristics that mark the "involved man." One way or another, explicitly or implicitly, these elements figure in the careers of each man and woman in our roster of successful people, and explain their involvement:

They Take the "Business Game" Seriously. Says Dr. Harry Levinson, head of the Menninger Foundation's Industrial Health Division: "A man works when he is hungry; and it is equally obvious that he continues to work when he is well fed, well clothed, well housed. A man devotes nearly half of his waking hours to work. Some men make work out of play, and some make play out of work." For the business executive pressing for the heights of achievement, the distinction between work and play disappears. It's all one ball of wax. His life is the "business game."

In order for the individual to throw himself wholeheartedly into any kind of game he must find it interesting and exciting. He must be willing to accept the worthwhileness of the "play." This means, among other things, that he must feel it's important to score, and even more important, to win. The game of tennis affords a good example of this principle. Mr. A feels that tennis is good exercise but can't get too worked up about the game itself. He'll get out on the court, volley for a half hour until he's worked up a good sweat, then retire to the clubhouse for a shower and convivial friends at the bar.

Mr. B behaves altogether differently. He's hooked on tennis. He's out there practicing his strokes, taking lessons from the pro, looking for the toughest competition he can get so that he can improve his game and take on even more impressive competitors. He may not end up being a Bill Tilden or a Don Budge, but he will certainly get as close to it as his potential will allow. In the same way, it's the man who finds the business field the most acceptable arena in which to act out his life's achievement who will get the farthest.

They're "Building Something." Whether an individual works for a company or has started his own enterprise, his involvement is intensified by the feeling that he is creating a personal monument. To the extent that he helps the company profit and grow and expands his own capabilities, he sees a direct relationship between what he does and the results he gets. Top executives in large companies don't feel they're working for "somebody else." It's *their* company. There is an identification of self with the organization.

They March to the Beat of Their Own Drum; they don't follow the band. David Riesman, author of *The Lonely Crowd,* puts people into three classifications: tradition-directed, inner-directed, and other-directed. Applied to behavior on the work scene, Riesman's trichotomy may be illustrated as follows:

The man who is tradition-directed takes a job because it's the thing to do, and it's what most people in his family or community seem to be doing. The other-directed person seeks a career for the material rewards it brings—status, high pay, or security. He may also choose an occupation because it's been recommended to him, or he sees someone else doing it and it appears attractive. The inner-directed man, on the other hand, is guided in his choice of work mainly by the desire to find an outlet for his own capabilities and inclinations. The twenty-one roads to the top described in this book in almost all cases were followed by men and women who are inner-directed. If success has a "secret," it is the successful man's feeling that he's guiding himself along a road that is the right one for him.

THE BLINDING EFFECT OF INVOLVEMENT

Although involvement has the effect of heightening motivation and tends to make the individual more effective, Dr. Feinberg points out that the highly involved executive is frequently misled by his own outlook: "In my experience," says the psychologist, "the highly involved executive has no perception of individual differences. For example, he doesn't perceive himself as unusual. He sees himself merely as a well-organized, well-integrated executive and, as a consequence, the successful executive often develops the feeling that 'anyone can do what I've done. It's just that most people are lazy or backward, or they drink too much, or have a health problem.' "

It's as a result of this blind spot that the successful executive often will drive his subordinates or make excessive demands. One says, cynically, about some of his young assistants: "Sure, I push them up against the wall and make them cry, but when it's all over their faces are cleaner."

CAN MOTIVATION BE ACQUIRED?

There are many people who would strongly deny that ambition, drive, or motivation can be developed in someone lacking it at the start. "You either have it, or you don't," is the idea. "Some people are born ambitious, some people are born lazy, and the rest of us are somewhere in between." That this commonly accepted "fact" may not be true at all, is being gradually proven by the social scientists. Research indicates that it *is* possible to "learn" drive, ambition, motivation.

A very interesting series of experiments in the motivation field is documented in the November–December 1965 issue of the *Harvard Business Review*, by David C. McClelland, Chairman of the Department of Social Relations at Harvard University. Several years ago, McClelland and his associates developed an intensive course, based on what they had learned about the achievement motive in people. First they tried their training course out on a group of executives in a large U.S. corporation and found that it did seem to make a difference in the men's subsequent behavior. Two years later, the executives who'd taken the course were doing better in terms of promotions, greater responsibility, etc., than those who had not. (The course consisted largely in teaching the participants what the achievement motive was, and how to think, talk, act, and see the world like a person with a high need for achievement.)

Then McClelland, under the aegis of the Indian government and the Carnegie Corp., tried the program out on a group consisting of the heads of some small businesses in India. One objective was to see if the same approach would work in an underdeveloped country, for the answer would be important to those providing foreign aid.

Here too, the sociologists got results. Six to ten months after taking the training in achievement motivation, two-thirds of the Indian businessmen had become unusually active in some measurable way; some had started a new business, or expanded their old business, others had increased profits, etc. Only one-third had shown similar enterprise in the two years before taking the course.

For example, one man who owned a small radio shop decided to start a paint and varnish factory. It succeeded and he opened another radio shop. A banker decided that he'd been too conservative in granting loans. He changed his approach and, instead of taking only wealthy landowners who could put up land as collateral, he took into account the quality of the project and the quality of the man requesting the loan. The banker's business flourished and his superiors offered him a better job.

Now, a group of people have formed a company, the Human Resources Development Corp. in Cambridge, Massachusetts, to provide such motivation training on a continuing basis. If such an approach proves successful on a broad scale, it is conceivable that many people who have the necessary talents, intelligence and skills to excel in a chosen field, will make their mark because they have also learned how to *desire* success as well as how to take the steps necessary to attain it.

A final aspect of the highly motivated achiever: self-doubt seldom drags him down. He sees himself as a worthy person. He likes what he is. Even when he doesn't see himself as an empire builder, he sees himself as a doer, a person who gets things done. In this self-image he finds pleasure, reward, and the incentive to become even more so. In terms of the "business game," the high achiever believes in his role, and furthermore feels he can influence the outcome of the "game."

25 { KEY ELEMENTS IN THE BREAKTHROUGH PATTERN

Patricia Murphy and Charles A. Berns made their breakthrough in the restaurant business. Donald Kendall scored his triumph in the soft-drink field, Solomon Dutka in the esoteric field of marketing information. But, regardless of the particular aspects of the business arena in which the successful man operates, key elements emerge that are shared by the success roster. These elements seem to represent the basic ingredients of success. Taken together, they form a grand design, a basic pattern of attitude and action of the successful man.

HE SEIZES THE REINS

"I want to control my own future," says the man who succeeds. He asserts in a figurative sense what Archimedes meant more literally: "Give me but one firm spot on which to stand, and I will move the earth." The ancient Greek was prepared to move the earth by application of the lever. The successful man intends to accomplish his objective by liberal amounts of the spirit of enterprise.

In some cases, the passion to be one's own boss is a reaction to an underprivileged childhood. Jeno Paulucci and Joseph Katz are two prime examples. Joseph Katz of Papercraft displays this urge to control very strongly. From the moment he was able to get hold of one hundred dollars in cash, he went into business for himself— making corn fritters. This "eagerness to run things" persisted from childhood to maturity. His souvenir magazine, *The Pittsburgh*

Flood, earned him four thousand dollars. But to him the money was only working capital—and the opportunity to be his own boss in a new enterprise.

Thomas Coe of Wakefield Engineering was so eager to start a business of his own that he went ahead before he even knew what form it would take. Where would the money come from? What kind of business would it be? Should he start from scratch or try to buy an existing business? Coe solved each problem in a practical way. But all decisions were subordinated to the principal one. He had to be his own boss, the master of his own fate, the captain of his business soul.

The fact that the success-seeker does well working for others doesn't alter his decision. The only way to be sure of where he is going is to take over the reins. Accordingly, he pushes upward in the company he's working for, seeking more responsibility, broader fields in which to operate, less likelihood of having his hands tied.

There's an important fact related to the desire to run things. When the successful man seizes the reins, he doesn't drive blind. He has a strong sense of his own destiny, an augury of his future triumph, a certainty about the direction he should go. As Owen Murphy describes it, he confronted himself in the bathroom mirror and assured himself that *he was going to be rich*. This "foreknowledge of success" has been dramatized in the story of a poor orphan named Dick Whittington, who sought his fortune in the city of London in the fourteenth century. Defeated, reduced to starvation, he was about to leave the city, when the famous Bow Bells rang out to him, predicting his eventual success. He stayed and lived to see the augury of the bells fulfilled. Call it insight, clairvoyance, or what you will—a kind of Whittington augury seems to guide many successful people to their breakthrough. Heartened by this inner assurance, they pursue the daily paths of business, confident that things will come out right, as long as they can "run things"— their way.

HE ANTICIPATES OPPORTUNITY

The successful businessman has a sixth sense, an early-warning system that helps him detect opportunity in its formative stages. This is quite different from the many people who view opportunity through a rearview mirror. "If I knew then what I know now, things would have been different." Because he recognizes opportunity while it's coming, not going, the successful person is able to exploit it. When Owen Murphy heard about a chair that could "increase blood circulation," he forgot about the auction going on around him. The average person would have been diverted by the auctioneer selling his wares. But Murphy, zeroed in by his inner radar, concentrated on the possibilities of the "circulating chair."

When William Rosenberg recognized opportunity, it was a case of "love at first taste." He was first struck by the popularity of doughnuts among customers of his trucks and his cafeterias. His fascination with it increased when he learned that there were small stores that actually specialized in coffee and doughnuts. Each additional fact enhanced his faith in the universal appeal of the doughnut. Viewing the product in the context of what he already knew about people's eating habits, he put two and two together and came up with "opportunity"—the chance to encircle the country with doughnut shops.

HE AVOIDS DEAD ENDS

The success-maker also has a penchant for telling when a situation offers *no* special opportunity for him. When a situation, a job, a company seems to be wrong, he doesn't wait until something better comes along—*he moves out.*

Young Charlie Berns not only proved to be a poor shoe salesman, he failed miserably at selling. But the failure was a learning experience. He became aware that while there were some things he could do well, there were some things he couldn't do at all. With this insight firmly established, he moved into areas that offered him greater opportunity for scoring a breakthrough.

HE GOES WHERE THE ACTION IS

The successful man is action-minded; he seeks out situations providing movement and change. He hungers for action as strongly as the salmon needs to seek the spawning grounds. However, the success-maker is not merely restless or adventurous. He is drawn to situations offering the biggest rewards—even if the hazards are equally large. To him, the phrase "calculated risk" is neither subtle nor figurative. It's a clear-cut description of what he's playing for. It would be inaccurate, however, to equate him with the gambler. Something special is added—and a recent *Wall Street Journal* piece on Texas oil millionaire John Mecom suggests what the extra ingredient is. "Like his fellows," says the *Journal,* "he is an innovator and perennial risk-taker—but he takes special pains to shave the odds as closely as he can before he gambles."

With his appraisal and manipulation of the gamble accomplished to the best of his ability—i.e., Solomon Dutka enlisted Elmo Roper's backing before starting his own company—the successful man develops the confidence that he will win. But win or lose, eventually he's willing to put the chips down and take his chances.

Patricia Murphy of the famed Candlelight Restaurants didn't hesitate to invest twenty-five dollars a week to start a new restaurant during the depression. The challenges of the business game were irresistible. In a more general sense, it is interesting to note that she left her Newfoundland fishing village, where opportunities were scarce, to come to New York. Even though business was not on her mind at this time, she was drawn instinctively to a center of activity.

Stanley Arnold is another "player" fascinated by action. When he left his native Cleveland for the greater opportunities of New

York, he sought out that business sage, the late Bernard Baruch; he wanted the latter's opinion as to where he could find the chance "to try for bigger stakes."

The career of Myra Janco also demonstrates the urge to strive, to compete, to swim in the racing currents of enterprise rather than the placid backwaters of academic life. Miss Janco could very well have foresworn the business life altogether. Her accomplishments and status in the academic world were quickly recognized. While in her twenties, she was successfully teaching marketing courses at Indiana University. A full professorship, and academic honors, were well within her grasp. But because she had a need for action, and knew she would find it in the business world, the academic life, attractive though it might be for others, held only a sideline interest for her. The successful man and woman learns early what many people never learn at all: that only those entering the race can win.

HE KNOWS HOW TO SNOWBALL SUCCESS

"Knowing what to do with money once you have it," says one top businessman, "that's the knack that separates the millionaire from the man who cuddles a nest-egg." No grass grows under the bank accounts of the man headed for the top. And, of course, it's not simply a matter of money. Look closely at the portrait of a successful man and you'll see a "repeater tendency": He works out a winning combination and sticks with it. "Nothing succeeds like success?" Right. "If at first you *do* succeed, try, try again?" Correct. This skill, using a little to make a lot, recurs explicitly in various biographies.

Patricia Murphy demonstrated the process when she used the proceeds of her first restaurant to start another. Jeno Paulucci got his "bean-sprouts factory" off to a flourishing start and then found that mushrooms were a natural second product for his indoor farm. He continued to add enterprises, growing first one ingredient, then another, as required for his food recipes. He even made a business out of selling his used-up soil. The mechanics of the snowballing concept are enlightening. It cuts down to reasonable size the classical problem of "making a million." The successful man *knows* that he doesn't need to make a million in one lump. Usually, that's too formidable an objective. But just let him get started in one profitable activity. The first dollar will be used to make a second. The two dollars will then be used to make four—and immediately the arithmetic of wealth is on his side.

HE SEES KNOWLEDGE AS A TOOL

The *need to know,* to be informed both intensively and extensively in his chosen field, marks the achiever. Many of the individuals in the roster are vociferous in their emphasis on education as a success touchstone. But in their own cases, learning is directed toward very specific objectives. Typically, the success-seeker learns by experience the hard facts of the business areas in which he's interested. He learns the business facts of life from a source that imprints the lessons indelibly on his mind. Time and time again, he returns to this core of experience for guidance and help in decision-making. This is education of the most practical kind.

Amelia Lobsenz got the business knowledge that equipped her to run her own company by doing research for clients. Rex Wood gained his know-how in sophisticated selling techniques by selling to that tough and wary customer, the American housewife. Regardless of how or from whom the achiever learns the core lessons about business, this education makes all the difference in the way he operates, and in his eventual achievement.

The professional-turned-businessman is an interesting special case of the role of education in success. For example, Solomon Dutka, a professional mathematician, transformed himself into an entrepreneur, head of a large service organization. Apparently, the professional who yearns for new fields to conquer can score a breakthrough by using his professional education as a platform.

HE BUILDS HIS COMPANY IN HIS OWN IMAGE

Is an enterprise the shadow of its founder? Eugene Denton's good taste in women's clothes and his desire for high quality are directly reflected in the policies, practices, and image of his store, The Tailored Woman. Customers flock to the store because *its* personality is sharply defined. Similarly, the world-famous Candlelight Restaurants are a direct expression of Patricia Murphy's personal interests and style. Everything from menus to decor spells one woman's tastes and preferences.

Personality can brand an organization in more subtle ways than decor, quality of goods, or company image, however. Jeno Paulucci, for example, has the businessman's equivalent of a green thumb. Everything he touches turns to enterprise. Almost every idea he has for new products in the food field, developed through his ardent, outgoing character, turns into a new enterprise, a new company. "Grow, build, flourish," he seems to say, and new companies are incorporated to satisfy not only his own needs, but those of the economy, the state of Minnesota, and the hundreds of people he employs.

HIS PERSONALITY ENABLES HIM TO ORGANIZE OTHER PEOPLE

The successful businessman builds into his enterprise the qualities that mirror his interests and values. McCormick & Company is a world-famous spice-importing firm headquartered in Baltimore. Under the leadership of Charles P. McCormick, the company became known for its multiple management concept, a unique approach to getting cooperation from all echelons, from the rank-and-file upward. Through a system of auxiliary management boards, all McCormick employees have the chance to participate in the operation and decision-making of the company. This concept, an earmark of the company, derived from McCormick's own strong feelings about the responsibility and dignity of the individual.

A competent psychologist very likely could study a Charles P. McCormick, a Van Andel, and De Vos and make fairly accurate predictions as to the character of the organizations they would create and run. The reverse process is also possible. Set an industrial psychologist to studying the character of an organization and he would be able to come up with fairly accurate predictions as to the personality make-up of the corporate head.

For the success-seeker, the company is a vehicle, the device for getting what he wants, in the way he wants to get it. He shapes and sharpens it to his unconscious needs and conscious wishes.

Leonard Reinsch demonstrated his organization skill at an early age. He quit a full-time job to take on a six-month assignment to reorganize and manage radio station WNBD. At the age of twenty-four, he waded into a messy organizational situation. A staff of twenty people was running a station in an erratic, almost comic manner. Reinsch sized up the situation in a way that would have warmed the hearts of the American Management Association officials. He evaluated the staff, dismissed those he felt were incapable of doing a good job, and undertook to retrain the balance, in line with his own feelings about appropriate business conduct and effectiveness. And, as part of his organizational skill, Reinsch demonstrated his ability to motivate people. He used the galvanizing effect of praise and encouragement, assigned specific tasks with clear-cut deadlines.

Rex Wood and Donald Kendall also showed that if one intends to climb up into the driver's seat of a business organization, one had better know what to do when arriving there. The surer the grasp of the organizational reins, the greater the ability to master and direct individuals within the corporate framework, the more certain the chance of a breakthrough.

HE CULTIVATES MENTORS

Repeatedly, one sees the successful individual getting a boost, direct or otherwise, from someone who has himself already made out. "Father-image!" exclaims the amateur psychologist. Possibly. But why deny the effectiveness of interest and encouragement of a strong and benevolent guide?

Stanley Arnold makes no secret of the fact that he constantly sought guidance from people of expertness and influence. His meeting with Bernard Baruch at a critical time in his career served to push him in a worthwhile direction. J. J. Mascuch makes a clear case for the advantages of getting to know the right people: ". . . a young man ought to try constantly to associate himself with people who are bigger than he is. . . . I don't mean he should kiss the boss's tail or be a social climber. . . . But he should get as close as he decently can to the man from whom he can learn the important things about life and business." The direct and friendly relations Mascuch developed with Alfred P. Sloan and other men were a strong boost upward. Leonard Reinsch found his mentor in the person of James Middleton Cox, ex-Governor of Ohio. Solomon Dutka, originally a scientist, found a guide through the unknown world of business in the person of Elmo Roper.

But the relationship between the man-on-his-way-up and his mentor is *not* a dependency of the kind that minimizes instead of motivates, that binds instead of liberates. The successful person has the ability to gain strength from an individual whose abilities and opinions he respects, and to avoid any "flypaper" side effects.

LUCK AND HARD WORK—HOW MUCH OF EACH?

"An unlucky man," said Harris H. Uris, founder of the New York building firm bearing his name, "falls into a sewer and comes up messy; the lucky man falls in in exactly the same place and comes up with a box of jewels." The turn-of-the-century writer Maude Wilder Goodwin expressed the same idea somewhat more poetically: "Luck is the pebble on which the traveller trips and slides into quicksands, or sands of gold." Luck in business has been discussed in dozens of contexts. Some people say that the only difference between the successful and unsuccessful man is that luck favors the former.

Many successful people, in want of a better explanation, attribute their achievements to a kind providence. Perhaps just as many, looking back on their years of toil and perseverence, unhesitatingly assert that hard work has been the secret of their success. Which is true? Both? Neither?

One's view of the role of luck and hard work in business is often formed by what one sees in everyday business life: "John X is a hard worker," says his superior. "He's here at eight and often works hours past quitting time. I couldn't do without John." Then in an aside to himself he adds, "Poor son-of-a-gun, he'll be in the same job for the next twenty years." Peter Y is a flamboyant, seems to put out a minimum of effort and yet his career prospects are bright. "Is that guy lucky," says an envious colleague. "His boss has a nervous breakdown and he gets a made-to-order promotion without having earned it."

Many other instances of "lucky breaks" come to the Peter Y's of the world. They just "happen" to be given an assignment that turns out to be a key to a company expansion plan and they're in the driver's seat. Or a chance bit of work experience, or education— the ability to speak fluent French, for example, wins them an important foreign assignment that heads them upward on the promotional ladder.

There is a vast difference between John X and Peter Y, between the "hard worker" and the "lucky worker." Both expend energy in their tasks. But the hard worker works to a different end than the man on whom luck smiles. The hard worker tends to bury himself in his work and not look beyond task objectives. The lucky worker may work just as diligently, but he doesn't bury himself in routines. His nose, rather than hugging the grindstone, is more likely to be up in the air, sniffing for favorable winds. Both the hard worker and lucky worker expend energy, but each has different aims. While the hard worker tends to see his work as an end in itself, the lucky man is more likely to see his work as a means to some gainful personal end.

There's no mystery about hard work or what it can produce. Ray Thompson, the Canadian "International Press Lord," whose vast communications network includes 128 newspapers, 15 radio and TV stations, and 150 trade magazines, has said: "Our family was very poor. I made up my mind that I would be a millionaire by the time I was thirty. I missed that mark, but I made it eventually. Most people would like to be rich and some of them start out just the way I did. The difference is that extremely few of these people are prepared to make the necessary sacrifices and to work hard enough. I was bloody well determined to succeed, and I made sacrifices anyone else would think unreasonable when I was young, just to make money."

Some people seem literally to be able to create their own luck, to turn, twist, or shape a situation to their advantage. Nothing may seem to happen to these luck builders that doesn't happen to other people. But they have a way of looking at things, of evaluating events, that invariably reveals an "angle," an opportunity for profitable development. Other people, looking at the same incident or set of circumstances, see nothing.

Consider the case of Joseph Katz of Papercraft, and his experience in the Pittsburgh flood. To the average person, the rising waters were an occasion for concern, or for picture-taking. Katz saw the chaos as a serious yet fascinating calamity that would prompt people in droves to purchase a photographic record of the event. This ability to see events or situations in terms of their potential for advantageous action is a recurring theme in many success stories. After World War II, some GIs were able to take advantage of war materials surpluses, and to make a profit by selling everything from life jackets to unassembled jeeps in the consumer market.

Every person who looked at the run-down, out-of-business restaurant in Brooklyn Heights saw a zero—except one. To Patricia Murphy, it represented an opportunity for a new kind of eating place that would tempt appetites and cause even the frugal-minded families of the depression to part with their hard-earned cash.

There is another approach to luck that seems somewhat similar to "angle" seeking, but it depends on an entirely different plan of action. "Luck favors the prepared mind," is one way of expressing the thought. The plan of action followed by Robert Huyot, of Interconcontinental Hotels, is an excellent example. Early in his career, Huyot systematically set about acquiring the skills and training he would need to function as a top man in the hotel business. He studied law, interior decoration, restaurant practice, public and customer relations. Then, when opportunity presented itself and a position opened up, he was the likely, even inevitable choice.

SPECIAL CASE OF THE SUCCESSFUL BUSINESSWOMAN

Of particular interest to feminists and antifeminists, the average man and the average woman, are the breakthroughs of the women in the roster—Patricia Murphy, Mildred Custin, Amelia Lobsenz, Myra Janco. What special factors mark their success?

Viewed as a group, it seems that being a woman had as many advantages as drawbacks. True, when "Pat" Murphy turned out to be a diminutive young woman, a renting agent refused her offer on a desirable restaurant site. On the other hand, when Miss Murphy started her enterprise, she probably had more male help than a man would have ever gotten. Male gallantry saved the day as everything from dishwashers to decorators appeared to lend a helping hand.

"You have to show a clear-out superiority," says one female vice-president of a California bank. "The only way you can beat out the competition for a promotion is to lead the pack by a mile." Myra Janco's career illustrates the point well.

"Willingness to play the business game." In the attitude of the typical successful businesswoman is a complete dedication to business goals. Any trace of dilettantism, any slight suggestion that in her business role she is "out of her natural element" creates tensions

and discomfort in those about her that would be a serious handicap to effectiveness.

"An abandonment of some feminine qualities." Some aspects of behavior that are thought of as feminine constitute a very definite handicap on the business scene. The "kaffee klatsch" tendency, for example, so common in housewives would be disastrous if the woman executive were to indulge this type of gregariousness on the work scene.

Amelia Lobsenz advises the female on her way up, "Never deliberately use 'feminity' or 'wiles.'"

"Know when to zip thy ruby lips and let the men do the talking," cautions another authority, Miss Jo Foxworth, vice-president of a New York advertising agency.

HE DOES EVERYTHING HE CAN

The elements just enumerated appear to various degrees and various ways in the profiles of the success roster. They sound again and again like a theme and variations.

The words of a Wimbledon tennis player following a victory in the early round of a 1965 tournament tell a great deal about how successful people put together the elements that make up their success pattern. The player was Christine Truman, an awkward, six-foot-tall English girl. According to the *New York Times* dispatch that described her winning game, "All England loves Miss Truman because she never has made an incorrect gesture or said the wrong thing on or off the court." When Miss Truman finally won the match against her tough opponent, she was asked to explain her victory. She said: "Really, I can't explain what I do, but I never actually feel as though I haven't done everything I could."

Like Miss Truman, the successful businessman cannot always pinpoint what he does or why he does it. But he knows one thing— he does everything he can.